LIFE AND TIMES OF
FREDERICK DOUGLASS

LIFE AND TIMES OF FREDERICK DOUGLASS

Frederick Douglass

WORDSWORTH AMERICAN LIBRARY

This edition published 1996 by
Wordsworth Editions Limited
Cumberland House, Crib Street
Ware, Hertfordshire SG12 9ET

ISBN 1 85326 869 1

© Wordsworth Editions Limited 1996

Wordsworth® is a registered trade mark of
Wordsworth Editions Ltd

Typeset by Antony Gray
Printed and bound in Great Britain by
Mackays of Chatham plc, Chatham, Kent

INTRODUCTION

Frederick Douglass' life intersects the most significant events in America's nineteenth-century social and political culture. His autobiography chronicles, to an extraordinary degree, the central importance of race to the American experience. We marvel, as he did, at his rise from the meanest sort of slavery, from the field-hand's labour and overseer's whip, to stirring abolitionist speaker, editor of the *North Star* and dedicated reformer; from ship's caulker to presidential adviser, race leader and Consul General to Haiti. We are unsettled, however, by the realisation that a life of such talent and achievement remained severely limited by the constrictions imposed by nineteenth-century racial mores.

Born a slave at Tuckahoe on Maryland's Eastern Shore in 1817, Douglass lived to speak at the first world's fair, the famous Columbian Exposition held in Chicago during 1893, dying shortly thereafter on 20 February 1895. Between those years he lived a life of moral courage and conviction; he refused to submit to bigotry or injustice and enthusiastically endorsed the struggles against slavery, for equal rights for women and against segregation. Like his friends and allies, William Lloyd Garrison, Wendell Phillips, Lucretia Mott, Elizabeth Cady Stanton and John Brown, Douglass was single-minded in his pursuit of social change; zealous in his hatred of perceived injustice.

These things and more can be found in this most famous of slave narratives. Published in three different editions, the *Life and Times of Frederick Douglass: Written by Himself* is his final autobiographical effort. It is remarkable because he did write it by himself, having never received a day of formal education in his life. Yet he attributed his later achievements to his determination to learn to read, write, and speak with authority and grace. After the Civil War, and the abolition of slavery, Douglass advocated an industrial education for the former slaves; an education comprised of practical industrial skills, coupled with learning both to read and write. He never forgot the lessons he received as a young person and the lessons he imparted to his brother-slaves: 'I began to address my companions on the subject of education, and the advantages of intelligence over ignorance, and, as far as I dared, I tried to show the agency of ignorance in keeping men in slavery.' [1]

His hard-won ability to read and write provided the essential written pass, knowledge and confidence to join other runaways in the flight North to freedom. But his reflections on slavery, the tragic separation from his mother and his family, the brutal life under the whip of several masters and overseers and the life-and-death struggle with Edward Covey, slave-breaker, provide some of the most vivid reflections left to anyone interested in the tragic details and legacy of American slavery.

Frederick Douglass was also a spellbinding orator in a time when oration was both art and necessity. His impassioned abolition speeches, delivered to crowds numbered in their thousands, in New England and the Northeast, in England, Scotland and Ireland, carried the authority of real experience and, increasingly, the conviction of one who forged his own path. Beginning as a Garrisonian moral disunionist, Douglass soon embraced the political abolitionism of Garritt Smith, Theodore Weld and the New York brothers, Arthur and Lewis Tappan; by the late 1850s, he could call John Brown a friend without fully embracing the violent and direct emancipationism of the stern New Englander.

Taking up a new home in Rochester, New York, Douglass turned his hand to publishing one of the earliest African-American newspapers and one of the most famous of abolitionist journals, the *North Star*, later *Frederick Douglass' Paper*. Appearing weekly, the *North Star* reached some three thousand subscribers. Despite financial problems, including the necessity to mortgage his home to keep the paper solvent, Douglass continuously published his anti-slavery views from 1847 to the end of the Civil War.

The Douglass home in Rochester was also an important stop on the underground railroad for escaping slaves. Never foolhardy, nevertheless Douglass often risked his life and fortune personally to hit 'that old enemy some telling blows . . .' [2] His account of rescuing three 'coloured men', who had killed one of the officers pursuing them, conveys the depth of his opposition to slavery and the odious Fugitive-Slave Law.

1 Frederick Douglass, *Life and Times of Frederick Douglass: Written by Himself*, page 109
2 ibid., page 204

John Brown's futile, but powerfully provocative, raid on the arsenal at Harper's Ferry, designed with the hope of rousing a slave uprising, put Frederick Douglass in immediate danger. Brown's captured carpet-bag contained numerous letters and documents that implicated other abolitionists, including Garritt Smith, Joshua R. Giddings, Samuel G. Howe, Frank P. Sanborn and Frederick Douglass, the other five of the famous Six Conspirators. Facing imminent arrest and prosecution, Douglass retraced the route he took many years before, following his own escape from slavery; Douglass fled America to England where he was greeted as an equal, and, on this occasion, as a hero.

Frederick Douglass lived to see the end of slavery and the extension of equal rights and suffrage to the former slaves. He also survived long enough, however, to experience the gradual and galling return of segregation, a condition he, and his family, first experienced during the pre-Civil War period in the free Northern states. Douglass fought the repeal of the Civil Rights Act of 1875 and physically resisted being placed in the Jim Crow railroad cars that began to appear in the 1880s. Even his proud example, however, could not halt the steady realignment of national politics that ended the reconstruction period and marked the triumph of 'separate but equal'.

In his retrospective, Frederick Douglass asked to be remembered for the example he believed his life provided for others of his race. His was a life, however, that inspires all persons in America, and elsewhere, who cherish a sense of decency and justice; who respect courage and integrity. His own words seem the most fitting epitaph: ' To those who have taken some risks and encountered hardships in the flight from bondage, I can say, I too have endured and risked. To those who have battled for liberty, brotherhood, and citizenship, I can say, I too have battled . . . If I have pushed my example too prominently for the good taste of my Caucasian readers, I beg them to remember that I have written in part for the encouragement of a class whose aspirations need the stimulus of success.' [3]

CORNEL J. REINHART
Canton, New York
Assistant Professor of History
St Lawrence University

---

3. *Life and Times of Frederick Douglass: Written by Himself*, op. cit.., page 391

FURTHER READING

Frederick Douglass, *Narrative of the Life of Frederick Douglass, an American Slave*, Boston 1845

Frederick Douglass, *My Bondage and My Freedom*, New York 1855

Waldo E. Martin, Jr, *The Mind of Frederick Douglass*, University of North Carolina Press, Chapel Hill 1984

William S. McFeely, *Frederick Douglass*, W. W. Norton, New York 1991

James Olney, 'I Was Born . . . Slave Narratives, Their Status as Autobiography and as Literature', *The Slave's Narrative*, Oxford University Press, London 1985

Benjamin Quarles, *Just Frederick Douglass*, Atheneum, New York 1969

CONTENTS

PART TWO: A SLAVE NO MORE

LIFE AND TIMES OF
FREDERICK DOUGLASS

INTRODUCTORY NOTE BY THE
RT. HON. JOHN BRIGHT MP

132 Piccadilly, London, 8 March 1882
To Mr John Lobb

DEAR SIR – I am glad to hear that you are about to publish an English edition of the *Life and Times of Frederick Douglass* – in his youth a slave in the State of Maryland, now holding an honourable office in the District of Columbia, in the United Sates of America.

I have read the book with great interest. It shows what may be done, and has been done, by a man born under the most adverse circumstances; done, not for himself alone, but for his race, and for his country. It shows also, how a great nation, persisting in a great crime, cannot escape the penalty inseperable from crime.

History has probably no more striking example of the manner in which an offence of the highest guilt may be followed by the most terrible punishment than is to be found in the events which make the history of the United States, from the year 1860 to the year 1865.

The book which you are about to offer to English readers is one which will stimulate the individual to noble effort and to virtue, whilst it will act as a lesson and a warning to every nation whose policy is based upon injustice and wrong.

I hope it may find its way into many thousands of English homes.

I am, with great respect,

Yours sincerely,

JOHN BRIGHT

PART ONE: LIFE AS A SLAVE

CHAPTER I

Birth and Parentage

Place of birth – Description of country – Its inhabitants –
Genealogical trees – Method of counting time in slave districts –
Date of birth – Names of grandparents – Their cabin – Home
with them – Slave practice of separating mothers from their
children – Recollections of his mother – Who was his father?

In Talbot County, Eastern Shore, State of Maryland, near Easton, the
County town, there is a small district of country, thinly populated, and
remarkable for nothing that I know of more than for the worn-out,
sandy, desert-like appearance of its soil, the general dilapidation of its
farms and fences, the indigent and spiritless character of its inhabitants,
and the prevalence of ague and fever. It was in this dull, flat, and
unthrifty district or neighbourhood, bordered by the Choptank river,
among the laziest and muddiest of streams, surrounded by a white
population of the lowest order, indolent and drunken to a proverb, and
among slaves who, in point of ignorance and indolence, were fully in
accord with their surroundings, that I, without any fault of my own,
was born, and spent the first years of my childhood.

The reader must not expect me to say much of my family.
Genealogical trees did not flourish among slaves. A person of some
consequence in civilised society, sometimes designated as father, was
literally unknown to slave law and slave practice. I never met with a
slave in that part of the country who could tell me with any certainty
how old he was. Few at that time knew anything of the months of the
year, or of the days of the month. They measured the ages of their
children by springtime, wintertime, harvest-time, planting-time, and
the like. Masters allowed no questions to be put to them by slaves
concerning their ages. Such questions were regarded by the masters as
evidence of an impudent curiosity. From certain events, however, the

dates of which I have since learned, I suppose myself to have been born in February, 1817.

My first experience of life, as I now remember it, and I remember it but hazily, began in the family of my grandmother and grandfather, Betsey and Isaac Bailey. They were considered old settlers in the neighbourhood, and from certain circumstances I infer that my grandmother, especially, was held in high esteem, far higher than was the lot of most coloured persons in that region. She was a good nurse, and a capital hand at making nets used for catching shad and herring, and was, withal, somewhat famous as a fisherwoman. I have known her to be in the water waist-deep, for hours seine-hauling. She was a gardener as well as a fisherwoman, and remarkable for her success in keeping her seedling sweet potatoes through the months of winter, and easily got the reputation of being born to 'good luck'. In planting time Grandmother Betsey was sent for in all directions, simply to place the seedling potatoes in the hills or drills; for superstition had it that her touch was needed to make them grow. This reputation was full of advantage to her and her grandchildren, for a good crop, after her planting for the neighbours, brought her a share of the harvest.

Whether because she was too old for field service, or because she had so faithfully discharged the duties of her station in early life, I know not, but she enjoyed the privilege of living in a cabin separate from the slave quarters, having only the charge of the young children and the burden of her own support imposed upon her. She esteemed it great good fortune to live there, and took much comfort in having the children. The practice of separating mothers from their children and hiring them out at distances too great to admit of their meeting, save at long intervals, was a marked feature of the cruelty and barbarity of the slave system, which always and everywhere sought to reduce man to a level with the brute. It had no interest in recognising or preserving any of the ties that bind families together or to their homes.

My grandmother's five daughters were hired out in this way, and my only recollections of my own mother are of a few hasty visits made in the night on foot, after the daily tasks were over, and when she was under the necessity of returning in time to respond to the driver's call to the field in the early morning. These little glimpses of my mother, obtained under such circumstances and against such odds, meagre as they were, are ineffaceably stamped upon my memory. She was tall and finely proportioned, of dark glossy complexion, with regular features and amongst the slaves was remarkably sedate and dignified. There is, in *Prichard's Natural History of Man*, the head of a figure, the features of which so resemble my mother's, that I often recur to it with something of the feeling which I suppose others experience when looking upon the likenesses of their own dear departed ones.

Of my father I know nothing. Slavery had no recognition of fathers, as none of families That the mother was a slave was enough for its deadly purpose. By its law the child followed the condition of its mother. The father might be a freeman and the child a slave. The father might be a white man, glorying in the purity of his Anglo-Saxon blood, and his child ranked with the blackest slaves. Father he might be, and not be husband, and could sell his own child without incurring reproach, if in its veins coursed one drop of African blood.

CHAPTER II

Removal from Grandmother's

Early home – Its charms – Ignorance of 'old master' – His gradual perception of the truth concerning him – His relations to Colonel Edward Lloyd – Removal to 'old master's' home – His journey thence – His separation from his grandmother – His grief

Living thus with my grandmother, whose kindness and love stood in place of my mother's, it was some time before I knew myself to be a slave. I knew many other things before I knew that. Her little cabin had to me the attractions of a palace. Its fence railed floor – which was equally floor and bedstead – upstairs, and its clay floor downstairs, its dirt, and straw chimney and windowless sides, and that most curious piece of workmanship, the ladder stairway, and the hole so strangely dug in front of the fireplace, beneath which grandmamma placed her sweet potatoes, to keep them from frost in winter, were full of interest to my childish observation. The squirrels, as they skipped the fences, climbed the trees or gathered their nuts, were an unceasing delight to me. There, too, right at the side of the hut, stood the old well, with its stately and skyward-pointing beam, so aptly placed between the limbs of what had once been a tree, and so nicely balanced, that I could move it up and down with only one hand, and could get a drink myself without calling for help. Nor were these all the attractions of the place. At a little distance stood Mr Lee's mill, where the people came in large numbers to get their corn ground. I can never tell the many things thought and felt, as I sat on the bank and watched that mill, and the turning of its ponderous wheel. The mill-pond, too, had its charms; and with my pin-hook and thread line I could get amusing nibbles if I could catch no fish.

It was not long, however, before I began to learn the sad fact that this house of my childhood belonged not to my dear old grandmother, but to someone I had never seen, and who lived a great distance off. I learned, too, the sadder fact, that not only the home and lot, but that grandmother herself and all the little children around her, belonged to a mysterious personage, called by grandmother, with every mark of reverence, 'old master'. Thus early, did clouds and shadows begin to fall upon my path.

I learned that this old master, whose name seemed ever to be mentioned with fear and shuddering, only allowed the little children to live with grandmother for a limited time, and that as soon as they were big enough they were promptly taken away to live with the said old master. These were distressing revelations indeed. My grandmother was all the world to me, and the thought of being separated from her was a most unwelcome suggestion to my affections and hopes. This mysterious old master was really a man of some consequence. He owned several farms in Tuckahoe, was the chief clerk and butler on the home plantation of Colonel Lloyd, had overseers as well as slaves on his own farms, and gave directions to the overseers on the farms owned by Colonel Lloyd. Captain Aaron Anthony, for such was the name and title of my old master, lived on Colonel Lloyd's plantation, which was situated on the Wye river, and which was one of the largest, most fertile, and best appointed in the State.

About this plantation and this old master I was most eager to know everything which could be known; and, unhappily for me, all the information I could get concerning him increased my dread of being separated from my grandmother and grandfather. I wished it was possible I could remain small all my life, knowing that the sooner I grew large the shorter would be my time to remain with them, Everything about the cabin became doubly dear, and I was sure there could be no other spot equal to it on earth. But the time came when I must go and my grandmother, knowing my fears, in pity for them, kindly kept me ignorant of the dreaded moment up to the morning, a beautiful summer morning, when we were to start, and indeed, during the whole journey, which, child, as I was, I remember as well as if it were yesterday, she kept the unwelcome truth hidden from me. The distance from Tuckahoe to Colonel Lloyd's, where my old master lived, was full twelve miles, and the walk was quite a severe test of the endurance of my young legs. The journey would have proved too severe for me, but that my dear old grandmother – blessings on her memory! – afforded occasional relief by 'toteing' me on her shoulder. Advanced in years as she was, as was evident from the more than one grey hair which peeped from between the ample, and graceful folds of her newly and smoothly ironed bandana turban, grandmother was yet a woman of power and spirit. She was remarkably straight in figure, elastic and muscular in movement. I seemed hardly to be a burden to her. She would have 'toted 'me farther, but I felt myself too much of a man to allow it. Yet while I walked I was not independent of her. She often found me holding her skirts lest something should come out of the woods and eat me up. Several old logs and stumps imposed upon me, and got themselves taken for enormous animals. I could plainly see their legs, eyes, ears, and teeth, till I got close enough to see that the eyes were knots washed with rain, and the legs were broken limbs, and the ears and teeth only such because of the point from which they were seen.

As the day advanced the heat increased, and it was not until the afternoon that we reached the much dreaded end of the journey. Here I found myself in the midst of a group of children of all sizes and of many colours, black, brown, copper coloured, and nearly white. I had not seen so many children before. As a newcomer I was an object of special interest. After laughing and yelling around me and playing all sorts of wild tricks they asked me to go out and play with them. This I refused to do. Grandmamma looked sad, and I could not help feeling that our being there boded no good to me. She was soon to lose another object of affection, as she had lost many before. Affectionately patting me on the head she told me to be a good boy and go out to play with the children. 'They are kin to you,' she said, 'go and play with them'. She pointed out to me my brother Perry, my sisters, Sarah and Eliza. I had never seen them before, and though I had sometimes heard of them and felt a curious interest in them, I really did not understand what they were to me or I to them. Brothers and sisters we were by blood, but slavery had made us strangers. They were already initiated into the mysteries of old master's domicile, and they seemed to look upon me with a certain degree of compassion. I really wanted to play with them, but they were strangers to me, and I was full of fear that my grandmother might leave for home without taking me with her. Entreated to do so, however, and that, too, by my dear grandmother, I went to the back part of the house to play with them and the other children. Play, however, I did not, but stood with my back against the wall witnessing the playing of the others. At last, while standing there, one of the children, who had been in the kitchen, ran up to me in a sort of roguish glee, exclaiming, 'Fed, Fed, grandmamma gone!' I could not believe it. Yet, fearing the worst, I ran into the kitchen to see for myself, and lo! she was indeed gone, and was now far away and 'clean' out of sight. I need not tell all that happened now. Almost heart-broken at the discovery, I fell upon the ground and wept a boy's bitter tears, refusing to be comforted. My brother gave me peaches and pears to quiet me, but I promptly threw them on the ground. I had never been deceived before, and something of resentment at this, mingled with my grief at parting with my grandmother.

It was now late in the afternoon. The day had been an exciting and wearisome one, and, I know not how, but I suppose I sobbed myself to sleep, and its balm was never more welcome to any wounded soul than to mine. The reader may be surprised that I relate so minutely an incident apparently so trivial and which must have occurred when I was less than seven years old, but as I wish to give a faithful history of my experience in slavery, I cannot withold a circumstance which at the time affected me so deeply, and which I still remember so vividly. Besides, this was my first introduction to the realities of the slave system.

CHAPTER III

Troubles of Childhood

Colonel Lloyd's plantation – Aunt Katy – Her cruelty and ill-nature – Captain Anthony's partiality to Aunt Katy – Allowance of food – Hunger – Unexpected rescue by his mother – The reproof of Aunt Katy – Sleep – A slave-mother's love – His inheritance – His mother's acquirements – Her death

Once established on the home plantation of Colonel Lloyd – I was with the children there, left to the tender mercies of Aunt Katy, a slave woman who was to my master, what he was to Colonel Lloyd. Disposing of us in classes or sizes, he left to Aunt Katy all the minor details concerning our management. She was a woman who never allowed herself to act greatly within the limits of delegated power, no matter how broad that authority might be. Ambitious of old master's favour, ill-tempered and cruel by nature, she found in her present position an ample field for the exercise of her ill-omened qualities. She had a strong hold upon old master, for she was a first-rate cook, and very industrious. She was therefore greatly favoured by him – and as one mark of his favour she was the only mother who was permitted to retain her children around her, and even to these, her own children, she was often fiendish in her brutality. Cruel, however, as she sometimes was to her own children, she was not destitute of maternal feeling, and in her instinct to satisfy their demands for food, she was often guilty of starving me and the other children. Want of food was my chief trouble during my first summer here. Captain Anthony, instead of allowing a given quantity of food to each slave, committed the allowance for all to Aunt Katy, to be divided by her, after cooking, amongst us. The allowance consisted of coarse corn-meal, not very abundant, and which by passing through Aunt Katy's hands, became more slender still for some of us. I have often been so pinched with hunger, as to dispute with old 'Nep' the dog, for the crumbs which fell from the kitchen table. Many times have I followed with eager step, the waiting-girl when she shook the table-cloth, to get the crumbs and small bones flung out for the dogs and cats. It was a great thing to have the privilege of dipping a piece of bread into the water in which meat had been boiled – and the skin taken from the rusty bacon was a positive luxury. With this description of the domestic arrangements of my new home, I may here recount a circumstance which is deeply impressed on my memory, as affording a bright gleam of a slave-mother's love, and the earnestness of a mother's care. I had offended Aunt Katy. I do not remember in what way, for my offences were numerous in that quarter, greatly depending upon her moods as to their heinousness; and she had adopted her usual mode of punishing me: namely, making me go all day without food. For the first hour or two after dinner time, I succeeded pretty well in keeping up my spirits; but as the day wore away, I found it quite impossible to do so any longer. Sundown came, but no bread; and in its stead came the threat from Aunt Katy, with a scowl well suited to its terrible import, that she would starve the life out of me. Brandishing her knife, she chopped off the heavy slices of bread for the other children, and put the loaf away, muttering all the while her savage designs upon myself. Against this disappointment, for I was expecting that her heart would relent at last, I made an extra effort to maintain my dignity; but when I saw the other children around me with satisfied faces, I could stand it no longer. I went out behind the kitchen wall and cried like a fine fellow. When wearied with this, I returned to the kitchen, sat by the fire and brooded over my hard lot. I was too hungry to sleep. While I sat in the corner, I caught sight of an ear of Indian corn upon an upper shelf. I watched my chance and got it; and shelling off a few grains, I put it back again. These grains I quickly put into the hot ashes to roast. I did this at the risk of getting a brutal thumping, for Aunt Katy could beat as well as starve me. My corn was not long in roasting, and I eagerly pulled it from the ashes, and placed it upon a stool in a clever little pile. I began to help myself, when who but my own dear mother should come in. The scene which followed is beyond my power to describe. The friendless and hungry boy, in his extremest need, found himself in the strong protecting arms of his mother. I have before spoken of my mother's dignified and impressive manner. I shall never forget the indescribable expression of her countenance when I told her that Aunt Katy had said she would starve the life out of me, There was deep and tender pity in her glance at me, and a fiery indignation at Aunt Katy at the same moment, and while she took the corn from me, and gave in its stead a large ginger cake, she read Aunt Katy a lecture which was never forgotten. That night I learned as I had never learned before, that I was not only a child, but somebody's child. I was grander upon my mother's knee than a king upon his throne. But my triumph was short. I dropped off to sleep, and waked in the morning to find my mother gone and myself at the mercy again of the virago in my master's kitchen, whose fiery wrath was my constant dread.

My mother had walked twelve miles to see me, and had the same distance to travel over again before the morning sunrise. I do not remember ever seeing her again. Her death soon ended the little communication that had existed between us, and with it, I believe, a life full of weariness and heartfelt sorrow. To me it has ever been a grief that I knew my mother so little, and have so few of her words treasured in my remembrance. I have since learned that she was the only one of all the coloured people of Tuckahoe who could read. How she acquired this knowledge I know not, for Tuckahoe was the last place in the world where she would have been likely to find facilities for learning. I can therefore fondly and proudly ascribe to her, an earnest love of knowledge.

That a field-hand should learn to read in any slave State is remarkable, but the achievements of my mother, considering the place and circumstances, were very extraordinary. In view of this fact, I am happy to attribute any love of letters I may have, not to my presumed Anglo-Saxon paternity, but to the native genius of my sable, unprotected, and uncultivated mother – a woman who belonged to a race whose mental endowments are still disparaged and despised.

CHAPTER IV

A General Survey of the Slave Plantation

Home plantation of Colonel Lloyd – Its isolation – Its industries – The slave rule – Power of overseers – Finds some enjoyment – Natural scenery – Sloop *Sally Lloyd* – Windmill – Slave quarter – 'Old master's' house – Stables, storehouses, &c., &c. – The 'great house' – Its surroundings – Lloyd – Burial-place – Superstition of slaves – Colonel Lloyd's wealth – Negro politeness – Doctor Copper – Captain Anthony – His family – Master Daniel Lloyd – His brothers – Social etiquette

It was generally supposed that slavery in the State of Maryland existed in its mildest form, and that it was totally divested of those harsh and terrible peculiarities which characterised the slave system in the Southern and South Western States of the American Union. The ground of this opinion was the contiguity of the free States, and the influence of their moral, religious, and humane sentiments. Public opinion was, indeed, a measurable restraint upon the cruelty and barbarity of masters, overseers, and slave-drivers, whenever and wherever it could reach them; but there were certain secluded and out-of-the-way places, even in the State of Maryland, fifty years ago, seldom visited by a single ray of healthy public sentiment, where slavery, wrapt in its own congenial darkness, could and did develop all its malign and shocking characteristics, where it could be indecent without shame, cruel without shuddering, and murderous without apprehension or fear of exposure or punishment. Just such a secluded, dark and out-of-the-way place, was the home plantation of Colonel Edward Lloyd, in Talbot county, Eastern Shore of Maryland. It was far away from all the great thoroughfares of travel and commerce, and proximate to no town or village. There was neither schoolhouse nor townhouse in its neighbourhood. The schoolhouse was unnecessary, for there were no children to go to school. The children and grandchildren of Colonel Lloyd were taught in the house by a private tutor, a Mr Page from Greenfield, Massachusetts, a tall, gaunt, sapling of a man, remarkably dignified, thoughtful, and reticent, and who did not speak a dozen words to a slave in a whole year. The overseer's children went off somewhere in the State to school, and therefore could bring no foreign or dangerous influence from abroad to embarrass the natural operation of the slave system of the place. Not even the commonest mechanics, from whom there might have been an occasional outburst of honest and telling indignation at cruelty and wrong on other plantations, were white men here. Its whole public was made up of and divided into three classes, slave-holders, slaves, and overseers. Its blacksmiths, wheelrights, shoemakers, weavers and coopers were slaves. Not even commerce, selfish and indifferent to moral considerations as it usually is, was permitted within its secluded precincts. Whether with a view of guarding against the escape of its secrets, I know not, but it is a fact, that every leaf and grain of the products of this plantation and those of the neighbouring farms, belonging to Colonel Lloyd, were transported to Baltimore in his own vessels, every man and boy on board of which, except the captain, were owned by him as his property. In return everything brought to the plantation came through the same channel. To make this isolation more apparent it may be stated that the adjoining estates to Colonel Lloyd's were owned and occupied by friends of his, who were as deeply interested as himself in maintaining the slave system in all its rigour. These were the Tilgmans, the Goldboroughs, the Lockermans, the Pacas, the Skinners, Gibsons and others of lesser affluence and standing.

The fact is, public opinion in such a quarter, the reader must see, was not likely to be very efficient in protecting the slave from cruelty. To be a restraint upon abuses of this nature, opinion must emanate from humane and virtuous communities, and to no such opinion or influence was Colonel Lloyd's plantation exposed. It was a little nation by itself, having its own language, its own rules, regulations, and customs. The troubles and controversies arising here were not settled by the civil power of the State. The overseer was the important dignitary. He was generally accuser, judge, jury, advocate, and executioner. The criminal was always dumb – and no slave was allowed to testify, other than against his brother slave.

There were, of course, no conflicting rights of property, for all the people were the property of one man, and they could themselves own no property. Religion and politics were largely excluded. One class of the population was too high to be reached by the common preacher, and the other class was too low in condition and ignorance to be much cared for by religious teachers, and yet some religious ideas did enter this dark corner.

This, however, is not the only view which the place presented. Though civilisation was in many respects shut out, nature could not be. Though separated from the rest of the world, though public opinion, as I have said, could seldom penetrate its dark domain, though the whole place was stamped with its own peculiar iron-like individuality, and though crimes, high-handed and atrocious, could be committed there with strange and shocking impunity, it was to outward seeming, a most strikingly interesting place, full of life, activity and spirit, and presented a very favourable contrast to the indolent monotony and languor of Tuckahoe. It resembled in some respects descriptions I have since read of the old baronial domains of Europe. Keen as was my regret, and great as was my sorrow, at leaving my old home, I was not long in adapting myself to my new one. A man's troubles are always half disposed of when he finds endurance the only alternative. I found myself there; there was no getting away; and naught remained for me but to make the best of it. There were plenty of children to play with, and plenty of pleasant resorts for boys of my age and older. The little tendrils of affection so rudely broken from the darling objects in and around my grandmother's home, gradually began to extend and twine themselves around the new surroundings. There for the first time I saw a large windmill, with its wide-sweeping white wings, a commanding object to a child's eye. This was situated on what was called Long Point – a tract of land dividing Miles river from the Wye. I spent many hours watching the wings of this wondrous mill. In the river, or what was called the 'Swash,' at a short distance from the shore, quietly lying at anchor, with her small row boat dancing at her stern, was a large sloop, the *Sally Lloyd*, called by that name in honour of the favourite daughter of the Colonel. These two objects, the sloop and mill, as I remember, awakened thoughts, ideas, and wondering. Then there were a great many houses, human habitations full of the mysteries of life at every stage of it. There was the little red house up the road, occupied by Mr Seveir, the overseer; a little nearer to my old master's stood a long, low, rough building literally alive with slaves of all ages, sexes, conditions, sizes, and colours. This was called the long quarter. Perched upon a hill east of our house, was a tall dilapidated old brick building, the architectural dimensions of which proclaimed its creation for a different purpose, now occupied by slaves, in a similar manner to the long quarters. Besides these, there were numerous other slave houses and huts, scattered around in the neighbourhood, every nook and corner of which were completely occupied.

Old master's house, a long brick building, plain but substantial, was centrally located, and was an independent establishment. Besides these houses there were barns, stables, storehouses, tobacco-houses, blacksmith shops, wheelwright shops, cooper shops; but above all there stood the grandest building my young eyes had ever beheld, called by everyone on the plantation the *great* house. This was occupied by Colonel Lloyd and his family. It was surrounded by numerous and variously shaped out-buildings. There were kitchens, wash-houses, dairies, summer-houses, greenhouses, hen-houses, turkey-houses, pigeon-houses, and arbours of many sizes and devices, all neatly painted or whitewashed – interspersed with grand old trees, ornamental and primitive, which afforded delightful shade in summer, and imparted to the scene a high degree of stately beauty. The *great* house itself was a large white wooden building with wings on three sides of it. In front a broad portico extended the entire length of the building, supported by a long range of columns, which gave to the Colonel's home an air of great dignity and grandeur. It was a treat to my young and gradually opening mind to behold this elaborate exhibition of wealth, power, and beauty.

The carriage entrance to the house was by a large gate, more than a quarter of a mile distant. The intermediate space was a beautiful lawn, very neatly kept and cared for. It was dotted thickly over with trees and flowers. The road or lane from the gate to the great house was richly paved with white pebbles from the beach, and in its course formed a complete circle around the lawn. Outside this select enclosure were parks, as about the residences of the English nobility, where rabbits, deer, and other wild game might be seen peering and playing about, with 'none to molest them or make them afraid'. The tops of the stately poplars were often covered with red-winged blackbirds, making all nature vocal with the joyous life and beauty of their wild, warbling notes. These all belonged to me as well as to Colonel Edward Lloyd, and, whether they did or not, I greatly enjoyed them. Not far from the great house were the stately mansions of the dead Lloyds – a place of sombre aspect. Vast tombs, embowered beneath the weeping willow and the fir tree, told of the generations of the family, as well as their wealth. Superstition was rife among the slaves about this family burying-ground. Strange sights had been seen there by some of the older slaves, and I was often compelled to hear stories of shrouded ghosts, riding on great black horses, and of balls of fire which had been seen to fly there at midnight, and of startling and dreadful sounds that had been repeatedly heard. Slaves knew enough of the orthodox theology at the time, to consign all bad slave-holders to hell, and they often fancied such persons wishing themselves back again to wield the lash. Tales of sights and sounds strange and terrible, connected with the huge black tombs, were a great security to the grounds about them, for few of the slaves had the courage to approach them during the daytime. It was a dark, gloomy and forbidding place, and it was difficult to feel that the spirits of the sleeping dust there deposited reigned with the blest in the realms of eternal peace.

Here was transacted the business of twenty or thirty different farms, which, with the slaves upon them, numbering, in all, not less than a thousand, all belonged to Colonel Lloyd. Each farm was under the management of an overseer, whose word was law.

Mr Lloyd at this time was very rich. His slaves alone, numbering as I have said not less than a thousand, were an immense fortune, and though scarcely a month passed without the sale of one or more lots to the Georgia traders, there was no apparent diminution in the number of his human stock. The selling of any to the State of Georgia was a sore and mournful event to those left behind, as well as to the victims themselves.

The reader has already been informed of the handicrafts carried on here by the slaves. 'Uncle' Toney was the blacksmith, 'Uncle' Harry the cartwright, and 'Uncle' Abel was the shoemaker, and these had assistants in their several departments. These mechanics are called 'Uncles' by all the younger slaves, not because they really sustained that relationship to any, but according to plantation etiquette as a mark of respect, due from the younger to the older slaves. Strange and even ridiculous as it may seem, among a people so uncultivated and with so many stern trials to look in the face, there is not to be found among any people a more rigid enforcement of the law of respect to elders than is maintained among them. I set this down as partly constitutional with the coloured race and partly conventional. There is no better material in the world for making a gentleman than is furnished in the African.

Among other slave notabilities, I found here one called by everybody, white and coloured, 'Uncle' Isaac Copper. It was seldom that a slave, however venerable, was honoured with a surname in Maryland, and so completely has the south shaped the manners of the north in this respect that their right to such honour is tardily admitted even now. It goes sadly against the grain to address and treat a negro as one would address and treat a white man. But once in a while, even in a slave state, a negro had a surname fastened to him by common consent. This was the case with 'Uncle' Isaac Copper. Where the 'Uncle' was dropped, he was called Doctor Copper. He was both our Doctor of Medicine and our Doctor of Divinity. When he took his degree I am unable to say, but he was too well established in his profession to permit question as to his native skill, or attainments. One qualification he certainly had. He was a confirmed cripple, wholly unable to work, and was worth nothing for sale in the market. Though lame, he was no sluggard. He made his crutches do him good service, and was always on the alert looking up the sick, and such as were supposed to need his aid and counsel. His remedial prescriptions embraced four articles. For diseases of the body, Epsom salts and castor oil; for those of the soul, the 'Lord's prayer' and a few stout hickory switches.

I was early sent to Doctor Isaac Copper, with twenty or thirty other children, to learn the Lord's prayer. The old man was seated on a huge three-legged oaken stool, armed with several large hickory switches, and from the point where he sat, lame as he was, he could reach every boy in the room. After standing a while to learn what was expected of us, he commanded us to kneel down. This done, he told us to say everything he said. 'Our Father'– this we repeated after him with promptness and uniformity – 'who art in Heaven', was less promptly and uniformly repeated, and the old gentleman paused in the prayer to give us a short lecture, and to use his switches on our backs.

Everybody in the South seemed to want the privilege of whipping somebody else. 'Uncle' Isaac, though a good old man, shared the common passion of his time and country. I cannot say I was much edified by attendance upon his ministry. There was even at that time something a little inconsistent and laughable, in my mind, in the blending of prayer with punishment. I was not long in my new home before I found that the dread I had conceived of Captain Anthony was in a measure groundless. Instead of leaping out from some hiding place and destroying me, he hardly seemed to notice my presence. He probably thought as little of my arrival there, as of an additional pig to his stock. He was the chief agent of his employer. The overseers of all the farms composing the Lloyd estate, were in some sort under him. The Colonel himself seldom addressed an overseer, or allowed himself to be addressed by one. To Captain Anthony, therefore, was committed the head-ship of all the farms. He carried the keys of all the storehouses, weighed and measured the allowances of each slave, at the end of each month; superintended the storing of all goods brought to the storehouse; dealt out the raw material to the different handicraftsmen, shipped the grain, tobacco, and all other saleable produce of the numerous farms to Baltimore, and had a general oversight of all the workshops of the place. In addition to all this he was frequently called abroad to Easton and elsewhere in the discharge of his numerous duties as chief agent of the estate.

The family of Captain Anthony consisted of two sons – Andrew and Richard, his daughter Lucretia and her newly-married husband, Captain Thomas Auld. In the kitchen were Aunt Katy, Aunt Esther, and ten or a dozen children, most of them older than myself. Captain Anthony was not considered a rich slave-holder, hough he was pretty well off in the world. He owned about thirty slaves and three farms in the Tuckahoe district. The more valuable part of his property was in slaves, of whom he sold one every year, which brought him in seven or eight hundred dollars, besides his yearly salary and other revenue from his lands.

I have been often asked during the earlier part of my free life at the North, how I happened to have so little of the slave accent in my speech. The mystery is in some measure explained by my association with Daniel Lloyd, the youngest son of Colonel Edward Lloyd. The law of compensation holds here as well as elsewhere. While this lad could not associate with ignorance without sharing its shade, he could not give his black playmates his company without giving them his superior intelligence as well. Without knowing this, or caring about it at the time, I, for some cause or other, was attracted to him and was much his companion.

I had little to do with the older brothers of Daniel – Edward and Murray. They were grown up and were fine-looking men. Edward was especially esteemed by the slave children and by me among the rest, not that he ever said anything to us or for us which could be called particularly kind. It was enough for us that he never looked or acted scornfully towards us. The idea of rank and station was rigidly maintained on this estate. The family of Captain Anthony never visited the great house, and the Lloyds never came to our house. Equal non-intercourse was observed between Captain Anthony's family and the family of Mr Seveir, the overseer.

Such, kind readers, was the community and such the place in which my earliest and most lasting impressions of the workings of slavery were received – of which impressions you will learn more in the after chapters of this book.

CHAPTER V

A Slave-holder's Character

Increasing acquaintance with old master – Evils of unresisted
passion – Apparent tenderness – A man of trouble – Custom of
muttering to himself – Brutal outrage – A drunken overseer –
Slave-holder's impatience – Wisdom of appeal – A base and
selfish attempt to break up a courtship

Although my old master, Captain Anthony, gave me, at the first of my
coming to him from my grandmother's, very little attention, and
although that little was of a remarkably mild and gentle description, a
few months only were sufficient to convince me that mildness and
gentleness were not the prevailing or governing traits of his character.
These excellent qualities were displayed only occasionally. He could,
when it suited him, appear to be literally insensible to the claims of
humanity. He could not only be deaf to the appeals of the helpless
against the aggressor, but he could himself commit outrages deep,
dark, and nameless. Yet he was not by nature worse than other men.
Had he been brought up in a free state, surrounded by the full
restraints of civilised society – restraints which are necessary to the
freedom of all its members, alike and equally, Captain Anthony might
have been as humane a man as are members of such society generally.
A man's character always takes its hue, more or less, from the form and
colour of things about him. The slave-holder, as well as the slave, was
the victim of the slave system. Under the whole heavens there could be
no relation more unfavourable to the development of honourable
character than that sustained by the slave-holder to the slave. Reason is
imprisoned here and passions run wild. Could the reader have seen
Captain Anthony gently leading me by the hand, as he sometimes did,
patting me on the head, speaking to me in soft, caressing tones and
calling me his little Indian boy, he would have deemed him a kind-
hearted old man, and really almost fatherly to the slave boy. But the
pleasant moods of a slave-holder are transient and fitful. They neither

come often nor remain long. The temper of the old man was subject to special trials, but since these trials were never borne patiently, they added little to his natural stock of patience. Aside from his troubles with his slaves and those of Mr Lloyd's, he made the impression upon me of being an unhappy man. Even to my child's eye he wore a troubled and at times a haggard aspect. His strange movements excited my curiosity and awakened my compassion. He seldom walked alone without muttering to himself, and he occasionally stormed about as if defying an army of invisible foes. Most of his leisure was spent in walking around, cursing and gesticulating as if possessed by a demon. He was evidently a wretched man, at war with his own soul and all the world around him. To be overheard by the children disturbed him very little. He made no more of our presence than that of the ducks and geese he met on the green. But when his gestures were most violent, ending with a threatening shake of the head and a sharp snap of his middle finger and thumb, I deemed it wise to keep at a safe distance from him.

One of the first circumstances that opened my eyes to the cruelties and wickedness of slavery and its hardening influences upon my old master, was his refusal to interpose his authority to protect and shield a young woman, a cousin of mine, who had been most cruelly abused and beaten by his overseer in Tuckahoe. This overseer, a Mr Plummer, was like most of his class, little less than a human brute; and in addition to his general profligacy and repulsive coarseness, he was a miserable drunkard, a man not fit to have the management of a drove of mules. In one of his moments of drunken madness he committed the outrage which brought the young woman in question down to my old master's for protection. The poor girl, on her arrival at our house, presented a most pitiable appearance. She had left in haste and without preparation, and probably without the knowledge of Mr Plummer. She had travelled twelve miles, bare-footed, bare-necked, and bare-headed. Her neck and shoulders were covered with scars newly made, and not content with marring her neck and shoulders with the cowhide, the cowardly wretch had dealt her a blow on the head with a hickory club, which cut a horrible gash and left her face literally covered with blood. In this condition the poor young woman came down to implore protection at the hands of my old master. I expected to see him boil over with rage at the revolting deed, and to hear him fill the air with curses upon the brutal Plummer; but I was disappointed. He sternly told her in an angry tone, 'She deserved every bit of it, and if she did not go home instantly he would himself take the remaining skin from her neck and back.' Thus the poor girl was compelled to return without redress, and perhaps to receive an additional flogging for daring to appeal to authority higher than that of the overseer.

I did not at that time understand the philosophy of this treatment of my cousin. I think I now understand it. This treatment was a part of the system, rather than a part of the man. To have encouraged appeals of this kind would have occasioned much loss of time, and left the overseer powerless to enforce obedience. Nevertheless, when a slave had nerve enough to go straight to his master, with a well-founded complaint against an overseer, though he might be repelled and have even that of which he complained at the time repeated, and though he might be beaten by his master as well as by the overseer, for his temerity, in the end, the policy of complaining was generally vindicated by the relaxed rigour of the overseer's treatment. The latter became more careful and less disposed to use the lash upon such slaves thereafter.

The overseer very naturally disliked to have the ear of the master disturbed by complaints, and either for this reason or because of advice privately given him by his employer, he generally modified the rigour of his rule after complaints of this kind had been made against him. For some cause or other the slaves, no matter how often they were repulsed by their masters, were ever disposed to regard them with less abhorrence than the overseer. And yet these masters would often go beyond their overseers in wanton cruelty. They wielded the lash without any sense of responsibility. They could cripple or kill without fear of consequences. I have seen my old master in a tempest of wrath, full of pride, hatred, jealousy, and revenge, when he seemed a very fiend.

The circumstances which I am about to narrate, and which gave rise to this fearful tempest of passion, were not singular, but very common in our slave-holding community.

The reader will have noticed that among the names of slaves, Esther is mentioned. This was a young woman who possessed that which was ever a curse to the slave girl – namely, personal beauty. She was tall, light-coloured, well-formed, and made a fine appearance. Esther was courted by 'Ned Roberts', the son of a favourite slave of Colonel Lloyd, who was as fine-looking a young man as Esther was a woman. Some slave-holders would have been glad to have promoted the marriage of two such persons, but for some reason, Captain Anthony disapproved of their courtship. He strictly ordered her to quit the company of young Roberts, telling her that he would punish her severely if he ever found her again in his company. But it was impossible to keep this couple apart. Meet they would, and meet they did. Had Mr Anthony been himself a man of honour, his motives in this matter might have appeared more favourably. As it was, they appeared as abhorrent as they were contemptible. It was one of the damning characteristics of slavery, that it robbed its victims of every earthly incentive to a holy life. The fear of God and the hope of heaven were sufficient to sustain many slave women amidst the snares and dangers of their strange lot; but they were ever at the mercy of the power, passion, and caprice of their owners. Slavery provided no means for the honourable perpetuation of the race. Yet despite of this destitution there were many men and women among the slaves who were true and faithful to each other through life.

But to the case in hand. Abhorred and circumvented as he was, Captain Anthony, having the power was determined on revenge. I happened to see its shocking execution, and shall never forget the scene. It was early in the morning, when all was still, and before any of the family in the house or kitchen had risen. I was, in fact, awakened by the heart-rending shrieks and piteous cries of poor Esther. My sleeping-place was on the dirt floor of a little rough closet which opened into the kitchen, and through the cracks in its unplaned boards I could distinctly see and hear what was going on, without being seen. Esther's wrists were firmly tied, and the twisted rope was fastened to a strong iron staple in a heavy wooden beam above, near the fireplace. Here she stood on a bench, her arms tightly drawn above her head. Her back and shoulders were perfectly bare. Behind her stood old master, with cowhide in hand, pursuing his barbarous work with all manner of harsh, coarse, and tantalising epithets. He was cruelly deliberate, and protracted the torture as one who was delighted with the agony of his victim. Again and again he drew the hateful scourge through his hand, adjusting it with a view of dealing the most pain-giving blow his strength and skill could inflict. Poor Esther had never before been severely whipped. Her shoulders were plump and tender. Each blow, vigorously laid on, brought screams from her as well as blood. 'Have mercy! Oh, mercy!' she cried. 'I won't do so no more.' But her piercing cries seemed only to increase his fury. The whole scene, with all its attendants, was revolting and shocking to the last degree, and when the motives for the brutal castigation are known, language has no power to convey a just sense of its dreadful criminality. After laying on I dare not say how many stripes, old master untied his suffering victim. When let down she could scarcely stand. From my heart I pitied her, and child as I was, and new to such scenes, the shock was tremendous. I was terrified, hushed, stunned, and bewildered. The scene here described was often repeated, for Edward and Esther continued to meet, notwithstanding all efforts to prevent their meeting.

CHAPTER VI

A Child's Reasoning

Early reflections on slavery – Aunt Jennie and Uncle Noah – Presentiment of one day becoming a freeman – Conflict between an overseer and a slave woman – Advantage of resistance – Death of an overseer – Colonel Lloyd's plantation home – Monthly distribution of food – Singing of Slaves – An explanation – The slave's food and clothing – Naked children – Life in the quarter – Sleeping-places – Not beds – Deprivation of sleep – Care of nursing babies – Ash cake – Contrast

The incidents in the foregoing chapter led me thus early to enquire into the origin and nature of slavery. Why am I a slave? Why are some people slaves and others masters? These were perplexing questions and very troublesome to my childhood. I was told by someone very early that '*God up in the sky*' had made all things, and had made black people to be slaves and white people to be masters. I was told too, that God was good and that He knew what was best for everybody. This was, however, less satisfactory than the first statement. It came point blank against all my notions of goodness. The case of Aunt Esther was in my mind. Besides, I could not tell how anybody could know that God made black people to be slaves. Then I found, too, that there were puzzling exceptions to this theory of slavery, in the fact that all black people were not slaves, and all white people were not masters. An incident occurred about this time that made a deep impression on my mind. One of the men slaves of Captain Anthony and my aunt Jennie ran away. A great noise was made about it. Old master was furious. He said he would follow them and catch them and bring them back, but he never did it, and somebody told me that Uncle Noah and Aunt Jennie had gone to the Free States and were free. Besides this occurrence, which brought much light to my mind on the subject, there were several slaves on Mr Lloyd's place who remembered being brought from Africa. There were others that told me that their fathers and mothers were stolen from Africa.

This to me was important knowledge, but not such as to make me feel very easy in my slave condition. The success of Aunt Jennie and Uncle Noah in getting away from slavery was, I think, the first fact that made me seriously think of escape for myself. I could not have been more than seven or eight years old at the time of this occurrence, but young as I was, I was already a fugitive from slavery in spirit and purpose.

Up to the time of the brutal treatment of my Aunt Esther, already narrated, and the shocking plight in which I had seen my cousin from Tuckahoe, my attention had not been especially directed to the grosser and more revolting features of slavery. I had, of course, heard of whippings and savage mutilation of slaves by brutal overseers, but happily for me I had always been out of the way of such occurrences. My play time was spent outside of the corn and tobacco fields, where the overseers and slaves were brought together and in conflict. But after the case of my Aunt Esther I saw others of the same disgusting and shocking nature. The one of these which agitated and distressed me most, Was the whipping of a woman, not belonging to my old master, but to Colonel Lloyd.

The charge against her was very common and very indefinite, namely, '*impudence*'. This crime could be committed by a slave in a hundred different ways, and depended much upon the temper and caprice of the overseer as to whether it was committed at all. He could create the offence whenever it pleased him. A look, a word, a gesture, accidental or intentional, never failed to be taken as 'impudence' when he was in the right mood for such an offence. In this case there were all the necessary conditions for the commission of the crime charged. The offender was nearly white, to begin with; she was the wife of a favourite hand on board of Mr Lloyd's sloop, and was besides the mother of five sprightly children. Vigorous and spirited woman that she was, a wife and a mother, she had a predominating share of the blood of the master running in her veins. Nellie, for that was her name, had all the qualities essential to 'impudence' to a slave overseer. My attention was called to the scene of the castigation by the loud screams and curses that proceeded from the direction of it. When I came near the parties engaged in the struggle, the overseer had hold of Nellie, endeavouring with his whole strength to drag her to a tree against her resistance.

Both his and her faces were bleeding, for the woman was doing her best. Three of her children were present, and though quite small, from seven to ten years old I should think, they gallantly took the side of their mother against the overseer, and pelted him with stones and epithets. Amid the screams of the children 'Let my mammy go! Let my mammy go!' the hoarse voice of the maddened overseer was heard in terrible oaths that he would teach her how to give a white man 'impudence'. The blood on his face and on hers attested her skill in the use of her nails, and his dogged determination to conquer. His purpose was to tie her up to a tree and give her, in slave-holding parlance, a 'genteel flogging'; and he evidently had not expected the stern and protracted resistance he was meeting, or the strength and skill needed to its execution. There were times when she seemed likely to get the better of the brute, but he finally overpowered her, and succeeded in getting her arms firmly tied to the tree towards which he had been dragging her. The victim was now at the mercy of his merciless lash. What followed I need not here describe. The cries of the now helpless woman, while undergoing the terrible infliction, were mingled with the hoarse curses of the overseer and the wild cries of her distracted children. When the poor woman was untied, her back was covered with blood. She was whipped, terribly whipped, but she was not subdued, and continued to denounce the overseer, and pour upon him every vile epithet she could think of. Such floggings are seldom repeated by overseers on the same persons. They preferred to whip those who were the most easily whipped. The doctrine that submission to violence is the best cure for violence did not hold good as between slaves and overseers. He was whipped oftener who was whipped easiest. That slave who had the courage to stand up for himself against the overseer, although he might have many hard stripes at first, became, while legally a slave, virtually, a freeman. 'You can shoot me,' said a slave to Rigby Hopkins, 'but you can't whip me,' and the result was he was neither whipped nor shot. I do not know that Mr Sevier ever attempted to whip Nellie again. He probably never did, for not long after he was taken sick and died. It was commonly said that his deathbed was a wretched one, and that the ruling passion being strong in death, he died flourishing the slave whip, and with horrid oaths upon his lips. Such a deathbed scene may only have been the imagining of the slaves. One thing is certain, that when he was in health his profanity was enough to chill the blood of an ordinary man. Nature, or habit had given to his face an expression of uncommon savageness. Tobacco and rage had ground his teeth short, and nearly every sentence that he uttered was commenced or completed with an oath. Hated for his cruelty, despised for his cowardice, he went to his grave lamented by nobody on the place outside of his own house, if, indeed, he was even lamented there.

In Mr James Hopkins, the succeeding overseer, we had a different and a better man, as good perhaps as any man could be in the position of a slave overseer. Though he sometimes wielded the lash, it was evident that he took no pleasure in it and did it with much reluctance. He stayed but a short time here, and his removal from the position was much regretted by the slaves generally. Of the successor of Mr Hopkins I shall have something to say at another time and in another place.

For the present we will attend to a further description of the business-like aspect of Colonel Lloyd's '*great house*' farm. There was always much bustle and noise there on the two days at the end of each month; for then the slaves belonging to the different branches of this great estate assembled there by their representatives to obtain their monthly allowances of corn-meal and pork. These were gala days for the slaves of the out-lying farms, and there was much rivalry among them as to who should be elected to go up to the great house farm for the '*Allowances*'; and indeed, to attend to any other business at this great place, to them the capitol of a little nation. Its beauty and grandeur, its immense wealth, its numerous population, and the fact that Uncles Harry, Peter and Jake, the sailors on board the sloop, usually kept trinkets on sale, which they bought in Baltimore to sell to their less fortunate fellow servants, made a visit to the great house farm a high privilege, and eagerly sought. It was valued, too, as a mark of distinction and confidence; but probably, the chief motive among the competitors for the office was the opportunity it afforded to shake off the monotony of the field, and to get beyond the overseer's eye and lash. Once on the road with an ox team, and seated on the tongue of the cart, with no overseer to look after him, he felt himself comparatively free.

Slaves were expected to sing as well as to work. A silent slave was not liked either by masters, or by overseers. '*Make a noise there! make a noise there!*' and '*Bear a hand*', were words usually addressed to slaves when they were silent. This, and the natural disposition of the negro to make a noise in the world, may account for the almost constant singing among them when at work. There was generally more or less singing among the teamsters at all times. It was a means of telling the overseer, in the distance, where they were, and what they were about. But on the allowance days those commissioned to the great house farm were peculiarly vocal. While on the way, they would make the grand old woods for miles around reverberate with their wild and plaintive notes. They were indeed both merry and sad. Child as I was, these wild songs greatly depressed my spirits. Nowhere outside of dear old Ireland, in the days of want and famine, have I heard sounds so mournful.

In all these slave songs there was ever some expression of praise of the great house farm – something that would please the pride of the Lloyds.

> I am going away to the great house farm,
> O, yea! O, yea! O, yea!
> My old master is a good old master,
> O, yea! O, yea! O, yea!

These words would be sung over and over again, with others, improvised as they went along – jargon, perhaps, to the reader, but full of meaning to the singers. I have sometimes thought, that the mere hearing of these songs would have done more to impress the good people of the North with the soul-crushing character of slavery, than whole volumes exposing the physical cruelties of the slave system; for the heart has no language like song. Many years ago, when recollecting my experience in this respect, I wrote of these slave songs in the following strain –

'I did not, when a slave, fully understand the deep meaning of those rude and apparently incoherent songs. I was, myself, within the circle, so that I could then neither hear nor see as those without might see and hear. They breathed the prayer and complaint of souls overflowing with the bitterest anguish. They depressed my spirits and filled my heart with ineffable sadness.'

The remark in the olden time was not unfrequently made, that slaves were the most contented and happy labourers in the world, and their dancing and singing were referred to in proof of this alleged fact; but it was a great mistake to suppose them happy because they sometimes made those joyful noises. The songs of the slaves represented their sorrows, rather than their joys. Like tears, they were a relief to their aching hearts. It is not inconsistent with the constitution of the human mind, that it avails itself of one and the same method for expressing opposite emotions. Sorrow and desolation have their songs, as well as joy and peace.

It was the boast of slave-holders that their slaves enjoyed more of the physical comforts of life than the peasantry of any country in the world.

My experience contradicts this. The men and the women slaves on Colonel Lloyd's farm received as their monthly allowance of food, eight pounds of pickled pork, or its equivalent in fish. The pork was often tainted, and the fish were of the poorest quality. With their pork or fish, they had given them one bushel of Indian meal, unbolted, of which quite fifteen per cent. was more fit for pigs than for men. With this, one pint of salt was given, and this was the entire monthly allowance of a full-grown slave, working constantly in the open field from morning till night every day in the month except Sunday. There is no kind of work which really requires a better supply of food to prevent physical exhaustion than the field work of a slave. The yearly allowance of clothing was not more ample than the supply of food. It consisted of two tow-linen shirts, one pair of trousers of the same coarse material, for summer, and a woollen pair of trousers and a woollen jacket for winter, with one pair of yarn stockings and a pair of the coarsest description. Children under ten years old had neither shoes, stockings, jackets, nor trousers. They had two coarse tow-linen shirts per year, and when these were worn out they went naked till the next allowance day – and this was the condition of the little girls as well as the boys. As to beds, they had none. One coarse blanket was given them, and this only to the men and women. The children stuck themselves in holes and corners about the quarters, often in the corners of huge chimneys, with their feet in the ashes to keep them warm. The want of beds, however, was not considered a great privation by the field-hands. Time to sleep was of far greater importance. For when the day's work was done most of them had their washing, mending, and cooking to do, and having few or no facilities for doing such things, very many of their needed sleeping hours were consumed in necessary preparations for the labours of the coming day. The sleeping apartments, if they could have been properly called such, had little regard to comfort or decency. Old and young, male and female, married and single, dropped down upon the common clay floor, each covered up with his or her blanket, their only protection from cold or exposure. The night, however, was shortened at both ends. The slaves worked often as long as they could see, and were late in cooking and mending for the coming day, and at the first grey streak of the morning they were summoned to the field by the overseer's horn. They were whipped for oversleeping more than for any other fault. Neither age nor sex found any favour. The overseer stood at the quarter door, armed with stick and whip, ready to deal heavy blows upon any who might be a little behind time. When the horn was blown there was a rush for the door, for the hindermost one was sure to get a blow from the overseer. Young mothers who worked in the field were allowed an hour about ten o'clock in the morning to go home to nurse their children. This was when they were not required to take them to the field with them, and leave them upon 'turning row', or in the corner of the fences.

As a general rule the slaves did not come to their quarters to take their meals, but took their ash-cake – called thus because baked in the ashes – and piece of pork, or their salt herrings, where they were at work.

But let us now leave the rough usage of the field, where vulgar coarseness and brutal cruelty flourished as rank as weeds in the tropics, where a vile wretch, in the shape of a man, rides, walks, and struts about, with whip in hand, dealing heavy blows and leaving deep gashes on the flesh of men and women, and turn our attention to the less repulsive slave life as it existed in the home of my childhood. Some idea of the splendour of that place sixty years ago has already been given. The contrast between the condition of the slaves and that of their masters was marvellously sharp and striking. There were pride, pomp, and luxury on the one hand, servility, dejection, and misery on the other.

CHAPTER VII

Luxuries at the Great House

Contrasts – Great-house luxuries – Its hospitality – Entertainments – Fault-finding – Shameful humiliation of an old and faithful coachman – William Wilks – Curious incident – Expressed satisfaction not always genuine – Reasons for suppressing the truth

The close-fisted stinginess that fed the poor slave on coarse corn-meal and tainted meat, that clothed him in trashy tow-linen, and hurried him on to toil through the field in all weathers, with wind and rain beating through his tattered garments, that scarcely gave even the young slave-mother time to nurse her infant in the fence-corner, wholly vanished on approaching the sacred precincts of the 'great house' itself. There, the scriptural phrase descriptive of the wealthy found exact illustration. The highly-favoured inmates of the mansion were literally arrayed in 'purple and fine linen, and fared sumptuously every day'. The table of the house groaned under the blood-bought luxuries gathered with pains-taking care at home and abroad. Fields, forests, rivers, and seas were made tributary. Immense wealth and its lavish expenditure filled the great house with all that could please the eye, or tempt the taste. Fish, flesh, and fowl were there in profusion. Chickens of all breeds; ducks of all kinds, wild and tame, the common and the huge Muscovite; Guinea fowls, turkeys, geese, and pea-fowls were fat, and fattening for the destined vortex. There the graceful swan, the mongrels, the black-necked wild goose, partridges, quails, pheasants, and pigeons, choice water-fowl, with all their strange varieties, were caught in the huge net. Beef, veal, mutton, and venison, of the most select kinds and quality, rolled in bounteous profusion to this grand consumer. The teeming riches of Chesapeake Bay, its rock-perch, drums, crocus, trout, oysters, crabs, and terrapin were drawn thither to adorn the glittering table. The dairy, too, the finest then on the Eastern Shore of Maryland, supplied by cattle of the best English stock, imported for the express purpose, poured its rich donations of fragrant cheese, golden butter, and delicious cream to heighten the attractions of the gorgeous, unending round of feasting. Nor were the fruits of the earth overlooked. The fertile garden, many acres in size, constituting a separate establishment distinct from the common farm, with its scientific gardener direct from Scotland, a Mr McDermott, and four men under his direction, was not behind, either in the abundance or in the delicacy of its contributions. The tender asparagus, the crispy celery, and the delicate cauliflower, egg plants, beets, lettuce, parsnips, peas, and French beans, early and late, radishes, cantelopes, melons of all kinds; and the fruits of all climes and of every description, from the hardy apples of the North to the lemon and orange of the South, culminated at this point. Here were gathered figs, raisins, almonds, and grapes from Spain, wines and brandies from France, teas of various flavour from China, and rich aromatic coffee from Java, all conspiring to swell the tide of high life, where pride and indolence lounged in magnificence and satiety.

Behind the tall-backed and elaborately wrought chairs stood the servants, fifteen in number, carefully selected, not only with a view to their capacity and adeptness, but with especial regard to their personal appearance, their graceful agility, and pleasing address. Some of these servants, armed with fans, wafted reviving breezes to the over-heated brows of the alabaster ladies, whilst others watched with eager eye and fawn-like step, anticipating and supplying wants before they were sufficiently formed to be announced by word or sign.

These servants constituted a sort of black aristocracy. They resembled the field-hands in nothing except their colour, and in this they held the advantage of a velvet-like glossiness, rich and beautiful. The hair, too, showed the same advantage. The delicately-formed coloured maid rustled in the scarcely-worn silk of her young mistress, while the servant men were equally well attired from the overflowing wardrobe of their young masters, so that in dress, as well as in form and feature, in manner and speech, in tastes and habits, the distance between these favoured few and the sorrow and hunger-smitten multitudes of the quarter and the field was immense.

In the stables and carriage-houses were to be found the same evidences of pride and luxurious extravagance. Here were three splendid coaches, soft within and lustrous without. Here, too, were gigs, phaetons, barouches, sulkeys, and sleighs. Here were saddles and harness, beautifully wrought and richly mounted. No less than thirty-five horses of the best approved blood, both for speed and beauty, were kept only for pleasure. The care of these horses constituted the entire occupation of two men, one or the other of them being always in the stable to answer any call which might be made from the great house. Over the way from the stable was a house built expressly for the hounds, a pack of twenty-five or thirty, the fare for which would have made glad the hearts of a dozen slaves. Horses and hounds, however, were not the only consumers of the slave's toil. The hospitality practised at the Lloyd's, would have astonished and charmed many a health-seeking divine or merchant from the North. Viewed from his table, and not from the field, Colonel Lloyd was, indeed, a model of generous hospitality. His house was literally a hotel for weeks, during the summer months. At these times, especially, the air was freighted with the rich fumes of baking, boiling, roasting, and broiling. It was something to me that I could share these odours with the winds, even if the meats themselves were under a more stringent monopoly. In master Daniel I had a friend at court, who would sometimes give me a cake, and who kept me well informed as to their guests and their entertainments. Viewed from Colonel Lloyd's table, who could have said that his slaves were not well clad and well cared for? Who would have said they did not glory in being the slaves of such a master? Who but a fanatic could have seen any cause for sympathy for either master or slave? Alas, this immense wealth, this gilded splendour, this profusion of luxury, this exemption from toil, this life of ease, this sea of plenty were not the pearly gates they seemed to a world of happiness and sweet content. The poor slave, on his hard pine plank, scantily covered with his thin blanket, slept more soundly than the feverish voluptuary who reclined upon his downy pillow. Food to the indolent is poison, not sustenance. Lurking beneath the rich and tempting viands were invisible spirits of evil, which filled the self-deluded gourmandiser with aches and pains, passions uncontrollable, fierce tempers, dyspepsia, rheumatism, lumbago and gout, and of these the Lloyds had a full share.

I had many opportunities of witnessing the restless discontent and capricious irritation of the Lloyds. My fondness for horses attracted me to the stables much of the time. The two men in charge of this establishment were old and young Barney – father and son. Old Barney was a fine looking, portly old man of a brownish complexion, and a respectful and dignified bearing. He was much devoted to his profession, and held his office as an honourable one. He was a farrier as well as an ostler, and could bleed, remove lampers from their mouths, and administer medicine to horses. No one on the farm knew so well as old Barney what to do with a sick horse; but his office was not an enviable one, and his gifts and acquirements were of little advantage to him. In nothing was Colonel Lloyd more unreasonable and exacting than in respect to the management of his horses. Any supposed inattention to these animals was sure to be visited with degrading punishment. His horses and dogs fared better than his men. Their beds were far softer and cleaner than those of his human cattle. No excuse could shield old Barney if the Colonel only suspected something wrong about his horses, and consequently he was often punished when faultless. It was painful to hear the unreasonable and fretful scoldings administered by Colonel Lloyd, his son Murray, and his sons-in-law, to this poor man. Three of the daughters of Colonel Lloyd were married, and they with their husbands remained at the great house a portion of the year, and enjoyed the luxury of whipping the servants when they pleased. A horse was seldom brought out of the stable to which no objection could be raised. 'There was dust in his hair'; 'there was a twist in his reins'; 'his foretop was not combed'; 'his mane did not lie straight'; 'his head did not look well'; 'his fetlocks had not been properly trimmed'. Something was always wrong. However groundless the complaint, Barney must stand, hat in hand, lips sealed, never answering a word in explanation or excuse. In a free State, a master thus complaining without cause, might be told by his ostler: 'Sir, I am sorry I cannot please you, but since I have done the best I can and fail to do so, your remedy is to dismiss me'. But here the ostler must listen and trem-blingly abide his master's behest. One of the most heart-saddening and humiliating scenes I ever witnessed was the whipping of old Barney by Colonel Lloyd. These two men were both advanced in years; there were the silver locks of the master, and the bald and toil-worn brow of the slave – superior and inferior here, powerful and weak here, but *equals* before God. 'Uncover your head,' said the imperious master; he was obeyed. 'Take off your jacket, you old rascal!' and off came Barney's jacket. 'Down on your knees!' down knelt the old man, his shoulders bare, his bald head glistening in the sunshine, and his aged knees on the cold, damp ground. In this humble and debasing attitude, that master, to whom he had devoted the best years and the best strength of his life, came forward and laid on thirty lashes with his horse-whip. The old man made no resistance, but bore it patiently, answering each blow with only a shrug of the shoulders and a groan. I do not think that the physical suffering from this infliction was severe, for the whip was a light riding-whip; but the spectacle of an aged man – a husband and a father – humbly kneeling before his fellow-man, shocked me at the time; and since I have grown older, few of the features of slavery have impressed me with a deeper sense of its injustice and barbarity than this exciting scene. I owe it to the truth, however, to say that this was the first and last time I ever saw a slave compelled to kneel to receive a whipping.

Another incident, illustrating a phase of slavery to which I have referred in another connection, I may here mention. Besides two other coachmen, Colonel Lloyd owned one named William Wilks, and his was one of the exceptional cases where a slave possessed a surname, and was recognised by it, by both coloured and white people. Wilks was a very fine-looking man. He was about as white as anyone on the plantation, and in form and feature bore a very striking resemblance to Murray Lloyd. It was whispered and generally believed that William Wilks was a son of Colonel Lloyd, by a highly favoured slave-woman, who was still on the plantation. There were many reasons for believing this whisper, not only from his personal appearance, but from the undeniable freedom which he enjoyed over all others, and his apparent consciousness of being something more than a slave to his master. It was notorious too, that William had a deadly enemy in Murray Lloyd, whom he so much resembled, and that the latter greatly worried his father with importunities to sell William. Indeed, he gave his father no rest, until he did sell him to Austin Woldfolk, the great slave-trader at that time. Before selling him, however, he tried to make things smooth by giving William a whipping, but it proved a failure. It was a compromise, and like most such, defeated itself – for soon after Colonel Lloyd atoned to William for the abuse, by giving him a gold watch and chain. Another fact somewhat curious was, that though sold to the remorseless Woldfolk, taken in irons to Baltimore, and cast into prison, with a view to being sent to the South, William outbid all his purchasers, paid for himself, and afterwards resided in Baltimore. How this was accomplished was a great mystery at the time, explained only on the supposition that the hand which had bestowed the gold watch and chain, had also supplied the purchase-money, but I have since learned that this was not the true explanation. Wilks had many friends in Baltimore and Annapolis, and they united to save him from a fate which was the one of all others most dreaded by the slaves. Practical amalgamation was however so common at the South, and so many circumstances pointed in that direction, that there was little reason to doubt that William Wilks was the son of Edward Lloyd.

The real feelings and opinions of the slaves were not much known or respected by their masters. The distance between the two was too great to admit of such knowledge; and in this respect Colonel Lloyd was no exception to the rule. His slaves were so numerous he did not know them when he saw them. Nor, indeed, did all his slaves know him. It is reported of him, that riding along the road one day he met a coloured man, and addressed him in what was the usual way of speaking to coloured people on the public highways of the South: 'Well, boy, who do you belong to?' 'To Colonel Lloyd,' replied the slave. 'Well, does the Colonel treat you well?' 'No, sir,' was the ready reply. 'What, does he work you hard?' 'Yes, sir.' 'Well, don't he give you enough to eat?' 'Yes, sir, he gives me enough to eat, such as it is.' The Colonel rode on; the slave also went on about his business, not dreaming that he had been conversing with his master. He thought and said nothing of the matter, until two or three weeks afterwards, he was informed by the overseer that for having found fault with his master, he was now to be sold to a Georgia trader. He was immediately chained and handcuffed; and thus without a moment's warning, he was snatched away, and forever sundered from his family and friends by a hand us unrelenting as that of death. This was the penalty of telling the simple truth, in answer to a series of plain questions. It was partly in consequence of such facts, that slaves, when enquired of as to their condition and the character of their masters, would almost invariably say that they were contented and their masters kind. Slave-holders are known to have sent spies among their slaves to ascertain if possible their views and feelings in regard to their condition; hence the maxim established among them, that 'a still tongue makes a wise head'. They would suppress the truth rather than take the consequence of telling it, and in so doing they proved themselves a part of the human family. I was frequently asked if I had a kind master, and I do not remember ever to have given a negative reply. I did not consider myself as uttering that which was strictly untrue, for I always measured the kindness of my master by the standard of kindness set by the slave-holders around us.

CHAPTER VIII

Characteristics of Overseers

Austin Gore – Sketch of his character – Overseers as a class – Their peculiar characteristics – The marked individuality of Austin Gore – His sense of duty – Murder of poor Denby – Sensation – How Gore made his peace with Colonel Lloyd – Other horrible murders – No laws for the protection of slaves could possibly be enforced

The comparatively moderate rule of Mr Hopkins as overseer on Colonel Lloyd's plantation was succeeded by that of another whose name was Austin Gore. I hardly know how to bring this man fitly before the reader, for under him there was more suffering from violence and bloodshed than had, according to the older slaves, ever been experienced before at that place. He was an overseer, and possessed the peculiar characteristics of his class, yet to call him merely an overseer would not give one a fair conception of the man. I speak of overseers as a class, for they were such. They were as distinct from the slave-holding gentry of the South as are the fish-women of Paris, and the coal-heavers of London, distinct from other grades of society. They constituted a separate fraternity at the South. They were arranged and classified by that great law of attraction which determines the sphere and affinities of men; which ordains that men whose malign and brutal propensities preponderate over their moral and intellectual

endowments shall naturally fall into those employments which promise
the largest gratification to those predominating instincts or propensities.
The office of overseer took this raw material of vulgarity and brutality,
and stamped it as a distinct class in Southern life. But in this class, as in
all other classes, there were sometimes persons of marked individuality,
yet with a general resemblance to the mass. Mr Gore was one of those
to whom a general characterisation would do no manner of justice. He
was an overseer, but he was something more. With the malign and
tyrannical qualities of an overseer he combined something of the lawful
master. He had the artfulness and mean ambition of his class, without
its disgusting swagger and noisy bravado. There was an easy air of
independence about him; a calm self-possession; at the same time a
sternness of glance which might well daunt less timid hearts than those
of poor slaves, accustomed from childhood to cower before a driver's
lash. He was one of those overseers who could torture the slightest
word or look into 'impudence', and he had the nerve not only to resent
but to punish promptly and severely. There could be no answering
back. Guilty or not guilty, to be accused was to be sure of a flogging.
His very presence was fearful, and I shunned him as I would have
shunned a rattlesnake. His piercing black eyes and sharp, shrill voice
ever awakened sensations of dread. Other overseers, how brutal soever
they might be, would sometimes seek to gain favour with the slaves by
indulging in a little pleasantry; but Gore never said a funny thing, or
perpetrated a joke. He was always cold, distant and unapproachable –
the overseer on Colonel Edward Lloyd's plantation – and needed no
higher pleasure than the performance of the duties of his office. When
he used the lash, it was from a sense of duty, without fear of
consequences. There was a stern will, an iron-like reality about him,
which would easily have made him chief of a band of pirates, had his
environments been favourable to such a sphere. Among many other
deeds of shocking cruelty committed by him was the murder of a
young coloured man named Bill Denby. He was a powerful fellow, full
of animal spirits, and one of the most valuable of Colonel Lloyd's
slaves. In some way – I know not what – he offended this Mr Austin
Gore, and in accordance with the usual custom the latter undertook to
flog him. He had given him but few stripes when Denby broke away
from him, plunged into the creek, and standing there with the water up
to his neck refused to come out; whereupon, for this refusal, Gore *shot
him dead*; It is said that Gore gave Denby three calls to come out,
telling him if he did not obey the last call he should shoot him. When
the last call was given Denby still stood his ground, and Gore, without

further parley, or without making any further effort to induce obedience, raised his gun deliberately to his face, took deadly aim at his standing victim, and with one click of the gun the mangled body sank out of sight, and only his warm red blood marked the place where he had stood.

This fiendish murder produced, as it could not help doing, a tremendous sensation. The slaves were panic-stricken, and howled with alarm. The atrocity roused my old master, and he spoke out in reprobation of it. Both he and Colonel Lloyd arraigned Gore for his cruelty; but he, calm and collected, as though nothing unusual had happened, declared that Denby had become unmanageable; that he set a dangerous example to the other slaves, and that unless some such prompt measure was resorted to, there would be an end to all rule and order on the plantation. That convenient covert for all manner of villainy and outrage, that cowardly alarm-cry, that the slaves would 'take the place', was pleaded, just us it had been in thousands of similar cases. Gore's defence was evidently considered satisfactory, for he was continued in his office, without being subjected to a judicial investigation. The murder was committed in the presence of slaves only, and they, being slaves, could neither institute a suit nor testify against the murderer. Mr Gore lived in St Michaels, Talbot Co., Maryland, and I have no reason to doubt, from what I know to have been the moral sentiment of the place, that he was us highly esteemed and as much respected us though his guilty soul had not been stained with innocent blood.

I speak advisedly when I say that killing a slave, or any coloured person, in Talbot Co., Maryland, was not treated as a crime, either by the courts or the community. Mr Thomas Lanman, ship carpenter of St Michael's, killed two slaves, one of whom he butchered with a hatchet, by knocking his brains out. He used to boast of having committed the awful and bloody deed. I have heard him do so laughingly, declaring himself a benefactor of his country, and that 'when others would do as much as he had done, they would be rid of the damned niggers.'

Another notorious fact which I may state was the murder of a young girl between fifteen and sixteen years of age, by her mistress, Mrs Giles Hicks, who lived but a short distance from Colonel Lloyd's. This wicked woman, in the paroxysm of her wrath, not content with killing her victim, literally mangled her face and broke her breast-bone. Wild and infuriated as she was, she took the precaution to cause the burial of the girl; but, the facts of the case getting abroad, the remains were

disinterred, and a coroner's jury assembled, who, after due deliberation, decided that 'the girl had come to her death from severe beating'.
The offence for which this girl was thus hurried out of the world was
this, she had been set that night, and several preceding nights, to mind
Mrs Hicks' baby, and having fallen into a sound sleep, the crying of the
baby did not wake her, as it did its mother. The tardiness of the girl
excited Mrs Hicks, who, after calling her many times, seized a piece of
fire-wood from the fireplace, and pounded in her skull and breast-bone
till death ensued. I will not say that this murder most foul produced no
sensation. It *did* produce a sensation. A warrant was issued for the arrest
of Mrs Hicks, but incredible to tell, for some reason or other, that
warrant was never served, and she not only escaped condign punishment, but also the pain and mortification of being arraigned before a
court of justice.

While I am detailing the bloody deeds that took place during my stay
on Colonel Lloyd's plantation, I will briefly narrate another dark
transaction, which occurred about the time of the murder of Denby.

On the side of the river Wye, opposite Colonel Lloyd's, there lived a
Mr Beal Bondley, a wealthy slave-holder. In the direction of his land,
and near the shore, there was an excellent oyster fishing-ground, and to
this some of Lloyd's slaves occasionally resorted in their little canoes at
night, with a view of making up the deficiency of their scanty allowance
of food by the oysters that they could easily get there. Mr Bondley took
it into his head to regard this as a trespass, and while an old man slave
was engaged in catching a few of the many millions of oysters that lined
the bottom of the creek, to satisfy his hunger, the rascally Bondley,
lying in ambush, without the slightest warning, discharged the contents
of his musket into the back of the poor old man. As good fortune would
have it, the shot did not prove fatal, and Mr Bondley came over, the
next day, to see Colonel Lloyd about it. What happened between them
I know not, but there was little said about it and nothing publicly done.
One of the commonest sayings to which my ears early became
accustomed, was that it was 'worth but half a cent to kill a nigger, and
half a cent to bury one'. While I heard of numerous murders
committed by slave-holders on the Eastern Shore of Maryland. I never
knew a solitary instance where a slave-holder was either hung or
imprisoned for having murdered a slave. The usual pretext for such
crimes was that the slave had offered resistance. Should a slave, when
assaulted, but raise his hand in self-defence, the white assaulting party
was fully justified by Southern law, and Southern public opinion, in
shooting the slave down, and for this there was no redress.

CHAPTER IX

Change of Location

I have nothing cruel or shocking to relate of my own personal
experience while I remained on Colonel Lloyd's plantation, at the
home of my old master. An occasional cuff from Aunt Katy, and a
regular whipping from old master, such as any heedless and mischievous boy might get from his father, is all that I have to say of this sort. I
was not old enough to work in the field, and there being little else than
field-work to perform, I had much leisure. The most I had to do was to
drive up the cows in the evening, to keep the front yard clean, and to
perform small errands for my young mistress, Lucretia Auld. I had
reasons for thinking this lady was very kindly disposed towards me, and
although I was not often the object of her attention, I constantly
regarded her as my friend, and was always glad when it was my
privilege to do her a service. In a family where there was so much that
was harsh and indifferent, the slightest word or look of kindness was of
great value. Miss Lucretia – as we all continued to call her long after
her marriage – had bestowed on me such looks and words as taught me
that she pitied me, if she did not love me. She sometimes gave me a
piece of bread and butter, an article not set down in our bill of fare, but
an extra ration aside from both Aunt Katy and old master, and given as
I believed solely out of the tender regard she had for me. Then too, I
one day got into the wars with Uncle Abel's son 'Ike', and had got sadly
worsted; the little rascal struck me directly in the forehead with a sharp
piece of cinder, fused with iron, from the old blacksmith's forge, which

made a cross in my forehead very plainly to be seen even now. The gash bled very freely, and I roared and betook myself home. The cold-hearted Aunt Katy paid no attention either to my wound or my roaring, except to tell me it 'served me right; and I had no business with Ike; it would do me good; I would now keep away from "dem Lloyd niggers" '. Miss Lucretia in this state of the case came forward, and called me into the parlour, an extra privilege of itself, and without using toward me any of the hard and reproachful epithets of Aunt Katy, quietly acted the good Samaritan. With her own soft hand she washed the blood from my head and face, brought her own bottle of balsam, and with the balsam wetted a nice piece of white linen and bound up my head. The balsam was not more healing to the wound in my head, than her kindness was healing to the wounds in my spirit, induced by the unfeeling words of Aunt Katy. After this Miss Lucretia was yet more my friend. I felt her to be such; and I have no doubt that the simple act of binding up my head did much to awaken in her heart an interest in my welfare. It is quite true that this interest seldom showed itself in anything more than in giving me a piece of bread and butter, but this was a great favour on a slave plantation, and I was the only one of the children to whom such attention was paid. When very severely pinched with hunger, I had the habit of singing, which the good lady very soon came to understand, and when she heard me singing under her window, I was very apt to be paid for my music. Thus I had two friends, both at important points – Mas'r Daniel at the great house, and Miss Lucretia at home. From Mas'r Daniel I got protection from the bigger boys, and from Miss Lucretia I got bread by singing when I was hungry, and sympathy when I was abused by the termagant in the kitchen. For such friendship I was deeply grateful, and bitter as are my recollections of slavery, it is true pleasure to recall any instances of kindness, any sunbeams of humane treatment, which found way to my soul, through the iron grating of my house of bondage. Such beams seem all the brighter from the general darkness into which they penetrate, and the impression they make there is vividly distinct.

As before intimated, I received no severe treatment from the hands of my master, but the insufficiency of both food and clothing was a serious trial to me, especially from the lack of clothing. In hottest summer and coldest winter, I was kept almost in a state of nudity. My only clothing – a little coarse sackcloth or tow-linen sort of shirt, scarcely reaching to my knees, was worn night and day and changed once a week. In the daytime I could protect myself by keeping on the sunny side of the house, or in stormy weather, in the corner of the kitchen chimney. But the great difficulty was to keep warm during the night. The pigs in the pen had leaves, and the horses in the stable had straw, but the children had no beds. They lodged anywhere in the ample kitchen. I slept generally in a little closet, without even a blanket to cover me. In very cold weather I sometimes got down the bag in which corn was carried to the mill, and crawled into that. Sleeping there with my head in and my feet out, I was partly protected, though never comfortable. My feet have been so cracked with the frost that the pen with which I am writing might be laid in the gashes. Our corn-meal mush, which was our only regular if not all-sufficing diet, when sufficiently cooled from the cooking, was placed in a large tray or trough. This was set down on the floor of the kitchen, or out of doors on the ground, and the children were called like so many pigs, and like so many pigs would come, some with oyster-shells, some with pieces of shingle, but none with spoons, and literally devour the mush. He who could eat fastest got most, and he that was strongest got the best place, but few left the trough really satisfied. I was the most unlucky of all, for Aunt Katy had no good feeling for me, and if I pushed the children, or if they told her of anything unfavourable of me, she always believed the worst, and was sure to whip me.

As I grew older and more thoughtful, I became more and more filled with a sense of my wretchedness. The unkindness of Aunt Katy, the hunger and cold I suffered, and the terrible reports of wrongs and outrages which came to my ear, together with what I almost daily witnessed, led me to wish I had never been born. I used to contrast my condition with that of the blackbirds, whose wild and sweet songs made me fancy them so happy. Their apparent joy only deepened the shades of my sorrow. There are thoughtful days in the lives of children – at least there were in mine – when they grapple with all the great primary subjects of knowledge, and reach in a moment conclusions which no subsequent experience can shake. I was just as well aware of the unjust, unnatural, and murderous character of slavery, when nine years old, as I am now. Without any appeal to books, to laws, or to authorities of any kind, to regard God as 'Our Father', condemned slavery as a crime.

I was in this unhappy state when I received from Miss Lucretia the joyful intelligence that my old master had determined to let me go to Baltimore to live with Mr Hugh Auld, a brother to Mr Thomas Auld, Miss Lucretia's husband. I shall never forget the ecstacy with which I received this information, three days before the time set for my departure. They were the three happiest days I had ever known. I spent the largest part of them in the creek, washing off the plantation scurf, and thus preparing for my new home. Miss Lucretia took a lively interest in getting me ready She told me I must get all the dead skin off my feet and knees, for the people in Baltimore were very cleanly, and would laugh at me if I looked dirty; and besides she was intending to give me a pair of trousers, but which I could not put on unless I got all the dirt off. This was a warning which I was bound to heed, for the thought of owning and wearing a pair of trousers was great indeed. So I went at it in good earnest, working for the first time in my life in the hope of reward. I was greatly excited, and could hardly consent to sleep lest I should be left. The ties that ordinarily bind children to their homes, had no existence in my case, and in thinking of a home elsewhere, I was confident of finding none that I should relish less than the one I was leaving, If I should meet with hardship, hunger, and nakedness, I had known them all before, and I could endure them elsewhere, especially in Baltimore, for I had something of the feeling about that city which is expressed in the saying that 'being hanged in England is better than dying a natural death in Ireland'. I had the strongest desire to see Baltimore. My cousin Tom, a boy two or three years older than I, had been there, and, though not fluent in speech – he stuttered immoderately – he had inspired me with that desire by his eloquent descriptions of the place. Tom was sometimes cabin-boy on board the sloop *Sally Lloyd*, which Captain Thomas Auld commanded, and when he came home from Baltimore he was always a sort of hero among us, at least till his trip to Baltimore was forgotten. I could never tell him anything, or point out anything that struck me as beautiful or powerful, but he had seen something in Baltimore far surpassing it. Even the 'great house', with all its pictures within, and pillars without, he had the hardihood to say, 'was nothing to Baltimore'. He bought a trumpet, worth sixpence, and brought it home; told what he had seen in the windows of the stores; that he had heard shooting-crackers, and seen soldiers; that he had seen a steamboat; that there were ships in Baltimore that could carry four such sloops as the *Sally Lloyd*. He said a great deal about the Market house; of the ringing of the bells; and of many other things which roused my curiosity very much, and indeed which brightened my hopes of happiness in my new home. We sailed out of Miles River for Baltimore early on Saturday morning. I remember only the day of the week, for at that time I had no knowledge of the days of the month, nor indeed of the months of the year. On setting sail I walked aft and gave to Colonel Lloyd's plantation what I hoped would be the last look I should give to it, or to any place like it. After taking this last view, I quitted the quarterdeck, made my way to the bow of the boat, and spent the remainder of the day in looking ahead; interesting myself in what was in the distance, rather than in what was near by, or behind. The vessels sweeping along the bay were objects full of interest to me. The broad bay opened like a shoreless ocean on my boyish vision, filling me with wonder and admiration.

Late in the afternoon we reached Annapolis, stopping there not long enough to admit of going ashore. It was the first large town I had ever seen, and though it was inferior to many a factory village in New England, my feelings on seeing it were excited to a pitch very little below that reached by travellers at the first view of Rome. The dome of the State house was especially imposing, and surpassed in grandeur the appearance of the 'great house' I had left behind. So the great world was opening upon me, and I was eagerly acquainting myself with its multifarious lessons.

We arrived in Baltimore on Sunday morning, and landed at Smith's wharf, not far from Bowly's wharf. We had on board a large flock of sheep, for the Baltimore market; and after assisting in driving them to the slaughter house of Mr Curtiss on London Slater's hill, I was conducted by Rich – one of the hands belonging to the sloop – to my new home on Alliciana Street, near Gardiner's shipyard, on Fell's point. Mr and Mrs Hugh Auld, my new master and mistress, were both at home and met me at the door with their rosy-cheeked little son Thomas, to take care of whom was to constitute my further occupation. In fact it was to 'little Tommy', rather than to his parents, that old master made a present of me, and, though there were no *legal* form or arrangement entered into, I have no doubt that Mr and Mrs Auld felt that in due time I should be the legal property of their bright-eyed and beloved boy Tommy. I was struck with the appearance especially of my new mistress. Her face was lighted with the kindliest emotions; and the reflex influence of her countenance, as well as the tenderness with which she seemed to regard me, while asking me sundry little questions, greatly delighted me, and lit up, to my fancy, the pathway of my future. Little Thomas was affectionately told by his mother that 'there was his Freddy', and that 'Freddy would take care of him'; and I was told to 'be kind to little Tommy', an injunction I scarcely needed, for I had already fallen in love with the dear boy. With these little ceremonies I was initiated into my new home, and entered upon my peculiar duties, then unconscious of a cloud to dim its broad horizon.

I may say here, that I regard my removal from Colonel Lloyd's plantation as one of the most interesting and fortunate events of my life. Viewing it in the light of human likelihoods, it is quite probable that but for the mere circumstance of being thus removed, before the rigours of slavery had fully fastened upon me; before my young spirit had been crushed under the iron control of the slave-driver. I might have continued in slavery until emancipated by the war.

CHAPTER X

Learning to Read

City annoyances – Plantation regrets – My mistress – Her history – Her kindness – My master – His sourness – My comforts – Increased sensitiveness – My occupation – Learning to read – Baneful effects of slave-holding on my dear, good mistress – Mr Hugh forbids Mrs Sophia to teach me further – Clouds gather on my bright prospects – Master Auld's exposition of the philosophy of slavery – City slaves – Country slaves – Contrasts – Exceptions – Mr Hamilton's two slaves – Mrs Hamilton's cruel treatment of them – Piteous aspect presented by them – No power to come between the slave and the slave-holder

Established in my new home in Baltimore, I was not very long in perceiving that in picturing to myself what was to be my life there, my imagination had painted only the bright side; and that the reality had its dark shades as well as its light ones. The open country, which had been so much to me, was all shut out. Walled in on every side by towering brick buildings, the heat of the summer was intolerable to me, and the hard brick pavements almost blistered my feet. If I ventured out to the streets, new and strange objects glared upon me at every step, and startling sounds greeted my ears from all directions. My country eyes and ears were confused and bewildered. Troops of hostile boys pounced upon me at every corner. They chased me, and called me 'Eastern-Shore man', till really I almost wished myself back on the Eastern Shore. My new mistress happily proved to be all she had seemed, and in her presence I easily forgot all the outside annoyances.

Mrs Sophia was naturally of an excellent disposition – kind, gentle, and cheerful. The supercilious contempt for the rights and feelings of others, and the petulance and bad humour which generally characterised slave-holding ladies, were all quite absent from her manner and bearing toward me. She had never been a slave-holder – a thing then quite unusual at the South – but had depended almost entirely upon her own industry for a living. To this fact the dear lady no doubt owed the excellent preservation of her natural goodness of heart, for slavery could change a saint into a sinner, and an angel into a demon. I hardly knew how to behave towards 'Miss Sophia', as I used to call Mrs Hugh Auld. I could not approach her even, as I had formerly approached Mrs Thomas Auld. Why should I hang down my head, and speak with bated breath, when there was no pride to scorn me, no coldness to repel me, and no hatred to inspire me with fear? I therefore soon came to regard her as something more akin to a mother than a slave-holding mistress. So far from deeming it impudent in a slave to look her straight in the face, she seemed ever to say, 'Look up, child; don't be afraid.' The sailors belonging to the sloop esteemed it a great privilege to be the bearers of parcels or messages to her, for whenever they came, they were sure of a most kind and pleasant reception. If little Thomas was her son, and her most dearly loved child, she made me something like his half-brother in her affections. If dear Tommy was exalted to a place on his mother's knee, 'Feddy' was honoured by a place at the mother's side. Nor did the slave-boy lack the caressing strokes of her gentle hand, soothing him into the consciousness that, though motherless, he was not friendless. Mrs Auld was not only kindhearted, but remarkably pious; frequent in her attendance at public worship, much given to reading the Bible, and to chanting hymns of praise when alone. Mr Hugh was altogether a different character. He cared very little about religion; knew more of the world, and was more a part of the world, than his wife. He set out doubtless to be, as the world goes, a respectable man, and to get on by becoming a successful shipbuilder, in that city of shipbuilding. This was his ambition, and it fully occupied him. I was of course of very little consequence to him, and when he smiled upon me, as he sometimes did, the smile was borrowed from his lovely wife, and like all borrowed light, was transient, and vanished with the source whence it was derived. Though I must, in truth, characterise Master Hugh as a sour man of forbidding appearance, it is due to him to acknowledge that he was never cruel to me, according to the notion of cruelty in Maryland. During the first year or two, he left me almost exclusively to the management of his wife. She was my law-giver. In hands so tender as hers, and in the absence of the cruelties of the plantation, I became both physically and mentally much more sensitive, and a frown from my mistress caused me far more suffering than Aunt Katy's hardest cuffs. Instead of the cold, damp floor of my old master's kitchen, I was on carpets; for the corn bag in winter, I had a good straw bed, well furnished with covers; for the coarse corn-meal in the morning, I had good bread and mush occasionally; for my old tow-linen shirt, I had good clean clothes. I was really well off. My employment was to run errands, and to take care of Tommy; to prevent his getting in the way of carriages, and to keep him out of harm's way generally. So for a time everything went well. I say for a time, because the fatal poison of irresponsible power, and the natural influence of slave customs, were not very long in making their impression on the gentle and loving disposition of my excellent mistress. She regarded me at first as a child, like any other. This was the natural and spontaneous thought; afterwards, when she came to consider me as property, our relations to each other were changed, but a nature so noble as hers could not instantly become perverted, and it took several years before the sweetness of her temper was wholly lost.

The frequent hearing of my mistress reading the Bible aloud, for she often read aloud when her husband was absent, awakened my curiosity in respect to this *mystery* of reading, and roused in me the desire to learn. Up to this time I had known nothing whatever of this wonderful art, and my ignorance and inexperience of what it could do for me, as well as my confidence in my mistress, emboldened me to ask her to teach me to read. With an unconsciousness and inexperience equal to my own, she readily consented, and in an incredibly short time, by her kind assistance, I had mastered the alphabet and could spell words of three or four letters. My mistress seemed almost as proud of my progress as if I had been her own child, and supposing that her husband would be as well pleased, she made no secret of what she was doing for me. Indeed, she exultingly told him of the aptness of her pupil, and of her intention to persevere in teaching me, as she felt it her duty to do, at least to read the Bible. And here arose the first dark cloud over my Baltimore prospects, the precursor of chilling blasts and drenching storms. Master Hugh was astounded beyond measure, and probably for the first time, proceeded to unfold to his wife the true philosophy of the slave system, and the peculiar rules necessary in the nature of the case to be observed in the management of human chattels. Of course he forbade her to give me any further instruction, telling her in the first place that to do so was unlawful, as it was also unsafe, 'For,' said he, 'if you give a nigger an inch he will take an ell. Learning will spoil the best nigger in the world. If he learns to read the Bible it will for ever unfit him to be a slave. He should know nothing but the will of his master, and learn to obey it. As to himself, learning will do him no good, but a great deal of harm, making him disconsolate and unhappy. If you teach him how to read, he'll want to know how to write, and this accomplished, he'll be running away with himself.' Such was the tenor of Master Hugh's oracular exposition; and it must be confessed that he very clearly comprehended the nature and the requirements of the relation of master and slave. His discourse was the first decidedly antislavery lecture to which it had been my lot to listen. Mrs Auld evidently felt the force of what he said, and like an obedient wife, began to shape her course in the direction indicated by him. The effect of his words *on me* was neither slight nor transitory. His iron sentences, cold and harsh, sunk like heavy weights deep into my heart, and stirred up within me a rebellion not soon to be allayed. This was a new and special revelation, dispelling a painful mystery against which my youthful understanding had struggled, and struggled in vain, to wit, the white man's power to perpetuate the enslavement of the black man. 'Very well,' thought I. 'Knowledge unfits a child to be a slave.' I instinctively assented to the proposition, and from that moment I understood the direct pathway from slavery to freedom. It was just what I needed, and it came to me at a time and from a source whence I least expected it. Of course I was greatly saddened at the thought of losing the assistance of my kind mistress, but the information so instantly derived, to some extent compensated me for the loss I had sustained in this direction. Wise as Mr Auld was, he underrated my comprehension, and had little idea of the use to which I was capable of putting the impressive lesson he was giving to his wife. He wanted me to be a slave; I had already voted against that on the home plantation of Colonel Lloyd. That which he most loved I most hated; and the very determination which he expressed to keep me in ignorance, only rendered me the more resolute to seek intelligence. In learning to read, therefore, I am not sure that I do not owe quite as much to the opposition of my master as to the kindly assistance of my amiable mistress. I acknowledge the benefit rendered me by the one, and by the other, believing that but for my mistress I might have grown up in ignorance.

CHAPTER XI

Growing in Knowledge

My mistress – Her slave-holding duties – The effects on her
originally noble nature – The conflict in her mind – She opposes
my learning to read – Too late – She had given me the 'inch', I
was resolved to take the 'ell' – How I pursued my study to read –
My tutors – What progress I made – Slavery – What I heard said
about it – Thirteen years old – Columbian Orator – Dialogue
Speeches – Sheridan – Pitt – Lords Chatham and Fox –
Knowledge increasing – Liberty – Singing – Sadness –
Unhappiness of Mrs Sophia – My hatred of slavery – One Upas
tree overshadows us all

I lived in the family of Mr Auld, at Baltimore, seven years, during
which time, as the almanac makers say of the weather, my condition
was variable. The most interesting feature of my history here, was my
learning to read and write under somewhat marked disadvantages. In
attaining this knowledge I was compelled to resort to indirections by
no means congenial to my nature, and which were really humiliating to
my sense of candour and uprightness. My mistress, checked in her
benevolent designs toward me, not only ceased instructing me herself,
but set her face as a flint against my learning to read by any means. It is
due to her to say, however, that she did not adopt this course in all its
stringency at first. She either thought it unnecessary, or she lacked the
depravity needed to make herself forget at once my human nature. She
was, as I have said, naturally a kind and tender-hearted woman, and in
the humanity of her heart and the simplicity of her mind, she set out,
when I first went to live with her, to treat me as she supposed one
human being ought to treat another.

Nature never intended that men and women should be either slaves
or slave-holders, and nothing but rigid training, long persisted in, can
perfect the character of the one or the other. Mrs Auld was singularly
deficient in the qualities of a slave-holder. It was no easy matter for her
to think or to feel that the curly-headed boy, who stood by her side,

and even leaned on her lap, who was loved by little Tommy, and who loved little Tommy in turn, sustained to her only the relation of a chattel. I was more than that; she felt me to be more than that. I could talk and sing; I could laugh and weep; I could reason and remember; I could love and hate. I was human, and she, dear lady, knew and felt me to be so. How could she then treat me as a brute, without a mighty struggle with all the noblest powers of her soul? That struggle came, and the will and power of the husband was victorious. Her noble soul was overcome, and he who wrought the wrong was injured in the fall, no less than the rest of the household. When I went into that household, it was the abode of happiness and contentment. The wife and mistress there was a model of affection and tenderness. Her fervent piety and watchful uprightness made it impossible to see her without thinking and feeling, 'that woman is a Christian'. There was no sorrow nor suffering for which she had not a tear, and there was no innocent joy for which she had not a smile. She had bread for the hungry, clothes for the naked, and comfort for every mourner who came within her reach. But slavery soon proved its ability to divest her of these excellent qualities, and her home of its early happiness. Conscience cannot stand much violence. Once thoroughly injured, who is he who can repair the damage? If it be broken toward the slave on Sunday, it will be toward the master on Monday. It cannot long endure such shocks. It must stand unharmed, or it does not stand at all. As my condition in the family waxed bad, that of the family waxed no better. The first step in the wrong direction was the violence done to nature and to conscience, in arresting the benevolence that would have enlightened my young mind. In ceasing to instruct me, my mistress had to seek to justify herself to herself; and once consenting to take sides in such a debate, she was compelled to hold her position. One needs little knowledge of moral philosophy to see where she inevitably landed. She finally became even more violent in her opposition to my learning to read, than was Mr Auld himself. Nothing now appeared to make her more angry than seeing me, seated in some nook or corner, quietly reading a book or newspaper. She would rush at me with the utmost fury, and snatch the book or paper from my hand, with something of the wrath and consternation which a traitor might be supposed to feel on being discovered in a plot by some dangerous spy. The conviction once thoroughly established in her mind, that education and slavery were incompatible with each other, I was most narrowly watched in all my movements. If I remained in a separate room from the family for any considerable time, I was sure to be suspected of having a book, and was at once called to give an account of myself. But this was too late: the first and never-to-be-retraced step had been taken. Teaching me the alphabet had been the 'inch' given, I was now waiting only for the opportunity to 'take the ell'.

Filled with the determination to learn to read at any cost, I hit upon many expedients to accomplish that much desired end. The plan which I mainly adopted, and the one which was most successful, was that of using my young white playmates, whom I met in the streets, as teachers. I used to carry almost constantly a copy of Webster's spelling-book in my pocket, and when sent on errands, or when playtime was allowed me, I would step aside with my young friends and take a lesson in spelling. I am greatly indebted to these boys – Gustavus Dorgan, Joseph Bailey, Charles Farity, and William Cosdry.

Although slavery was a delicate subject, and very cautiously talked about among grown-up people in Maryland, I frequently talked about it, and that very freely, with the white boys. I would sometimes say to them, while seated on a curbstone or a cellar door; 'I wish I could be free, as you will be when you get to be men.' 'You will be free, you know, as soon as you are twenty-one, and can go where you like, but I am a slave for life. Have I not as good a right to be free as you have?' Words like these, I observed, always troubled them; and I had no small satisfaction in drawing out from them, as I occasionally did, that fresh and bitter condemnation of slavery which ever springs from natures unseared and unperverted. Of all consciences, let me have those to deal with, which have not been seared and bewildered with the cares and perplexities of life. I do not remember ever to have met with a boy while I was in slavery who defended the system; but I do remember many times, when I was consoled by them, and by them encouraged to hope that something would yet occur by which I would be made free. Over and over again, they have told me that 'they believed I had as good a right to be free as they had', and that 'they did not believe God ever made anyone to be a slave'. It is easily seen that such little conversations with my playfellows had no tendency to weaken my love of liberty, nor to render me contented as a slave.

When I was about thirteen years old, and had succeeded in learning to read, every increase of knowledge, especially anything respecting the Free States, was an additional weight to the almost intolerable burden of my thought – 'I am a slave for life.' To my bondage I could see no end. It was a terrible reality, and I shall never be able to tell how sadly that thought chafed my young spirit. Fortunately, or unfortunately, I had earned a little money in blacking boots for some gentlemen, with which I purchased of Mr Knight, on Thames Street, what was then a very popular schoolbook, viz., *The Columbian Orator*, for which I paid fifty cents. I was led to buy this book by hearing some little boys say they were going to learn some pieces out of it for recitation. This volume was indeed a rich treasure, and every opportunity afforded me, for a time, was spent in diligently perusing it. Among much other interesting matter, that which I read again and again, with unflagging satisfaction, was a short dialogue between a master and his slave. The slave is represented as having been recaptured in a second attempt to run away; and the master opens the dialogue with an upbraiding speech, charging the slave with ingratitude, and demanding to know what he has to say in his own defence. Thus upbraided, and thus called upon to reply, the slave rejoins that he knows how little anything that he can say will avail, seeing that he is completely in the hands of his owner; and with noble resolution, calmly says, 'I submit to my fate.' Touched by the slave's answer, the master insists upon his further speaking, and recapitulates the many acts of kindness which he has performed toward the slave, and tells him he is permitted to speak for himself. Thus invited, the quondam slave makes a spirited defence of himself, and thereafter the whole argument for and against slavery is brought out. The master is vanquished at every turn in the argument, and appreciating the fact, he generously and meekly emancipates the slave, with his best wishes for his prosperity. It is unnecessary to say that a dialogue with such an origin and such an end, read by me when every nerve of my being was in revolt at my own condition as a slave, affected me most powerfully. I could not help feeling that the day might yet come, when the well-directed answers made by the slave to the master, in this instance, would find a counterpart in my own experience. This, however, was not all the fanaticism which I found in *The Columbian Orator*. I met there one of Sheridan's mighty speeches, on the subject of Catholic Emancipation, Lord Chatham's speech on the American War, and speeches by the great William Pitt, and by Fox. These were all choice documents to me, and I read them over and over again, with an interest ever increasing, because it was ever gaining in intelligence; for the more I read them the better I understood them. The reading of these speeches added much to my limited stock of language, and enabled me to give tongue to many interesting thoughts which had often flashed through my mind and died away for want of words in which to give them utterance. The mighty power and heart-searching directness of truth penetrating the heart of a slave-holder, compelling him to yield up his earthly interests to the claims of eternal justice, were finely illustrated in the dialogue; and from the speeches of Sheridan I got a bold and powerful denunciation of oppression and a most brilliant vindication of the rights of man. Here was indeed a noble acquisition. If I had ever wavered under the consideration that the Almighty, in some way, had ordained slavery, and willed my enslavement for His own glory, I wavered no longer. I had now penetrated to the secret of all slavery and all oppression, and had ascertained their true foundation to be in the pride, the power, and the avarice of man. With a book in my hand so redolent of the principles of liberty, with a perception of my own human nature, and the facts of my past and present experience, I was equal to a contest with the religious advocates of slavery, whether white or black – for blindness in this matter was not confined to the white people. I have met many good religious coloured people at the South, who were under the delusion that God required them to submit to slavery, and to wear their chains with meekness and humility. I could entertain no such nonsense as this; and I quite lost my patience when I found a coloured man weak enough to believe such stuff. Nevertheless, eager as I was to partake of the tree of knowledge, its fruits were bitter as well as sweet. 'Slave-holders,' thought I, 'are only a band of successful robbers, who, leaving their own homes, went into Africa for the purpose of stealing and reducing my people to slavery.' I loathed them as the meanest and the most wicked of men. And as I read, behold! the very discontent so graphically predicted by Master Hugh had already come upon me. I was no longer the light-hearted gleesome boy, full of mirth and play, as when I landed in Baltimore. Light had penetrated the moral dungeon where I had lain, and I saw the bloody whip for my back, and the iron chain for my feet, and my *good, kind* master, he was the author of my situation. The revelation haunted me, stung me, and made me gloomy and miserable. As I writhed under the sting and torment of this knowledge, I almost envied my fellow slaves their stupid indifference. It opened my eyes to the horrible pit, and revealed the teeth of the frightful dragon that was ready to pounce upon me; but alas, it opened no way for my escape. I wished myself a beast, a bird, anything rather than a slave. I was wretched and gloomy beyond my ability to describe. This everlasting thinking distressed and tormented me; and yet there was no getting rid of this subject of my thoughts. Liberty, as the inestimable birthright of every man, converted every object into an asserter of this right. I heard it in every sound, and saw it in every object. It was ever present to torment me with a sense of my wretchedness. The more beautiful and charming the smiles of nature, the more horrible and desolate my condition. I saw nothing without seeing it, and I heard nothing without hearing it. I do not exaggerate when I say it looked at me in every star, it smiled in every calm, breathed in every wind, and moved in every storm. I have no doubt that my state of mind had something to do with the change in treatment which my mistress adopted towards me. I can easily believe that my leaden, downcast, and disconsolate look was very offensive to her. Poor lady! She did not understand my trouble, and I could not tell her. Could I have made her acquainted with the real state of my mind and given her the reason for it, it might have been well for both of us. As it was, her abuse fell upon me like the blows of the false prophet upon his ass; she did not know that an angel stood in the way. Nature made us friends, but slavery had made us enemies. My interests were in a direction opposite to hers, and we both had our private thoughts and plans. She aimed to keep me ignorant, and I resolved to *know*, although knowledge only increased my misery. My feelings were not the result of any marked cruelty in the treatment I received; they sprang from the consideration of my being a slave at all. It was *slavery*, not its mere *incidents* I hated. I had been cheated. I saw through the attempt to keep me in ignorance. I saw that slave-holders would have gladly made me believe that they were merely acting under the authority of God in making a slave of me and in making slaves of others, and I felt to them as to robbers and deceivers. The feeding and clothing me well could not atone for taking my liberty from me. The smiles of my mistress could not remove the deep sorrow that dwelt in my young bosom. Indeed, these came in time but to deepen my sorrow. She had changed, and the reader will see that I had changed, too. We were both victims to the same overshadowing evil, *she* as mistress, I as slave. I will not censure her harshly.

CHAPTER XII

Religious Nature Awakened

Abolitionists spoken of – Eagerness to know the meaning of word – Consults the dictionary – Incendiary information – The enigma solved – 'Nat Turner' insurrection – Cholera – Religion – Methodist minister – Religious impressions – Father Lawson – His character and occupation – His influence over me – Our mutual attachment – New hopes and aspirations – Heavenly light – Two Irishmen on wharf – Conversation with them – Learning to write – My aims.

In the unhappy state of mind described in the foregoing chapter, regretting my very existence because doomed to a life of bondage, so goaded and so wretched as to be even tempted at times to take my own life, I was most keenly sensitive to know any and everything possible that had any relation to the subject of slavery. I was all ears, all eyes, whenever the words slave or slavery dropped from the lips of any white person, and the occasions became more and more frequent when these words became leading ones in high social debate at our house. Very often I would overhear Master Hugh, or some of his company, speak with much warmth of the '*abolitionists*'. Who or what the abolitionists were, I was totally ignorant. I found, however, that whoever or whatever they might be, they were most cordially hated and abused by slave-holders of every grade. I very soon discovered, too, that slavery was, in some sort, under consideration whenever the abolitionists were alluded to. This made the term a very interesting one to me. If a slave had made good his escape from slavery, it was generally alleged that he had been persuaded and assisted to do so by the abolitionists. If a slave killed his master, or struck down his overseer, or set fire to his master's dwelling, or committed any violence or crime out of the common way, it was certain to be said that such a crime was the legitimate fruits of the abolition movement. Hearing such charges often repeated, I, naturally enough, received the impression that abolition – whatever else it might be – was not unfriendly to the slave, nor very friendly to the slave-holder. I therefore set about finding out, if possible, *who* and *what* the abolitionists were, and *why* they were so obnoxious to the slave-holders. The dictionary offered me very little help. It taught me that abolition was 'the act of abolishing'; but it left me in ignorance at the very point where I most wanted information, and that was, as to the thing to be abolished. A city newspaper – the 'Baltimore *American*' – gave me the incendiary information denied me by the dictionary. In its columns I found that on a certain day a vast number of petitions and memorials had been presented to congress, praying for the abolition of slavery in the District of Columbia, and for the abolition of the slave trade between the States of the Union. This was enough. The vindictive bitterness, the marked caution, the studied reserve, and the ambiguity practised by our white folks when alluding to this subject, was now fully explained. Ever after that, when I heard the word abolition, I felt the matter one of a personal concern, and I drew near to listen whenever I could do so, without seeming too solicitous and prying. There was HOPE in those words. Ever and anon, too, I could see some terrible denunciation of slavery in our papers – copied from abolition papers at the North – and the injustice of such denunciation commented on. These I read with avidity. I had a deep satisfaction in the thought that the rascality of slave-holders was not concealed from the eyes of the world, and that I was not alone in abhorring the cruelty and brutality of slavery. A still deeper train of thought was stirred. I saw that there was fear as well as rage in the manner of speaking of the abolitionists, and from this I inferred that they must have some power in the country, and I felt that they might perhaps succeed in their designs. When I met with a slave to whom I deemed it safe to talk on the subject, I would impart to him so much of the mystery as I had been able to penetrate. Thus the light of this grand movement broke in upon my mind by degrees; and I must say that, ignorant as I was of the philosophy of that movement, I believed in it from the first, and I believed in it partly because I saw that it alarmed the consciences of the slave-holders. The insurrection of Nat Turner had been quelled, but the alarm and terror which it occasioned had not subsided. The cholera was then on its way to this country, and I remember thinking that God was angry with the white people because of their slave-holding wickedness, and therefore his judgements were abroad in the land. Of course it was impossible for me not to hope much for the abolition movement when I saw it supported by the Almighty, and armed with DEATH.

Previously to my contemplation of the anti-slavery movement and its probable results, my mind had been seriously awakened to the subject of religion. I was not more than thirteen years old when, in my loneliness and destitution, I longed for someone to whom I could go, as to a father and protector. The preaching of a white Methodist minister, named Hanson, was the means of causing me to feel that in God I had such a friend. He taught that all men, great and small, bond and free, were sinners in the sight of God; that they were but natural rebels against his government; and that they must repent of their sins, and be reconciled to God through Christ. I cannot say that I had a very distinct notion of what was required of me, but one thing I did know well: I was wretched and had no means of making myself otherwise. I consulted a good coloured man named Charles Lawson, and in tones of holy affection he told me to pray, and to 'cast all my care upon God'. This I sought to do; and though for weeks I was a poor, broken-hearted mourner, travelling through doubts and fears, I finally found my burden lightened, and my heart relieved. I loved all mankind, slave-holders not excepted, though I abhorred slavery more than ever. I saw the world in a new light, and my great concern was to have everybody converted. My desire to learn increased, and especially did I want a thorough acquaintance with the contents of the Bible. I have gathered scattered pages of the Bible from the filthy street-gutters, and washed and dried them, that in moments of leisure I might get a word or two of wisdom from them. While thus religiously seeking knowledge, I became acquainted with a good old coloured man named Lawson. This man not only prayed three times a day, but he prayed as he walked through the streets, at his work, on his dray – everywhere. His life was a life of prayer, and his words when he spoke to anyone, were about a better world. Uncle Lawson lived near Master Hugh's house, and, becoming deeply attached to him, I went often with him to prayer-meeting, and spent much of my leisure time with him on Sunday. The old man could read a little, and I was a great help to him in making out the hard words, for I was a better reader than he. I could teach him 'the letter', but he could teach me 'the spirit', and refreshing times we had together, in singing and praying. These meetings went on for a long time without the knowledge of Master Hugh or my mistress. Both knew, however, I had become religious, and seemed to respect my conscientious piety. My mistress was still a professor of religion, and belonged to class. Her leader was no less a person than Revd Beverly Waugh, the presiding elder, and afterwards one of the bishops of the Methodist Episcopal Church.

In view of the cares and anxieties incident to the life she was leading, and especially in view of the separation from religious associations to which she was subjected, my mistress had, as I have before stated, become lukewarm, and needed to be looked up by her leader. This often brought Mr Waugh to our house, and gave me an opportunity to hear him extort and pray. But my chief instructor in religious matters was Uncle Lawson. He was my spiritual father and I loved him intensely, and was at his house every chance I could get. This pleasure, however, was not long unquestioned, Master Hugh became averse to our intimacy, and threatened to whip me if I ever went there again. I now felt myself persecuted by a wicked man, and I *would* go. The good old man had told me that the 'Lord had a great work for me to do,' and I must prepare to do it; that he had been shown that I must preach the gospel. His words made a very deep impression upon me, and I verily felt that some work was before me, though I could not see how I could ever engage in its performance. 'The good Lord would bring it to pass in His own time,' he said, and I must go on reading and studying the scriptures. This advice and these suggestions were not without their influence on my character and destiny. He fanned my already intense love of knowledge into a flame by assuring me that I was to be a useful man in the world. When I would say to him, 'How can these things be? and what can I do?' his simple reply was, '*Trust in the Lord.*' When I would tell him, 'I am a slave, and a slave for life, how can I do anything?' he would quietly answer, 'The *Lord* can make you free, my dear; all things are possible with Him; only have *faith* in God. "Ask, and it shall be given you." If you want liberty, ask the Lord for it *in* FAITH, *and he will give it to you.*'

Thus assured and thus cheered on, under the inspiration of hope, I worked and prayed with a light heart, believing that my life was under the guidance of a wisdom higher than my own. With all other blessings sought at the mercy seat, I always prayed that God would, of His great mercy and in His own good time, deliver me from my bondage.

I went one day to the wharf of Mr Waters, and seeing two Irishmen unloading a scow of stone or ballast, I went on board, unasked, and helped them. When we had finished the work, one of the men came to me, aside, and asked me a number of questions, and among them if I were a slave? I told him I was 'a slave for life'. The good Irishman gave a shrug, and seemed deeply affected. He said it was a pity so fine a little fellow as I was should be a slave for life. They both had much to say about the matter, and expressed the deepest sympathy with me, and the most decided hatred of slavery. They went so far as to tell me that I ought to run away and go to the North; that I should find friends there, and that I should be as free as anybody. I pretended not to be interested in what they said, for I feared they might be treacherous. White men were not unfrequently known to encourage slaves to escape, and then, to get the reward, they would kidnap them and return them to their masters. While I mainly inclined to the notion that these men were honest and meant me no ill, I feared it might be otherwise. I nevertheless remembered their words and their advice, and looked forward to an escape to the North as a possible means of gaining the liberty for which my heart panted. It was not my enslavement at the then present time which most affected me; the being a slave *for life* was the saddest thought. I was too young to think of running away immediately; besides I wished to learn to write before going, as I might have occasion to write my own pass. I now not only had the hope of freedom, but a foreshadowing of the means by which I might someday gain that inestimable boon. Meanwhile, I resolved to add to my educational attainments the art of writing.

After this manner I began to learn to write. I was much in the shipyards – Master Hugh's, and that of Durgan & Bailey – and I observed that the carpenters after hewing and getting ready a piece of timber to use, wrote on it the initials of the name of that part of the ship for which it was intended. When, for instance, a piece of timber was ready for the starboard side, it was marked with a capital 'S'. A piece for the larboard side was marked 'L'; larboard-forward was marked 'LF'; larboard-aft was marked 'LA'; starboard-as 'SA'; and starboard-forward 'SF'. I soon learned these letters, and for what they were placed on the timbers.

My work now was to keep fire under the steam-box, and to watch the shipyard while the carpenters were gone to dinner. This interval gave me a fine opportunity for copying the letters named. I soon astonished myself at the ease with which I made the letters, and the thought was soon present, 'If I can make four letters, I can make more.' Having made these readily and easily, when I met boys about the Bethel church or on any of our playgrounds, I entered the lists with them in the art of writing, and would make the letters which I had been so fortunate as to learn, and ask them to 'beat that if they could'. With playmates for my teachers, fences and pavements for my copybooks, and chalk for my pen and ink, I learned to write. I however adopted, afterwards, various methods for improving my hand. The most successful was copying the *italics* in Webster's spelling-book until I could make them all without looking on the book. By this time my little 'Master Tommy' had grown to be a big boy, and had written over a number of copy-books and brought them home. They had been shown to the neighbours, had elicited due praise, and had been laid carefully away. Spending part of my time both at the shipyard and the house, I was often the keeper of the latter as of the former. When my mistress left me in charge of the house I had a grand time. I got Master Tommy's copy-books and a pen and ink, and in the ample space between the lines I wrote other lines as nearly like his as possible. The process was a tedious one, and I ran the risk of getting a flogging for marking the highly-prized copy-books of the eldest son. In addition to these opportunities, sleeping as I did in the kitchen loft, a room seldom visited by any of the family, I contrived to get a flour-barrel up there and a chair, and upon the head of that barrel I have written, or endeavoured to write, copying from the Bible and the Methodist hymn-book, and other books which I had accumulated, till late at night, and when all the family were in bed and asleep. I was supported in my endeavours by renewed advice and by holy promises from the good father Lawson, with whom I continued to meet, and pray, and read the Scriptures. Although Master Hugh was aware of these meetings, I must say, to his credit, that he never executed his threats to whip me for having thus innocently employed my leisure time.

CHAPTER XIII

The Vicissitudes of Slave Life

Death of old master's son Richard, speedily followed by that of
old master – Valuation and division of all the property, including
the slaves – Sent for, to come to Hillsborough to be valued and
divided – Sad prospects and grief – Parting – Slaves have no
voice in deciding their own destinies – General dread of falling
into Master Andrew's hands – His drunkenness – Good fortune
in falling to Miss Lucretia – She allows my return to Baltimore –
Joy at Master Hugh's – Death of Miss Lucretia – Master
Thomas Auld's second marriage – The new wife unlike the old –
Again removed from Master Hugh's – Reasons for regret – Plan
of escape

I must now ask the reader to go back with me a little in point of time, in
my humble story, and notice another circumstance that entered into
my slavery experience, and which, doubtless, has had a share in
deepening my horror of slavery, and my hostility toward those men
and measures that practically uphold the slave system.

It has already been observed that though I was, after my removal
from Colonel Lloyd's plantation, in *form* the slave of Master Hugh
Auld, I was in *fact* and in *law* the slave of my old master, Captain
Anthony. Very well. In a very short time after I went to Baltimore my
old master's youngest son, Richard, died; and in three years and six
months after, my old master himself died, leaving only his daughter
Lucretia and his son Andrew to share the estate. The old man died
while on a visit to his daughter in Hillsborough, where Captain Auld
and Mrs Lucretia now lived. Master Thomas having given up the
command of Colonel Lloyd's sloop was now keeping store in that
town.

Cut off thus unexpectedly, Captain Anthony died intestate, and his
property must be equally divided between his two children, Andrew
and Lucretia.

The valuation and division of slaves among contending heirs was a most important incident in slave life. The characters and tendencies of the heirs were generally well understood by the slaves who were to be divided, and all had their aversions and their preferences. But neither their aversions nor their preferences availed anything.

On the death of old master, I was immediately sent for to be valued and divided with the other property. Personally, my concern was mainly about my possible removal from the home of Master Hugh, for up to this time there had no dark clouds arisen to darken the sky of that happy abode. It was a sad day to me when I left for the Eastern Shore, to be valued and divided, as it was for my dear mistress and teacher, and for little Tommy. We all three wept bitterly, for we were parting, and it might be we were parting for ever. No one could tell amongst which pile of chattels I might be flung. Thus early, I got a foretaste of that painful uncertainty which in one form or another was ever obtruding itself in the pathway of the slave. It furnished me a new insight into the unnatural power to which I was subjected. Sickness, adversity, and death may interfere with the plans and purposes of all, but the slave had the added danger of changing homes, in the separations unknown to other men. Then, too, there was the intensified degradation of the spectacle. What an assemblage! Men and women, young and old, married and single; moral and thinking human beings, in open contempt of their humanity, levelled at a blow with horses, sheep, horned cattle, and swine. Horses and men, cattle and women, pigs and children – all holding the same rank in the scale of social existence, and all subjected to the same narrow inspection, to ascertain their value in gold and silver – the only standard of worth applied by slave-holders to their slaves. Personality swallowed up in the sordid idea of property! Manhood lost in chattel-hood!

The valuation over, then came the division and apportionment. Our destiny was to be *fixed for life*, and we had no more voice in the decision of the question than the oxen and cows that stood chewing at the hay-mow. One word of the appraisers, against all preferences and prayers, could rend asunder all the ties of friendship and affection, even to separating husbands and wives, parents and children. We were all appalled before that power which, to human seeming, could bless or blast us in a moment. Added to this dread of separation, most painful to the majority of the slaves, we all had a decided horror of falling into the hands of Master Andrew, who was distinguished for his cruelty and intemperance.

Slaves had a great dread, very naturally, of falling into the hands of drunken owners. Master Andrew was a confirmed sot, and had already, by his profligate dissipation, wasted a large portion of his father's property. To fall into his hands, therefore, was considered as the first step toward being sold away to the far South. He would no doubt spend his fortune in a few years, it was thought, and his farms and slaves would be sold at public auction, and the slaves hurried away to the cotton-fields and rice-swamps of the burning South. This was cause of deep consternation.

The people of the North, and free people generally, I think, have less attachment to the places where they are born and brought up, than had the slaves. Their freedom to come and go, to be here or there, as they list, prevents any extravagant attachment to any one particular place. On the other hand, the slave was a fixture; he had no choice, no goal, but was pegged down to one single spot, and must take root there or nowhere. The idea of removal elsewhere came, generally, in shape of a threat, and in punishment for crime. It was therefore attended with fear and dread. The enthusiasm which animates the bosoms of young freemen, when they contemplate a life in the far West, or in some distant country, where they expect to rise to wealth and distinction, could have no place in the thoughts of the slave; nor could those from whom they separated know anything of that cheerfulness with which friends and relations yield each other up, when they feel that it is good for the departing one that he is removed from his native place. Then, too, there is correspondence and the hope of reunion, but with the slaves all these mitigating circumstances were wanting. There was no improvement in condition *probable* – no correspondence *possible* – no reunion attainable. His going out into the world was like a living man going into the tomb, who, with open eyes, sees himself buried out of sight and hearing of wife, children, and friends of kindred tie.

In contemplating the likelihoods and possibilities of our circumstances, I probably suffered more than most of my fellow-servants. I had known what it was to experience kind and even tender treatment; they had known nothing of the sort. Life to them had been rough and thorny, as well as dark. They had – most of them – lived on my old master's farm in Tuckahoe, and had felt the rigours of Mr Plummer's rule. He had written his character on the living parchment of most of their backs, and left them seamed and callous; my back, thanks to my early removal to Baltimore, was yet tender. I had left a kind mistress in tears when we parted, and the probabil/**ity of never seeing her again, trembling in the balance as it were, could not fail to excite in me alarm and agony. The thought of becoming the slave of Andrew Anthony – who but a few days before the division had in my presence seized my brother Perry by the throat, dashed him on the ground, and with the heel of his boot stamped him on the head, until the blood gushed from his nose and ears – was terrible! This fiendish proceeding had no better apology than the fact that Perry had gone to play when Master Andrew wanted him for some trifling service. After inflicting this cruel treatment on my brother, observing me, as I looked at him in astonishment, he said: '*That's* the way I'll serve you, one of these days'; meaning, probably, when I should come into his possession. This threat, the reader may well suppose, was not very tranquillising to my feelings.

At last, the anxiety and suspense were ended; and ended, thanks to a kind Providence, in accordance with my wishes. I fell to the portion of Mrs Lucretia, the dear lady who bound up my head in her father's kitchen, and shielded me from the maledictions of Aunt Katy.

Captain Thomas Auld and Mrs Lucretia at once decided on my return to Baltimore. They knew how warmly Mrs Hugh Auld was attached to me, and how delighted Tommy would be to see me, and withal, having no immediate use for me, they willingly concluded this arrangement.

I need not stop to narrate my joy on finding myself back in Baltimore. I was just one month absent, but the time seemed fully six months.

I had returned to Baltimore but a short time when the tidings reached me that my kind friend, Mrs Lucretia, was dead. She left one child, a daughter, named Amanda, of whom I shall speak again. Shortly after the death of Mrs Lucretia, Master Andrew died, leaving a wife and one child. Thus the whole family of Anthonys, as it existed when I went to Colonel Lloyd's place, was swept away during the first five years' time of my residence at Master Hugh Auld's in Baltimore.

No especial alteration took place in the condition of the slaves, in consequence of these deaths, yet I could not help the feeling that I was less secure now that Mrs Lucretia was gone. While she lived, I felt that I had a strong friend to plead for me in any emergency.

In a little book which I published six years after my escape from slavery, entitled 'Narrative of Frederick Douglass' – when the distance between the past then described, and the present was not so great as it is now – speaking of these changes in my master's family, and their results, I used this language: 'Now all the property of my old master, slaves included, was in the hands of strangers – strangers who had nothing to do in accumulating it. Not a slave was left free. All remained slaves, from the youngest to the oldest. If any one thing in my experience, more than another, has served to deepen my conviction of

the infernal character of slavery, and to fill me with unutterable
loathing of slave-holders, it was their base ingratitude to my poor old
grandmother. She had served my old master faithfully from youth to
old age. She had been the source of all his wealth; she had peopled his
plantation with slaves, she had become a great-grandmother in his
service. She had rocked him in his infancy, attended him in his
childhood, served him through life, and at his death wiped from his icy
brow the cold death-sweat, and closed his eyes for ever. She was
nevertheless a slave – a slave for life – a slave in the hands of strangers;
and in their hands she saw her children, her grandchildren, and her
great-grandchildren, divided like so many sheep, without being gratified with the small privilege of a single word as to their or her own
destiny. And to cap the climax of their base ingratitude, my grandmother, who was now very old, having outlived my old master and all
his children, having seen the beginning and end of them, and her
present owner – his grandson – finding she was of but little value – her
frame already racked with the pains of old age, and complete helplessness fast stealing over her once active limbs – took her to the woods,
built her a little hut with a mud chimney, and then gave her the
bounteous privilege of supporting herself there in utter loneliness; thus
virtually turning her out to die. If my poor, dear old grandmother now
lives, she lives to remember and mourn over the loss of children, the
loss of grandchildren, and the loss of great-grandchildren. They are, in
the language of Whittier, the slave's poet:

> Gone, gone, sold and gone,
> To the rice-swamp dank and lone;
> Where the slave-whip ceaseless swings,
> Where the noisome insect stings,
> Where the fever-demon strews
> Poison with the falling dews,
> Where the sickly sunbeams glare
> Through the hot and misty air –

>> Gone, gone, sold and gone,
>> To the rice-swamp, dank and lone,
>> From Virginia's hills and waters –
>> Woe is me, my stolen daughters!

The hearth is desolate. The unconscious children who once sang and
danced in her presence are gone. She gropes her way, in the darkness

of age, for a drink of water. Instead of the voices of her children, she hears by day the moans of the dove, and by night the screams of the hideous owl. All is gloom. The grave is at the door; and now, weighed down by the pains and aches of old age, when the head inclines to the feet, when the beginning and ending of human existence meet, and helpless infancy, and painful old age combine together; at this time – this most needed time for the exercise of that tenderness and affection which children only can bestow on a declining parent – my poor old grandmother, the devoted mother of twelve children, is left all alone, in yonder little hut, before a few dim cinders.

Two years after the death of Mrs Lucretia, Master Thomas married his second wife. Her name was Rowena Hamilton, the eldest daughter of Mr William Hamilton, a rich slave-holder on the Eastern Shore of Maryland, who lived about five miles from St Michaels, the then place of Master Thomas Auld's residence.

Not long after his marriage, Master Thomas had a misunderstanding with Master Hugh, and as a means of punishing him, he ordered him to send me home. As the ground of the misunderstanding will serve to illustrate the character of Southern chivalry and Southern humanity, fifty years ago, I will relate it.

Among the children of my Aunt Milly, was a daughter named Henny. When quite a child, Henny had fallen into the fire and had burnt her hands so badly that they were of very little use to her. Her fingers were drawn almost into the palms of her hands. She could make out to do something, but she was considered hardly worth the having – of little more value than a horse with a broken leg. This unprofitable piece of property, ill-shapen and disfigured, Captain Auld sent off to Baltimore.

After giving poor Henny a fair trial, Master Hugh and his wife came to the conclusion that they had no use for the poor cripple, and they sent her back to Master Thomas. This the latter took as an act of ingratitude on the part of his brother, and as a mark of his displeasure, he required him to send me immediately to St Michaels, saying, 'If he cannot keep Hen, he shan't have Fred.'

Here was another shook to my nerves, another breaking up of plans, and another severance of my religious and social alliances. I was now a big boy. I had become quite useful to several young coloured men, who had made me their teacher. I had taught some of them to read, and was accustomed to spend many of my leisure hours with them. Our attachment was strong, and I greatly dreaded the separation. But regrets with slaves were unavailing: my wishes were nothing; my happiness was the sport of my master.

My regrets at leaving Baltimore now, were not for the same reasons as when I before left the city to be valued and handed over to a new owner.

A change had taken place, both in Master Hugh and in his once pious and affectionate wife. The influence of brandy and bad company on him, and of slavery and social isolation on her, had wrought disastrously upon the characters of both. Thomas was no longer 'little Tommy', but was a big boy, and had learned to assume the airs of his class towards me. My condition, therefore, in the house of Master Hugh was not by any means so comfortable as in former years. My attachments were now outside of our family: They were fixed upon those to whom I imparted instruction, and to those little white boys, from whom I received instruction. There, too, was my dear old father, the pious Lawson, who was in all the Christian graces the very counterpart of 'Uncle Tom' – the resemblance so perfect that he might have been the original of Mrs Stowe's Christian hero. The thought of leaving these dear friends greatly troubled me, for I was going without the hope of ever returning again; the feud being most bitter, and apparently wholly irreconcilable.

In addition to the pain of parting from friends, as I supposed, for ever, I had the added grief of neglected chances of escape to brood over. I had put off running away until I was now to be placed where opportunities for escape would be much more difficult, and less frequent.

As we sailed down the Chesapeake Bay, on board the sloop Amanda, to St Michaels, and were passed by the steamers plying between Baltimore and Philadelphia, I formed many a plan for my future, beginning and ending in the same determination – yet to find some way of escape from slavery.

CHAPTER XIV

Experience in St Michaels

St Michaels and its inhabitants – Captain Auld – His new wife –
Sufferings from hunger – Forced to steal – Argument in
vindication thereof – Southern camp-meeting – What Captain
Auld did there – Hopes – Suspicions – The result – Faith
and works at variance – Position in the church – Poor Cousin
Henry – Methodist preachers – Their disregard of the slaves –
One exception – Sabbath-school – How and by whom broken
up – Sad change in my prospects – Covey, the negro-breaker

St Michaels, the village in which was now my new home, compared
favourably with villages in slave States generally, at this time – 1833.
There were a few comfortable dwellings in it, but the place as a whole
wore a dull, slovenly, enterprise-forsaken, aspect. The mass of the
buildings were of wood; they had never enjoyed the artificial adorn-
ment of paint, and time and storms had worn off the bright colour of
the wood, leaving them almost as black as buildings charred by a
conflagration.

St Michaels had, in former years, enjoyed some reputation as a
shipbuilding community, but that business had almost entirely given
place to oyster-fishing for the Baltimore and Philadelphia markets, a
course of life highly unfavourable to morals, industry, and manners.
Miles River was broad, and its oyster-fishing grounds were extensive,
and the fishermen were out often all day and a part of the night, during
autumn, winter, and spring. This exposure was an excuse for carrying
with them, in considerable quantities, spirituous liquors, the then
supposed best antidote for cold. Each canoe was supplied with its jug of
rum, and tippling among this class of the citizens became general. This
drinking habit, in an ignorant population, fostered coarseness, vulgarity, and an indolent disregard for the social improvement of the place,
so that it was admitted by the few sober thinking people who remained
there, that St Michaels was an unsaintly, as well as unsightly place.

I went to St Michaels to live in March 1838. I know the year, because it was the one succeeding the first cholera in Baltimore, and it was also the year of that strange phenomenon, when the heavens seemed about to part with its starry train. I witnessed this gorgeous spectacle, and was awestruck. The air seemed filled with bright descending messengers from the sky. It was about daybreak when I saw this sublime scene. I was not without the suggestion that it might be the harbinger of the coming of the Son of Man; and in my then state of mind I was prepared to hail Him as my friend and deliverer. I had read that the 'stars shall fall from heaven', and they were now falling. I was suffering very much in my mind. It did seem that every time the young tendrils of my affection became attached they were rudely broken by some unnatural outside power; and I was looking away to heaven for the rest denied me on earth.

But to my story. It was now more than seven years since I had lived with Master Thomas Auld, in the family of my old master, Captain Anthony, on the home plantation of Colonel Lloyd. As I knew him then it was as the husband of old master's daughter; I had now to know him as my master. All my lessons concerning his temper and disposition, and the best methods of pleasing him, were yet to be learned. Slave-holders, however, were not very ceremonious in approaching a slave, and my ignorance of the new material in the shape of a master was but transient. Nor was my new mistress long in making known her animus. Unlike Miss Lucretia, whom I remembered with the tenderness which departed blessings leave, Mrs Rowena Auld was cold and cruel, as her husband was stingy, and possessed the power to make him as cruel as herself, while she could easily descend to the level of his meanness.

As long as I had lived in Mr Hugh Auld's family, whatever changes had come over them, there had been always a bountiful supply of food; and now, for the first time in seven years, I realised the pitiless pinchings of hunger. So wretchedly starved were we, that we were compelled to live at the expense of our neighbours, or to steal from the home larder. This was a hard thing to do; but after much reflection I reasoned myself into the conviction that there was no other way to do, and that after all there was no wrong in it. Considering that my labour and person were the property of Master Thomas, and that I was deprived of the necessaries of life – necessaries obtained by my own labour, it was easy to deduce the right to supply myself with what was my own. It was simply appropriating what was my own to the use of my master, since the health and strength derived from such food were exerted in his service. To be sure this was stealing, according to the law and gospel I heard from the pulpit; but I had begun to attach less importance to what dropped from that quarter on such points. It was not always convenient to steal from master, and the same reason why I might innocently steal from him did not seem to justify me in stealing from others. In the case of my master it was a question of removal – the taking his meat out of one tub and putting it into another; the ownership of the meat was not affected by the transaction. At first he owned it in the tub, and last he owned it in me. His meat-house was not always open. There was a strict watch kept at that point, and the key was carried in Mrs Auld's pocket. We were oftentimes severely pinched with hunger, when meat and bread were mouldering under lock and key. This was so, when she knew we were nearly half starved; and yet with saintly air would she kneel with her husband and pray each morning that a merciful God would 'bless them in basket and store, and save them at last in His kingdom'. But I proceed with my argument.

It was necessary that the right to steal from others should be established; and this could only rest upon a wider range of generalisation than that which supposed the right to steal from my master. It was some time before I arrived at this clear right. To give some idea of my train of reasoning, I will state the case as I laid it out in my mind. 'I am,' I thought, 'not only the slave of Master Thomas, but I am the slave of society at large. Society at large has bound itself, in form and in fact, to assist Master Thomas in robbing me of my rightful liberty, and of the just reward of my labour; therefore, whatever rights I have against Master Thomas I have equally against those confederated with him in robbing me of liberty. As society has marked me out as privileged plunder, on the principle of self-preservation, I am justified in plundering in turn. Since each slave belongs to all, all must therefore belong to each.' I reasoned further, 'that within the bounds of his just earnings the slave was fully justified in helping himself to the gold and silver, and the best apparel of his master, or that of any other slaveholder; and that such taking was not stealing, in any just sense of the word.'

The morality of free society could have no application to slave society. Slave-holders made it almost impossible for the slave to commit any crime, known either to the laws of God or to the laws of man. If he stole he but took his own; if he killed his master, he only imitated the heroes of the Revolution. Slave-holders I held to be individually and collectively responsible for all the evils which grew out of the horrid relation, and I believed they would be so held in the sight of God. To make a man a slave was to rob him of moral responsibility.

Freedom of choice is the essence of all accountability; but my kind readers are probably less concerned about what were my opinions than about that which more nearly touched my personal experience, albeit my opinions have, in some sort, been the outgrowth of my experience.

When I lived with Captain Auld I thought him incapable of a noble action. His leading characteristic was intense selfishness. I think he was fully aware of this fact himself, and often tried to conceal it. Captain Auld was not a born slave-holder – not a birthright member of the slave-holding oligarchy. He was only a slave-holder by marriage-right; and of all slave-holders these were by far the most exacting. There was in him all the love of domination, the pride of mastery, and the swagger of authority; but his rule lacked the vital element of consistency. He could be cruel: but his methods of showing it were cowardly, and evinced his meanness, rather than his spirit. His commands were strong, his enforcements weak.

Slaves were not insensible to the whole-souled qualities of a generous, dashing slave-holder, who was fearless of consequences, and they preferred a master of this bold and daring kind, even with the risk of being shot down for impudence, to the fretful little soul who never used the lash but at the suggestion of a love of gain.

Slaves, too, readily distinguished between the birthright bearing of the original slave-holder, and the assumed attributes of the accidental slave-holder; and while they could have no respect for either, they despised the latter more than the former.

The luxury of having slaves to wait upon him was new to Master Thomas, and for it he was wholly unprepared. He was a slave-holder, without the ability to hold or manage his slaves. Failing to command their respect, both himself and wife were ever on the alert lest some indignity should be offered them by the slaves.

It was in the month of August 1838, when I had become almost desperate under the treatment of Master Thomas, and entertained more strongly than ever the oft-repeated determination to run away – a circumstance occurred which seemed to promise brighter and better days for us all. At a Methodist camp-meeting, held in the Bayside, a famous place for camp-meetings, about eight miles from St Michaels, Master Thomas came out with a profession of religion. He had long been an object of interest to the church, and to the ministers, as I had seen by the repeated visits and lengthy exhortations of the latter. He was a fish quite worth catching, for he had money and standing. In the community of St Michaels he was equal to the best citizen. He was strictly temperate, and there was little to do for him, to give the appearance of piety, and to make him a pillar of the church. Well, the camp-meeting continued a week; people gathered from all parts of the country, and two steamboats came loaded from Baltimore. The ground was happily chosen; seats were arranged; a stand erected; a rude altar fenced in, fronting the preacher's stand, with straw in it, making a soft kneeling-place for the accommodation of mourners. This place would have held at least one hundred persons. In front and on the sides of the preacher's stand, and outside the long rows of seats, rose the first class of stately tents, each vieing with the other in strength, neatness, and capacity for accommodation, Behind this first circle of tents, was another less imposing, which reached round the camp ground to the speaker's stand. Outside this second class of tents were covered wagons, ox-carts, and vehicles of every shape and size. These served as tents to their owners. Outside of these, huge fires were burning in all directions, where roasting and boiling and frying were going on, for the benefit of those who were attending to their spiritual welfare within the circle. *Behind* the preacher's stand, a narrow space was marked out for the use of the coloured people. There were no seats provided for this class of persons, and if the preachers addressed them at all, it was in an *aside*. After the preaching was over, at every service, an invitation was given to mourners to come forward into the pen; and in some cases, ministers went out to persuade men and women to come in. By one of these ministers, Master Thomas was persuaded to go inside the pen. I was deeply interested in that matter, and followed; and, though coloured people were not allowed either in the pen or in front of the preacher's stand, I ventured to take my stand at a sort of half-way place between the blacks and whites, where I could distinctly see the movements of the mourners, and especially the progress of Master Thomas. 'If he has got religion,' thought I, 'he will emancipate his slaves; or, if he should not do as much as this, he will at any rate behave towards us more kindly, and feed us more generously than he has heretofore done.' Appealing to my own religious experience, and judging my master by what was true in my own case, I could not regard him as soundly converted, unless some such good results followed his profession of religion. But in my expectations I was doubly disappointed: Master Thomas was *Master Thomas* still. The fruits of his righteousness were to show themselves in no such way as I had anticipated. His conversion was not to change his relation toward men – at any rate not toward BLACK men – but toward God. My faith I confess was not great. There was something in his appearance that, in my mind, cast a doubt over his conversion. Standing where I did, I could see his every movement. I watched very narrowly while he remained in the pen; and although I saw that his face was extremely red, and his hair dishevelled, and though I heard him groan, and saw a stray tear halting on his cheek, as if enquiring, 'which way shall I go?' – I could not wholly confide in the genuineness of the conversion. The hesitating behaviour of that tear-drop, and its loneliness, distressed me, and cast a doubt upon the whole transaction, of which it was a part. But people said, 'Captain Auld has come through', and it was for me to hope for the best. I was bound to do this in charity, for I, too, was religious, and had been in the church full three years, although now I was not more than sixteen years old. Slave-owners might sometimes have confidence in the piety of some of their slaves, but the slaves seldom had confidence in the piety of their masters. 'He can't go to heaven without blood on his skirts', was a settled point in the creed of every slave, which rose superior to all teaching to the contrary, and stood for ever as a fixed fact. The highest evidence the slave-holder could give the slave of his acceptance with God, was the emancipation of his slaves. This was proof to us that he was willing to give up all to God, and for the sake of God; and not to do this was, in our estimation, an evidence of hard-heartedness, and was wholly inconsistent with the idea of genuine conversion. I had read somewhere in the Methodist Discipline, the following question and answer: 'Question – What shall be done for the extirpation of slavery?' 'Answer – We declare that we are as much as ever convinced of the great evil of slavery; therefore no slave-holder shall be eligible to any official office in our church.' These words sounded in my ears for a long time, and encouraged me to hope. But as I have before said, I was doomed to disappointment. Master Thomas seemed to be aware of my hopes and expectations concerning him. I have thought before now that he looked at me in answer to my glances, as much as to say, 'I will teach you, young man, that though I have parted with my sins, I have not parted with my sense. I shall hold my slaves, and go to heaven too.'

There was always a scarcity of good nature about the man; but now his whole countenance was *soured* all over with the *seemings* of piety and he became more rigid and stringent in his exactions. If religion had any effect at all on him, it made him more cruel and hateful in all his ways. Do I judge him harshly? God forbid. Captain Auld made the greatest professions of piety. His house was literally a house of prayer. In the morning and in the evening loud prayers and hymns were heard there, in which both himself and wife joined: yet no more nor better meal was distributed at the quarters, no more attention was paid to the moral welfare of the kitchen, and nothing was done to make us feel that the heart of Master Thomas was one whit better than it was before he went into the little pen, opposite the preacher's stand on the camp-ground. Our hopes, too, founded on the discipline, soon vanished; for he was taken into the church at once, and before he was out of his term of probation, he lead in class. He quite distinguished himself among the brethren as a fervent exhorter. His progress was almost as rapid as the growth of the fabled Jack and the beanstalk. No man was more active in revivals, nor would go more miles to assist in carrying them on, and in getting outsiders interested in religion. His house, being one of the holiest in St Michaels, became the 'preachers' home'. They evidently liked to share his hospitality; for while he *starved* us, he stuffed them – three or four of these 'ambassadors' being there not unfrequently at a time – all living on the fat of the land, while we in the kitchen were worse than hungry. Not often did we get a smile of recognition from these holy men. They seemed about as unconcerned about our getting to heaven, as about our getting out of slavery. To this general charge, I must make one exception – the Reverend George Cookman. Unlike Revd Messrs Storks, Ewry, Nicky, Humphrey and Cooper, all of whom were on the St Michaels circuit, he kindly took an interest in our temporal and spiritual welfare. Our souls and our bodies were alike sacred in his sight, and he really had a good deal of genuine anti-slavery feeling mingled with his colonisation ideas. There was not a slave in our neighbourhood who did not love and venerate Mr Cookman. It was pretty generally believed that he had been instrumental in bringing one of the largest slave-holders in the neighbourhood – Mr Samuel Harrison – to emancipate all his slaves; and the general impression about Mr Cookman was, that whenever he met slave-holders, he laboured faithfully with them, as a religious duty, to induce them to liberate their bondsmen. When this good man was at our house, we were all sure to be called in to prayers in the morning; and he was not slow in making enquiries as to the state of our minds, nor in giving us a word of exhortation and of encouragement. Great was the sorrow of all the slaves when this faithful preacher of the gospel was removed from the circuit. He was an eloquent preacher, and possessed what few ministers, south of Mason and Dixon's line, possessed or dared to show – viz., a warm and philanthropic heart. This Mr Cookman was an Englishman by birth, and perished on board the ill-fated steamship *President*, while on his way to England.

But to return to my experience with Master Thomas after his conversion. In Baltimore I could occasionally get into a

Sabbath-school, amongst the free children, and receive lessons with the rest; but having learned to read and write already, I was more a teacher than a scholar, even there. When, however, I went back to the Eastern shore and was at the house of Master Thomas, I was not allowed either to teach or to be taught. The whole community, with but one exception among the whites, frowned upon everything like imparting instruction, either to slaves or to free coloured persons. That single exception, a pious young man named Wilson, asked me one day if I would like to assist him in teaching a little Sabbath-school, at the house of a free coloured man named James Mitchell. The idea was to me a delightful one, and I told him I would gladly devote as much of my Sabbaths as I could command to that most laudable work. Mr Wilson soon mustered up a dozen old spelling-books and a few testaments, and we commenced operations, with some twenty scholars in our school. Here, thought I, is something worth living for; here is a chance for usefulness. The first Sunday passed delightfully, and I spent the week after, very joyously. I could not go to Baltimore, where I and the little company of young friends who had been so much to me there, and from whom I felt parted for ever, but I could make a little Baltimore here. At our second meeting I learned there were some objections to the existence of our school; and sure enough we had scarcely got to work – *good* work, simply teaching a few coloured children how to read the gospel of the Son of God – when in rushed a mob, headed by two class-leaders, Mr Wright Fairbanks and Mr Garrison West, and with them Master Thomas. They were armed with sticks and other missiles, and drove us off, commanding us never to meet for such a purpose again. One of this pious crew told me that as for me, I wanted to be another Nat Turner, and if I did not look out I should get as many balls in me as Nat did into him. Thus ended the Sabbath-school; and the reader will not be surprised that this conduct, on the part of class-leaders and professedly holy men, did not serve to strengthen my religious convictions. The cloud over my St Michaels home grew heavier and blacker than ever.

It was not merely the agency of Master Thomas in breaking up our Sabbath-school, that shook my confidence in the power of that kind of Southern religion to make men wiser or better, but I saw in him all the cruelty and meanness *after* his conversion which he had exhibited before. His cruelty and meanness were especially displayed in his treatment of my unfortunate cousin Henny, whose lameness made her a burden to him. I have seen him tie up this lame and maimed woman and whip her in a manner most brutal and shocking; and then with blood-chilling blasphemy he would quote the passage of Scripture, 'That servant which knew his lord's will and prepared not himself, neither did according to his will, shall be beaten with many stripes.' He would keep this lacerated woman tied up by her wrists to a bolt in the joist, three, four, and five hours at a time. He would tie her up early in the morning, whip her with a cowskin before breakfast, leave her tied up, go to his store, and returning to dinner repeat the same castigation, laying on the rugged lash on flesh already raw by repeated blows. He seemed desirous to get the poor girl out of existence, or at any rate off his hands. In proof of this, he afterwards gave her away to his sister Sarah – Mrs Cline – but as in the case of Mr Hugh, Henny was soon returned on his hands. Finally, upon a pretence that he could do nothing for her, I use his own words, he 'set her adrift to take care of herself.' Here was a recently converted man, holding with tight grasp the well-framed and able-bodied slaves left him by old master – the persons who in freedom could have taken care of themselves; yet turning loose the only cripple among them, virtually to starve and die. No doubt, had Master Thomas been asked by some pious Northern brother, *why* he held slaves? his reply would have been precisely that which many another slave-holder has returned to the same enquiry, viz., 'I hold my slaves for their own good.'

The many differences springing up between Master Thomas and myself, owing to the clear perception I had of his character, and the boldness with which I defended myself against his capricious complaints, led him to declare that I was unsuited to his wants; that my city life had affected me perniciously; that in fact it had almost ruined me for every good purpose, and had fitted me for everything bad. One of my greatest faults, or offences, was that of letting his horse get away and go down to the farm which belonged to his father-in-law. The animal had a liking for that farm with which I fully sympathised. Whenever I let it out it would go dashing down the road to Mr Hamilton's as if going on a grand frolic. My horse gone, of course I must go after it. The explanation of our mutual attachment to the place is the same – the horse found good pasturage, and I found there plenty of bread. Mr Hamilton had his faults, but starving his slaves was not one of them. He gave food in abundance, and of excellent quality. In Mr Hamilton's cook – Aunt Mary – I found a generous and considerate friend. She never allowed me to go there without giving me bread enough to make good the deficiencies of a day or two. Master Thomas at last resolved to endure my behaviour no longer; he could keep neither me nor his horse, we liked so well to be at his father-in-law's farm. I had now lived with him nearly nine months, and he had given me a number of severe whippings, without any visible improvement in my character or conduct, and now he was resolved to put me out, as he said, '*to be broken*'.

There was, in the Bay-side, very near the camp-ground where my master received his religious impressions, a man named Edward Covey, who enjoyed the reputation of being a first-rate hand at breaking young negroes. This Covey was a poor man, a farm renter; and his reputation for being a good hand to break in slaves was of immense pecuniary advantage to him, since it enabled him to get his farm tilled at very little expense, compared with what it would have cost him otherwise. Some slave-holders thought it an advantage to let Mr Covey have the government of their slaves a year or two, almost free of charge, for the sake of the excellent training they had under his management. Like some horse-breakers noted for their skill, who ride the best horses in the country without expense, Mr Covey could have under him the most fiery bloods of the neighbourhood, for the reward of returning them to their owners *well broken*. Added to the natural witness of Mr Covey for the duties of his profession, he was said 'to enjoy religion', and he was as strict in the cultivation of piety as he was in the cultivation of his farm. I was made aware of these traits in his character by some who had been under his hand, and while I could not look forward to going to him with any degree of pleasure, I was glad to get away from St Michaels. I believed I should get enough to eat at Covey's, even if I suffered in other respects, and this to a hungry man is not a prospect to be regarded with indifference.

CHAPTER XV

Covey, the Negro Breaker

Journey to Covey's – Meditations by the way – Covey's house –
Family – Awkwardness as a field-hand – A cruel beating – Why
given – Description of Covey – First attempt at driving oxen –
Hair's-breadth escape – Ox and man alike property – Hard
labour more effective than the whip for breaking down the
spirit – Cunning and trickery of Covey – Family worship –
Shocking and indecent contempt for chastity – Great mental
agitation – Anguish beyond description

The morning of January 1, 1834, with its chilling wind and pinching
frost, quite in harmony with the winter in my own mind, found me,
with my little bundle of clothing on the end of a stick swung across my
shoulder, on the main road bending my way toward's Covey's, whither
I had been imperiously ordered by Master Thomas. He had been as
good as his word, and had committed me without reserve to the
mastery of that hard man. Eight or ten years had now passed since I
had been taken from my grandmother's cabin in Tuckahoe; and these
years, for the most part, I had spent in Baltimore, where, as the reader
has already seen, I was treated with comparative tenderness. I was now
about to sound profounder depths in slave life. My new master was
notorious for his fierce and savage disposition, and my only consolation
in going to live with him was the certainty of finding him precisely as
represented by common fame. There was neither joy in my heart nor
elasticity in my frame as I started for the tyrant's home. Starvation
made me glad to leave Thomas Auld's, and the cruel lash made me
dread to go to Covey's. Escape, however, was impossible; so, heavy and
sad, I paced the seven miles which lay between his house and St
Michaels, *thinking* much by the solitary way of my adverse condition.
But *thinking* was all I could do. Like a fish in a net, allowed to play for a
time, I was now drawn rapidly to the shore, secured at all points. 'I am,'
thought I, 'but the sport of a power which makes no account either of
my welfare or my happiness. By a law which I can comprehend, but

cannot evade or resist, I am ruthlessly snatched from the hearth of a fond grandmother and hurried away to the home of a mysterious old master; again I am removed from there to a master in Baltimore; thence I am snatched away to the Eastern Shore to be valued with the beasts of the field, and with them to be divided and set apart for a possessor; then I am sent back to Baltimore, and by the time I have formed new attachments and have begun to hope that no more rude shocks shall touch me, a difference arises between brothers, and I am again broken up and sent to St Michaels; and now from the latter place I am footing my way to the home of another master, where I am given to understand that like a wild young working animal I am to be broken to the yoke of a bitter and life-long bondage.' With thoughts and reflections like these, I came in sight of a small wood-coloured building, about a mile from the main road, which, from the description I had received at starting, I easily recognised as my new home. The Chesapeake Bay, upon the jutting banks of which the little wood-coloured house was standing, was white with foam raised by the heavy north-west wind; Poplar Island, covered with a thick black pine forest, standing out amid this half ocean; and Keat Point, stretching its sandy, desert-like shores out into the foam-crested bay, were all in sight, and served to deepen the wild and desolate scene.

The good clothes I had brought with me from Baltimore were now worn thin, and had not been replaced; for Master Thomas was as little careful to provide against cold as hunger. Met here by a north wind, sweeping through an open space of forty miles, I was glad to make any port, and, therefore, I speedily pressed on to the wood-coloured house. The family consisted of Mr and Mrs Covey; Mrs Hemp, a broken-backed woman, sister to Mrs Covey; William Hughes, cousin to Mr Covey; Caroline, the cook; Bill Smith, a hired man, and myself. Bill Smith, Bill Hughes, and myself were the working force of the farm, which comprised three or four hundred acres. I was now for the first time in my life to be a field-hand; and in my new employment I found myself even more awkward than a green country boy may be supposed to be upon his first entrance into the bewildering scenes of city life; and my awkwardness gave me much trouble. Strange and unnatural as it may seem, I had been in my new home but three days before Mr Covey, my brother in the Methodist Church, gave me a bitter foretaste of what was in reserve for me. I presume he thought that since he had but a single year in which to complete his work, the sooner he began the better. Perhaps he thought by coming to blows at once we should mutually understand better our relations to each other. But to whatever motive, direct or indirect, the cause may be referred, I had not been in his possession three whole days before he subjected me to a most brutal chastisement. Under his heavy blows blood flowed freely, and wales were left on my back as large as my little finger. The sores from this flogging continued for weeks, for they were kept open by the rough and coarse cloth which I wore for shirting. The occasion and details of this first chapter of my experience as a field-hand must be told, that the reader may see how unreasonable, as well as how cruel, my new master, Covey, was. The whole thing I found to be characteristic of the man, and I was probably treated no worse by him than scores of lads who had previously been committed to him, for reasons similar to those which induced my master to place me with him. But here are the facts connected with the affair, precisely as they occurred.

On one of the coldest mornings of the whole month of January 1834, I was ordered at daybreak to get a load of wood from a forest about two miles from the house. In order to perform this work, Mr Covey gave me a pair of unbroken oxen, for it seemed that his breaking abilities had not been turned in that direction. In due form, and with all proper ceremony, I was introduced to this huge yoke of unbroken oxen, and was carefully made to understand which was 'Buck' and which was 'Darby' – which was the 'in-hand' and which was the 'off-hand' ox. The master of this important ceremony was no less a person than Mr Covey himself; and the introduction was the first of the kind I had ever had.

My life, hitherto, had been quite away from horned cattle, and I had no knowledge of the art of managing them. What was meant by the 'in ox', as against the 'off ox', when both were equally fastened to one cart, and under one yoke, I could not very easily divine; and the difference implied by the names, and the peculiar duties of each, were alike *Greek* to me. Why was not the 'off ox' called the 'in ox'? Where and what is the reason for this distinction in names, when there is none in the things themselves? After initiating me into the use of the 'whoa', 'back', 'gee', 'hither' – the entire language spoken between oxen and driver – Mr Covey took a rope about ten feet long and one inch thick, and placed one end of it around the horns of the 'in-hand ox', and gave the other end to me, telling me that if the oxen started to run away, as the scamp knew they would, I must hold on to the rope and stop them. I need not tell anyone who is acquainted with either the strength or the disposition of an untamed ox, that this order was about as unreasonable as a command to shoulder a mad bull. I had never driven oxen before, and I was as awkward a driver as it is possible to conceive. I could not plead my ignorance to Mr Covey; there was that in his manner which forbade any reply. Cold, distant, morose, with a face wearing all the marks of captious pride and malicious sternness, he repelled all advances. He was not a large man – not more than five feet ten inches in height, I should think; short-necked, round-shouldered, of quick and wiry motion, of thin and wolfish visage, with a pair of small, greenish-grey eyes, set well back under a forehead without dignity, and which were constantly in motion, expressing his passions rather than his thoughts in looks, but denying them utterance in words. The creature presented an appearance altogether ferocious and sinister, disagreeable and forbidding, in the extreme. When he spoke, it was from the corner of his mouth, and in a sort of light growl, like a dog, when an attempt is made to take a bone from him. I already believed him a worse fellow than he had been represented to be. With his directions, and without stopping to question, I started for the woods, quite anxious to perform my first exploit in driving in a creditable manner. The distance from the house to the wood's gate – a full mile, I should think – was passed over with little difficulty: for, although the animals ran, I was fleet enough in the open field to keep pace with them, especially as they pulled me along at the end of the rope; but on reaching the woods, I was speedily thrown into a distressing plight. The animals took fright, and started off ferociously into the woods, carrying the cart full tilt against trees, over stumps, and dashing from side to side in a manner altogether frightful. As I held the rope I expected every moment to be crushed between the cart and the huge trees, among which they were so furiously dashing. After running thus for several minutes, my oxen were finally brought to a stand by a tree, against which they dashed themselves with great violence, upsetting the cart, and entangling themselves among sundry young saplings. By the shock the body of the cart was flung in one direction and the wheels and tongue in another, and all in the greatest confusion. There I was, all alone in a thick wood to which I was a stranger; my cart upset and shattered, my oxen entangled, wild, and enraged, and I, poor soul, but a green hand to set all this disorder right. I knew no more of oxen than the ox-driver is supposed to know of wisdom.

After standing a few minutes, surveying the damage, and not without a presentiment that this trouble would draw after it others even more distressing, I took one end of the cart body and, by an extra outlay of strength, I lifted it toward the axle-tree, from which it had been violently flung; and after much pulling and straining, I succeeded in getting the body of the cart in its place. This was an important step out of the difficulty, and its performance increased my courage for the work which remained to be done. The cart was provided with an axe, a tool with which I had become pretty well acquainted in the shipyard at Baltimore. With this I cut down the saplings by which my oxen were entangled, and again pursued my journey, with my heart in my mouth, lest the oxen should again take it into their senseless heads to cut up a caper. But their spree was over for the present, and the rascals now moved off as soberly as though their behaviour had been natural and exemplary. On reaching the part of the forest where I had been the day before chopping wood, I filled the cart with a heavy load, as a security against another runaway. But the neck of an ox is equal in strength to iron: it defies ordinary burdens. Tame and docile to a proverb when *well* trained, the ox is the most sullen and intractable of animals when but half-broken to the yoke. I saw in my own situation several points of similarity with that of the oxen. They were property: so was I. Covey was to break me – I was to break them. Break and be broken was the order.

Half of the day was already gone and I had not yet turned my face homeward. It required only two days' experience and observation to teach me that no such apparent waste of time would be lightly overlooked by Covey. I therefore hurried toward home; but in reaching the lane gate I met the crowning disaster of the day. This gate was a fair specimen of Southern handicraft. There were two huge posts eighteen inches in diameter, rough hewed and square, and the heavy gate was so hung on one of these that it opened only about half the proper distance. On arriving here it was necessary for me to let go the end of the rope on the horns of the 'in hand ox'; and now as soon as the gate was open and I let go of it to get the rope again, off went my oxen, making nothing of their load, full tilt; and in so doing they caught the huge gate between the wheel and the cart body, literally crushing it to splinters, and coming only within a few inches of subjecting me to a similar crushing, for I was just in advance of the wheel when it struck the left gate post. With these two hair's-breadth escapes I thought I could successfully explain to Mr Covey the delay, and avert punishment – I was not without a faint hope of being commended for the stern resolution which I had displayed in accomplishing the difficult task – a task which I afterwards learned even Covey himself would not have undertaken without first driving the oxen for some time in the open field, preparatory to their going to the woods. But in this I was disappointed. On coming to him his countenance assumed an aspect of rigid displeasure, and as I gave him a history of the casualties of my trip, his wolfish face, with his greenish eyes, became intensely ferocious. 'Go back to the woods again,' he said, muttering something else about wasting time. I hastily obeyed, but I had not gone far on my way when I saw him coming after me. My oxen now behaved themselves with singular propriety, contrasting their present conduct to my representation of their former antics. I almost wished, now that Covey was coming, they *would* do something in keeping with the character I had given them; but no, they had already had their spree, and they could afford now to be extra good, readily obeying orders, and seeming to understand them quite as well as I did myself. On reaching the woods my tormentor, who seemed all the time to be remarking to himself upon the good behaviour of the oxen, came up to me and ordered me to stop the cart, accompanying the same with the threat that he would now teach me how to break gates and idle away my time when he sent me to the woods. Suiting the action to the words, Covey paced off, in his own wiry fashion, to a large gum tree, the young shoots of which are generally used for *ox goads*, they being exceedingly tough. Three of these *goads*, from four to six feet long, he cut off and trimmed up with his large jack-knife. This done, he ordered me to take off my clothes. To this unreasonable order I made no reply, but in my apparent unconsciousness and inattention to this command I indicated very plainly a stern determination to do no such thing. 'If you will beat me,' thought I, 'you shall do so over my clothes.' After many threats, which made no impression on me, he rushed at me with something of the savage fierceness of a wolf, tore off the few and thinly worn clothes I had on, and proceeded to wear out on my back the heavy goads which he had cut from the gum tree. This flogging was the first of a series of floggings, and though very severe, it was no less so than many which came after it, and these for offences far lighter than the gate-breaking.

I remained with Mr Covey one year – I cannot say I *lived* with him – and during the first six months that I was there I was whipped, either with sticks or cow-skins, every week. Aching bones and a sore back were my constant companions. Frequently as the lash was used, Mr Covey thought less of it as a means of breaking down my spirit than that of hard and continued labour. He worked me steadily up to the point of my powers of endurance. From the dawn of day in the morning till the darkness was complete in the evening I was kept at hard work in the field or the woods. At certain seasons of the year we were all kept in the field till eleven and twelve o'clock at night. At these times Covey would attend us in the field and urge us on with words or blows, as it seemed best to him. He had, in his life, been an overseer, and he well understood the business of slave-driving. There was no deceiving him. He knew just what a man or boy could do, and he held both to strict account. When he pleased he would work himself like a very Turk, making everything fly before him. It was, however, scarcely necessary for Mr Covey to be really present in the field to have his work go on industriously. He had the faculty of making us feel that he was always present. By a series of adroitly managed surprises which he practised, I was prepared to expect him at any moment. His plan was never to approach the spot where his hands were at work in an open, manly, and direct manner. No thief was ever more artful in his devices than this man Covey. He would creep and crawl in ditches and gullies, hide behind stumps and bushes, and practise so much of the cunning of the serpent, that Bill Smith and I, between ourselves, never called him by any other name than 'the snake'. We fancied that in his eyes and his gait we could see a snakish resemblance. One half of his proficiency in the art of negro-breaking consisted, I should think, in this species of cunning. We were never secure. He could see or hear us nearly all the time. He was to us behind every stump, tree, bush, and fence on the plantation. He carried this kind of trickery so far that he would sometimes mount his horse and make believe he was going to St Michaels, and in thirty minutes afterwards you might find his horse tied in the woods, and the snake-like Covey lying flat in the ditch with his head lifted above its edge, or in a fence-corner, watching every movement of the slaves. I have known him walk up to us and give us special orders as to our work in advance, as if he were leaving home with a view to being absent several days, and before he got half way to the house he would avail himself of our inattention to his movements to turn short on his heel, conceal himself behind a fence-corner, or a tree, and watch us until the going down of the sun. Mean and contemptible as is all this, it is in keeping with the character which the life of a slave-holder was calculated to produce. There was no earthly inducement in the slave's condition to incite him to labour faithfully. The fear of punishment was the sole motive of any sort of industry with him. Knowing this fact as the slave-holder did, and judging the slave by himself, he naturally concluded that the slave would be idle whenever the cause for this fear was absent. Hence all sorts of petty deceptions were practised to inspire fear.

But with Mr Covey trickery was natural. Everything in the shape of learning or religion which he possessed was made to conform to this semi-lying propensity. He did not seem conscious that the practice had anything unmanly, base, or contemptible about it. It was a part of an important system with him, essential to the relation of master and slave. I thought I saw, in his very religious devotions, this controlling element of his character. A long prayer at night made up for a short prayer in the morning, and few men could seem more devotional than he, when he had nothing else to do.

Mr Covey was not content with the cold style of family worship adopted in the cold latitudes, which begin and end with a simple prayer. No! the voice of praise as well as of prayer must be heard in his house night and morning. At first I was called upon to bear some part in these exercises; but the repeated floggings given me turned the whole thing into mockery. He was a poor singer, and mainly relied on me for raising the hymn for the family, and when I failed to do so he was thrown into much confusion. I do not think he ever abused me on account of these vexations. His religion was a thing altogether apart from his worldly concerns. He knew nothing of it as a holy principle directing and controlling his daily life, making the latter conform to the requirements of the Gospel. One or two facts will illustrate his character better than a volume of generalities.

I have already implied that Mr Edward Covey was a poor man. He was, in fact, just commencing to lay the foundation of his fortune, as fortune was regarded in a slave state. The first condition of wealth and respectability there being the ownership of human property, every nerve was strained by the poor man to obtain it, with little regard sometimes as to the means. In pursuit of this object, pious as Mr Covey was, he proved himself as unscrupulous and base as the worst of his neighbours. In the beginning he was only able – as he said – 'to buy one slave'; and scandalous and shocking as is the fact, he boasted that he bought her simply 'as a breeder'. But the worst of this is not told in this naked statement. This young woman, Caroline was her name, was virtually compelled by Covey to abandon herself to the object for which he had purchased her; and the result was the birth of twins at the end of the year. At this addition to his human stock Covey and his wife were ecstatic with joy. No one dreamed of reproaching the woman, or of finding fault with the hired man, Bill Smith, the father of the children, for Mr Covey himself had locked the two up together every night, thus inviting the result.

But I will pursue this revolting subject no farther. No better illustration of the unchaste, demoralising, and debasing character of slavery can be found, than is furnished in the fact that this professedly Christian slave-holder, amidst all his prayers and hymns, was shamelessly and boastfully encouraging and actually compelling, in his own house, undisguised and unmitigated unchastity, as a means of increasing his stock. It was the system of slavery which made this allowable, and which no more condemned the slave-holder for buying a slave-woman and devoting her to this life, than for buying a cow and raising stock from her; and the same rules were observed, with a view to increasing the number and quality of the one, as of the other.

If at any one time in my life, more than another, I was made to drink the bitterest dregs of slavery, that time was during the first six months of my stay with this man Covey. We were worked in all weathers. It was never too hot, nor too cold; it could never rain, blow, snow, nor hail too hard to prevent us from working in the field. Work, work, work, was scarcely more the order of the day than of the night. The longest days were too short for him, and the shortest nights were too long for him. I was somewhat unmanageable at the first, but a few months of this discipline tamed me. Mr Covey succeeded in *breaking* me – in body, soul, and spirit. My natural elasticity was crushed; my intellect languished; the disposition to read departed, the cheerful spark that lingered about my eye died out; the dark night of slavery closed in upon me, and beheld a man transformed to a brute.

Sunday was my only leisure time. I spent this in a sort of beast-like stupor, between sleeping and waking under some large tree. At times I would rise up, a flash of energetic freedom would dart through my soul, accompanied with a faint beam of hope that flickered for a moment, and then vanished. I sank down again, mourning over my wretched condition. I was sometimes tempted to take my life and that of Covey, but was prevented by a combination of hope and fear. My sufferings, as I remember them now, seem like a dream rather than a stern real reality.

Our house stood within a few rods of the Chesapeake Bay, whose broad bosom was ever white with sails from every quarter of the habitable globe. Those beautiful vessels, robed in white, and so delightful to the eyes of freemen, were to me so many shrouded ghosts, to terrify and torment me with thoughts of my wretched condition. I have often, in the deep stillness of a summer's Sabbath, stood all alone upon the banks of that noble bay, and traced, with saddened heart and tearful eye, the countless number of sails moving off to the mighty ocean. The sight of these always affected me powerfully. My thoughts would compel utterance; and there, with no audience but the Almighty, I would pour out my soul's complaint in my rude way with an apostrophe to the moving multitude of ships –

'You are loosed from your moorings, and free. I am fast in my chains, and am a slave! You move merrily before the gentle gale, and I sadly before the bloody whip. You are freedom's swift-winged angels, that fly around the world; I am confined in bonds of iron. O, that I were free! O, that I were on one of your gallant decks, and under your protecting wing! Alas! betwixt me and you the turbid waters roll. Go on, go on; O, that I could also go! Could I but swim! If I could fly! O, why was I born a man, of whom to make a brute? The glad ship is gone: she hides in the dim distance. I am left in the hell of unending slavery. O, God, save me! God, deliver me! Let me be free! – Is there any God? Why am I a slave? I will run away. I will not stand it. Get caught or get clear, I'll try it. I may as well die with ague as with fever. I have only one life to lose. I may as well be killed running as die standing. Only think of it: one hundred miles north, and I am free! Try it? Yes! God helping me, I will. It cannot be that I shall live and die a slave. I will take to the water. This very day shall yet bear me into freedom. The steamboats steer in a north-east course from North Point; I will do the same; and when I get to the head of the bay, I will turn my canoe adrift, and walk straight through Delaware into Pennsylvania. When I get there I shall not be required to have a pass: I will travel there without being disturbed. Let but the first opportunity offer, and come what will, I am off. Meanwhile I will try the yoke. I am not the only slave in the world. Why should I fret? I can bear as much as any of them. Besides, I am but a boy yet, and all boys are bound out to someone. It may be that my misery in slavery will only increase my happiness when I get free. There is a better day coming.'

I shall never be able to narrate half the mental experience through which it was my lot to pass, during my stay at Covey's. I was completely wrecked, changed, and bewildered; goaded almost to madness at one time, and at another, reconciling myself to my wretched condition. All the kindness I had received at Baltimore, all my former hopes and aspirations for usefulness in the world, and even the happy moments spent in the exercises of religion, contrasted with my then present lot, served but to increase my anguish.

I suffered bodily as well as mentally. I had neither sufficient time in which to eat, nor to sleep, except on Sundays. The overwork, and the brutal chastisement of which I was the victim, combined with that ever-gnawing and soul-devouring thought – '*I am a slave – a slave for life – a slave with no rational ground to hope for freedom*'– rendered me a living embodiment of mental and physical wretchedness.

CHAPTER XVI

Another Pressure of the Tyrant's Vice

Experience at Covey's summed up – First six months severer
than the remaining six – Preliminaries to the change – Reasons
for narrating the circumstances – Scene in the treading-yard –
Taken ill – Escapes to St Michaels – The pursuit – Suffering in
the woods – Talk with Master Thomas – His beating – Driven
back to Covey's – The slaves never sick – Natural to expect them
to feign sickness – Laziness of slave-holders

The reader has but to repeat, in his mind, once a week the scene in the
woods, where Covey subjected me to his merciless lash, to have a true
idea of my bitter experience during the first six months of the breaking
process through which he carried me. I have no heart to repeat each
separate transaction. Such a narration would fill a volume much larger
than the present one. I aim only to give the reader a truthful impression
of my slave-life without unnecessarily affecting him with harrowing
details.

As I have intimated, my hardships were much greater during the first
six months of my stay at Covey's than during the remainder of the year,
and as the change in my condition was owing to causes which may help
the reader to a better understanding of human nature, when subjected
to the terrible extremities of slavery, I will narrate the circumstances of
this change, although I may seem thereby to applaud my own courage.

The reader has seen me humbled, degraded, broken down, enslaved,
and brutalised; and understands how it was done; now let us see the
converse of all this, and how it was brought about; and this will take us
through the year 1834.

On one of the hottest days in the month of August, of the year just
mentioned, had the reader been passing through Covey's farm, he
might have seen me at work in what was called the 'treading-yard' – a
yard upon which wheat was trodden out from the straw by the horses'
feet. I was there at work feeding the 'fan', or rather bringing wheat to
the fan, while Bill Smith was feeding. Our force consisted of Bill

Hughes, Bill Smith, and a slave by the name of Eli, the latter having been hired for the occasion. The work was simple, and required strength and activity, rather than any skill or intelligence; and yet to one entirely unused to such work, it came very hard. The heat was intense and overpowering, and there was much hurry to get the wheat trodden out that day through the fan; since if that work was done an hour before sundown, the hands would have, according to a promise of Covey, that hour added to their night's rest I was not behind any of them in the wish to complete the day's work before sundown, and hence I struggled with all my might to get it forward. The promise of one hour's repose on a week day was sufficient to quicken my pace, and to spur me on to extra endeavour. Besides, we had all planned to go fishing, and I certainly wished to have a hand in that. But I was disappointed, and the day turned out to be one of the bitterest I ever experienced. About three o'clock, while the sun was pouring down his burning rays, and not a breeze was stirring, I broke down; my strength failed me; I was seized with a violent aching of the head, attended with extreme dizziness, and trembling in every limb. Finding what was coming, and feeling it would never do to stop work, I nerved myself up, and staggered on, until I fell by the side of the wheat fan, with a feeling that the earth had fallen in upon me. This brought the entire work to a dead stand. There was work for four: each one had his part to perform, and each part depended on the other, so that when one stopped, all were compelled to stop. Covey, who had become my dread, was at the house, about a hundred yards from where I was fanning, and instantly, upon hearing the fan stop he came down to the treading-yard to enquire into the cause of the stopping. Bill Smith told him I was sick, and that I was unable longer to bring wheat to the fan.

I had by this time crawled away under the side of a post-and-rail fence in the shade, and was exceedingly ill. The intense heat of the sun, the heavy dust rising from the fan, the stooping to take up the wheat from the yard, together with the hurrying to get through, had caused a rush of blood to my head. In this condition Covey, finding out where I was, came to me; and after standing over me a while he asked me what the matter was. I told him as well as I could, for it was with difficulty that I could speak. He gave me a savage kick in the side which jarred my whole frame, and commanded me to get up. The monster had obtained complete control over me, and if he had commanded me to do any possible thing I should, in my then state of mind, have endeavoured to comply. I made an effort to rise, but fell back in the attempt before gaining my feet. He gave me another heavy kick, and again told me to rise. I again tried, and succeeded in standing up; but upon stooping to get the tub with which I was feeding the fan I again staggered and fell to the ground; and I must have so fallen had I been sure that a hundred bullets would have pierced me through as the consequence. While down in this sad condition, and perfectly helpless, the merciless negro-breaker took up the hickory slab with which Hughes had been striking off the wheat to a level with the sides of the half-bushel measure – a very hard weapon – and with the edge of it he dealt me a heavy blow on my head, which made a large gash and caused the blood to run freely, saying at the same time, 'If you have the headache I'll cure you.' This done, he ordered me again to rise; but I made no effort to do so, for I had now made up my mind that it was useless, and that the heartless villain might do his worst, he could but kill me and that might put me out of my misery. Finding me unable to rise, or rather despairing of my doing so, Covey left me, with a view to getting on with the work without me. I was bleeding very freely, and my face was soon covered with my warm blood. Cruel and merciless as was the motive that dealt that blow, the wound was a fortunate one for me. Bleeding was never more efficacious. The pain in my head speedily abated, and I was soon able to rise. Covey had, as I have said, left me to my fate, and the question was, shall I return to my work, or shall I find my way to St Michaels and make Captain Auld acquainted with the atrocious cruelty of his brother Covey and beseech him to get me another master? Remembering the object he had in view in placing me under the management of Covey, and further his cruel treatment of my poor crippled cousin Henny, and his meanness in the matter of feeding and clothing his slaves, there was little ground to hope for a favourable reception at the hands of Captain Thomas Auld. Nevertheless, I resolved to go straight to him, thinking that, if not animated by motives of humanity, he might be induced to interfere on my behalf from selfish considerations. 'He cannot,' I thought, 'allow his property to be thus bruised and battered, marred and defaced, and I will go to him about the matter.' In order to get to St Michaels by the most favourable and direct road I must walk seven miles, and this, in my sad condition, was no easy performance. I had already lost much blood, I was exhausted by over exertion, my sides were sore from the heavy blows planted there by the stout boots of Mr Covey, and I was in every way in an unfavourable plight for the journey. I, however, watched my chance, while the cruel and cunning Covey was looking in an opposite direction, and started off across the field for St Michaels. This was a daring step. If it failed it would only exasperate Covey, and increase the rigours of my bondage during the remainder of my term of service under him; but the step was taken, and I must go forward. I succeeded in getting nearly half way across the broad field towards the woods, when Covey observed me. I was still bleeding, and the exertion of running had started the blood afresh. *'Come back! Come back!'* he vociferated, with threats of what he would do if I did not return instantly. But disregarding his calls and threats, I pressed on towards the woods as fast as my feeble state would allow. Seeing no signs of my stopping he caused his horse to be brought out and saddled, as if he intended to pursue me. The race was now to be an unequal one, and thinking I might be overhauled by him if I kept the main road I walked nearly the whole distance in the woods, keeping far enough from the road to avoid detection and pursuit. But I had not gone far before my little strength again failed me, and I was obliged to lie down. The blood was still oozing from the wound in my head, and for a time I suffered more than I can describe. There I was in the deep woods, sick and emaciated, pursued by a wretch whose character for revolting cruelty beggars all opprobrious speech, bleeding and almost bloodless. I was not without the fear of bleeding to death. The thought of dying in the woods all alone, and of being torn in pieces by the buzzards, had not yet been rendered tolerable by my many troubles and hardships, and I was glad when the shade of the trees and the cool evening breeze combined with my matted hair to stop the flow of blood. After lying there about three quarters of an hour brooding over the singular and mournful lot to which I was doomed, my mind passing over the whole scale or circle of belief and unbelief, from faith in the over-ruling Providence of God to the blackest atheism, I again took up my journey toward St Michaels, more weary and sad than on the morning when I left Thomas Auld's for the home of Covey. I was bare-footed, bare-headed, and in my shirt sleeves. The way was through briars and bogs, and I tore my feet often during the journey. I was full five hours in going the seven or eight miles; partly because of the difficulties of the way, and partly because of the feebleness induced by my illness, bruises, and loss of blood.

On gaining my master's store, I presented an appearance of wretchedness and woe calculated to move any but a heart of stone. From the crown of my head to the sole of my feet there were marks of blood. My hair was all clotted with dust and blood, and the back of my shirt was literally stiff with the same. Briars and thorns had scarred and torn my feet and legs. Had I escaped from a den of tigers, I could not have looked worse. In this plight I appeared before my professedly *Christian* master, humbly to invoke the interposition of his power and authority, to protect me from further abuse and violence. During the latter part of my tedious journey, I had begun to hope that my master. would now show himself in a nobler light than I had before seen him. But I was disappointed. I had jumped from a sinking ship into the sea; I had fled from a tiger to something worse. I told him all the circumstances, as well as I could: how I was endeavouring to please Covey; how hard I was at work in the present instance; how unwillingly I sank down under the heat, toil, and pain; the brutal manner in which Covey had kicked me in the side, the gash cut in my head; my hesitation about troubling him, Captain Auld, with complaints; but that now I felt it would not be best longer to conceal from him the outrages committed on me from time to time. At first Master Thomas seemed somewhat affected by the story of my wrongs, but he soon repressed whatever feeling he may have had, and became as cold and hard as iron. It was impossible, *at first*, as I stood before him, to seem indifferent. I distinctly saw his human nature asserting its conviction against the slave system, which made cases like mine *possible*; but, as I have said, humanity fell before the systematic tyranny of slavery. He first walked the floor, apparently much agitated by my story, and the spectacle I presented; but soon it was *his* turn to talk. He began moderately by finding excuses for Covey, and ended with a full justification of him, and a passionate condemnation of me. He had no doubt I deserved the flogging. He did not believe I was sick; I was only endeavouring to get rid of work. My dizziness was laziness, and Covey did right to flog me as he had done. After thus fairly annihilating me, and arousing himself by his eloquence, he fiercely demanded what I wished *him* to do in the case! With such a knockdown to all my hopes, and feeling as I did my entire subjection to his power, I had very little heart to reply. I must not assert my innocence of the allegations he had piled up against me, for that would be impudence. The guilt of a slave was always and everywhere presumed, and the innocence of the slave-holder, or employer, was always asserted. The word of the slave against this presumption was generally treated as impudence, worthy of punishment. 'Do you dare to contradict me, you rascal?' was a final silencer of counter-statements from the lips of a slave. Calming down a little, in view of my silence and hesitation, and perhaps a little touched at my forlorn and miserable appearance, he enquired again, what I wanted him to do? Thus invited a second time, I told him I wished him to allow me to get a new home, and to find a new master; that as sure as I went back to live again with Mr Covey, I should be killed by him; that he would never forgive my coming home with complaints; that since I had lived with him he had almost crushed my spirit, and I believed he would ruin me for future service, and that my life was not safe in his hands. This Master Thomas, *my brother in the church*, regarded as 'nonsense'. There was no danger that Mr Covey would kill me; he was a good man, industrious, and religious; and he would not think of removing me from that home; 'Besides,' said he – and this I found was the most distressing thought of all to him – 'if you should leave Covey now that your year is but half expired, I should lose your wages for the entire year. You belong to Mr Covey for one year, and you *must go back* to him, come what will; and you must not trouble me with any more stories; and if you don't go immediately home, I'll get hold of you myself.' This was just what I expected when I found he had *prejudged* the case against me. 'But, sir,' I said, 'I am sick and tired, and I *cannot* get home to night.' At this he somewhat relented, and finally allowed me to stay the night, but said I must be off early in the morning, and concluded his directions by making me swallow a huge dose of Epsom salts, which was about the only medicine ever administered to slaves.

It was quite natural for Master Thomas to presume I was feigning sickness to escape work, for he probably thought that were he in the place of a slave, with no wages for his work, no praise for well doing, no motive for toil but the lash, he would try every possible scheme by which to escape labour. I say I have no doubt of this; the reason is that there were not, under the whole heavens, a set of men who cultivated such a dread of labour as did the slave-holders. The charge of laziness against the slaves was ever on their lips, and was the standing apology for every species of cruelty and brutality. These men did, indeed, literally 'bind heavy burdens, grievous to be borne, and laid them upon men's shoulder's, but they themselves would not move them with one of their fingers'.

CHAPTER XVII

The Last Flogging

A sleepless night – Return to Covey's – Punished by him –
The chase defeated – Vengeance postponed – Musings in the
woods – The alternative – Deplorable spectacle – Night in the
woods – Expected attack – Accosted by Sandy – A friend,
not a master – Sandy's hospitality – The ash-cake supper –
Interview with Sandy – His advice – Sandy a conjurer as well as a
Christian – The magic root – Strange meeting with Covey – His
manner – Covey's Sunday face – Defensive resolve – The fight –
The victory, and its results

Sleep does not always come to the relief of the weary in body and
broken in spirit; especially is it so when past troubles only foreshadow
coming disasters. My last hope had been extinguished. My master,
whom I did not venture to hope would protect me as *a man*, had now
refused to protect me as *his property*, and had cast me back, covered
with reproaches and bruises, into the hands of one who was a stranger
to that mercy which is the soul of the religion he professed. May the
reader never know what it is to spend such a night as that was to me,
which heralded my return to the den of horrors from which I had made
a temporary escape.

I remained – sleep I did not – all night at St Michaels, and in the
morning I started off, obedient to the order of Master Thomas, feeling
that I had no friend on earth, and doubting if I had one in heaven. I
reached Covey's about nine o'clock; and just as I stepped into the field,
before I had reached the house, true to his snakish habits, Covey darted
out at me from a fence-corner, in which he had secreted himself for the
purpose of securing me. He was provided with a cowskin and a rope,
and he evidently intended to *tie me up*, and wreak his vengeance on me
to the fullest extent. I should have been an easy prey had he succeeded
in getting his hands upon me, for I had taken no refreshment since the
previous noon; and this, with the other trying circumstances had
greatly reduced my strength. I, however, darted back into the woods

before the ferocious hound could reach me, and buried myself in a thicket, where he lost sight of me. The cornfield afforded me shelter in getting to the woods. But for the tall corn, Covey would have overtaken me, and made me his captive. He was much chagrined that he did not, and gave up the chase very reluctantly, as I could see by his angry movements as he returned to the house.

Well, now I am clear of Covey and his lash, for a little time. I am in the wood, buried in its sombre gloom, and hushed in its solemn silence; hidden from all human eyes, shut in with nature, and with nature's God, and absent from all human contrivances. Here was a good place to pray; to pray for help, for deliverance – a prayer I had often made before. But how could I pray? Covey could pray – Captain Auld could pray. I would fain pray; but doubts arising, partly from my neglect of the means of grace, and partly from the sham religion which everywhere prevailed, cast in my mind a doubt upon all religion, and led me to the conviction that prayers were unavailing and delusive.

Life in itself had almost become burdensome to me. All my outward relations were against me; I must stay here and starve, or go home to Covey's and have my flesh torn to pieces and my spirit humbled under the cruel lash of Covey. These were the alternatives before me. The day was long and irksome. I was weak from the toils of the previous day, and from want of food and sleep, and I had been so little concerned about my appearance that I had not yet washed the blood from my garments. I was an object of horror, even to myself. Life in Baltimore, when most oppressive, was a paradise to this. What had I done, what had my parents done, that such a life as this should be mine? That day, in the woods, I would have exchanged my manhood for the brutehood of an ox.

Night came. I was still in the woods, and still unresolved what to do. Hunger had not yet pinched me to the point of going home, and I laid myself down in the leaves to rest; for I had been watching for hunters all day, but not being molested by them during the day, I expected no disturbance from them during the night. I had come to the conclusion that Covey relied upon hunger to drive me home, and in this I was quite correct, for he made no effort to catch me after the morning.

During the night I heard the step of a man in the woods. He was coming toward the place where I lay. A person laying still has the advantage over one walking in the woods in the daytime, and this advantage is much greater at night. I was not able to engage in physical struggle, and I had recourse to the common resort of the weak. I hid myself in the leaves to prevent discovery. But as the night rambler in the woods drew nearer I found him to be a *friend*, not an enemy, a slave of Mr William Groomes, of Easton, a kind-hearted fellow named 'Sandy'. Sandy lived with Mr Kemp that year, about four miles from St Michaels. He, like myself, had been hired out that year, but unlike myself had not been hired out to be broken. He was the husband of a free woman who lived in the lower part of 'Poppie Neck', and he was now on his way through the woods to see her and spend the Sabbath with her.

As soon as I had ascertained that the disturber of my solitude was not an enemy, but the good-hearted Sandy – a man as famous among the slaves of the neighbourhood for his good nature as for his good sense – I came out from my hiding-place and made myself known to him. I explained the circumstances of the past two days which had driven me to the woods, and he deeply compassionated my distress. It was a bold thing for him to shelter me, and I could not ask him to do so, for had I been found in his hut he would have suffered the penalty of thirty-nine lashes on his bare back, if not something worse. But Sandy was too generous to permit the fear of punishment to prevent his relieving a brother bondman from hunger and exposure, and therefore, on his own motion, I accompanied him home to his wife – for the house and lot were hers, as she was a free woman. It was about midnight, but his wife was called up, a fire was made, some Indian meal was soon mixed with salt and water, and an ash-cake was baked in a hurry, to relieve my hunger. Sandy's wife was not behind him in kindness; both seemed to esteem it a privilege to succour me, for although I was hated by Covey and by my master, I was loved by the coloured people, because they thought I was hated for my knowledge, and persecuted because I was feared. I was the only slave in that region who could read or write. There had been one other man, belonging to Mr Hugh Hamilton, who could read, but he, poor fellow, had shortly after coming into the neighbourhood been sold off to the far South, I saw him ironed, in the cart, to be carried to Easton for sale, pinioned like a yearling for the slaughter. My knowledge was now the pride of my brother slaves, and no doubt Sandy felt something of the general interest in me on that account. The supper was soon ready, and though I have since feasted with honourables, lord mayors, and aldermen over the sea, my supper on ash-cake and cold water, with Sandy, was the meal of all my life most sweet to my taste, and now most vivid to my memory.

Supper over, Sandy and I went to a discussion of what was *possible* for me, under the perils and hardships which overshadowed my path. The question was, must I go back to Covey, or must I attempt to run away?

Upon a careful survey the latter was found to be impossible; for I was on a narrow neck of land, every avenue from which would bring me in sight of pursuers. There was Chesapeake Bay to the right, and 'Pot-pie' river to the left, and St Michaels and its neighbourhood occupied the only space through which there was any retreat.

I found Sandy an old adviser. He was not only a religious man, but he professed to believe in a system for which I have no name. He was a genuine African, and had inherited some of the so-called magical powers said to be possessed by the eastern nations. He told me that he could help me; that in those very woods there was an herb which in the morning might be found, possessing all the powers required for my protection – I put his words in my own language – and that if I would take his advice he would procure me the root of the herb of which he spoke. He told me, further, that if I would take that root and wear it on my right side it would be impossible for Covey to strike me a blow; that with this root about my person no white man could whip me. He said he had carried it for years, and that he had fully tested its virtues. He had never received a blow from a slave-holder since he had carried it, and he never expected to receive one, for he meant always to carry that root for protection. He knew Covey well, for Mrs Covey was the daughter of Mrs Kemp; and he, Sandy, had heard of the barbarous treatment to which I had been subjected, and he wanted to do something for me.

Now all this talk about the root was to me very absurd and ridiculous, if not positively sinful. I at first rejected the idea that the simple carrying a root on my right side – a root, by-the-way, over which I walked every time I went into the woods – could possess any such magic power as he ascribed to it, and I was, therefore, not disposed to cumber my pocket with it. I had a positive aversion to all pretenders to '*divination*'. It was beneath one of my intelligence to countenance such dealings with the devil as this power implied. But with all my learning – it was really precious – Sandy was more than a match for me. 'My book-learning,' he said, 'had not kept Covey off me' – a powerful argument just then – and he entreated me, with flashing eyes, to try this. If it did me no good it could do me no harm, and it would cost me nothing anyway. Sandy was so earnest and so confident of the good qualities of this weed that, to please him, I was induced to take it. He had been to me the good Samaritan, and had, almost providentially, found me and helped me when I could not help myself; how did I know but that the hand of the Lord was in it? With thoughts of this sort I took the root from Sandy and put them in my right hand pocket.

This was Sunday morning. Sandy now urged me to go home with all speed, and to walk up bravely to the house, as though nothing had happened. I saw in Sandy too deep an insight into human nature, with all his superstition, not to have some respect for his advice; and perhaps, too, a slight gleam or shadow of his superstition had fallen on me. At any rate, I started off toward Covey's as directed. Having, the previous night, poured my griefs into Sandy's ears and enlisted him in my behalf, having made his wife a sharer in my sorrows, and having also become well refreshed by sleep and food, I moved off quite courageously toward the dreaded Covey's. Singularly enough, just as I entered the yard gate I met him and his wife, dressed in their Sunday best, looking as smiling as angels, on their way to church. His manner perfectly astonished me. There was something really benignant in his countenance. He spoke to me as never before, told me that the pigs had got into the lot and he wished me to go and drive them out; enquired how I was, and seemed an altered man. This extraordinary conduct really made me begin to think that Sandy's herb had more virtue in it than I, in my pride, had been willing to allow, and had the day been other than Sunday I should have attributed Covey's altered manner solely to the power of the root. I suspected, however, that the Sabbath, not the root, was the real explanation of the change. His religion hindered him from breaking the *Sabbath*, but not from breaking my skin on any other day than Sunday. He had more respect for the day than for the man for whom the day was mercifully given; for while he would out and slash my body during the week, he would on Sunday teach me the value of my soul, and the way of life and salvation by Jesus Christ.

All went well with me till Monday morning; and then, whether the root had lost its virtue, or whether my tormenter had gone deeper into the black art than I had – as was sometimes said of him – or whether he had obtained a special indulgence for his faithful Sunday's worship, it is not necessary for me to know or to inform the reader; but this much I may say, the pious and benignant smile which graced the face of Covey on *Sunday* wholly disappeared on *Monday*.

Long before daylight I was called up to feed, rub, and curry the horses. I obeyed the call, as I should have done had it been made at an earlier hour, for I had brought my mind to a firm resolve during that Sunday's reflection to obey every order, however unreasonable, if it were possible, and if Mr Covey should then undertake to beat me to defend and protect myself to the best of my ability. My religious views on the subject of resisting my master had suffered a serious shock by the savage persecution to which I had been subjected, and my hands were no longer tied by my religion. Master Thomas's indifference had severed the last link. I had backslidden from this point in the slaves' religious creed, and I soon had occasion to make my fallen state known to my Sunday-pious brother, Covey.

While I was obeying his order to feed and get the horses ready for the field, and when I was in the act of going up the stable loft, for the purpose of throwing down some blades, Covey sneaked into the stable, in his peculiar way, and seizing me suddenly by the leg, he brought me to the stable-floor, giving my newly-mended body a terrible jar. I now forgot all about my *roots*, and remembered my pledge to stand up in my own defence. The brute was skilfully endeavouring to get a slip-knot on my legs, before I could draw up my feet. As soon as I found what he was up to, I gave a sudden spring – my two days' rest had been of much service to me – and by that means, no doubt, he was able to bring me to the floor so heavily. He was defeated in his plan of tying me. While down, he seemed to think he had me very securely in his power. He little thought he was – as the rowdies say – 'in' for a 'rough and tumble' fight: but such was the fact. Whence came the daring spirit necessary to grapple with a man, who eight-and-forty hours before, could, with his slightest word, have made me tremble like a leaf in a storm, I do not know; at any rate I *was resolved to fight*, and what was better still, I actually was hard at it. The fighting madness had come upon me, and I found my strong fingers firmly attached to the throat of the tyrant, as heedless of consequences, at the moment, as if we stood as equals before the law. The very colour of the man was forgotten, I felt supple as a cat, and was ready for him at every turn. Every blow of his was parried, though I dealt no blows in return. I was strictly on the *defensive*, preventing him from injuring me, rather than trying to injure him. I flung him on to the ground several times when he meant to have hurled me there. I held him so firmly by the throat that his blood followed my nails. He held me, and I held him.

All was fair thus far, and the contest was about equal. My resistance was entirely unexpected, and Covey was taken all aback by it, and he trembled in every limb. '*Are you going to resist*, you scoundrel?' said he. To which I returned a polite '*Yes, sir*,' steadily gazing my interrogator in the eye, to meet the first approach or dawning of the blow which I expected my answer would call forth. But the conflict did not long remain equal. Covey soon cried lustily for help; not that I was obtaining any marked advantage over him, or was injuring him, but because he was gaining none over me, and was not able, single-handed, to conquer me. He called for his cousin Hughes to come to his assistance, and now the scene was changed. I was compelled to give blows, as well as to parry them, and since I was in any case to suffer for resistance, I felt – as the musty proverb goes – that I 'might as well be hanged for an old sheep as a lamb'. I was still defensive toward Covey, but aggressive toward Hughes, on whom at his first approach, I dealt a blow which fairly sickened him. He went off, bending over with pain, and manifesting no disposition to come again within my reach. The poor fellow was in the act of trying to catch and tie my right hand, and while flattering himself with success, I gave him a kick which sent him staggering away in pain, at the same time that I held Covey with a firm hand.

Taken completely by surprise, Covey seemed to have lost his usual strength and coolness. He was frightened, and stood puffing and blowing, seemingly unable to command words or blows. When he saw that Hughes was standing half bent with pain, his courage quite gone, the cowardly tyrant asked if I 'meant to persist in my resistance'. I told him I *did mean to resist*, come what might; that I had been treated like a brute during the last six months, and that I should stand it no longer'. With that he gave me a shake, and attempted to drag me toward a stick of wood that was lying just outside the stable door. He meant to knock me down with it, but just as he leaned over to get the stick, I seized him with both hands, by the collar, and with a vigorous and sudden snatch, I brought my assailant harmlessly, his full length, on the not over clean ground, for we were now in the cow-yard. He had selected the place for the fight, and it was but right that he should have the advantages of his own selection.

By this time Bill, the hired man, came home. He had been to Mr Helmsley's to spend Sunday with his nominal wife. Covey and I had been at skirmishing from before daybreak till now, and the sun was now shooting his beams almost over the eastern woods, and we were still at it. I could not see where the matter was to terminate. He evidently was afraid to let me go, lest I should again make off to the woods, otherwise he would probably have obtained arms from the house to frighten me. Holding me, he called upon Bill to assist him. The scene here had something comic about it. Bill, who knew precisely what Covey wished him to do, affected ignorance, and pretended he did not know what to do. 'What shall I do, Master Covey?' said Bill. 'Take hold of him! – take hold of him!' said Covey. With a toss of his head, peculiar to Bill, he said, 'indeed Master Covey, I want to go to work.' '*This is your work*,' said Covey; 'take hold of him.' Bill replied, with spirit: 'My master hired me to work, and not to help you whip Frederick.' It was my turn to speak. 'Bill,' said I, 'don't put your hands on me.' To which he replied: 'My God, Frederick, I ain't goin' to tech ye;' and Bill walked off, leaving Covey and myself to settle our differences as best we might.

But my present advantage was threatened when I saw Caroline – the slave woman of Covey – coming to the cow-shed to milk, for she was a powerful woman, and could have mastered me easily, exhausted as I was.

As soon as she came near, Covey attempted to rally her to his aid. Strangely and fortunately, Caroline was in no humour to take a hand in any such sport. We were all in open rebellion that morning. Caroline answered the command of her master 'to take hold of me', precisely as Bill had done, but in her it was at far greater peril, for she was the slave of Covey, and he could do what he pleased with her. It was not so with Bill, and Bill knew it. Samuel Harris, to whom Bill belonged, did not allow his slaves to be beaten, unless they were guilty of some crime which the law would punish. But poor Caroline, like myself, was at the mercy of the merciless Covey, nor did she escape the dire effects of her refusal: he gave her several sharp blows.

At length, after two hours had elapsed, the contest was given over. Letting go of me, puffing and blowing at a great rate, Covey said: 'Now, you scoundrel, go to your work; I would not have whipped you half as hard if you had not resisted.' The fact was, he had not whipped me at all. He had not, in all the scuffle, drawn a single drop of blood from me. I had drawn blood from him, and should even without this satisfaction have been victorious, because my aim had not been to injure him, but to prevent his injuring me.

During the whole six months I lived with Covey after this transaction, he never again laid the weight of his finger on me in anger. He would occasionally say he did not want to have to get hold of me again – a declaration which I had no difficulty in believing; and I had a secret feeling which answered, 'you had better not wish to get hold of me again, for you will be likely to come off worse in a second fight than you did in the first.'

Well, my dear reader, this battle with Mr Covey, undignified as it was, and as I fear my narration of it is, was the turning point in my 'life as a slave'. It rekindled in my breast the smouldering embers of liberty; it brought up my Baltimore dreams, and revived a sense of my own manhood. I was a changed being after that fight. I was *nothing* before; I was *a man* now. It recalled to life my crushed self-respect, and my self-confidence, and inspired me with a renewed determination to be a *free man*. A man without force is without the essential dignity of humanity. Human nature is so constituted, that it cannot *honour* a helpless man, though it can *pity* him, and even this it cannot do long if signs of power do not arise.

He only can understand the effect of this combat on my spirit, who has himself incurred something, hazarded something, in repelling the unjust and cruel aggressions of a tyrant. Covey was a tyrant and a cowardly one withal. After resisting him, I felt as I never felt before. It was a resurrection from the dark and pestiferous tomb of slavery, to the heaven of comparative freedom. I was no longer a servile coward, trembling under the frown of a brother worm of the dust, but my long-cowed spirit was roused to an attitude of independence. I had reached the point at which I was *not afraid to die*. This spirit made me a freeman in *fact*, though I still remained a slave in *form*. When a slave cannot be flogged, he is more than half free. He has a domain as broad as his own manly heart to defend, and he is really 'a power on the earth'. From this time until my escape from slavery, I was never fairly whipped. Several attempts were made, but they were always unsuccessful. Bruises I did get, but the instance I have described was the end of that brutification to which slavery had subjected me.

The reader may like to know why, after I had so grievously offended Mr Covey, he did not have me taken in hand by the authorities; indeed, why the law of Maryland, which assigned hanging to the slave who resisted his master, was not put in force against me; at any rate why I was not taken up, as was usual in such cases, and publicly whipped, as an example to other slaves, and as a means of deterring me from committing the same offence again. I confess that the easy manner in which I got off was always a surprise to me, and even now I cannot fully explain the cause, though the probability is that Covey was ashamed to have it known that he had been mastered by a boy of sixteen. He enjoyed the unbounded and very valuable reputation of being a first-rate overseer and negro-breaker, and by means of this reputation he was able to procure his hands at very trifling compensation and with very great ease. His interest and his pride would mutually suggest the wisdom of passing the matter by in silence. The story that he had undertaken to whip a lad and had been resisted, would of itself be damaging to him in the estimation of slave-holders.

It is perhaps not altogether creditable to my natural temper that after this conflict with Mr Covey I did, at times, purposely aim to provoke him to an attack, by refusing to keep with the other hands in the field, but I could never bully him to another battle. I was determined on doing him serious damage if he ever again attempted to lay violent hands on me.

> Hereditary bondmen know ye not
> Who would be free, themselves must strike the blow?

CHAPTER XVIII

New Relations and Duties

Change of masters – Benefits derived by change – Fame of the fight with Covey – Reckless unconcern – Abhorrence of slavery – Ability to read a cause of prejudice – The holidays – How spent – Sharp hit at slavery – Effects of holidays – Difference between Covey and Freeland – An irreligious master preferred to a religious one – Hard life at Covey's useful – Improved condition does not bring contentment – Congenial society at Freeland's – Sabbath-school – Secrecy necessary – Affectionate relations of tutor and pupils – Confidence and friendship among slaves – Slavery the inviter of vengeance

My term of service with Edward Covey expired on Christmas day, 1834. I gladly enough left him, although he was by this time as gentle as a lamb. My home for the year 1835 was already secured, my next master selected. There was always more or less excitement about the changing of hands, but I had become somewhat reckless and cared little into whose hands I fell, determined to fight my way. The report got abroad that I was hard to whip, that I was guilty of kicking back, that though generally a good-natured negro, I sometimes 'got the devil in me'. These sayings were rife in Talbot County, and they distinguished me among my servile brethren. Slaves would sometimes fight with each other, and even die at each other's hands, but there were very few who were not held in awe by a white man. Trained from the cradle to think and feel that their masters were superior, and invested with a sort of sacredness, there were few who could rise above the control which that sentiment exercised. I had freed myself from it, and the thing was known. One bad sheep will spoil a whole flock. I was a bad sheep. I hated slavery, slave-holders, and all pertaining to them; and I did not fail to inspire others with the same feeling wherever and whenever opportunity was presented. This made me a marked lad among the slaves, and a suspected one among slave-holders. A knowledge of my ability to read and write got pretty widely spread, which was very much against me.

The days between Christmas and New Year's day were allowed the slaves as holidays. During these days all regular work was suspended, and there was nothing to do but keep fires and look after the stock. We regarded this time as our own by the grace of our masters, and we therefore used it or abused it as we pleased. Those who had families at a distance were expected to visit them and spend with them the entire week. The younger slaves or the unmarried ones were expected to see to the cattle, and to attend to incidental duties at home. The holidays were variously spent. The sober, thinking, industrious ones would employ themselves in manufacturing corn brooms, mats, horse collars, and baskets, and some of these were very well made. Another class spent their time in hunting opossums, coons, rabbits, and other game. But the majority spent the holidays in sports, ball-playing, wrestling, boxing, running foot-races, dancing, and drinking whiskey; and this latter mode was generally most agreeable to their masters. A slave who would work during the holidays was thought by his master undeserving of holidays. There was in this simple act of continued work an accusation against slaves, and a slave could not help thinking that if he made three dollars during the holidays he might make three hundred during the year. Not to be drunk during the holidays was disgraceful.

The fiddling, dancing, and 'jubilee beating' was carried on in all directions. This latter performance was strictly southern. It supplied the place of violin, or of other musical instruments, and was played so easily that almost every farm had its 'Juba' beater. The performer improvised as he beat the instrument, marking the words as he sang so as to have them fall pat with the movement of his hands. Among a mass of nonsense and wild frolic, once in a while a sharp hit was given to the meanness of slave-holders. Take the following for example:

> We raise de wheat,
> Dey gib us de corn;
> We bake de bread,
> Dey gib us de crust;
> We sif de meal,
> Dey gib us de huss;

> We peel de meat,
> Dey gib us de skin;
> And dat's de way
> Dey take us in;
> We skim de pot,
> Dey give us de liquor,
> And say dat's good enough for nigger.
>
> Walk over! walk over!
> Your butter and de fat
> Poor nigger you can't get over dat.
> Walk over –

This is not a summary of the palpable injustice and fraud of slavery, giving, as it does, to the lazy and idle the comforts which God designed should be given solely to the honest labourer. But to the holidays. Judging from my own observation and experience, I believe those holidays were among the most effective means in the hands of slave-holders of keeping down the spirit of insurrection among the slaves.

To enslave men successfully and safely it is necessary to keep their minds occupied with thoughts and aspirations short of the liberty of which they are deprived. A certain degree of attainable good must be kept before them. These holidays served the purpose of keeping the minds of the slaves occupied with prospective pleasure within the limits of slavery. The young man could go wooing, the married man to see his wife, the father and mother to see their children, the industrious and money-loving could make a few dollars, the great wrestler could win laurels, the young people meet and enjoy each other's society, the drunken man could get plenty of whiskey, and the religious man could hold prayer-meetings, preach, pray, and exhort. Before the holidays there were pleasures in prospect; after the holidays they were pleasures of memory, and they served to keep out thoughts and wishes of a more dangerous character. These holidays were also conductors or safety-valves, to carry off the explosive elements inseparable from the human mind when reduced to the condition of slavery. But for these the rigours of bondage would have become too severe for endurance, and the slave would have been forced to dangerous desperation.

Thus they became a part and parcel of the gross wrongs and inhumanity of slavery. Ostensibly they were institutions of benevolence designed to mitigate the rigours of slave life, but practically they were a fraud instituted by human selfishness, the better to secure the ends of injustice and oppression. The slave's happiness was not the end sought, but the master's safety. It was not from a generous unconcern for the slave's labour, but from a prudent regard for the slave system. I am strengthened in this opinion from the fact that most slave-holders liked to have their slaves spend the holidays in such a manner as to be of no real benefit to them. Everything like rational enjoyment was frowned upon. and only those wild and low sports peculiar to semi-civilised people were encouraged. The licence allowed appeared to have no other object than to disgust the slaves with their temporary freedom, and to make them as glad to return to their work as they were to leave it. I have known slave-holders resort to cunning tricks, with a view of getting their slaves deplorably drunk. The usual plan was to make bets on a slave that he could drink more whiskey than any other, and so induce a rivalry among them for the mastery in this degradation. The scenes brought about in this way were often scandalous and loathsome in the extreme. Whole multitudes might be found stretched out in brutal, drunkenness, at once helpless and disgusting. Thus, when the slave asked for hours of 'virtuous liberty', his cunning master took advantage of his ignorance and cheered him with a dose of vicious and revolting dissipation artfully labelled with the name of '*liberty*'.

We were induced to drink, I among the rest, and when the holidays were over we all staggered up from our filth, and wallowing, took a long breath, and went away to our various fields of work, feeling, upon the whole, rather glad to go from that which our masters had artfully deceived us into the belief was freedom, back again to the arms of slavery. It was not what we had taken it to be, nor what it would have been, had it not been abused by us. It was about as well to be a slave to a master, as to be a slave to whiskey and rum. When the slave was drunk the slave-holder had no fear that he would escape to the North. It was the sober, thoughtful slave who was dangerous, and needed the vigilance of his master to keep him a slave.

On the first of January 1835, I proceeded from St Michaels to Mr William Freeland's – my new home. Mr Freeland lived only three miles from St Michaels, on an old, worn-out farm, which required much labour to render it anything like a self-supporting establishment.

I found Mr Freeland a different man from Covey. Though not rich, he was what might have been called a well-bred Southern gentleman. Though a slave-holder and sharing in common with them many of the vices of his class, he seemed alive to the sentiment of honour, and had also some sense of justice, and some feelings of humanity. He was fretful, impulsive, and passionate, but free from the mean and selfish characteristics which distinguished the creature from whom I had happily escaped. Mr Freeland was open, frank, imperative, and practised no concealments, and disdained to play the spy; in all these qualities he was the opposite of Covey.

My poor weather-beaten bark now reached smoother water and gentler breezes. My stormy life at Covey's had been of service to me. The things that would have seemed very hard had I gone direct to Mr Freeland's from the home of Master Thomas were now 'trifles light as air'. I was still a field-hand, and had come to prefer the severe labour of the field to the enervating duties of a house servant. I had become large and strong, and had begun to take pride in the fact that I could do as much hard work as some of the older men. There was much rivalry among slaves at times as to which could do the most work, and masters generally sought to promote such rivalry. But some of us were too wise to race with each other very long. Such racing, we had the sagacity to see, was not likely to pay. We had our times for measuring each other's strength, but we knew too much to keep up the competition so long as to produce an extraordinary day's work. We knew that if by extraordinary exertion a large quantity of work was done in one day, on its becoming known to the master, it might lead him to require the same amount every day. This thought was enough to bring us to a dead halt when ever so much excited in the race.

At Mr Freeland's my condition was every way improved. I was no longer the scapegoat that I was when at Covey's, where every wrong thing done was saddled upon me, and where other slaves were whipped over my shoulders. Bill Smith was protected by a positive prohibition, made by his rich master, and the command of the *rich* slave-holder was *law* to the poor one. Hughes was favoured by his relationship to Covey, and the hands hired temporarily escaped flogging. I was the general pack horse; but Mr Freeland held every man individually responsible for his own conduct. Mr Freeland, like Mr Covey, gave his hands enough to eat, but, unlike Mr Covey, he gave them time to take their meals. He worked us hard during the day, but gave us the night for rest. We were seldom in the field after dark in the evening, or before sunrise in the morning, Our implements of husbandry were of the most improved pattern, and much superior to those used at Covey's.

Notwithstanding all the improvement in my relations, notwithstanding the many advantages I had gained by my new home and my new master, I was still restless and discontented. I was about as hard to please with a master as a master is with a slave. The freedom from bodily torture and unceasing labour had given my mind an increased sensibility, and imparted to it greater activity. I was not yet exactly in right relations. 'Howbeit, that was not first which is spiritual, but that which is natural, and afterward that which is spiritual.' When entombed at Covey's, shrouded in darkness and physical wretchedness, temporal well-being was the grand desideratum; but, temporal wants supplied, the spirit puts in its claim. Beat and cuff your slave, keep him hungry and spiritless, and he will follow the lead of his master like a dog; but feed and clothe him well, work him moderately, surround him with physical comfort, and dreams of freedom intrude. Give him a *bad* master, and he wishes for a good master; give him a good master and he aspires to become his own master. Such is human nature. You may place a man so far beneath the level of his kind, that he loses all just ideas of his natural position, but elevate him a little, and the clear conception of rights rises to life and power, and leads him onward. Thus, elevated a little at Freeland's, the dreams called into being by that good man, Father Lawson, when in Baltimore, began to visit me again; shoots from the tree of liberty began to put forth buds, and dim hopes of the future began to dawn.

I found myself in congenial society. There were Henry Harris, John Harris, Handy Caldwell, and Sandy Jenkins, this last of the root-preventive memory.

Henry and John Harris were brothers, and belonged to Mr Freeland. They were both remarkably bright and intelligent, though neither of them could read. Now for my mischief! I had not been long there before I was up to my old tricks. I began to address my companions on the subject of education, and the advantages of intelligence over ignorance, and, as far as I dared, I tried to show the agency of ignorance in keeping men in slavery. Webster's spelling-book and *The Columbian Orator* were looked into again. As summer came on, and the long Sabbath days stretched themselves over our idleness, I became uneasy, and wanted a Sabbath-school, wherein to exercise my gifts, and to impart the little knowledge I possessed to my brother slaves. A house was hardly necessary in the summer time; I could hold my school under the shade of an old oak as well as anywhere else. The thing was to get the scholars, and to have them thoroughly imbued with the desire to learn. Two such boys were quickly found in Henry and John, and from them the contagion spread. I was not long in bringing around me twenty or thirty young men, who enrolled themselves gladly in my Sabbath-school, and were willing to meet me regularly under the trees or elsewhere, for the purpose of learning to read. It was surprising with what ease they provided themselves with spelling-books. These were mostly the cast-off books of their young masters or mistresses. I taught at first on our own farm. All were impressed with the necessity of keeping the matter as private as possible, for the fate of the St Michaels attempt was still fresh in the minds of all. Our pious masters at St Michaels must not know that a few of their dusky brothers were learning to read the Word of God, lest they should come down upon us with the lash and chain. We might have met to drink whiskey, to wrestle, fight, and to do other unseemly things, with no fear of interruption from the saints or the sinners of St Michaels. But to meet for the purpose of improving the mind and heart, by learning to read the sacred Scriptures, was a nuisance to be instantly stopped. The slave-holders there, like slave-holders elsewhere, preferred to see the slaves engaged in degrading sports, rather than acting like moral and accountable beings. Had anyone asked a religious white man in St Michaels at that time the names of three men in that town whose lives were most after the pattern of our Lord and Master Jesus Christ, the reply would have been: Garrison West, class-leader, Wright Fairbanks, and Thomas Auld, both also class-leaders; and yet these men ferociously rushed in upon my Sabbath-school, armed with mob-like missiles, and forbade our meeting again on pain of having our backs subjected to the bloody lash. This same Garrison West was my class-leader, and I had thought him a Christian until he took part in breaking up my school. He led me no more after that.

The plea for this outrage was then, as it is always, the tyrant's plea of necessity. If the slaves learned to read they would learn something more and something worse. The peace of slavery would be disturbed; slave rule would be endangered. I do not dispute the soundness of the reasoning. If slavery were right, Sabbath-schools for teaching slaves to read were wrong, and ought to have been put down. These Christian class-leaders were, to this extent, consistent. They had settled the question that slavery was right, and by that standard they determined that Sabbath-schools were wrong. To be sure they were Protestants, and held to the great protestant right of every man to 'search the Scriptures' for himself; but then, to all general rules there are exceptions. How convenient! What crimes may not be committed under such ruling! But my dear class-leading Methodist brethren did not condescend to give me a reason for breaking up the school at St Michaels; they had determined its destruction, and that was enough. However, I am digressing.

After getting the school nicely started a second time, holding it in the woods behind the barn, and in the shade of trees, I succeeded in inducing a free coloured man who lived several miles from our house to permit me to hold my school in a room at his house. He incurred much peril in doing so, for the assemblage was an unlawful one. I had at one time more than forty scholars, all of the right sort, and many of them succeeded in learning to read. I have had various employments during my life, but I look to none with more satisfaction. An attachment, deep and permanent, sprung up between me and my persecuted pupils, which made my parting from then intensely painful.

Besides my Sunday-school, I devoted three evenings a week to my other fellow slaves during the winter. Those dear souls who came to my Sabbath-school came not because it was popular or reputable to do so, for they came with a liability of having forty stripes laid on their naked backs. In this Christian country men and women were obliged to hide in barns and woods and trees from professing Christians, in order to learn to read the Holy Bible. Their minds had been cramped and starved by their cruel masters; the light of education had been completely excluded, and their hard earnings had been taken to educate their master's children. I felt a delight in circumventing the tyrants, and in blessing the victims of their curses.

The year at Mr Freeland's passed off very smoothly, to outward seeming. Not a blow was given me during the whole year. To the credit of Mr Freeland, irreligious though he were, it must be stated that he was the best master I ever had, until I became my own master and assumed for myself, as I had a right to do, the responsibility of my own existence and the exercise of my own powers.

For much of the happiness, or absence of misery, with which I passed this year, I am indebted to the genial temper and ardent friendship of my brother slaves. They were every one of them manly, generous, and brave; yes, I say they were brave, and I will add fine looking. It is seldom the lot of any to have truer and better friends than were the slaves on this farm. It was not uncommon to charge slaves with great treachery toward each other, but I must say I never loved, esteemed, or confided in men more than I did in these. They were as true as steel, and no band of brothers could be more loving. There were no mean advantages taken of each other, no tattling, no giving each other bad names to Mr Freeland, and no elevating one at the expense of the other. We never undertook anything of any importance which was likely to affect each other without mutual consultation. We were generally a unit, and moved together. Thoughts and sentiments were exchanged between us which might well have been considered incendiary had they been known by our masters. The slave-holder, were he kind or cruel, was a slave-holder still, the every-hour-violator of the just and inalienable rights of man, and he was therefore every hour silently but surely whetting the knife of vengeance for his own throat. He never lisped a syllable in commendation of the fathers of this republic without inviting the sword and asserting the right of rebellion for his own slaves.

CHAPTER XIX

The Runaway Plot

New year's thoughts and meditations – Again hired by Freeland – Kindness no compensation for slavery – Incipient steps toward escape – Considerations leading thereto – Hostility to slavery – Solemn vow taken – Plan divulged to slaves – Columbian Orator again – Scheme gains favour – Danger of discovery – Skill of slave-holders – Suspicion and coercion – Hymns with double meaning – Consultation – Password – Hope and fear – Ignorance of Geography – Imaginary difficulties – Patrick Henry – Sandy, a dreamer – Route to the North mapped out – Objections – Frauds – Passes – Anxieties – Fear of failure – Strange presentiment – Coincidence – Betrayal – Arrests – Resistance – Mrs Freeland – Prison – Brutal jests – Passes eaten – Denial – Sandy – Dragged behind horses – Slave-traders – Alone in prison – Sent to Baltimore

I am now at the beginning of the year – 1836 – when the mind naturally occupies itself with the mysteries of life in all its phases – the ideal, the real, and the actual. Sober people look both ways at the beginning of a new year, surveying the errors of the past, and providing against the possible errors of the future. I, too, was thus exercised. I had little pleasure in retrospect, and the future prospect was not brilliant. 'Notwithstanding,' thought I, 'the many resolutions and prayers I have made in behalf of freedom, I am, this first day of the year 1836, still a slave, still wandering in the depths of a miserable bondage. My faculties and powers of body and soul are not my own, but are the property of a fellow-mortal in no sense superior to me, except that he has the physical power to compel me to be owned and controlled by him. By the combined physical force of the community I am his slave – a slave for life.' With thoughts like these I was chafed and perplexed, and they rendered me gloomy and disconsolate. The anguish of my mind cannot be written.

At the close of the year, Mr Freeland renewed the purchase of my services from Mr Auld for the coming year. His promptness in doing so would have been flattering to my vanity had I been ambitious to win the reputation of being a valuable slave. Even as it was, I felt a slight degree of complacency at the circumstance. It showed him to be as well pleased with me as a slave as I with him as a master. But the kindness of the slave-master only gilded the chain, it detracted nothing from its weight or strength. The thought that men are made for other and better uses than slavery throve best under the gentle treatment of a kind master. Its grim visage could assume no smiles able to fascinate the partially enlightened slave into a forgetfulness of his bondage, or of the desirableness of liberty.

I was not through the first month of my second year with the kind and gentlemanly Mr Freeland, before I was earnestly considering and devising plans for gaining that freedom, which, when I was but a mere child, I had ascertained to be the natural and inborn right of every member of the human family. The desire for this freedom had been benumbed while I was under the brutalising dominion of Covey, and it had been postponed and rendered inoperative by my truly pleasant Sunday-school engagements with my friends during the year at Mr Freeland's. It had, however, never entirely subsided. I hated slavery *always* and my desire for freedom needed only a favourable breeze to fan it into a blaze at any moment. The thought of being only a creature of the *present* and the *past* troubled me, and I longed to have a *future* – a future with hope in it. To be shut up entirely to the past and present is to the soul whose life and happiness is unceasing progress – what the prison is to the body – a blight and mildew, a hell of horrors. The dawning of this, another year, awakened me from my temporary slumber, and roused into life my latent but long-cherished aspirations for freedom. I became not only ashamed to be contented in slavery, but ashamed to *seem* to be contented, and in my present favourable condition under the mild rule of Mr Freeland, I am not sure that some kind reader will not condemn me for being over ambitious, and greatly wanting in humility, when I say the truth, that I now drove from me all thoughts of making the best of my lot, and welcomed only such thoughts as led me away from the house of bondage. The intensity of my desire to be free, quickened by my present favourable circumstances, brought me to the determination to *act* as well as to think and speak. Accordingly, at the beginning of this year 1836, I took upon me a solemn vow, that the year which had just now dawned upon me should not close without witnessing an earnest attempt, on my part, to gain my liberty, This vow only bound me to make good my own individual escape, but my friendship for my brother-slaves was so affectionate and confiding that I felt it my duty, as well as my pleasure, to give them an opportunity to share in my determination. Toward Harry and John Harris I felt a friendship as strong as one man can feel for another, for I could have died with and for them. To them, therefore, with suitable caution, I began to disclose my sentiments and plans, sounding them the while on the subject of running away, provided a good chance should offer. I need not say that I did my *very best* to imbue the minds of my dear friends with my own views and feelings. Thoroughly awakened now, and with a definite vow upon me, all my little reading which had any bearing on the subject of human rights was rendered available in my communications with my friends. That gem of a book, *The Columbian Orator*, with its eloquent orations and spicy dialogues denouncing oppression and slavery – telling what had been dared, done, and suffered by men, to obtain the inestimable boon of liberty, was still fresh in my memory, and whirled into the ranks of my speech with the aptitude of well-trained soldiers going through the drill. I here began my public speaking. I canvassed with Henry and John the subject of slavery, and dashed against it the condemning brand of God's eternal justice. My fellow-servants were neither indifferent, dull, nor inapt. Our feelings were more alike than our opinions. All, however, were ready to act when a feasible plan should be proposed. 'Show us how the thing is to be done,' said they, 'and all else is clear.'

We were all, except Sandy, quite clear from slave-holding priest-craft. It was in vain that we had been taught from the pulpit at St Michaels the duty of obedience to our masters; to recognise God as the author of our enslavement; to regard running away as an offence, alike against God and man; to deem our enslavement a merciful and beneficial arrangement; to esteem our condition in this country a paradise to that from which we had been snatched in Africa; to consider our hard hands and dark colour as God's displeasure, and as pointing us out as the proper subjects of slavery; that the relation of master and slave was one of reciprocal benefits; that our work was not more serviceable to our masters than our masters' thinking was to us. I say it was in vain the pulpit of St Michaels had constantly inculcated these plausible doctrines. Nature laughed them to scorn. For my part, I had become altogether too big for my chains. Father Lawson's solemn words of what I ought to be, and what I might be in the providence of God, had not fallen dead on my soul. I was fast verging toward manhood, and the prophecies of my childhood were still unfulfilled. The thought that year after year had passed away, and my best resolutions to run away had failed and faded, that I was still a slave, with chances for gaining my freedom diminished and still diminishing – was not a matter to be slept over easily. But here came a trouble. Such thoughts and purposes as I now cherished could not agitate the mind long, without making themselves manifest to scrutinising and un-friendly observers. I had reason to fear that my sable face might prove altogether too transparent for the safe concealment of my hazardous enterprise. Plans of great moment have leaked through stone walls, and revealed their projectors. But here was no stone wall to hide my purpose. I would have given my poor tell-tale face for the immovable countenance of an Indian, for it was far from proof against the daily searching glances of those whom I met.

It was the interest and business of slave-holders to study human nature, and the slave nature in particular, with a view to practical results; and many of them attained astonishing proficiency in this direction. They had to deal not with earth, wood, and stone, but with *men*; and by every regard they had for their own safety and prosperity, they had need to know the material on which they were to work. So much intellect as slave-holders had round them required watching. Their safety depended on their vigilance. Conscious of the injustice and wrong they were every hour perpetrating, and knowing what they themselves would do if they were victims of such wrongs, they were constantly looking out for the first signs of the dread retribution. They watched, therefore, with skilled and practised eyes, and learned to read, with great accuracy, the state of mind and heart of the slave through his sable face. Unusual sobriety, apparent abstraction, sullenness, or indif-ference – indeed, any mood out of the common way – afforded ground for suspicion and enquiry. Relying on their superior position and wisdom, they would often hector the slave into a confession by affecting to know the truth of their accusations. 'You have got the devil in you, and we'll whip him out of you,' they would say. I have often been put thus to the torture on bare suspicion. This system had its disadvantages as well as its opposite – the slave being sometimes whipped into the confession of offences which he never committed. It will be seen that the good old rule, 'A man is to be held innocent until proved to be guilty', did not hold good on the slave plantation. Suspicion and torture were the approved methods of getting at the truth there. It was necessary, therefore, for me to keep a watch over my deportment, lest the enemy should get the better of me. But with all our caution and studied reserve, I am not sure that Mr Freeland did not suspect that all was not right with us. It *did* seem that he watched us more narrowly after the plan of escape had been conceived and discussed amongst us. Men seldom see themselves as others see them; and while to ourselves everything connected with our contemplated escape appeared concealed, Mr Freeland may, with the peculiar prescience of a slave-holder, have mastered the huge thought which was disturbing our peace. As I now look back, I am the more inclined to think he suspected us, because, prudent as we were, I can see that we did many silly things very well calculated to awaken suspicion. We were at times remarkably buoyant, singing hymns, and making joyous exclamations, almost as triumphant in their tone as if we had reached a land of freedom and safety. A keen observer might have detected in our repeated singing of

> O Canaan, sweet Canaan,
> I am bound for the land of Canaan,

something more than a hope of reaching heaven. We meant to reach the *North*, and the North was our Canaan.

> I thought I heard them say
> There were lions in the way;
> I don't expect to stay
> Much longer here.
> Run to Jesus, shun the danger –
> I don't expect to stay
> Much longer here,

was a favourite air, and had a double meaning. In the lips of some, it meant the expectation of a speedy summons to a world of spirits; but in the lips of our company, it simply meant a speedy pilgrimage to a free State, and deliverance from all the evils and dangers of slavery.

I had succeeded in winning to my scheme a company of five young men, the very flower of the neighbourhood, each one of whom would have commanded one thousand dollars in the home market. At New Orleans they would have brought fifteen hundred dollars apiece, and perhaps more. Their names were as follows: Henry Harris, John Harris, Sandy Jenkins, Charles Roberts and Henry Bailey. I was the youngest but one of the party. I had, however, the advantage of them all in experience, and in a knowledge of letters. This gave me a great influence over them. Perhaps not one of them, left to himself, would have dreamed of escape as a thing. They all wanted to be free, but the serious thought of running away had not entered into their minds until I won them to the undertaking. They all were tolerably well off – for slaves – and had dim hopes of being set free someday by their masters. If anyone is to blame for disturbing the quiet of the slaves and slave-masters of the neighbourhood of St Michaels, I AM THE MAN. I claim to be the instigator of the high crime – as slave-holders regarded it – and I kept life in it till life could be kept in it no longer.

Pending the time of our contemplated departure out of our Egypt, we met often by night, and on every Sunday. At these meetings we talked the matter over, told our hopes and fears, and the difficulties discovered or imagined; and like men of sense, we counted the cost of the enterprise to which we were committing ourselves. These meetings must have resembled, on a small scale, the meetings of the revolution-ary conspirators in their primary condition. We were plotting against our, so-called, lawful rulers, with this difference – we sought our own good, and not the harm of our enemies. We did not seek to overthrow them, but to escape from them. As for Mr Freeland, we all liked him, and would gladly have remained with him *as free men. Liberty* was our aim, and we had now come to think that we had a right to it against every obstacle, even against the lives of our enslavers.

We had several words, expressive of things important to us, which we understood, but which, even if distinctly heard by an outsider, would have conveyed no certain meaning. I hated this secrecy, but where slavery was powerful, and liberty weak, the latter was driven to concealment to escape destruction.

The prospect was not always bright. At times we were almost tempted to abandon the enterprise, and try to get back to that comparative peace of mind which even a man under the gallows might feel, when all hope of escape had vanished. We were confident, bold, and determined at times, and again, doubting, timid, and wavering, whistling, like the boy in the graveyard, to keep away the spirits.

To look at the map and observe the proximity of Eastern Shore, Maryland, to Delaware and Pennsylvania, it may seem to the reader quite absurd to regard the proposed escape as a formidable undertak-ing. But to *understand*, someone has said, a man must *stand under*. The real distance was great enough, but the imagined distance was, to our ignorance, much greater. Slave-holders sought to impress their slaves with a belief in the boundlessness of slave territory, and of their own limitless power. Our notions of the geography of the country were very vague and indistinct. The distance, however, was not the chief trouble, for the nearer the lines of a slave State to the borders of a free State, the greater was the trouble. Hired kidnappers infested the borders. Then, too, we knew that merely reaching a free State did not free us, that wherever caught we could be returned to slavery. We knew of no spot this side the ocean where we could be safe. We had heard of Canada, then the only real Canaan of the American bondsman, simply as a country to which the wild goose and the swan repaired at the end of winter to escape the heat of summer, but not as the home of man. I knew something of Theology, but nothing of Geography. I really did not know that there was a State of New York or a State of Massachusetts. I had heard of Pennsylvania, Delaware, and New Jersey, and all the Southern States, but was utterly ignorant of the Free States. New York City was our northern limit, and to go there and to be for ever harassed with the liability of being hunted down and returned to slavery, with the certainty of being treated ten times worse than ever before, was a prospect which might well cause some hesitation. The case sometimes, to our excited visions, stood thus: At every gate through which we had to pass we saw a watchman; at every ferry a guard; on every bridge a sentinel, and in every wood a patrol or slave-hunter. We were hemmed in on every side. The good to be sought and the evil to be shunned, were flung in the balance and weighed against each other. On the one hand stood slavery, a stern reality glaring rightfully upon us, with the blood of millions in its polluted skirts, terrible to behold, greedily devouring our hard earnings and feeding itself upon our flesh. This was the evil from which to escape. On the other hand, far away, back in the hazy distance, where all forms seemed but shadows under the flickering light of the north star, behind the craggy hill or snow capped mountain, stood a doubtful freedom, half frozen, beckoning us to her icy domain. This was the good to be sought. The inequality was as great as that between certainty and uncertainty. This in itself was enough to stagger us; but when we came to survey the untrodden road and conjecture the many possible difficulties, we were appalled, and at times, as I have said, were upon the point of giving over the struggle altogether. The reader can have little idea of the phantoms which would flit, in such circumstances, before the uneducated mind of the slave. Upon either side we saw grim death, assuming a variety of horrid shapes. Now it was starvation, causing us, in a strange and friendless land, to eat our own flesh. Now we were contending with the waves and were drowned. Now we were hunted by dogs and overtaken, and torn to pieces by their merciless fangs. We were stung by scorpions, chased by wild beasts, bitten by snakes, and worst of all, after having succeeded in swimming rivers, encountering wild beasts, sleeping in the woods, suffering hunger, cold, heat, and nakedness, overtaken by hired kidnappers, who in the name of law and for the thrice-cursed reward, would, perchance, fire upon us, kill some, wound others, and capture all. This dark picture, drawn by ignorance and fear, at times greatly shook our determination, and not unfrequently caused us to

> Rather bear the ills we had,
> Than flee to others which we knew not of.

I am not disposed to magnify this circumstance in my experience, and yet I think I shall seem to be so disposed to the reader, but no man can tell the intense agony which was felt by the slave when wavering on the point of making his escape. All that he has is at stake, and even that which he has not, is at stake also. The life which he has may be lost, and the liberty which he seeks may not be gained.

Patrick Henry, to a listening senate which was thrilled by his magic eloquence and ready to stand by him in his boldest flights, could say, 'Give me liberty or give me death,' and this saying was a sublime one, even for a free man; but incomparably more sublime is the same sentiment when *practically* asserted by men accustomed to the lash and chain, men whose sensibilities must have become more or less deadened by their bondage. With us it was a doubtful liberty, at best, that we sought, and a certain lingering death in the rice-swamps and sugar-fields if we failed. Life is not lightly regarded by men of sane minds. It is precious both to the pauper and to the prince, to the slave and to his master; and yet I believe there was not one among us who would not rather have been shot down than pass away life in hopeless bondage.

In the progress of our preparations Sandy, the root man, became troubled. He began to have distressing dreams. One of these, which happened on a Friday night, was to him of great significance, and I am quite ready to confess that I felt somewhat damped by it myself. He said, 'I dreamed last night that I was roused from sleep by strange noises like the noises of a swarm of angry birds that caused a roar as they passed, and which fell upon my ear like a coming gale over the tops of the trees. Looking up to see what it could mean I saw you, Frederick, in the claws of a huge bird, surrounded by a large number of birds of all colours and sizes. These were all pecking at you, while you, with your arms, seemed to be trying to protect your eyes. Passing over me, the birds flew in a south-westerly direction, and I watched them until they were clean out of sight. Now I saw this as plainly as I now see you and furder, honey, watch de Friday-night dream; dare is sumpon in it shose you born; dare is indeed, honey.' I did not like the dream, but I showed no concern, attributing it to the general excitement and perturbation consequent upon our contemplated plan to escape. I could not, however, shake off its effect at once. I felt that it boded no good. Sandy was unusually emphatic and oracular, and his manner had much to do with the impression made upon me.

The plan which I recommended, and to which my comrades consented, for our escape, was to take a large canoe owned by Mr Hamilton, and on the Saturday night previous to the Easter holiday launch out into the Chesapeake Bay and paddle for its head, a distance of seventy miles, with all our might. On reaching this point we were to turn the canoe adrift and bend our steps toward the north star till we reached a Free State.

There were several objections to this plan. In rough weather the waters of the Chesapeake are much agitated, and there would be danger, in a canoe, of being swamped by the waves. Another objection was that the canoe would soon be missed, the absent slaves would at once be suspected of having taken it, and we should be pursued by some of the fast-sailing craft out of St Michaels. Then again, if we reached the head of the bay and turned the canoe adrift, she might prove a guide to our track and bring the hunters after us.

These and other objections were set aside by the stronger ones, which could be urged against every other plan that could then be suggested. On the water we had a chance of being regarded as fishermen, in the service of a master. On the other hand, by taking the land route, through the counties adjoining Delaware, we should be subjected to all manner of interruptions, and many disagreeable questions, which might give us serious trouble. Any white man if he pleased, was authorised to stop a man of colour on any road, and examine and arrest him. By this arrangement many abuses, considered such even by slave-holders, occurred. Cases have been known where freemen, being called upon to show their free papers by a pack of ruffians, and on the presentation of the papers, the ruffians have torn them up, and seized the victim and sold him to a life of endless bondage.

The week before our intended start, I wrote a pass for each of our party, giving them permission to visit Baltimore during the Easter holidays. The pass ran after this manner:

> This is to certify that I, the undersigned, have given the bearer, my servant John, full liberty to go to Baltimore to spend the Easter holidays.
>
> W. H.
> *Near St Michaels, Talbot Co., Md*

Although we were now going to Baltimore, and were intending to land east of North Point, in the direction I had seen the Philadelphia steamers go, these passes might be useful to us in the lower part of the bay, while steering towards Baltimore. These were not, however, to be shown by us, until all other answers failed to satisfy the enquirers. We were all fully alive to the importance of being calm and self-possessed when accosted, if accosted we should be; and we more than once rehearsed to each other how we should behave in the hour of trial.

Those were long, tedious days and nights. The suspense was painful in the extreme. To balance probabilities, where life and liberty hang on the result, requires steady nerves. I panted for action, and was glad when the day, at the close of which we were to start, dawned upon us. Sleeping the night before, was out of the question. I probably felt more deeply than any of my companions, because I was the instigator of the movement. The responsibility of the whole enterprise rested on my shoulders. The glory of success, and the shame and confusion of failure, could not be matters of indifference to me. Our food was prepared, our clothes were packed; we were all ready to go, and impatient for Saturday morning – considering *that* the last of our bondage.

I cannot describe the tempest and tumult of my brain that morning. The reader will please bear in mind that in a slave State an unsuccessful runaway was not only subject to cruel torture, and sold away to the far South, but he was frequently execrated by the other slaves. He was charged with making the condition of the other slaves intolerable, by laying them all under the suspicion of their masters – subjecting them to greater vigilance, and imposing greater limitations on their privileges. I dreaded murmurs from this quarter. It was difficult, too, for a slave-master to believe that slaves escaping had not been aided in their flight by some one of their fellow-slaves. When, therefore, a slave was missing, every slave on the place was closely examined as to his knowledge of the undertaking.

Our anxiety grew more and more intense, as the time of our intended departure drew nigh. It was truly felt to be a matter of life and death with us, and we fully intended to *fight*, as well as *run*, if necessity should arise for that extremity. But the trial hour had not yet come. It was easy to resolve, but not so easy to act. I expected there might be some drawing back at the last; it was natural there should be; therefore, during the intervening time, I lost no opportunity to explain away difficulties, remove doubts, dispel fears, and inspire all with firmness. It was too late to look back, and now was the time to go forward. I appealed to the pride of my comrades by telling them, that, if after having solemnly promised to go, as they had done, they now failed to make the attempt, they would in effect brand themselves with cowardice, and might well sit down, fold their arms, and acknowledge themselves fit only to be slaves. This detestable character all were unwilling to assume. Every man except Sandy – he, much to our regret, withdrew – stood firm, and at our last meeting we pledged ourselves afresh, and in the most solemn manner, that at the time appointed we *would* certainly start on our long journey for a free country. This meeting was in the middle of the week, at the end of which we were to start.

Early on the appointed morning we went as usual to the field, but with hearts that beat quickly and anxiously. Anyone intimately acquainted with us might have seen that all was not well with us, and that some monster lingered in our thoughts. Our work that morning was the same as it had been for several days past – drawing out and spreading manure. While thus engaged, I had a sudden presentiment, which flashed upon me like lightning in a dark night, revealing to the lonely traveller the gulf before, and the enemy behind. I instantly turned to Sandy Jenkins, who was near me, and said: '*Sandy, we are betrayed!* something has just told me so.' I felt as sure of it as if the officers were in sight. Sandy said: 'Man, dat is strange; but I feel just as you do.' If my mother – then long in her grave – had appeared before me and told me that we were betrayed, I could not at that moment have felt more certain of the fact.

In a few minutes after this, the long, low, and distant notes of the horn summoned us from the field to breakfast. I felt as one may be supposed to feel before being led forth to be executed for some great offence. I wanted no breakfast, but I went with the other slaves towards the house for form's sake, My feelings were not disturbed as to the right of running away; on that point I had no misgiving whatever, but from a sense of the consequences of failure.

In thirty minutes after that vivid impression, came the apprehended crash. On reaching the house, and glancing my eye toward the lane gate, the worst was at once made known. The lane gate to Mr Freeland's house was nearly half a mile from the door, and much shaded by the heavy wood which bordered the main road. I was, however, able to descry four white men and two coloured men approaching. The white men were on horseback, and the coloured men were walking behind, and seemed to be tied. '*It is indeed all over with us; we are surely betrayed,*' I thought to myself. I became composed, or at least comparatively so, and calmly awaited the result. I watched the ill-omened company entering the gate. Successful flight was impossible, and I made up my mind to stand and meet the evil, whatever it might be, for I was not altogether without a slight hope that things might turn out differently from what I had at first feared. In a few moments in came Mr William Hamilton, riding very rapidly and evidently much excited. He was in the habit of riding very slowly, and was seldom known to gallop his horse. This time his horse was nearly at full speed, causing the dust to roll thick behind him. Mr Hamilton, though one of the most resolute men in the whole neighbourhood, was, nevertheless, a remarkably mild-spoken man, and, even when greatly excited, his language was cool and circumspect. He came to the door, and enquired if Mr Freeland was in. I told him that Mr Freeland was at the barn. Off the old gentleman rode towards the barn, with unwonted speed. In a few moments Mr Hamilton and Mr Freeland came down from the barn to the house, and just as they made their appearance in the front yard, three men, who proved to be constables, came dashing into the lane on horseback, as if summoned by a sign requiring quick work. A few seconds brought them into the front yard, where they hastily dismounted and tied their horses. This done they joined Mr Freeland and Mr Hamilton, who were standing a short distance from the kitchen. A few moments were spent as if in consulting how to proceed, and then the whole party walked up to the kitchen door. There was now no one in the kitchen but myself and John Harris; Henry and Sandy were yet in the barn. Mr Freeland came inside the kitchen door, and with an agitated voice called me by name, and told me to come forward, that there were some gentlemen who wished to see me. I stepped towards them at the door, and asked what they wanted, when the constables grabbed me, and told me I had better not resist; that I had been in a scrape, or was said to have been in one; that they were merely going to take me where I could be examined;

that they would have me brought before my master at St Michaels, and if the evidence against me was not proved true, I should be acquitted. I was now firmly tied, and completely at the mercy of my captors. Resistance was idle. They were five in number, armed to the teeth. When they had secured me, they turned to John Harris, and in a few moments succeeded in tying him as firmly as they had tied me. They next turned toward Henry Harris, who had now returned from the barn. 'Cross your hands,' said the constable to Henry. 'I won't,' said Henry, in a voice so firm and clear, and in a manner so determined, as for a moment to arrest all proceedings. 'Won't you cross your hands?' said Tom Graham, the constable. '*No, I won't,*' said Henry, with increasing emphasis. Mr Hamilton, Mr Freeland, and the officers now came near to Henry. Two of the constables drew out their shining pistols, and swore, by the name of God, that he should cross his hands or they would shoot him down. Each of these hired ruffians now cocked their pistols, and, with fingers apparently on the triggers, presented their deadly weapons to the breast of the unarmed slave, saying, if he did not cross his hands, they would 'blow his damned heart out of him'. '*Shoot me, shoot me,*' said Henry; 'you can't kill me but once. *Shoot, shoot,* and be damned! I won't be tied!' This the brave fellow said in a voice as defiant and heroic in its tones as was the language itself; and at the moment of saying this, with the pistol at his very breast, he quickly raised his arms, and dashed them from the puny hands of his assassins, the weapons flying in all directions. Now came the struggle. All hands rushed upon the brave fellow, and after beating him for some time they succeeded in overpowering and tying him. Henry put me to shame; he fought, and fought bravely. John and I had made no resistance. The fact is, I never saw much use in fighting where there was no reasonable probability of whipping anybody. Yet there was something almost providential in the resistance made by Henry. But for that resistance every soul of us would have been hurried off to the far South. Just a moment previous to the trouble with Henry, Mr Hamilton *mildly* said – and this gave me the unmistakable clue to the cause of our arrest – 'Perhaps we had now better make a search for those protections, which we understand Frederick has written for himself and the rest.' Had these Passes been found, they would have been point-blank proof against us, and would have confirmed all the statements of our betrayer. Thanks to the resistance of Henry, the excitement produced by the scuffle drew all attention in that direction, and I succeeded in flinging my pass, unobserved, into the fire. The confusion attendant on the scuffle, and the apprehension of still further trouble, perhaps, led our captors to forego, for the time, any search for 'those protections' which Frederick was said to have written for his companions'; so we were not yet convicted of the purpose to run away, and it was evident that there was some doubt on the part of all whether we had been guilty of such purpose.

Just as we were all completely tied, and about ready to start toward St Michaels, and thence to gaol, Mrs Betsey Freeland, mother to William, who was much attached, after the Southern fashion, to Henry and John, they having been reared from childhood in her house, came to the kitchen door with her hands full of biscuits, for we had not had our breakfast that morning, and divided them between Henry and John. This done, the lady made the following parting address to me, pointing her bony finger at me: 'You devil, you yellow devil! It was you who put it into the heads of Henry and John to run away. But for *you, you long-legged yellow devil*, Henry and John would never have thought of running away.' I gave the lady a look which called forth from her a scream of mingled wrath and terror, as she slammed the kitchen door and went in, leaving me, with the rest, in hands as harsh as her own broken voice.

Could the kind reader have been riding along the main road to or from Easton that morning, his eye would have met a painful sight. He would have seen five young men, guilty of no crime save that of preferring *liberty* to *slavery*, drawn along the public highway – firmly bound together, tramping through dust and heat, barefooted and bareheaded – fastened to three strong horses, whose riders were armed with pistols and daggers, on their way to prison like felons, and suffering every possible insult from the crowds of idle, vulgar people, who clustered round, and heartlessly made their failure to escape, the occasion for all manner of ribaldry and sport. As I looked upon this crowd of vile persons, and saw myself and friends thus assailed and persecuted, I could not help seeing the fulfilment of Sandy's dream. I was in the hands of moral vultures, and held in their sharp talons, and was being hurried away towards Easton, in a south-easterly direction, amid the jeers of new birds of the same feather, through every neighbourhood we passed. It seemed to me that everybody was out, and knew the cause of our arrest, and awaited our passing in order to feast their vindictive eyes on our misery.

Some said '*I ought to be hanged*'; and others, '*I ought to be burned*'; others, 'I ought to have the "hide" taken off my back'; while no one gave us a kind word or sympathising look, except the poor slaves who were lifting their heavy hoes, and who cautiously glanced at us through the post-and-rail fences, behind which they were at work. Our sufferings that morning can be more easily imagined than described. Our hopes were all blasted at one blow. The cruel injustice, the victorious crime, and the helplessness of innocence, led me to ask in my ignorance and weakness: Where is now the God of justice and mercy? and why have these wicked men the power thus to trample upon our rights, and to insult our feelings? and yet in the next moment came the consoling thought, 'the day of the oppressor will come at last'. Of one thing I could be glad: not one of my dear friends upon whom I had brought this great calamity, either by word or look, reproached me for having led them into it. We were a band of brothers, and never dearer to each other than now. The thought which gave us the most pain, was the probable separation which would now take place in case we were sold off to the far South, as we were likely to be. While the constables were looking forward, Henry and I, being fastened together, could occasionally exchange a word without being observed by the kidnappers who had us in charge. 'What shall I do with my pass?' said Henry. 'Eat it with your biscuit,' said I; 'it won't do to tear it up.' We were now near St Michaels. The direction concerning the passes was passed around, and executed. 'Own nothing,' said I. 'Own nothing' was passed round, enjoined, and assented to. Our confidence in each other was unshaken, and we were quite resolved to succeed or fail together, as much after the calamity which had befallen us as before.

On reaching St Michaels we underwent a sort of examination at my master's store, and it was evident to my mind that Master Thomas suspected the truthfulness of the evidence upon which they had acted in arresting us, and that he only affected, to some extent, the positiveness with which he asserted our guilt. There was nothing said by any of our company, which could, in any manner, prejudice our cause, and there was hope yet that we should be able to return to our homes, if for nothing else, at least to find out the guilty man or woman who betrayed us.

To this end we all denied that we had been guilty of intended flight. Master Thomas said that the evidence he had of our intention to run away was strong enough to hang us in a case of murder. 'But,' said I, 'the cases are not equal; if murder were committed – the thing is done! but we have not run away. Where is the evidence against us? We were quietly at our work.' I talked thus, with unusual freedom, to bring out the evidence against us, for we all wanted, above all things, to know who had betrayed us, that we might have something tangible on which to pour our execrations. From something which dropped, in the course of the talk, it appeared that there was but one witness against us, and that that witness could not be produced. Master Thomas would not tell us who his informant was, but we suspected, and suspected *one* person only. Several circumstances seemed to point Sandy out as our betrayer. His entire knowledge of our plans, his participation in them, his withdrawal from us, his dream, and his simultaneous presentiment that we were betrayed, the taking us and the leaving him, were calculated to turn suspicion towards him, and yet we could not suspect him. We all loved him too well to think it possible that he could have betrayed us. So we rolled the guilt on other shoulders.

We were literally dragged, that morning, behind horses, a distance of fifteen miles, and placed in the Easton gaol. We were glad to reach the end of our journey, for our pathway had been full of insult and mortification. Such is the power of public opinion that it is hard, even for the innocent, to feel the happy consolations of innocence when they fall under the maledictions of this power. How could we regard ourselves as in the right, when all about us denounced us as criminals, and had the power and the disposition to treat us as such.

In gaol we were placed under the care of Mr Joseph Graham, the sheriff of the county. Henry and John and myself were placed in one room, and Henry Bailey and Charles Roberts in another by themselves. This separation was intended to deprive us of the advantage of concert, and to prevent trouble in gaol.

Once shut up, a new set of tormentors came upon us. A swarm of imps in human shape – the slave-traders and agents of slave-traders – who gathered in every country town of the state, watching for chances to buy human flesh, as buzzards watch for carrion, flocked in upon us to ascertain if our masters had placed us in gaol to be sold. Such a set of debased and villainous creatures I never saw before, and hope never to see again. I felt as if surrounded by a pack of *fiends* fresh from *perdition*. They laughed, leered, and grinned at us, saying, 'Ah, boys, we have got you, haven't we? So you were about to make your escape? Where were you going to?' After taunting us in this way as long as they liked, they one by one subjected us to an examination, with a view to ascertaining our value, feeling our arms and legs and shaking us by the shoulders, to see if we were sound and healthy, impudently asking us, 'how we would like to have them for masters?' To such questions we were quite dumb, much to their annoyance. One fellow told me, 'if he had me he would cut the devil out of me pretty quick'.

These negro-buyers were very offensive to the genteel Southern Christian public. They were looked upon in respectable Maryland society as necessary but detestable characters. As a class, they were hardened ruffians, made such by nature and by occupation. Yes, they were the legitimate fruit of slavery, and were second in villainy only to the slave-holders themselves, who made such a class *possible*. They were mere hucksters of the slave produce of Maryland and Virginia – coarse, cruel, and swaggering bullies, whose very breathing was of blasphemy and blood.

Aside from these slave-buyers who infested the prison from time to time, our quarters were much more comfortable than we had any right to expect them to be. Our allowance of food was small and coarse, but our room was the best in the gaol – neat and spacious, and with nothing about it necessarily reminding us of being in prison but its heavy locks and bolts and the black iron lattice work at the windows. We were prisoners of state compared with most slaves who were put into the Easton gaol. But the place was not one of contentment. Bolts, bars, and grated windows are not acceptable to freedom-loving people of any colour. The suspense, too, was painful. Every step on the stairway was listened to, in the hope that the comer would cast a ray of light on our fate. We would have given the hair of our heads for half a dozen words with one of the waiters in Sol Lowe's hotel. Such waiters were in the way of hearing, at the table, the probable course of things. We could see them flitting about in their white jackets in front of this hotel, but could speak to none of them.

Soon after the holidays were over, contrary to all our expectations, Messrs Hamilton and Freeland came up to Easton; not to make a bargain with the 'Georgia traders', nor to send us up to Austin Woldfolk, as was usual in the case of runaway-slaves, but to release Charles, Henry Harris, Henry Bailey, and John Harris from prison, and this, too, without the infliction of a single blow. I was left alone in prison. The innocent had been taken, and the guilty left. My friends were separated from me, and apparently for ever. This circumstance caused me more pain than any other incident connected with our capture and imprisonment. Thirty-nine lashes on my naked and bleeding back would have been joyfully borne, in preference to this separation from these, the friends of my youth. And yet I could not but feel that I was the victim of something like justice. Why should these young men, who were led into this scheme by me, suffer as much as the instigator? I felt glad that they were released from prison, and from the dread prospect of a life, or death I should rather say, in the rice-swamps. It is due to the noble Henry to say that he was almost as reluctant to leave the prison with me in it as he had been to be tied and dragged to prison. But we all knew that we should, in all the likelihoods of the case, be separated, in the event of being sold; and since we were completely in the hands of our owners, they concluded it would be the best to go peaceably home.

Not until this last separation, dear reader, had I touched those profounder depths of desolation which it is the lot of slaves often to reach. I was solitary and alone, within the walls of a stone prison, left to a fate of life-long misery. I had hoped and expected much, for months before; but my hopes and expectations were now withered and blasted. The ever dreaded slave life in Georgia, Louisiana, and Alabama – from which escape was next to impossible – now in my loneliness stared me in the face. The possibility of ever becoming anything but an abject slave, a mere machine in the hands of an owner, had now fled, and it seemed to me it had fled for ever. A life of living death, beset with the innumerable horrors of the cotton-field and the sugar-plantation, seemed to be my doom. The fiends who rushed into the prison when we were first put there, continued to visit me and ply me with questions and tantalising remarks. I was insulted, but helpless; keenly alive to the demands of justice and liberty, but with no means of asserting them. To talk to those imps about justice or mercy would have been as absurd as to reason with bears and tigers. Lead and steel were the only arguments that they were capable of appreciating, as the events of the subsequent years have proved.

After remaining in this life of misery and despair about a week, which seemed a month, Master Thomas, very much to my surprise, and greatly to my relief, came to the prison and took me out for the purpose, as he said, of sending me to Alabama with a friend of his, who would emancipate me at the end of eight years. I was glad enough to get out of prison, but I had no faith in the story that his friend would emancipate me. Besides, I had never heard of his having a friend in Alabama, and I took the announcement simply as an easy and comfortable method of shipping me off to the far South. There was a little scandal, too, connected with the idea of one Christian selling another to the Georgia traders, while it was deemed every way proper for them to sell to others. I thought this friend in Alabama was an invention to meet this difficulty, for Master Thomas was quite jealous of his religious reputation, however unconcerned he might have been about his real Christian character. In these remarks it is possible I did him injustice. He certainly did not exert his power over me as he might have done in the case, but acted, upon the whole, very generously, considering the nature of my offence. He had the power and the provocation to send me, without reserve, into the very everglades of Florida, beyond the remotest hope of emancipation; and his refusal to exercise that power must be set down to his credit.

After lingering about St Michaels a few days, and no friend from Alabama appearing, Master Thomas decided to send me back again to Baltimore, to live with his brother Hugh, with whom he was now at peace; possibly he became so by his profession of religion at the camp-meeting in the Bayside. Master Thomas told me he wished me to go to Baltimore and learn a trade; and that if I behaved myself properly he would *emancipate me at twenty-five*. Thanks for this one beam of hope in the future. The promise had but one fault – it seemed too good to be true.

CHAPTER XX

Apprenticeship Life

> Nothing lost by my attempt to run away – Comrades at home – Reasons for sending me away – Return to Baltimore – Tommy changed – Caulking in Gardiner's shipyard – Desperate fight – Its causes – Conflict between white and black labour – Outrage – Testimony – Master Hugh – Slavery in Baltimore – My condition improves – New associations – Slave-holder's right to the slave's wages – How to make a discontented slave

Our little domestic revolution, notwithstanding the sudden snub it got by the treachery of somebody, did not, after all, end so disastrously as when in the iron cage at Easton I conceived it would. The prospect from that point did look about as dark as any that ever cast its gloom over the vision of an anxious, out-looking human spirit. 'All's well that ends well!' My affectionate friends, Henry and John Harris, were still with Mr Freeland. Charles Roberts and Henry Bailey were safe at their homes. I had not, therefore, anything to regret on their account. Their masters had mercifully forgiven them, probably on the ground suggested in the spirited little speech of Mrs Freeland made to me just before leaving for the gaol. My friends had nothing to regret either: for while they were watched more closely, they were doubtless treated more kindly than before, and got new assurances that they should someday be legally emancipated, provided their behaviour from that time forward should make them deserving. Not a blow did any one of them receive. As for Master Freeland, good soul, he did not believe we were intending to run away at all. Having given – as he thought – no occasion to his boys to leave him, he could not think it possible that they had entertained a design so grievous.

This, however, was not the view taken of the matter by 'Mars'r Billy', as we used to call the soft-spoken, but crafty and resolute Mr William Hamilton. He had no doubt that the crime had been meditated, and regarding me as the instigator of it, he frankly told Master Thomas that he must remove me from that neighbourhood or he would shoot me. He would not have one so dangerous as 'Frederick' tampering with his slaves. William Hamilton was not a man whose threat might be safely disregarded. I have no doubt he would have proved as good as his word, had the warning given been disregarded. He was furious at the thought of such a piece of high-handed *theft* as we were about to perpetrate – the stealing of our own bodies and souls. The feasibility of the plan, too, could the first steps have been taken, was marvellously plain. Besides, this was a *new* idea, this use of the Bay. Slaves escaping, until now, had taken to the woods; they had never dreamed of profaning or abusing the waters of the noble Chesapeake, by making them the highway from slavery to freedom. Here was a broad road leading to the destruction of slavery, which hitherto had been looked upon as a wall of security by the slave-holders. But Master Billy could not get Mr Freeland to see matters precisely as he did, nor could he get Master Thomas, excited as he was. The latter, I must say it to his credit, showed much humane feeling, and atoned for much that had been harsh, cruel, and unreasonable in his former treatment of me and of others. My 'Cousin Tom' told me that while I was in gaol Master Thomas was very unhappy, and that the night before his going up to release me he had walked the floor nearly all night, evincing great distress; that very tempting offers had been made to him by the negro-traders, but he had rejected them all, saying that *money could not tempt him to sell me to the far South*. I can easily believe all this, for he seemed quite reluctant to send me away at all. He told me that he only consented to do so because of the very strong prejudice against me in the neighbourhood, and that he feared for my safety if I remained there.

Thus after three years spent in the country, roughing it in the fields, and experiencing all sorts of hardships, I was again permitted to return to Baltimore, the very place of all others, short of a Free State, where I most desired to live. The three years spent in the country had made some difference in me, and in the household of Master Hugh. 'Little Tommy' was no longer little Tommy; and I was not the slender lad who had left the Eastern Shore just three years before. The loving relations between Master Tommy and myself were broken up. He was no longer dependent on me for protection, but felt himself a *man*, with other and more suitable associates. In childhood he had considered me scarcely inferior to himself – certainly quite as good as any other boy with whom he played – but the time had come when his *friend* must be his slave. So we were cold to each other, and parted. It was a sad thing to me, that loving each other as we had done, we must now take different roads. To him, a thousand avenues were open. Education had made him acquainted with all the treasures of the world, and liberty had flung open the gates thereunto; but I, who had attended him seven years, had watched over him with the care of a big brother, fighting his battles in the street, and shielding him from harm to an extent which induced his mother to say, 'Oh, Tommy is always safe when he is with Freddy' – I must be confined to a single condition. He had grown and become a *man*; I, though grown to the stature of manhood, must all my life remain a minor – a mere boy. Thomas Auld, junior, obtained a situation on board the brig *Tweed*, and went to sea. I have since heard of his death. There were few persons to whom I was more sincerely attached, than to him.

Very soon after I went to Baltimore to live, Master Hugh succeeded in getting me hired to Mr William Gardiner, an extensive shipbuilder on Fell's Point. I was placed there to learn to caulk; a trade of which I already had some knowledge, gained while in Mr Hugh Auld's shipyard. Gardiner's, however, proved a very unfavourable place for the accomplishment of the desired object. Mr Gardiner was that season engaged in building two large man-of-war vessels, professedly for the Mexican government. These vessels were to be launched in the month of July of that year, and in failure thereof, Mr Gardiner would forfeit a very considerable sum of money. So when I entered the shipyard, all was hurry and driving. There were in the yard about one hundred men; of these, seventy or eighty were regular carpenters – privileged men. There was no time for a raw hand to learn anything. Every man had to do that which he knew how to do, and in entering the yard, Mr Gardiner had directed me to do whatever the carpenters told me to do. This was placing me at the beck and call of about seventy-five men. I was to regard all these as my masters. Their word was to be my law. My situation was a trying one. I was called a dozen ways in the space of a single minute. I needed a dozen pairs of hands. Three or four voices would strike my ear at the same moment. It was 'Fred, come help me to cant this timber here' – 'Fred, come carry this timber yonder' – 'Fred, bring that roller here' – 'Fred, go get a fresh can of water' – 'Fred, come help saw off the end of this timber' – 'Fred, go quick and get the crowbar' – 'Fred, hold on the end of this fall' – 'Fred, go to the blacksmith's shop and get a new punch' – 'Halloo, Fred! run and bring me a cold-chisel' – 'I say, Fred, bear a hand, and get up a fire under the steam-box as quick as lightning' – 'Hullo, nigger! come turn this grindstone' – 'Come, come; move, move! and *bowse* this timber forward' – 'I say, darkey, blast your eyes! why don't you heat up some pitch?' – 'Halloo! halloo! halloo!' (three voices at the same time) – 'Come here; go there; hold on where you are. Damn you, if you move I'll knock your brains out!' Such, my dear reader, is a glance at the school which was mine, during the first eight months of my stay at Gardiner's shipyard. At the end of eight months Master Hugh refused longer to allow me to remain with Gardiner. The circumstances which led to this refusal was the committing of an outrage upon me, by the white apprentices of the shipyard. The fight was a desperate one, and I came out of it shockingly mangled. I was cut and bruised in sundry places, and my left eye was nearly knocked out of its socket. The facts which led to this brutal outrage upon me, illustrate a phase of slavery which was destined to become an important element in the overthrow of the slave system, and I may therefore state them with some minuteness. That phase was this – the conflict of slavery with the interests of white mechanics and labourers. In the country this conflict was not so apparent; but in cities, such as Baltimore, Richmond, New Orleans, Mobile, etc., it was seen pretty clearly. The slave-holders, with a craftiness peculiar to themselves, by encouraging the enmity of the poor labouring white man against the blacks, succeeded in making the said white man almost as much a slave as the black slave himself. The difference between the white slave and the black slave was this: the latter belonged to one slave-holder, and the former belonged to the slave-holders collectively. The white slave had taken from him by indirection what the black slave had taken from him directly and without ceremony. Both were plundered, and by the same plunderers. The slave was robbed by his master of all his earnings, above what was required for his bare physical necessities, and the white labouring man was robbed by the slave system of the just results of his labour, because he was flung into competition with a class of labourers who worked without wages. The slave-holders blinded them to this competition by keeping alive their prejudice against the slaves as *men* – not against them as slaves. They appealed to their pride, often denouncing emancipation as tending to place the white working man on an equality with negroes, and by this means they succeeded in drawing off the minds of the poor whites from the real fact, that, by the rich slave-master, they were already regarded as but a single remove from equality with the slave. The impression was cunningly made, that slavery was the only power that could prevent the labouring white man from falling to the level of the slave's poverty and degradation. To make this enmity deep and broad between the slave and the poor white man, the latter was allowed to abuse and whip the former without hindrance. But, as I have said, this state of affairs prevailed *mostly* in the country. In the city of Baltimore, there were not unfrequent murmurs that educating slaves to be mechanics might, in the end, give slave-masters power to dispose altogether with the services of the poor white man. But with characteristic dread of offending the slave-holders, these poor white mechanics in Mr Gardiner's shipyard, instead of applying the natural, honest remedy for the apprehended evil, and objecting at once to work there by the side of slaves, made a cowardly attack upon the free coloured mechanics, saying they were eating the bread which should be eaten by American freemen, and swearing that they would not work with them. The feeling was *really* against having their labour brought into competition with that of the coloured freeman, and aimed to prevent him from serving himself, in the evening of life, with the trade with which he had served his master, during the more vigorous portion of his days. Had they succeeded in driving the black freemen out of the shipyard, they would have determined also upon the removal of the black slaves. The feeling was very bitter toward all coloured people in Baltimore about this time, 1836, and they – free and slave – suffered all manner of insult and wrong.

Until a very little time before I went there, white and black carpenters worked side by side in the shipyards of Mr Gardiner, Mr Duncan, Mr Walter Price and Mr Robb. Nobody seemed to see any impropriety in it. Some of the blacks were first rate workmen, and were given jobs requiring the highest skill. All at once, however, the white carpenters knocked off, and swore that they would no longer work on the same stage with negroes. Taking advantage of the heavy contract resting upon Mr Gardiner to have the vessels for Mexico ready to launch in July, and of the difficulty of getting other hands at that season of the year, they swore they would not strike another blow for him, unless he would discharge his free coloured workmen. Now, although this movement did not extend to me *in form*, it did reach me in *fact*. The spirit which it awakened was one of malice and bitterness toward coloured people *generally*, and I suffered with the rest, and suffered severely. My fellow-apprentices very soon began to feel it to be degrading to work with me. They began to put on high looks, and to talk contemptuously and maliciously of 'the niggers', saying that they would take the 'country', that they 'ought to be killed'. Encouraged by workmen who, knowing me to be a slave, made no issue with Mr Gardiner about my being there, these young men did their utmost to make it impossible for me to stay. They seldom called me to do anything, without coupling the call with a curse, and Edward North, the biggest in everything, rascality included, ventured to strike me, whereupon I picked him up and threw him into the dock. Whenever any of them struck me, I struck back at them, regardless of consequences. I could manage any of them *singly*, and so long as I could keep them from combining I got on pretty well. In the conflict which ended my stay at Mr Gardiner's, I was beset by four of them at once – Ned North, Ned Hays, Bill Stewart and Tom Humphreys. Two of them were as big as myself, and they came near killing me in broad daylight. One came in front, armed with a brick; there was one at each side and one behind, and they closed up all around me. I was struck on all sides; and while I was attending to those in front, I received a blow on my head from behind, dealt with a heavy hand-spike. I was completely stunned by the blow, and fell heavily on the ground among the timbers. Taking advantage of my fall they rushed upon me and began to pound me with their fists. I let them lay on for a while after I came to myself, with a view of gaining strength. They did me little damage so far; but finally getting tired of that sport I gave a sudden surge, and despite their weight I rose to my hands and knees. Just as I did this one of their number planted a blow with his boot in my left eye, which for a time seemed to have burst my eyeball. When they saw my eye completely closed, my face covered with blood, and I staggering under the stunning blows they had given me, they left me. As soon as I gathered strength I picked up the hand-spike and madly enough attempted to pursue them; but here the carpenters interfered, and compelled me to give up my pursuit. It was impossible to stand against so many.

Dear reader, you can hardly believe the statement, but it is true, and therefore I write it down: no fewer than fifty white men stood by and saw this brutal and shameful outrage committed, and not a man of them all interposed a single word of mercy. There were four against one, and that one's face was beaten and battered most horribly, and no one said 'that is enough'; but some cried out, 'Kill him! kill him! kill the damn nigger! knock his brains out! he struck a white person!' I mention this inhuman outcry to show the character of the men and the spirit of the times at Gardiner's shipyard; and, indeed, in Baltimore generally, in 1836. As I look back to the period, I am almost amazed that I was not murdered outright, so reckless was the spirit which prevailed there. On two other occasions while there I came near losing my life, on one of which I was driving bolts in the hold through the keelson with Hays. In its course the bolt bent. Hays cursed me, and said that it was my blow which bent the bolt. I denied this, and charged it upon him. In a fit of rage he seized an adze and darted towards me. I met him with a maul, and parried his blow, or I should have lost my life.

After the united attack of North, Stewart, Hays, and Humphreys, finding that the carpenters were as bitter toward me as the apprentices, and that the latter were probably set on by the former, I found my only chance for life was in flight. I succeeded in getting away without an additional blow. To strike a white man was death by lynch law, in Gardiner's shipyard; nor was there much of any other law toward the coloured people at that time, in any other part of Maryland.

After making my escape from the shipyard I went straight home and related my story to Master Hugh; and to his credit I say it, that his conduct, though he was not a religious man, was every way more humane than that of his brother Thomas, when I went to him in a somewhat similar plight, from the hands of his 'Brother Edward Covey'. Master Hugh listened attentively to my narration of the circumstances leading to the ruffianly assault, and gave many evidences of his strong indignation at what was done. He was a rough but manly-hearted fellow, and at this time his best nature showed itself.

The heart of my once kind mistress Sophia was again melted in pity toward me. My puffed-out eye and my scarred and blood-covered face moved the dear lady to tears. She kindly drew a chair by me, and with friendly and consoling words, she took water and washed the blood from my face. No mother's hand could have been more tender than hers. She bound up my head and covered my wounded eye with a lean piece of fresh beef. It was almost compensation for all I had suffered, that it occasioned the manifestation once more of the originally characteristic kindness of my mistress. Her affectionate heart was not yet dead, though much hardened by time and circumstances.

As for Master Hugh he was furious, and gave expression to his feelings in the forms of speech usual in that locality. He poured curses on the whole of the shipyard company, and swore that he would have satisfaction. His indignation was really strong and healthy; but unfortunately it resulted from the thought that his rights of property, in my person, had not been respected; more than from any sense of the outrage perpetrated upon me *as a man*. I had reason to think this from the fact that he could himself beat and mangle, when it suited him to do so.

Bent on having satisfaction, as he said, just as soon as I got a little the better of my bruises, Master Hugh took me to Esquire Watson's office on Bond Street, Fell's Point, with a view of procuring the arrest of those who had assaulted me. He related the outrage to the magistrate as I had related it to him, and seemed to expect that a warrant would at once be issued for the arrest of the lawless ruffians. Mr Watson heard all he had to say, then coolly enquired – 'Mr Auld, who saw this assault of which you speak?' 'It was done, sir, in the presence of a shipyard full of hands.' 'Sir,' said Mr Watson, 'I am sorry, but I cannot move in this matter, except upon the oath of white witnesses.' 'But here's the boy; look at his head and face,' said the excited Master Hugh; '*they* show *what* has been done.' But Watson insisted that he was not authorised to do anything, unless white witnesses of the transaction would come forward and testify to what had taken place. He could issue no warrant on my word, against white persons, if I had been killed in the presence of a *thousand blacks*; their testimony combined would have been insufficient to condemn a single murderer. Master Hugh was compelled to say, for once, that this state of things was *too bad*, and he left the office of the magistrate disgusted.

Of course it was impossible to get any white man to testify against my assailants. The carpenters saw what was done; but the actors were but the agents of their malice, and did only what the carpenters sanctioned. They had cried with one accord, 'Kill the nigger! kill the nigger!' Even those who may have pitied me, if any such were among them, lacked the moral courage to volunteer their evidence. The slightest show of sympathy or justice toward a person of colour was denounced as abolitionism; and the name of abolitionist subjected its hearer to frightful liabilities. 'Damn abolitionists', and 'kill the niggers', were the watchwords of the foul-mouthed ruffians of those days. Nothing was done, and probably there would not have been, had I been killed in the affray. The laws and the morals of the Christian city of Baltimore afforded no protection to the sable denizens of that city.

Master Hugh, on finding he could get no redress for the cruel wrong, withdrew me from the employment of Mr Gardiner, and took me into his own family, Mrs Auld kindly taking care of me and dressing my wounds until they were healed, and I was ready to go to work again.

While I was on the Eastern Shore, Master Hugh had met with reverses which overthrew his business; and he had given up shipbuilding in his own yard, on the City Block, and was now acting as foreman of Mr Walter Price. The best he could do for me was to take me into Mr Price's yard, and afford me the facilities there for completing the trade which I began to learn at Gardiner's. Here I rapidly became expert in the use of caulker's tools, and in the course of a single year, I was able to command the highest wages paid to journeymen caulkers in Baltimore.

The reader will observe that I was now of some pecuniary value to my master. During the busy season I was bringing six or seven dollars per week. I have sometimes brought him as much as nine dollars a week, for the wages were a dollar and a half per day.

After learning to caulk, I sought my own employment, made my own contracts, and collected my own earnings – giving Master Hugh no trouble in any part of the transactions to which I was a party.

Here, then, were better days for the Eastern Shore *slave*. I was free from the vexatious assaults of the apprentices at Mr Gardiner's, and free from the perils of plantation life, and once more in favourable condition to increase my little stock of education, which had been at a dead stand since my removal from Baltimore. I had on the Eastern Shore been only a teacher, when in company with other slaves, but now there were coloured persons here who could instruct me. Many of the young caulkers could read, write, and cipher. Some of them had high notions about mental improvement, and the free ones on Fell's Point organised what they called the 'East Baltimore Mental Improvement Society'. To this society, notwithstanding it was intended that only free persons should attach themselves, I was admitted, and was several times assigned a prominent part in its debates. I owe much to the society of these young men.

The reader already knows enough of the *ill* effects of good treatment on a slave, to anticipate what was now the case in my improved condition. It was not long before I began to show signs of disquiet with slavery, and to look around for means to get out of it by the shortest route. I was living among *freemen*, and was in all respects equal to them by nature and attainments. *Why should I be a slave?* There was *no* reason why I should be the thrall of any man. Besides, I was now getting, as I have said, a dollar and fifty cents per day. I contracted for it, worked for it, collected it; it was paid to me, and it was *rightfully* my own; and yet upon every returning Saturday night, this money – my own hard earnings, every cent of it – was demanded of me, and taken from me, by Master Hugh. He did not earn it; he had no hand in earning it; why, then, should he have it? I owed him nothing. He had given me no schooling, and I had received from him only my food and raiment; and for these my services were supposed to pay from the first. The right to take my earnings was the right of the robber. He had the *power* to compel me to give him the fruits of my labour, and this power was the only right in the case. I became more and more dissatisfied with this state of things, and in so becoming, I only gave proof of the same human nature which every reader of this chapter in my life – slave-holder, or non-slave-holder – is conscious of possessing.

To make a contented slave, you must make a thoughtless one. It is necessary to darken his moral and mental vision, and, as far as possible, annihilate his power of reason. He must be able to detect no inconsistencies in slavery. The man who takes his earnings must be able to convince him that he has a perfect right to do so. It must not depend upon mere force: the slave must know no higher law than his master's will. The whole relationship must not only demonstrate to his mind its necessity, but its absolute rightfulness. If there be one crevice through which a single drop can fall, it will certainly rust off the slave's chain.

CHAPTER XXI

Escape from Slavery

Closing incidents in my 'life as a slave' – Discontent – Suspicions – Master's generosity – Difficulties in the way of escape – Plan to obtain money – Allowed to hire my time – A gleam of hope – Attend camp-meeting – Anger of Master Hugh – The result – Plans of escape – Day for departure fixed – Harassing doubts and fears – Painful thoughts of separation from friends

My condition during the year of my escape, 1838, was comparatively a free and easy one, so far, at least, as the wants of the physical man were concerned; but the reader will bear in mind that my troubles from the beginning had been less physical than mental, and he will thus be prepared to find slave life was adding nothing to its charms for me as I grew older, and became more and more acquainted with it. The practice from week to week of openly robbing me of all my earnings, kept the nature and character of slavery constantly before me. I could be robbed by indirection, but this was too open and barefaced to be endured. I could see no reason why I should, at the end of each week, pour the reward of my honest toil into the purse of my master. My obligation to do this vexed me, and the manner in which Master Hugh received my wages vexed me yet more. Carefully counting the money, and rolling it out dollar by dollar, he would look me in the face as if he would search my heart as well as my pocket, and reproachfully ask me, 'Is that all?' – implying that I had perhaps kept back part of my wages; or, if not so, the demand was made possibly to make me feel that, after all, I was an 'unprofitable servant'. Draining me of the last cent of my hard earnings, he would, however, occasionally, when I brought home an extra large sum, dole out to me a sixpence or a shilling, with a view, perhaps, of enkindling my gratitude. But it had the opposite effect; it was an admission of my right to the whole sum. The fact that he gave me any part of my wages, was proof that he suspected I had a right to the whole of them; and I always felt uncomfortable after having received anything in this way, lest his giving me a few cents might possibly ease his conscience, and make him feel himself to be a pretty honourable robber, after all.

Held to a strict account, and kept under a close watch – the old suspicion of my running away not having been entirely removed – to accomplish my escape seemed a very difficult thing. The railroad from Baltimore to Philadelphia was under regulations so stringent, that even *free* coloured travellers were almost excluded. They must have free papers; they must be measured, and carefully examined, before they could enter the cars, and could go only in the daytime, even when so examined. The steamboats were under regulations equally stringent. And still more, and worse than all, all the great turnpikes leading Northward, were beset with kidnappers; a class of men who watched the newspapers for advertisements for runaway slaves, thus making their living by the accursed reward of slave-hunting.

My discontent grew upon me, and I was on the constant look-out for means to get away. With money I could easily have managed the matter, and from this consideration I hit upon the plan of soliciting the privilege of hiring my time. It was quite common in Baltimore to allow slaves this privilege, and was the practice also in New Orleans. A slave who was considered trustworthy could, by paying his master a definite sum regularly, at the end of each week, dispose of his time as he liked.

It so happened that I was not in very good odour, and I was far from being a trustworthy slave. Nevertheless, I watched my opportunity when Master Thomas came to Baltimore – for I was still his property, Hugh only acting as his agent – in the spring of 1838, to purchase his spring supply of goods, and applied to him directly for the much-coveted privilege of hiring my time. This request Master Thomas unhesitatingly refused to grant; and he charged me, with some sternness, with inventing this stratagem to make my escape. He told me I could go *nowhere* but he would catch me; and, in the event of my running away, I might be assured he should spare no pains in his efforts to recapture me. He recounted, with a good deal of eloquence, the many kind offices he had done me, and exhorted me to be contented and obedient. 'Lay out no plans for the future,' said he; 'if you behave yourself properly, I will take care of you.' Now, kind and considerate as this offer was, it failed to soothe me into repose. In spite of all Master Thomas had said, and in spite of my own efforts to the contrary, the injustice and wickedness of slavery was always uppermost in my thoughts, strengthening my purpose to make my escape at the earliest moment possible.

About two months after applying to Master Thomas for the privilege of hiring my time, I applied to Master Hugh for the same liberty, supposing him to be unacquainted with the fact, that I had made a similar application to Master Thomas, and had been refused. My boldness in making this request fairly astounded him at first. He gazed at me in amazement. But I had many good reasons for pressing the matter, and, after listening to them awhile, he did not absolutely refuse, but told me he would think of it. There was hope for me in this. Once master of my own time, I felt sure that I could make over and above my obligation to him – a dollar or two every week. Some slaves had made enough in this way to purchase their freedom. It was a sharp spur to their industry; and some of the most enterprising coloured men in Baltimore hired themselves in that way.

After mature reflection, as I suppose it was, Master Hugh granted me the privilege in question, on the following terms: I was to be allowed all my time; to make all bargains for work, and to collect my own wages; and in return for this liberty, I was required or obliged to pay him three dollars at the end of each week, and to board and clothe myself, and buy my own caulking tools. A failure in any of these particulars would put an end to the privilege. This was a hard bargain. The wear and tear of clothing, the losing and breaking of tools, and the expense of board made it necessary for me to earn at least six dollars per week to keep even with the world. All who are acquainted with caulking know how uncertain and irregular that employment is. It can be done to advantage only in dry weather, for it is useless to put wet oakum into a ship's seam. Rain or shine, however, work or no work, at the end of each week the money must be forthcoming.

Master Hugh seemed much pleased with this arrangement for a time; and well he might be, for it was decidedly in his favour. It relieved him of all anxiety concerning me. His money was sure. He had armed my love of liberty with a lash and a driver far more efficient than any I had before known; and while he derived all the benefits of slaveholding by the arrangement, without its evils, I endured all the evils of being a slave, and yet suffered all the care and anxiety of a responsible freeman. 'Nevertheless,' thought I, 'it is a valuable privilege – another step in my career toward freedom.' It was something, even to be permitted to stagger under the disadvantages of liberty, and I was determined to hold on to the newly-gained footing by all proper industry. I was ready to work by night as by day, and being in the possession of excellent health, I was not only able to meet my current expenses, but also to lay by a small sum at the end of each week. All went on thus from the month of May till August; then, for reasons which will become apparent as I proceed, my much-valued liberty was wrested from me.

During the week previous to this calamitous event, I had made arrangements with a few young friends to accompany them on Saturday night to a camp-meeting, to be held about twelve miles from Baltimore. On the evening of our intended start for the camp-ground, something occurred in the shipyard where I was at work, which detained me unusually late, and compelled me either to disappoint my friends, or to neglect carrying my weekly dues to Master Hugh. Knowing that I had the money and could hand it to him on another day, I decided to go on the camp-meeting, and to pay him the three dollars for the past week on my return. Once on the camp-ground, I was induced to remain one day longer than I intended when I left home. But as soon as I returned I went directly to his home in Fell Street, to hand him his (my) money. Unhappily the fatal mistake had been made. I found him exceedingly angry. He exhibited all the signs of apprehension and wrath which a slave-holder might be surmised to exhibit on the supposed escape of a favourite slave. 'You rascal! I have a great mind to give you a sound whipping. How dare you go out of the city without first asking and obtaining my permission?' 'Sir,' I said, 'I hired my time and paid you the price you asked for it. I did not know that it was any part of the bargain that I should ask you when or where I should go.' 'You did not know, you rascal! You are bound to show yourself here every Saturday night.' After reflecting a few moments, he became somewhat cooled down; but evidently greatly troubled, and said: 'Now, you scoundrel, you have done for yourself; you shall hire your time no longer. The next thing I shall hear of, will be your running away. Bring home your tools at once. I'll teach you how to go off in this way.'

Thus ended my partial freedom. I could hire my time no longer; and I obeyed my master's orders at once. The little taste of liberty which I had had – although as it will be seen, that taste was far from being unalloyed – by no means enhanced my contentment with slavery. Punished by Master Hugh, it was now my turn to punish him. 'Since,' thought I, 'you *will* make a slave of me, I will await your order in all things.' So, instead of going to look for work on Monday morning, as I had formerly done, I remained at home during the entire week, without the performance of a single stroke of work. Saturday night came, and he called upon me as usual for my wages. I, of course, told him I had done no work, and had no wages. Here we were at the point of coming to blows. His wrath had been accumulating during the whole week; for he evidently saw that I was making no effort to get work, but was most aggravatingly awaiting his orders in all things. As I look back to this behaviour of mine, I scarcely know what possessed me, thus to trifle with one who had such unlimited power to bless or blast me. Master Hugh raved, and swore he would 'get hold of me', but wisely for *him*, and happily for *me*, his wrath employed only those harmless, impalpable missiles which roll from a limber tongue. In my desperation I had fully made up my mind to measure strength with him, in case he should attempt to execute his threats. I am glad there was no occasion for this, for resistance to him could not have ended so happily for me, as it did in the case of Covey. Master Hugh was not a man to be safely resisted by a slave; and I freely own that in my conduct toward him, in this instance, there was more folly than wisdom. He closed his reproof, by telling me that hereafter I need give myself no uneasiness about getting work; he 'would himself see to getting work for me, and enough of it at that'. This threat, I confess, had some terror in it, and on thinking the matter over during the Sunday, I resolved not only to save him the trouble of getting me work, but that on the third day of September I would attempt to make my escape. His refusal to allow me to hire my time therefore hastened the period of my flight. I had three weeks in which to prepare for my journey.

Once resolved, I felt a certain degree of repose, and on Monday morning, instead of waiting for Master Hugh to seek employment for me, I was up by break of day, and off to the shipyard of Mr Butler, on the City Block, near the drawbridge. I was a favourite with Mr Butler, and, young as I was, I had served as his foreman, on the float-stage, at caulking. Of course I easily obtained work, and at the end of the week, which, by-the-way, was exceedingly fine, I brought Master Hugh nine dollars. The effect of this mark of returning good sense on my part, was excellent. He was very much pleased; he took the money, commended me, and told me I might have done the same thing the week before. It is a blessed thing that the tyrant may not always know the thoughts and purposes of his victim. Master Hugh little knew my plans. The going to camp-meeting without asking his permission, the insolent answers to his reproaches, the sulky deportment of the week, after being deprived of the privilege of hiring my time, had awakened the suspicion that I might be cherishing disloyal purposes. My object, therefore, in working steadily, was to remove suspicion; and in this I succeeded admirably. He probably thought I was never better satisfied with my condition than at the very time I was planning my escape. The second week passed, and I again carried him my full week's wages – *nine dollars*; and so well pleased was he that he gave me *twenty-five cents*! and bade me 'make good use of it'. I told him I would do so; for one of the uses to which I intended to put it was to pay my fare on the 'underground railroad'.

Things without went on as usual; but I was passing through the same internal excitement and anxiety which I had experienced two years and a half before. The failure in that instance was not calculated to increase my confidence in the success of this, my second attempt; and I knew that a second failure could not leave me where my first did. I must either get to the *far North* or *be sent* to the *far South*. Besides the exercise of mind from this state of facts, I had the painful sensation of being about to separate from a circle of honest and warm-hearted friends. The thought of such a separation, where the hope of ever meeting again was excluded, and where there could be no correspondence was very painful. It is my opinion that thousands more would have escaped from slavery but for the strong affection which bound them to their families, relatives, and friends. The daughter was hindered by the love she bore her mother, and the father by the love he bore his wife and children, and so on to the end of the chapter. I had no relations in Baltimore, and I saw no probability of ever living in the neighbourhood of sisters and brothers; but the thought of leaving my friends was the strongest obstacle to my running away. The last two days of the week, Friday and Saturday, were spent mostly in collecting my things together for my journey. Having worked four days that week for my master, I handed him six dollars on Saturday night. I seldom spent my Sundays at home, and for fear that something might be discovered in my conduct, I kept up my custom and absented myself all day. On Monday, the third day of September 1838, in accordance with my resolution, I bade farewell to the city of Baltimore, and to that slavery which had been my abhorrence from childhood.

PART TWO: A SLAVE NO MORE

CHAPTER I

Escape from Slavery

Reasons for not having revealed the manner of escape – Nothing of romance in the method – Danger – Free Papers – Unjust tax – Protection papers – 'Free trade and sailors' rights'– American eagle – Railroad train – Unobserving conductor – Captain McGowan – Honest German – Fears – Safe arrival in Philadelphia – Ditto in New York

In the first narrative of my experience in slavery, written nearly forty years ago, and in various writings since, I have given the public what I considered very good reasons for withholding the manner of my escape. In substance these reasons were, first, that such publication at any time during the existence of slavery might be used by the master against the slave, and prevent the future escape of any who might adopt the same means that I did. The second reason was, if possible, still more binding to silence – for publication of details would certainly have put in peril the persons and property of those who assisted. Murder itself was not more sternly and certainly punished in the State of Maryland, than that of aiding and abetting the escape of a slave. Many coloured men, for no other crime than that of giving aid to a fugitive slave, have, like Charles T. Torrey, perished in prison. The abolition of slavery in my native state and throughout the country, and the lapse of time, render the caution hitherto observed no longer necessary. But even since the abolition of slavery, I have sometimes thought it well enough to baffle curiosity, by saying that while slavery existed there were good reasons for not telling the manner of my escape, and since slavery had ceased to exist, there was no reason for telling it. I shall now, however, cease to avail myself of this formula, and as far as I can, endeavour to satisfy this very natural curiosity. I should perhaps have yielded to that feeling sooner, had there been anything very heroic or thrilling in the incidents connected with my escape, but I am sorry to say I have nothing of that sort to tell; and yet, the courage that could risk betrayal, and the bravery which was ready to encounter death, if need be, in pursuit of freedom, were essential features in the undertaking. My success was due to address rather than courage; to good luck rather than bravery. My means of escape were provided for me by the very men who were making laws to hold and bind me more securely in slavery. It was the custom in the State of Maryland to require the free coloured people to have what were called free papers. This instrument they were required to renew very often, and by charging a fee for this writing, considerable sums, from time to time, were collected by the State. In these papers the name, age, colour, height, and form of the free man were described, together with any scars or other marks upon his person, which could assist in his identification. This device of slave-holding ingenuity, like other devices of wickedness, in some measure defeated itself – since more than one man could be found to answer the same general description. Hence many slaves could escape by personating the owner of one set of papers; and this was often done as follows: A slave nearly or sufficiently answering the description set forth in papers, would borrow or hire them till he could by their means escape to a free State, and then, by mail or otherwise, return them to the owner. The operation was a hazardous one for the lender as well as the borrower. A failure on the part of the fugitive to send back the papers would imperil his benefactor, and the discovery of the papers in possession of the wrong man, would imperil both the fugitive and his friend. It was, therefore, an act of supreme trust on the part of a freeman of colour thus to put in jeopardy his own liberty, that another might be free. It was, however, not unfrequently bravely done, and was seldom discovered. I was not so fortunate to sufficiently resemble any of my free acquaintances as to answer the description of their papers. But I had one friend – a sailor – who owned a sailor's protection, which answered somewhat the purpose of free papers – describing his person, and certifying to the fact that he was a free American sailor. The instrument had at its head the American eagle, which gave it the appearance at once of an authorised document. This protection did not, when in my hands, describe its bearer very accurately. Indeed, it culled for a man much darker than myself, and close examination of it would have caused my arrest at the start. In order to avoid this fatal scrutiny on the part of the railroad official, I had arranged with Isaac Rolls, a hackman, to bring my baggage to the train just on the moment of its starting, and I jumped upon the car myself when the train was already in motion. Had I gone into the station and offered to purchase a ticket, I should have been instantly and carefully examined, and undoubtedly arrested. In choosing this plan upon which to act, I considered the jostle of the train, and the natural haste of the conductor, in a train crowded with passengers, and relied upon my skill and address in playing the sailor as described in my protection, to do the rest. One element in my favour, was the kind feeling which prevailed in Baltimore and other seaports at the time, towards 'those who go down to the sea in ships'. 'Free trade and sailors' rights' expressed the sentiment of the country just then. In my clothing, I was rigged out in sailor style. I had on a red shirt and a tarpaulin hat and black cravat, tied in sailor fashion, carelessly and loosely about my neck. My knowledge of ships and sailor's talk came much to my assistance, for I knew a ship from stem to stern, and from keelson to cross-trees, and could talk sailor like an 'old salt'. On sped the train, and I was well on the way to Havre de Grace before the conductor came into the negro car to collect tickets and examine the papers of his black passengers. This was a critical moment in the drama. My whole future depended upon the decision of this conductor. Agitated I was while this ceremony was proceeding, but still externally, at least, I was apparently calm and self-possessed. He went on with his duty – examining several coloured passengers before reaching me. He was somewhat harsh in tone, and peremptory in manner until he reached me, when, strangely enough, and to my surprise and relief, his whole manner changed. Seeing that I did not readily produce my free papers, as the other coloured persons in the car had done, he said to me, in a friendly contrast with that observed towards the others: 'I suppose you have your free papers?' To which I answered: 'No, sir; I never carry my free papers to sea with me.' 'But you have something to show that you are a free man, have you not?' 'Yes, sir,' I answered; 'I have a paper with the American eagle on it, and that will carry me round the world.' With this I drew from my deep sailor's pocket my seaman's protection, as before described. The merest glance at the paper satisfied him, and he took my fare and went on about his business. This moment of time was one of the most anxious I ever experienced. Had the conductor looked closely at the paper, he could not have failed to discover that it called for a very different looking person from myself, and in that case, it would have been his duty to arrest me on that instant, and send me back to Baltimore from the first station. When he left me with the assurance that I was all right, though much relieved, I realised that I was still in great danger. I was still in

Maryland, and subject to arrest at any moment. I saw on the train several persons who would have known me in any other clothes, and I feared they might recognise me, even in my sailor 'rig', and report me to the conductor, who would then subject me to a closer examination, which I knew well would be fatal to me.

Though I was not a murderer fleeing from justice, I felt perhaps quite as miserable as such a criminal. The train was moving at a very high rate of speed for that time of railroad travel, but to my anxious mind, it was moving far too slowly. Minutes were hours, and hours were days, during this part of my flight. After Maryland, I was to pass through Delaware – another slave State, where slave-catchers generally awaited their prey, for it was not in the interior of the State, but on its borders, that these human hounds were most vigilant and active. The border lines between slavery and freedom were the dangerous ones, for the fugitives. The heart of no fox or deer, with hungry hounds on his trail in full chase, could have beaten more anxiously or noisily than did mine, from the time I left Baltimore till I reached Philadelphia. The passage of the Susquehanna river at Havre de Grace was made by ferry boat at that time, on board of which I met a young coloured man by the name of Nichols, who came very near betraying me. He was a 'hand' on the boat, but instead of minding his business, he insisted upon knowing me, and asking me dangerous questions as to where I was going, and when I was coming back, etc. I got away from my old and inconvenient acquaintance as soon as I could decently do so, and went to another part of the boat. Once across the river I encountered a new danger. Only a few days before, I had been at work on a revenue-cutter, in Mr Price's shipyard, under the care of Captain McGowan. On the meeting at this point of the two trains, the one going South stopped on the track just opposite to the one going North, and it so happened that this Captain McGowan sat at a window where he could see me very distinctly, and would certainly have recognised me had he looked at me but for a second. Fortunately, in the hurry of the moment, he did not see me; and the trains soon passed each other on their respective ways. But this was not my only hair's breadth escape. A German blacksmith whom I knew well, was on the train with me, and looked at me very intently, as if he thought he had seen me somewhere before in his travels. I really believe he knew me, but had no heart to betray me. At any rate he saw me escaping and held his peace.

The last point of imminent danger, and the one I dreaded most, was Wilmington. Here we left the train, and took the steamboat for Philadelphia. In making the change here I again apprehended arrest, but no one disturbed me, and I was soon on the broad and beautiful Delaware, speeding away to the Quaker City. On reaching Philadelphia in the afternoon, I enquired of a coloured man how I could get on to New York. He directed me to the William Street depot, and thither I went, taking the train that night. I reached New York on Tuesday morning, having completed the journey in less than twenty-four hours. Such is briefly the manner of my escape from slavery – and the end of my experience as a slave. Other chapters will tell the story of my life as a freeman.

CHAPTER II

Life as a Freeman

Loneliness and insecurity – 'Allender's Jake'– Succoured by a sailor – David Ruggles – Marriage – Steamer *J. W. Richmond* – Stage to New Bedford – Arrival there – Driver's detention of baggage – Nathan Johnson – Change of Name – Why called 'Douglass' – Obtaining work – The *Liberator* and its editor

My free life began on the third of September 1838. On the morning of the 4th of that month, after an anxious and most perilous, but safe journey, I found myself in the big city of New York, a *free man*; one more added to the mighty throng which, like the confused waves of the troubled sea, surged to and fro between the lofty walls of Broadway. Though dazzled with the wonders which met me on every hand, my thoughts could not be much withdrawn from my strange situation. For the moment, the dreams of my youth, and the hopes of my manhood, were completely fulfilled. The bonds that had held me to 'old master' were broken. No man now had a right to call me his slave, or assert mastery over me. I was in the rough and tumble of an out-door world, to take my chance with the rest of its busy number. I have often been asked how I felt, when first I found myself on free soil; and my readers may share the same curiosity. There is scarcely anything in my experience about which I could not give a more satisfactory answer. A new world had opened upon me. If life is more than breath, and the 'quick round of blood', I lived more in one day than in a year of my slave life. It was a time of joyous excitement which words can but tamely describe. In a letter written to a friend soon after reaching New York, I said: 'I felt as one might feel upon escape from a den of hungry lions.' Anguish and grief, like darkness and rain, may be depicted; but gladness and joy, like the rainbow, defy the skill of pen or pencil. During ten or fifteen years I had, as it were, been dragging a heavy chain, which no strength of mine could break; I was not only a slave, but a slave for life. I might become a husband, a father, an aged man, but through all, from birth to death, from the cradle to the grave, I had felt myself doomed. All efforts I had previously made to secure my freedom, had not only failed, but had seemed only to rivet my fetters the more firmly, and to render my escape more difficult. Baffled, entangled, and discouraged, I had at times asked myself the question: may not my condition after all be God's work, and ordered for a wise purpose, and if so, was not submission my duty? A contest had in fact been going on in my mind for a long time, between the clear consciousness of right, and the plausible makeshifts of theology and superstition. The one held me an abject slave – a prisoner for life, punished for some transgression in which I had no lot or part; and the other counselled me to manly endeavour to secure my freedom. This contest was now ended: my chains were broken, and the victory brought me unspeakable joy. But my gladness was short lived, for I was not yet out of the reach and power of the slave-holders. I soon found that New York was not quite so free, or so safe a refuge as I had supposed, and a sense of loneliness and insecurity, again oppressed me most sadly. I chanced to meet on the street, a few hours after my landing, a fugitive slave, whom I had once known well in slavery. The information received from him alarmed me. The fugitive in question was known in Baltimore as 'Allender's Jake', but in New York he bore the more respectable name of 'William Dixon'. Jake, in law, was the property of Doctor Allender, and Tolly Allender, the son of the doctor, had once made an effort to recapture *Mr Dixon*, but had failed for want of evidence to support his claim. Jake told me the circumstances of this attempt, and how narrowly he escaped being sent back to slavery and torture. He told me that New York was then full of Southerners returning from the watering places North; that the coloured people of New York were not to be trusted; that there were hired men of my own colour who would betray me for a few dollars; that there were hired men ever on the look-out for fugitives; that I must trust no man with my secret; that I must not think of going either upon the wharves, or into any coloured boarding-house, for all such places were closely watched; that he was himself unable to help me; and, in fact, he seemed while speaking to me to fear lest I myself might be a spy, and a betrayer. Under this apprehension, as I suppose, he showed signs of wishing to be rid of me, and with whitewash-brush in hand, in search of work, he soon disappeared. This picture, given by poor 'Jake', of New York, was a damper to my enthusiasm. My little store of money would soon be exhausted, and since it would be unsafe for me to go on the wharves for work, and I had no introductions elsewhere, the prospect for me was far from cheerful. I saw the wisdom of keeping away from the shipyards, for, if pursued, as I felt certain I should be, Mr Auld would naturally seek me there, among the caulkers. Every door seemed closed against me. I was in the midst of an ocean of my fellow men, and yet a perfect stranger to everyone. I was without home, without acquaintance, without money, without credit, without work, and without any definite knowledge as to what course to take, or where to look for succour. In such an extremity, a man has something beside his new-born freedom to think of. While wandering about the streets of New York, and lodging at least one night among the barrels on one of the wharves, I was indeed free from slavery – but free from food and shelter as well. I kept my secret to myself as long as I could, but was compelled at last to seek someone who would befriend me, without taking advantage of my destitution to betray me. Such an one I found in a sailor named Stuart, a warm-hearted and generous fellow, who from his humble home on Centre Street, saw me standing on the opposite sidewalk, near 'The Tombs'. As he approached me, I ventured a remark to him which at once enlisted his interest in me. He took me to his home to spend the night, and in the morning went with me to Mr David Ruggles, the secretary of the New York Vigilance Committee, a co-worker with Isaac T. Hopper, Lewis and Arthur Tappan, Theodore S. Wright, Samuel Cornish, Thomas Downing, Phillip A. Bell and other true men of their time. All these 'save Mr Bell, who still lives, and is editor and publisher of a paper called the *Elevator*, in San Francisco', have finished their work on earth. Once in the hands of these brave and wise men, I felt comparatively safe. With Mr Ruggles, on the corner of Lispenard and Church Streets, I was hidden several days, during which time my intended wife came on from Baltimore at my call, to share the burdens of life with me. She was a free woman, and came at once on getting the good news of my safety. We were married by Revd J. W. C. Pennington, then a well-known and respected Presbyterian minister. I had no money with which to pay the marriage fee, but he seemed well pleased with our thanks.

Mr Ruggles was the first officer on the underground railroad with whom I met after coming North; and was indeed the only one with whom I had anything to do, till I became *such* an officer myself. Learning that my trade was that of a caulker, he promptly decided that the best place for me was in New Bedford, Mass. He told me that many ships for whaling voyages were fitted out there, that I might there find work at my trade, and make a good living. So on the day of the marriage ceremony, we took our little luggage to the steamer *John W. Richmond*, which at that time was one of the line running between New York and Newport, R. I. Forty-three years ago coloured travellers were not permitted in the cabin, nor allowed abaft the paddle-wheels of a steam vessel. They were compelled, whatever the weather might be, whether cold or hot, wet or dry, to spend the night on deck. Unjust as this regulation was, it did not trouble us much. We had fared much harder before. We arrived at Newport the next morning, and soon after an old-fashioned stage-coach with 'New Bedford' in large yellow letters on its sides, came down to the wharf. I had not money enough to pay our fare, and stood hesitating to know what to do. Fortunately for us, there were two Quaker gentlemen who were about to take passage on the stage – Friends William C. Taber and Joseph Ricketson – who at once discerned our true situation, and in a peculiarly quiet way, addressing me, Mr Taber said: 'Thee get in.' I never obeyed an order with more alacrity, and we were soon on our way to our new home. When we reached 'Stone Bridge', the passengers alighted for breakfast, and paid their fares to the driver. We took no breakfast, and when asked for our fares I told the driver I would make it right with him when we reached New Bedford. I expected some objection to this on his part, but he made none. When, however, we reached New Bedford he took our baggage, including three music books – two of them collections by Dyer, and one by Shaw – and held them until I was able to redeem them by paying to him the sums due for our rides. This was soon done, for Mr Nathan Johnson not only received me kindly, and hospitably, but, on being informed about our baggage, at once loaned me the two dollars with which to square accounts with the stage-driver. Mr and Mrs Nathan Johnson reached a good old age, and now rest from their labours. I am under many grateful obligations to them. They not only 'took me in when a stranger', and 'fed me when hungry', but taught me how to make an honest living.

Thus, in a fortnight after my flight from Maryland, I was safe in New Bedford – a citizen of the grand old commonwealth of Massachussetts.

Once initiated into my new life of freedom, and assured by Mr Johnson that I need not fear recapture in that city, a comparatively unimportant question arose, as to the name by which I should be known thereafter, in my new relation as a free man. The name given me by my dear mother was no less pretentious and long than Frederick Augustus Washington Bailey. I had, however, while living in Maryland dispensed with the Augustus Washington, and retained only Frederick Bailey. Between Baltimore and New Bedford, the better to conceal myself from the slave-hunters, I had parted with Bailey and called myself Johnson; but finding that in New Bedford the Johnson family was already so numerous, as to cause some confusion in distinguishing one from another, a change in this name seemed desirable. Nathan Johnson, mine host, was emphatic as to this necessity, and wished me to allow him to select a name for me. I consented, and he called me by my present name, the one by which I have been known for three and forty years – Frederick Douglass. Mr Johnson had just been reading the *Lady of the Lake*, and so pleased was he with its great character, that he wished me to bear his name. Since reading that charming poem myself, I have often thought that, considering the noble hospitality and manly character of Nathan Johnson, black man though he was, he, far more than I, illustrated the virtues of the Douglas of Scotland. Sure am I that if any slave-catcher had entered his domicile with a view to my recapture, Johnson would have been like him of the 'stalwart hand'.

The reader may be surprised – living in Baltimore as I had done for many years – when I tell the honest truth of the impressions I had in some way conceived of the social and material condition of the people at the North. I had no proper idea of the wealth, refinement, enterprise, and high civilisation of this section of the country. My *Columbian Orator*, almost my only book, had done nothing to enlighten me concerning Northern society. I had been taught that slavery was the bottom-fact of all wealth. With this foundation idea, I came naturally to the conclusion, that poverty must be the general condition of the people of the free States. A white man holding no slaves in the country from which I came, was usually an ignorant and poverty-stricken man. Men of this class were contemptuously called 'poor white trash'. Hence I supposed, that since the non-slave-holders at the South were ignorant, poor, and degraded as a class, the non-slave-holders at the North, must be in a similar condition. New Bedford therefore, which at that time was really the richest city in the Union, in proportion to its population, took me greatly by surprise, in the evidences it gave, of its solid wealth and grandeur. I found that even the labouring classes lived in better houses, that their houses were more elegantly furnished, and were more abundantly supplied with conveniences and comforts, than the houses of many who owned slaves on the Eastern Shore of Maryland. This was true, not only of the white people of that city, but it was so of my friend, Mr Johnson. He lived in a nicer house, dined at a more ample board, was the owner of more books, the reader of more newspapers, was more conversant with the moral, social, and political condition of the country and the world, than nine-tenths of the slave-holders in all Talbot county. I was not long in finding the cause of the difference in these respects, between the people of the North and South. It was the superiority of educated mind over mere brute force. I will not detain the reader by extended illustrations as to how my understanding was enlightened on this subject. On the wharves of New Bedford I received my first light. I saw there industry without bustle, labour without noise, toil – honest, earnest, and exhaustive, without the whip. There was no loud singing or hallooing, as at the wharves of Southern ports when ships were loading or unloading; no loud cursing or quarrelling; everything went on as smoothly as well-oiled machinery. One of the first incidents which impressed me with the superior mental character of labour in the North, over that of the South, was in the manner of loading and unloading vessels. In a Southern port twenty or thirty hands would be employed to do what five or six men, with the help of one ox, would do at the wharf in New Bedford. Main strength – human muscle – unassisted by intelligent skill, was slavery's method of labour. With a capital of about sixty dollars, in the shape of a good-natured old ox, attached to the end of a stout rope, New Bedford did the work of ten or twelve thousand dollars, represented in the bones and muscles of slaves, and did it far better. In a word, I found everything managed with a much more scrupulous regard to economy, both of men and things, time and strength, than in the country from which I had come. Instead of going a hundred yards to the spring, the maidservant had a well or pump at her elbow. The wood used for fuel was kept dry, and snugly piled away for winter. Here were sinks, drains, self-shutting gates, pounding-barrels, washing-machines, wringing-machines, and a hundred other contrivances for saving time and money. The ship-repairing docks showed the same thoughtful wisdom as was seen elsewhere. Everybody seemed in earnest. The carpenter struck the nail on its head, and the caulkers wasted no strength in idle flourishes of their mallets. Ships brought here for repairs, were made stronger and better than when new. I could have landed in no part of the United States where I should have found a more striking and gratifying contrast, not only to life generally in the South, but in the condition of the coloured people, than in New Bedford. No coloured man was really free, while residing in a slave State. He was ever more or less subject to the condition of his slave brother. In his colour was his badge of bondage. I saw in New Bedford the nearest approach to freedom and equality that I had ever seen. I was amazed when Mr Johnson told me that there was nothing in the laws or constitution of Massachusetts, that would prevent a coloured man from being governor of the State, if the people should see fit to elect him. There too the black man's children attended the same public schools with the white man's children, and apparently without objection from any quarter. To impress me with my security from recapture, and return to slavery, Mr Johnson assured me that no slave-holder could take a slave out of New Bedford; that there were men there who would lay down their lives to save me from such a fate. A threat was once made by a coloured man, to inform a Southern master where his runaway slave could be found. As soon as this threat became known to the coloured people, they were furious. A notice was read from the pulpit of the Third Christian Church – coloured – for a public meeting, when important business would be transacted – not stating what the important business was. In the meantime special measures had been taken to secure the attendance of the would-be Judas, and these had proved successful, for when the hour of meeting arrived, ignorant of the object for which they were called together, the offender was promptly in attendance. All the usual formalities were gone through, the prayer, appointments of president, secretaries, etc. Then the president, with an air of great solemnity, rose and said: 'Well, friends and brethren, we have got him here, and I would recommend that you young men should take him outside the door and kill him.' This was enough, there was a rush for the villain, who would probably have been killed but for his escape by an open window. He was never seen again in New Bedford.

The fifth day after my arrival I put on the clothes of a common labourer, and went upon the wharves in search of work. On my way down Union Street, I saw a large pile of coal in front of the house of the Revd Ephraim Peabody, the Unitarian minister. I went to the kitchen door, and asked the privilege of bringing in and putting away this coal. 'What will you charge?' said the lady. 'I will leave that to you, madam.' 'You may put it away,' she said. I was not long in accomplishing the job, when the dear lady put into my hand *two silver half-dollars*. To understand the emotion which swelled my heart as I clasped this

money, realising that I had no master who could take it from me – *that
it was mine – that my hands were my own*, and could earn more of the
precious coin – one must have been in some sense himself a slave. My
next job was stowing a sloop, at Uncle Gid Howland's wharf, with a
cargo of oil for New York. I was not only a freeman, but a free-working
man, and no Master Hugh stood ready at the end of the week to seize
my hard earnings,

The season was growing late and work was plenty. Ships were being
fitted out for whaling, and much wood was used in storing them. The
sawing of this wood was considered a good job. With the help of old
Friend Johnson – blessings on his memory! I got a 'saw' and 'buck', and
went at it. When I went into a store to buy a cord with which to brace
up my saw in the frame, I asked for a 'fip's' worth of cord. The man
behind the counter looked rather sharply at me, and said with equal
sharpness, 'You don't belong about here.' I was alarmed, and thought I
had betrayed myself. A fip in Maryland was six and a quarter cents,
called fourpence in Massachusetts, But no harm came, except my fear,
from the 'fipenny-bit' blunder, and I confidently and cheerfully went to
work with my saw and buck. It was new business to me, but I never did
better work, or more of it in the same space of time for Covey, the
negro-breaker, than I did for myself in these earliest years of my
freedom.

Notwithstanding the just and humane sentiment of New Bedford
three and forty years ago, the place was not entirely free from race and
colour prejudice. The good influence of the Roaches, Rodmans,
Arnolds, Grinnells, and Robesons did not pervade all classes of its
people. The test of the real civilisation of the community came when I
applied for work at my trade, and then my repulse was emphatic and
decisive. It so happened that Mr Rodney French, a wealthy and
enterprising citizen, distinguished as an anti-slavery man, was fitting
out a vessel for a whaling voyage, upon which there was a heavy job of
caulking and coppering to be done. I had some skill in both branches,
and applied to Mr French for work. He, generous man that he was,
told me he would employ me, and I might go at once to the vessel. I
obeyed him, but upon reaching the float-stage, where other caulkers
were at work, I was told that every white man would leave the ship in
her unfinished condition, if I struck a blow at my trade upon her. This
uncivil, inhuman, and selfish treatment was not so shocking and
scandalous in my eyes at the time as it now appears to me. Slavery had
inured me to hardships that made ordinary trouble sit lightly upon me.
Could I have worked at my trade, I could have earned two dollars a day,

but as a common labourer, I received but one dollar. The difference was of great importance to me, but if I could not get two dollars, I was glad to get one; and so I went to work for Mr French as a common labourer. The consciousness that I was free – no longer a slave – kept me cheerful under this, and many similar proscriptions, which I was destined to meet in New Bedford, and elsewhere on the free soil of Massachusetts. For instance, though white and coloured children attended the same schools, and were treated kindly by their teachers, the New Bedford Lyceum refused, till several years after my residence in that city, to allow any coloured person to attend the lectures delivered in its hall. Not until such men as Hon. Chas. Sumner, Theodore Parker, Ralph W. Emerson and Horace Mann refused to lecture in their course while there was such a restriction, was it abandoned.

Becoming satisfied that I could not rely on my trade in New Bedford to give me a living, I prepared myself to do any kind of work that came to hand. I sawed wood, shovelled coal, dug cellars, moved rubbish from backyards, worked on the wharves, loaded and unloaded vessels, and scoured their cabins.

This was an uncertain and unsatisfactory mode of life, for it kept me too much of the time in search of work. Fortunately it was not to last long. One of the gentlemen of whom I have spoken as being in company with Mr Taber on the Newport wharf, when he said to me 'thee get in', was Mr Joseph Ricketson; and he was the proprietor of a large candle-works in the south part of the city. In this 'candle-works' as it was called, though no *candles* were manufactured there, by the kindness of Mr Ricketson, I found what is of the utmost importance to a young man just starting in life – constant employment and regular wages. My work in this oil refinery required good wind and muscle. Large casks of oil were to be moved from place to place, and much heavy lifting to be done. Happily I was not deficient in the requisite qualities. Young, twenty-one years old, strong, and active, and ambitious to do my full share, I soon made myself useful, and, I think, was liked by the men who worked with me, though they were all white. I was retained here as long as there was anything for me to do; when I went again to the wharves, and obtained work as a labourer on two vessels which belonged to Mr George Howland, and which were being repaired and fitted up for whaling. My employer was a man of great industry: a hard driver, but a good paymaster, and I got on well with him. I was not only fortunate in finding work with Mr Howland, but in my work-fellows. I have seldom met three working-men more intelligent than were John Briggs, Abraham Rodman, and Solomon Pennington, who laboured with me on the *Java* and *Golconda*. They were sober, thoughtful, and upright, thoroughly imbued with the spirit of liberty, and I am much indebted to them, for many valuable ideas and impressions. They taught me that all coloured men were not light-hearted triflers, incapable of serious thought or effort. My next place of work, was at the brass-foundry owned by Mr Richmond. My duty here was to blow the bellows, swing the crane, and empty the flasks in which castings were made; and at times this was hot and heavy work. The articles produced here were mostly for ship work, and in the busy season, the foundry was in operation night and day. I have often worked two nights and each working day of the week. My foreman, Mr Cobb, was a good man, and more than once protected me from abuse that one or more of the hands was disposed to throw upon me. While in this situation I had little time for mental improvement. Hard work, night and day, over a furnace hot enough to keep the metal running like water, was more favourable to action than thought; yet here, I often nailed a newspaper to the post near my bellows, and read while I was performing the up and down motion of the heavy beam, by which the bellows was inflated and discharged. It was the pursuit of knowledge under difficulties, and I look back to it now, after so many years, with some complacency and a little wonder, that I could have been so earnest and persevering in any pursuit, other than for my daily bread. I certainly saw nothing in the conduct of those around to inspire me with such interest: they were all devoted exclusively to what their hands found to do. I am glad to be able to say that during my engagement in this foundry, no complaint was ever made against me, that I did not do my work, and do it well. The bellows which I worked by main strength was, after I left, moved by a steam engine.

I had been living four or five months in New Bedford when there came a young man to me with a copy of the *Liberator*, the paper edited by William Lloyd Garrison, and published by Isaac Knapp, and asked me to subscribe for it. I told him I had but just escaped from slavery, and was of course very poor, and had no money then to pay for it. He was very willing to take me as a subscriber, notwithstanding, and from this time I was brought into contact with the mind of Mr Garrison, and his paper took a place in my heart, second only to the Bible. It detested slavery, and made no truce with the traffickers in the bodies and souls of men. It preached human brotherhood; it exposed hypoc-risy and wickedness in high places; it denounced oppression, and with all the solemnity of 'Thus saith the Lord', demanded the complete emancipation of my race. I loved this paper and its editor. He seemed to me, an all-sufficient match for every opponent, whether they spoke in the name of the law, or the gospel. His words were full of holy fire, and straight to the point. Something of a hero-worshipper by nature, here was one to excite my admiration and reverence.

Soon after becoming a reader of the *Liberator*, it was my privilege to listen to a lecture in Liberty Hall, by Mr Garrison, its editor. He was then a young man, of a singularly pleasing countenance, and earnest and impressive manner. On this occasion he announced nearly all his heresies. His Bible was his text book – held sacred as the very word of the Eternal Father. He believed in sinless perfection, complete submission to insults and injuries, and literal obedience to the injunction 'if smitten on one cheek, to turn the other also'. Not only was Sunday a Sabbath, but all days were Sabbaths, and to be kept holy. All sectarianism was false and mischievous – the regenerated throughout the world, being members of one body, and the head Christ Jesus. *Prejudice against colour, was rebellion against God.* Of all men beneath the sky, the slaves – because most neglected and despised – were nearest and dearest to His great heart. Those ministers who defended slavery from the Bible, were of their 'father, the devil'; and those churches which fellow-shipped slave-holders as Christians, were synagogues of Satan, and our nation was a nation of liars. He was never loud and noisy, but calm and serene as a summer sky, and as pure. 'You are the man – the Moses, raised up by God, to deliver his modern Israel from bondage,' was the spontaneous feeling of my heart, as I sat away back in the hall and listened to his mighty words – mighty in truth – mighty in their simple earnestness. I had not long been a reader of the *Liberator*, and a listener to its editor, before I got a clear comprehension of the principles of the anti-slavery movement. I had already its spirit, and only needed to understand its principles and measures, and as I became acquainted with these my hope for the ultimate freedom of my race increased. Every week the *Liberator* came, and every week I made myself master of its contents. All the anti-slavery meetings held in New Bedford I promptly attended, my heart bounding at every true utterance against the slave system, and every rebuke of it by its friends and supporters. Thus passed the first three years of my free life. I had not then dreamed of the possibility of my becoming a public advocate of the cause so deeply imbedded in my heart. It was enough for me to listen, to receive, and applaud the great words of others, and only whisper in private, among the white labourers on the wharves and elsewhere, the truths which burned in my heart.

CHAPTER III

Introduced to the Abolitionists

Anti-slavery convention at Nantucket – First speech – Much
sensation – Extraordinary speech of Mr Garrison – Anti-slavery
agency – Youthful enthusiasm – Fugitive slaveship doubted –
Experience in slavery written – Danger of recapture

In the summer of 1841, a grand anti-slavery convention was held in
Nantucket, under the auspices of Mr Garrison and his friends. I had
taken no holiday since establishing myself in New Bedford, and feeling
the need of a little rest, I determined on attending the meeting, though
I had no thought of taking part in any of its proceedings. Indeed, I was
not aware that anyone connected with the convention so much as knew
my name. Mr William C. Coffin, a prominent abolitionist in those
days of trial, had heard me speaking to my coloured friends in the little
schoolhouse on Second Street, where we worshipped. He sought me
out in the crowd, and invited me to say a few words to the convention.
Thus sought out, and thus invited, I was induced to express the feelings
inspired by the occasion, and the fresh recollection of the scenes
through which I had passed as a slave. It was with the utmost difficulty
that I could stand erect, or that I could command and articulate two
words without hesitation or stammering. I trembled in every limb. I am
not sure that my embarrassment was not the most effective part of my
speech, if speech it could be called. At any rate, this is about the only
part of my performance that I now distinctly remember. The audience
sympathised with me at once, and from having been remarkably quiet,
became much excited. Mr Garrison followed me, taking me as his text,
and now, whether I had made an eloquent plea in behalf of freedom, or
not, his was one, never to be forgotten. Those who had heard him
oftenest, and had known him longest, were astonished at his masterly
effort. For the time, he possessed that almost fabulous inspiration,
often referred to, but seldom attained, by which a public meeting is
transformed, as it were, into a single individuality, the orator swaying a
thousand heads and hearts at once, and by the simple majesty of his

all-controlling thought, converting his hearers into the express image of his own soul. That night there were at least a thousand Garrisonians in Nantucket!

At the close of this great meeting, I was duly waited on by Mr John A. Collins, then the general agent of the Massachusetts Anti-Slavery Society, and urgently solicited by him to become an agent of that society, and publicly advocate its principles. I was reluctant to take the proffered position. I had not been quite three years from slavery and was honestly distrustful of my ability, and I wished to be excused. Besides, publicity might discover me to my master, and many other objections presented themselves. But Mr Collins was not to be refused, and I finally consented to go out for three months, supposing I should, in that length of time, come to the end of my story and my consequent usefulness.

Here opened for me a new life – a life for which I had had no preparation. Mr Collins used to say, when introducing me to an audience, I was a 'graduate from the peculiar institution, with my diploma *written on my back*'. The three years of my freedom had been spent in the hard school of adversity. My hands seemed to be furnished with something like a leather coating, and I had marked out for myself a life of rough labour, suited to the hardness of my hands, as a means of supporting my family and rearing my children.

Young, ardent, and hopeful, I entered upon this new life in the full gush of unsuspecting enthusiasm. The cause was good, the men engaged in it were good, the means to attain its triumph, good. Heaven's blessing must attend all, and freedom must soon be given to the millions pining under a ruthless bondage. My whole heart went with the holy cause, and my most fervent prayer to the Almighty Disposer of the hearts of men, was continually offered for its early triumph. In this enthusiastic spirit I dropped into the ranks of freedom's friends, and went forth to the battle. For a time, I was made to forget that my skin was dark and my hair crisped. For a time, I regretted that I could not have shared the hardships and dangers endured by the earlier workers for the slave's release. I found, however, full soon, that my enthusiasm been extravagant, that hardships and dangers were not all over, and that the life now before me had its shadows also, as well as its sunbeams.

Among the first duties assigned me on entering the ranks, was to travel in company with Mr George Foster to secure subscribers to the *Anti-Slavery Standard* and the *Liberator*. With him I travelled and lectured through the eastern counties of Massachusetts. Much interest was awakened – large meetings assembled. Many came, no doubt from curiosity, to hear what a negro could say his own cause. I was generally introduced as a 'chattel' – 'a thing'– a piece of Southern property – the chairman assuring the audience that *it* could speak. *Fugitive slaves* were rare then, and as a fugitive-slave lecturer, I had the advantage of being a 'brand-new fact' – the first one out. Up to that time, a coloured man was deemed a fool who confessed himself a runaway slave, not only because of the danger to which he exposed himself of being retaken, but because it was a confession of a very low origin. Some of my coloured friends in New Bedford thought very badly of my wisdom, in thus exposing and degrading myself. The only precaution I took at the beginning, to prevent Master Thomas from knowing where I was and what I was about, was the withholding my former name, my master's name, and the name of the State and county from which I came. During the first three or four months, my speeches were almost exclusively made up of narrations of my own personal experience as a slave. 'Let us have the facts,' said the people. So also said friend George Foster, who always wished to pin me down to my simple narrative. 'Give us the facts,' said Collins, 'we will take care of the philosophy.' Just here arose some embarrassment. It was impossible for me to repeat the same old story, month after month, and to keep up an interest in it. It was new to the people, it is true, but it was an old story to me; and to go through with it night after night, was a task altogether too mechanical for my nature. 'Tell your story, Frederick,' would whisper my revered friend, Mr Garrison, as I stepped upon the platform. I could not always follow the injunction, for I was now reading and thinking. New views of the subject were being presented to my mind. It did not entirely satisfy me to *narrate* wrongs; I felt like *denouncing* them. I could not always curb my moral indignation for the perpetrators of slave-holding villainy, long enough for a circumstantial statement of the facts, which I felt almost sure everybody must know. Besides, I was growing, and needed room. 'People won't believe you ever were a slave, Frederick, if you keep on this way,' said friend Foster. 'Be yourself,' said Collins, 'and tell your story.' 'Better have a little of the plantation speech than not,' it was said to me; 'it is not best that you seem too learned.' These excellent friends were actuated by the best of motives, and were not altogether wrong in their advice; and still, I must speak just the word that seemed to *me* the word to be spoken *by* me.

At last the apprehended trouble came. People doubted if I had ever been a slave. They said I did not talk like a slave, look like a slave, nor act like a slave, and that they believed I had never been south of Mason and Dixon's line. 'He don't tell us where he came from – what his master's name was, nor how he got away; besides, he is educated, and is, in this, a contradiction of all the facts we have concerning the ignorance of the slaves.' Thus I was in a pretty fair way to be denounced as an impostor. The committee of the Massachusetts Anti-Slavery knew all the facts in my case, and agreed with me thus far in the prudence of keeping them private; but going down the aisles of the churches in which my meetings were held, and hearing the out-spoken Yankees repeatedly saying, 'He's never been a slave, I'll warrant you,' I resolved to dispel all doubt at no distant day, by such a revelation of facts as could not be made by any other than a genuine fugitive. In a little less than four years, therefore, after becoming a public lecturer, I was induced to write out the leading facts connected with my experience in slavery, giving names of persons, place and dates – thus putting it in the power of any who doubted, to ascertain the truth or falsehood of my story. This statement soon became known in Maryland, and I had reason to believe that an effort would be made to recapture me.

It is not probable that any open attempt to secure me as a slave could have succeeded, further than the obtainment by my master, of the money value of my bones and sinews. Fortunately for me, in the four years of my labours in the abolition cause, I had gained many friends, who would have suffered themselves to be taxed to almost any extent to save me from slavery. It was felt that I had committed the double offence of running away and of exposing the secrets and crimes of slavery and slave-holders. There was a double motive for seeking my re-enslavement – avarice and vengeance; and while, as I have said, there was little probability of successful recapture, if attempted openly, I was constantly in danger of being spirited away, at a moment when my friends could render me no assistance. In travelling about from place to place, often alone, I was much exposed to this sort of attack. Anyone cherishing the design to betray me, could easily do so, by simply tracking my whereabouts through the anti-slavery journals, for my movements and meetings were made known through these in advance. My friends, Mr Garrison and Mr Phillips, had no faith in the power of Massachusetts to protect me in my right to liberty. Public sentiment and the law, in their opinion, would hand me over to the tormentors. Mr Phillips especially considered me in danger, and said, when I showed him the manuscript of my story, if in my place, he would 'throw it into the fire'. Thus, the reader will observe, that overcoming one difficulty only opened the way for another; and that though I had reached a free State, and had attained a position for public usefulness, I was still under the liability of losing all I had gained.

CHAPTER IV

Recollections of Old Friends

Work in Rhode Island – Dorr war – Further labours in Rhode Island and elsewhere in New England

In the State of Rhode Island, under the leadership of Thomas W. Dorr, an effort was made in 1841 to set aside the old colonial charter, under which that State had lived and flourished since the Revolution, and to replace it with a new constitution having such improvements as it was thought that time and experience had shown to be wise and necessary. This new constitution was especially framed to enlarge the basis of representation so far as the white people of the State were concerned – to abolish an odious property qualification, and to confine the right of suffrage to white male citizens only. Mr Dorr was himself a well-meaning man, and, after his fashion, a man of broad and progressive views, quite in advance of the party with which he acted. To gain their support, he consented to this restriction to a class, of a right which ought to be enjoyed by all citizens. In this he consulted policy rather than right, and at last shared the fate of all compromisers and trimmers, for he was disastrously defeated. The prospective features of his constitution shocked the sense of right, and roused the moral indignation of the abolitionists of the State, a class which would otherwise have gladly co-operated with him, at the same time that it did nothing to win support from the conservative class which clung to the old charter. Anti-slavery men wanted a new constitution, but they did not want a defective instrument, which required reform at the start. The result was that such men as William M. Chase, Thomas Davis, George L. Clark, Asa Fairbanks, Alphonso Janes, and others, of Providence; the Perry brothers of Westerly; John Brown and C. C. Eldridge of East Greenwich; Daniel Mitchell, William Adams, and Robert Shove of Pawtucket; Peleg Clark, Caleb Kelton, G. J. Adams, and the Anthonys and Goulds of Coventry and vicinity; Edward Norris of Woonsocket; and other abolitionists of the State, decided that the time had come, when people of Rhode Island might be taught a more comprehensive gospel of human rights than had gotten itself into this Dorr constitution. The public mind was awake, and one class of its people least, was ready to work with us to the extent of seeking to defeat the proposed constitution, though their reasons for such work were far different from ours. Stephen S. Foster, Parker Pillsbury, Abby Kelley, James Monroe and myself were called to the State to advocate equal rights, as against this narrow and proscriptive constitution. The work to which we were invited was not free from difficulty. The majority of the people were evidently with the new constitution; even the word *white* in it chimed well with the popular prejudice against the coloured race, and at the first, helped to make the movement popular. On the other hand. the arguments which the Dorr men could urge against a property qualification for suffrage were equally cogent against a colour qualification, and this was our advantage. But the contest was intensely bitter and exciting. We were as usual denounced as intermeddlers – carpet-bagger had not come into use at that time – and were told to mind our own business, and the like; a mode defence common to men when called to account for mean and discreditable conduct. Stephen S. Foster, Parker Pillsbury, and the rest of us were not the kind of men to be ordered off by that sort of opposition. We cared nothing for the Dorr party on the one hand, nor the 'law and order party' on the other. What we wanted, and what we laboured to obtain, was a constitution free from the narrow, selfish, and senseless limitation of the word *white*. Naturally enough when we said a strong and striking word against the Dorr Constitution, the conservatives were pleased and applauded, while the Dorr men were disgusted and indignant. Foster and Pillsbury were like the rest of us, young, strong, and at their best in this contest. The splendid vehemence of the one, and the weird and terrible denunciations of the other, never failed to stir up mob-ocratic wrath wherever they spoke. Foster especially was effective in this line His theory was that he must make converts or mobs. If neither came, he charged it either to his want of skill or his unfaithfulness. I was much with Mr Foster during the tour in Rhode Island, and though at times he seemed to me extravagant and need-lessly offensive in his manner of presenting his ideas, yet take him for all in all, he was one of the most impressive advocates the cause of the American slave ever had. No white man ever made the black man's cause more completely his own. Abby Kelley, since Abby Kelley Foster, was perhaps the most successful of any of us. Her youth and simple Quaker beauty, combined with her wonderful earnestness, her large knowledge and great logical power, bore down all opposition in the end, wherever she spoke, though she had been pelted with foul eggs, and no less foul words, from the noisy mobs which attended us.

Monroe and I were less aggressive than either of our co-workers, and of course did not provoke the same resistance. He at least, had the eloquence that charms, and the skill that disarms. I think that our labours in Rhode Island during this Dorr excitement did more to abolitionise the State than any previous, or subsequent work. It was the 'tide taken at the flood'. One effect of these labours was to induce the old 'Law and Order' party, when it set about making its new constitution, to avoid the narrow folly of the Dorrites, and make a constitution which should not abridge any man's rights on account of race or colour. Such a constitution was finally adopted.

Owing perhaps to my efficiency in this campaign I was, for a while, employed in farther labours in Rhode Island by the State Anti-Slavery Society, and made there many friends to my cause as well as to myself. As a class, the abolitionists of this State partook of the spirit of its founder. They had their own opinions, were independent, and called no man master. I have reason to remember them most gratefully. They received me as a man and a brother, when I was new from the house of bondage, and had few of the graces derived from free and refined society. They took me with earnest hand to their homes and hearths, and made me feel that though I wore the burnished livery of the sun, I was still a countryman and kinsman of whom they were never ashamed. I can never forget the Clarks, Keltons, Chaces, Browns, Adams, Greenes, Sissons, Eldredges, Mitchells, Shoves, Anthonys, Applins, Janes, Goulds and Fairbanks, and many others.

While thus remembering the noble anti-slavery men and women of Rhode Island, I do not forget that I suffered much rough usage within her borders. It was, like all the Northern States at that time, under the influence of slave power, and often showed a proscription and persecuting spirit, especially upon its railways, steamboats, and public-houses. The Stonington route was a 'hard road' for a coloured man 'to travel' in that day. I was several times dragged from the cars for the *crime* of being coloured. On the Sound, between New York and Stonington, there were the same proscriptions which I have before named, as enforced on the steamboats running between New York and Newport. No coloured man was allowed abaft the wheel, and in all seasons of the year, in heat or cold, wet or dry, the deck was his only place. If I would lie down at night, I must do so upon the freight on deck, and this in cold weather was not a very comfortable bed. When travelling in company with my white friends I always urged them to leave me, go into the cabin and take their comfortable berths. I saw no reason why they should be miserable because I was. Some of them took my advice very readily. I confess, however, that while I was entirely honest in urging them to go, and saw no principle that should bind them to stay and suffer with me, I always felt a little nearer to those who did not take my advice, and persisted in sharing my hardships with me.

There is something in the world above fixed rules and the logic of right and wrong, and there is some foundation for recognising works, which may be called works of supererogation. Wendell Phillips, James Monroe and William White were always dear to me for their nice feeling on this point. I have known James Monroe to pull his coat about him, crawl upon the cotton bales between decks, and pass the night with me, without a murmur. Wendell Phillips would never go into a first-class car while I was forced into what was called the Jim Crow car. True men they were, who could accept welcome at no man's table where I was refused. I speak of these gentlemen, not as singular or exceptional cases, but as representatives of a large class of the early workers for the abolition of slavery. As a general rule, there was little difficulty in obtaining suitable places in New England after 1840, where I could plead the cause of my people. The abolitionists had passed the Red Sea of mobs, and had conquered the right of a respectful hearing. I, however, found several towns in which the people closed their doors, and refused to entertain the subject. Notably among these was Hartford, Conn., and Grafton, Mass. In the former place, Messrs Garrison, Hudson, Foster, Abby Kelley and myself determined to hold our meetings under the open sky, which we did in a little court under the eaves of the 'sanctuary', where the Revd Dr Hawes ministered, with much satisfaction to ourselves, and I think with advantage to our cause. In Grafton I was alone, and there was neither house, hall, church, nor market-place, in which I could speak to the people; but *determined to speak*, I went to the hotel and borrowed a dinner bell, with which in hand, I passed through the principal streets, ringing the bell and crying out, '*Notice!* Frederick Douglass, recently a slave, will lecture on American Slavery, on Grafton Common, this evening at 7 o'clock. Those who would like to hear of the workings of slavery, by one of the slaves, are respectfully invited to attend.' This notice brought out a large audience, after which the largest church in the town was open to me. Only in one instance was I compelled to pursue this course thereafter, and that was in Manchester, N.H., and my labours there were followed by similar results. When people found that I would be heard, they saw it was the part of wisdom to open the way for me.

My treatment in the use of public conveyances about these times was extremely rough, especially on the 'Eastern Railroad, from Boston to Portland'. On that road, as on many others, there was a mean, dirty, and uncomfortable car set apart for coloured travellers, called the 'Jim Crow' car. Regarding this as the fruit of slave-holding prejudice, and being determined to fight the spirit of slavery wherever I might find it, I resolved to avoid this car, though it sometimes required some courage to do so. The coloured people generally accepted the situation, and complained of me as making matters worse, rather than better, by refusing to submit to this proscription. I, however, persisted, and sometimes was soundly beaten by conductor and brakeman. On one occasion, six of these 'fellows of the baser sort', under the direction of the conductor, set out to eject me from my seat. As usual, I had purchased a first-class ticket, and paid the required sum for it, and on the requirement of the conductor to leave, refused to do so, when he called on these men 'to snake me out'. They attempted to obey with an air which plainly told me they relished the job. They, however, found me *much attached* to my seat, and in removing me I tore away two or three of the surrounding ones, on which I held with a firm grasp, and did the car no service in some other respects. I was strong and muscular, and the seats were not then so firmly attached or of as solid make as now. The result was that Stephen A. Chase, superintendent of the road, ordered all passenger trains to pass through Lynn, where I then lived, without stopping. This was a great inconvenience to the people, large numbers of whom did business in Boston, and other points of the road. Led on, however, by James N. Buffum, Jonathan Buffum, Christopher Robinson, William Bassett and others, the people of Lynn stood bravely by me, and denounced the railroad management in emphatic terms. Mr Chase made reply that a railroad corporation was neither a religious nor reformatory body; that the road was run for the accommodation of the public, and that *it* required the exclusion of coloured people from its cars. With an air of triumph he told us that we ought not to expect a railroad company to be better than the Evangelical Church, and that until the churches abolished the 'negro pew', we ought not to expect the railroad company to abolish the negro car. This argument was certainly good enough against the church, but good for nothing as against the demands of justice and equality. My old and dear friend, J. N. Buffum, made a point against the company that they 'often allowed dogs and monkeys to ride in first-class cars, and yet excluded a man like Frederick Douglass!' In a

very few years this barbarous practice was put away, and I think there
have been no instances of such exclusion during the past thirty years;
and coloured people now, everywhere in New England, ride upon
equal terms with other passengers.

CHAPTER V

One Hundred Conventions

Anti-slavery conventions held in parts of New England, and in
some of the Middle and Western States – Mobs, incidents, etc.

The year 1843 was one of remarkable anti-slavery activity. The New
England Anti-Slavery Society at its annual meeting, held in the spring
of that year, resolved, under the auspices of Mr Garrison and his
friends, to hold a series of one hundred conventions. The territory
embraced in this plan for creating anti-slavery sentiment included New
Hampshire, Vermont, New York, Ohio, Indiana and Pennsylvania. I
had the honour to be chosen one of the agents to assist in these
proposed conventions, and I never entered upon any work with more
heart and hope. All that the American people needed, I thought, was
light. Could they know slavery as I knew it, they would hasten to the
work of its extinction. The corps of speakers who were to be associated
with me in carrying on these conventions were Messrs George
Bradburn, John A. Collins, James Monroe, William A. White, Charles
L. Remond and Sydney Howard Gay. They were all masters of the
subject, and some of them able and eloquent orators. It was a piece of
great good fortune to me, only a few years from slavery as I was, to be
brought into contact with such men. It was a real campaign, and
required nearly six months for its accomplishment.

Those who only know the State of Vermont as it is today, can hardly
understand, and must wonder that there was need for anti-slavery
effort within its borders forty years ago. Our first convention was held
in Middlebury, its chief seat of learning, and the home of William
Slade, who was for years the co-worker with John Quincy Adams in
Congress; and yet in this town the opposition to our anti-slavery

convention was intensely bitter and violent. The only man of note in
the town whom I now remember as giving us sympathy or welcome
was Mr Edward Barber, who was a man of courage as well as ability,
and did his best to make our convention a success. In advance of our
arrival, the college students had very industriously and mischievously
placarded the town with violent aspersions of our characters, and the
grossest misrepresentations of our principles, measures, and objects. I
was described as an escaped convict from the State Prison, and the
other speakers were assailed not less slanderously. Few people attended
our meeting, and apparently little was accomplished by it. In the
neighbouring town of Ferrisburgh the case was different and more
favourable. The way had been prepared for us by such stalwart anti-
slavery workers as Orson S. Murray, Charles C. Burleigh, Rowland T.
Robinson and others. Upon the whole, however, the several towns
visited showed that Vermont was surprisingly under the influence of
the slave power. Her proud boast that no slave had ever been delivered
up to his master within her borders did not hinder her hatred of *anti*-
slavery. What was true of the Green Mountain State in this respect,
was most discouragingly true of New York, the State next visited. All
along the Erie canal, from Albany to Buffalo, there was apathy,
indifference, aversion, and sometimes mob-ocratic spirit evinced. Even
Syracuse, afterwards the home of the humane Samuel J. May, and the
scene of the 'Jerry rescue', where Gerrit Smith, Beriah Greene,
William Goodell, Alvin Stewart and other able men afterwards taught
their noblest sons, would not at that time furnish us with church,
market, house or hall in which to hold our meetings. Discovering this
state of things, some of our number were disposed to turn their backs
upon the town, and shake its dust from their feet, but of these, I am
glad to say, I was not one. I had somewhere read of a command to go
into the hedges and highways and compel men to come in. Mr Stephen
Smith, under whose hospitable roof we were made at home, thought as
I did. It would be easy to silence anti-slavery agitation if refusing its
agents the use of halls and churches could effect that result. The house
of our friend Smith stood on the south-west corner of the park, which
was well covered with young trees, too small to furnish shade or
shelter, but better than none. Taking my stand under a small tree, in
the south-east corner of this park, I began to speak in the morning to
an audience of five persons, and before the close of the afternoon
meeting I had before me not less than five hundred. In the evening I
was waited upon by the officers of the Congregational Church, who
tendered the use of an old wooden building, which they had deserted

for a better, but still owned; and here our convention was continued during three days. I believe there has been no trouble to find places in Syracuse in which to hold anti-slavery meetings since. I never go there without endeavouring to see that tree, which, like the cause it sheltered, has grown large and strong and imposing.

I believe my first offence against our Anti-Slavery Israel, was committed during these Syracuse meetings. It was on this wise: Our general agent, John A. Collins, had recently returned from England full of communistic ideas, which ideas would do away with individual property, and have all things in common. He had arranged a corps of speakers of his communistic persuasion, consisting of John O. Wattles, Nathaniel Whiting and John Orvis to follow our anti-slavery conventions, and while our meeting was in progress in Syracuse, a meeting, as the reader will observe, obtained under much difficulty, Mr Collins came in with his new friends and doctrines, and proposed to adjourn our anti-slavery discussions and take up the subject of communism. To this I ventured to object. I held that it was imposing an additional burden of unpopularity on our cause, and an act of bad faith with the people, who paid the salary of Mr Collins, and were responsible for these hundred conventions. Strange to say, my course in this matter did not meet the approval of Mrs W. H. Chapman, an influential member of the board of managers of the Massachusetts Anti-Slavery Society, and called out a sharp reprimand from her, for my insubordination to my superiors. This was a strange and distressing revelation to me, and one of which I was not soon relieved. I thought I had only done my duty, and I think so still. The chief reason for the reprimand was the use which the liberty party papers would make of my seeming rebellion against the commanders of our Anti-Slavery Army.

In the growing city of Rochester we had in every way a better reception. Abolitionists of all shades of opinion were broad enough to give the Garrisonians, for such we were, a hearing. Samuel D. Porter and the Avery family, though they belonged to the Gerrit Smith, Myron Holly and William Goodell school, were not so narrow as to refuse us the use of their church for the convention. They heard our moral suasion arguments, and in a manly way met us in debate. We were opposed to carrying the anti-slavery cause to the ballot-box, and they believed in carrying it there. They looked at slavery as a creature of *law*; we regarded it as a creature of public opinion. It is surprising how small the difference appears as I look back to it, over the space of forty years; yet at the time, this difference was immense.

During our stay at Rochester we were hospitably entertained by Isaac and Amy Post, two people of all-bounding benevolence, the truest and best of Long Island, and Elias Hicks, Quakers. They were not more amiable than brave, for they never seemed to ask, What will the world say? but walked straight forward in what seemed to them the line of duty, please or offend whomsoever it might. Many a poor fugitive slave found shelter under their roof, when such shelter was hard to find elsewhere, and I mention them here in the warmth and fulness of earnest gratitude.

Pleased with our success in Rochester, we – that is Mr Bradburn and myself – made our way to Buffalo, then a rising city of steamboats, bustle, and business. Buffalo was too busy to attend to such matters as we had in hand. Our friend, Mr Marsh, had been able to secure for our convention only an old dilapidated and deserted room, formerly used as a post office. We went at the time appointed, and found seated a few cabmen in their coarse, everyday clothes, whips in hand, while their teams were standing on the street waiting for a job. Friend Bradburn looked around upon this unpromising audience, and turned upon his heel, saying he would not speak to 'such a set of ragamuffins', and took the first steamer to Cleveland, the home of his brother Charles, and left me to 'do' Buffalo alone. For nearly a week I spoke every day in this old post office, to audiences constantly increasing in numbers and respectability, till the Baptist Church was thrown open to me; and when this became too small, I went on Sunday into the open park and addressed an assembly of four or five thousand persons. After this my coloured friends, Charles L. Remond, Henry Highland Garnett, Theodore S. Wright, Amos G. Beaman, Charles M. Ray and other well-known coloured men, held a convention here, and then Remond and myself left for our next meeting in Chester county, Ohio. This was held in a great shed, built by the abolitionists, of whom Dr Abram Brook and Valentine Nicholson were the most noted, for this special purpose. Thousands gathered here and were addressed by Bradburn, White, Monroe, Remond, Gay and myself. The influence of this meeting was deep and widespread. It would be tedious to tell of all, or a small part of all that was interesting and illustrative of the difficulties encountered by the early advocates of anti-slavery in connection with this campaign, and hence I leave this part of it at once.

From Ohio we divided our forces and went into Indiana. At our first meeting we were mobbed, and some of us got our good clothes spoiled by evil-smelling eggs. This was at Richmond, where Henry

Clay had been recently invited to the high seat of the Quaker meeting-house, just after his gross abuse of Mr Mendenhall, because of his presenting him a respectful petition, asking him to emancipate his slaves. At Pendleton this mob-ocratic spirit was even more pronounced. It was found impossible to obtain a building in which to hold our convention, and our friends, Dr Fussell and others, erected a platform in the woods, where quite a large audience assembled. Mr Bradburn, Mr White, and myself were in attendance. As soon as we began to speak, a mob of about sixty of the roughest characters I ever looked upon ordered us, through its leaders, to 'be silent', threatening us, if we were not, with violence. We attempted to dissuade them, but they had not come to parley but to fight, and were well armed. They tore down the platform on which we stood, assaulted Mr White, knocking out several of his teeth; dealt a heavy blow on William A. White, striking him on the back part of the head badly cutting his scalp and felling him to the ground. Undertaking to fight my way through the crowd with a stick which I caught up in the *mêlée*, I attracted the fury of the mob, which laid me prostrate on the ground under a torrent of blows. Leaving me thus, with my right hand broken, and in a state of unconsciousness, the mob-ocrats hastily mounted their horses and rode to Andersonville, where most of them resided. I was soon raised up and revived by Neal Hardy, a kind-hearted member of the Society of Friends, and carried by him in his wagon about three miles in the country to his home, where I was tenderly nursed and bandaged by good Mrs Hardy, till I was again on my feet, but as the bones broken were not properly set my hand has never recovered its natural strength and dexterity. We lingered long in Indiana, and the good effects of our labours there are felt at this day. I have lately visited Pendleton, now one of the best Republican towns the State, and looked again upon the spot where I was beaten down, and have again taken by the hand some of the witnesses of that scene, amongst whom was the kind, good lady – Mrs Hardy who, so like the good Samaritan of old, bound up my wounds, and cared for me so kindly. A complete history of these hundred conventions would fill a volume far larger than the one in which this simple reference is to find a place. It would be a grateful duty to speak of the noble young men, who forsook ease and pleasure, as did White, Gay and Monroe, and endured all manner of privations in the cause of the enslaved and downtrodden of my race. Gay, Monroe and myself are the only ones who participated as agents in the one hundred conventions who now survive. Mr Monroe was for many years consul to Brazil, and has since been a faithful member of Congress from the Oberlin District, Ohio, and has filled other important positions in his State. Mr Gay was managing editor of the *National Anti-Slavery Standard*, and afterwards of the New York *Tribune*, and still later of the New York *Evening Post*.

CHAPTER VI

Impressions Abroad

Danger to be averted – A refuge sought abroad – Voyage on the steamship *Cambria*– Refusal of first-class passage – Attractions of the forecastle deck – Hutchinson family – Invited to make a speech – Southerners feel insulted – Captain threatens to put them in irons – Experiences abroad – Attentions received – Impressions of different Member of Parliament, and of other public men – Contrast with life in America – Kindness of friends – Their purchase of my person, and the gift of the same to myself – My return

As I have before intimated, the publishing of my 'Narrative' was regarded by my friends with mingled feelings of satisfaction and apprehension. They were glad to have the doubts and insinuations which the advocates and apologists of slavery had made against me, proved to the world to be false, but they had many fears lest this very proof should endanger my safety, and make it necessary for me to leave a position which in a signal manner had opened before me, and one in which I had thus far been efficient in assisting and arousing the moral sentiment of the community against a system which had deprived me, in common with my fellow-slaves, of all the attributes of manhood.

I became myself painfully alive to the liability which surrounded me, and which might at any moment scatter all my proud hopes, and return me to a doom worse than death. It was thus I was led to seek a refuge in monarchical England, from the dangers of Republican slavery. A rude, uncultivated fugitive slave, I was driven to that country to which American young gentlemen go to increase their stock of knowledge – to seek pleasure, and to have their rough democratic manners softened by contact with English aristocratic refinement.

My friend, James N. Buffum, of Lynn, Mass., who was to accompany me, applied on board the steamer *Cambria*, of the Cunard line, for tickets, and was told that I could not be received as a cabin passenger. American prejudice against colour had triumphed over British liberality and civilisation, and had erected a colour test as condition for crossing the sea in the cabin of a British vessel.

The insult was keenly felt by my white friends, but to me such insults were so frequent, and expected, that it was of no great consequence whether I went into the cabin or into the steerage. Moreover, I felt that if I could not go into the first cabin, first cabin passengers could come into the second cabin, and in this thought I was not mistaken, as I soon found myself an object of more general interest than I wished to be, and, so far from being degraded by being placed in the second cabin, that part of the ship became the scene of as much pleasure and refinement as the cabin itself. The Hutchinson family from New Hampshire – sweet singers of anti-slavery songs, and the 'good time coming' – were fellow-passengers, and often came to my rude forecastle-deck and sang their sweetest songs, making the place eloquent with music and alive with spirited conversation. They not only visited me, but invited me to visit them; and in two days after leaving Boston one part of the ship was about as free to me as another. My visits there, however, were but seldom. I preferred to live within my privileges, and keep upon my own premises. This course was quite as much in accord with good policy as with my own feelings. The effect was, that with the majority of the passengers all colour distinctions were flung to the winds, and I found myself treated with every mark of respect from the beginning to the end of the voyage, except in one single instance; and in that I came near being mobbed for complying with an invitation given me by the passengers and the captain of the *Cambria* to deliver a lecture on slavery. There were several young men – passengers from Georgia and New Orleans; and they were pleased to regard my lecture as an insult offered to them, and swore I should not speak. They went so far as to threaten to throw me overboard, and but for the firmness of Captain Judkins, they would probably, under the inspiration of slavery and brandy, have attempted to put their threats into execution. I have no space to describe this scene, although its tragic and comic features are well worth description. An end was put to the *mêlée* by the captain's call to the ship's company to put the salt-water mob-ocrats in irons, at which determined order the gentlemen of the lash scampered, and for the remainder of the voyage conducted themselves very decorously.

This incident of the voyage brought me, within two days after landing at Liverpool, before the British public. The gentlemen so promptly withheld in their attempted violence toward me, flew to the press to justify their conduct, and to denounce me as a worthless and insolent negro. This course was even less wise than the conduct it was intended to sustain; for, besides awakening something like a national interest in me, and securing me an audience, it brought out counter statements, and threw the blame upon themselves, which they had sought to fasten upon me and the gallant captain of the ship.

My visit to England did much for me every way. Not the least among the many advantages derived from it was the opportunity it afforded me of becoming acquainted with educated people, and of seeing and hearing many of the most distinguished men of that country. My friend, Mr Wendell Phillips, knowing something of my appreciation of orators and oratory, had said to me before leaving Boston: 'Although Americans are generally better speakers than Englishmen, you will find in England individual orators superior to the best of ours.' I do not know that Mr Phillips was quite just to himself in this remark, for I found in England few, if any, superior to him in the gift of speech. When I went to England that country was in the midst of a tremendous agitation. The people were divided by two great questions of 'Repeal'– the repeal of the corn laws, and the repeal of the union between England and Ireland.

Debate ran high in Parliament, and among the people everywhere, especially concerning the corn laws. Two powerful interests of the country confronted each other: one venerable from age, and the other young, stalwart, and growing. Both strove for ascendancy. Conservatism united for retaining the corn laws, while the rising power of commerce and manufactures demanded repeal. It was interest against interest, but something more and deeper: for, while there was an aggrandisement of the landed aristocracy on the one side, there was famine and pestilence on the other. Of the anti-corn-law movement, Richard Cobden and John Bright, both then Member of Parliament, were the leaders. They were the rising statesmen of England, and possessed a very friendly disposition toward America. Mr Bright, who is now the Right Honourable John Bright, and occupies a high place in the British Cabinet, was friendly to the loyal and progressive spirit which abolished our slavery and saved our country from dismemberment. I have seen and heard both of these great men, and if I may be allowed so much egotism, I may say I was acquainted with both of them. I was, besides, a welcome guest at the house of Mr Bright, in

Rochdale, and treated as a friend and brother among his brothers and sisters. Messrs Cobden and Bright were well-matched leaders. One was in large measure the complement of the other. They were spoken of usually as Cobden and Bright, but there was no reason, except that Cobden was the elder of the two, why their names might not have been reversed.

They were about equally fitted for their respective parts in the great movement of which they were the distinguished leaders, and either was likely to encroach upon the work of the other. The contrast was quite marked in their persons as well as in their oratory. The powerful speeches of the one, as they travelled together over the country, heightened the effect of the speeches of the other, so that their difference was as effective for good, as was their agreement. Mr Cobden – for an Englishman – was lean, tall, and slightly sallow, and might have been taken for an American or Frenchman. Mr Bright was, in the broadest sense, an Englishman, abounding in all the physical perfections peculiar to his countrymen – full, round and ruddy. Cobden had dark eyes and hair, a well-formed head, high above his shoulders, and, when sitting quiet, had a look of sadness and fatigue. In the House of Commons, he often sat with one hand supporting his head. Bright appeared the very opposite in this and other respects. His eyes were blue, his hair light, his head massive, and firmly set upon his shoulders, suggesting immense energy and determination. In his oratory Mr Cobden was cool, candid, deliberate, straightforward, yet at times slightly hesitating. Bright, on the other hand, was fervid, fluent, rapid; always ready in thought or word. Mr Cobden was full of facts and figures, dealing in statistics by the hour. Mr Bright was full of wit, knowledge and pathos, and possessed amazing power of expression. One spoke to the cold, calculating side of the British nation, which asks 'if the new idea will pay?' The other spoke to the infinite side of human nature – the side which asks, first of all, 'is it right? is it just? is it humane?' Wherever these two great men appeared, the people assembled in thousands. They could, at an hour's notice, pack the Town Hall of Birmingham, which would hold seven thousand persons, or the Free Trade Hall in Manchester, and Covent Garden Theatre, London, each of which was capable of holding eight thousand.

One of the first attentions shown me by these gentlemen, was to make me welcome at the Free Trade Club in London.

I was not long in England before a crisis was reached in the anti-corn-law movement. The announcement that Sir Robert Peel, then Prime Minister of England, had become a convert to the views of Messrs

Cobden and Bright, came upon the country with startling effect, and formed the turning point in the anti-corn-law question. Sir Robert had been the strong defence of the landed aristocracy of England, and his defection left them without a competent leader, and just here came the opportunity for Mr Benjamin Disraeli, the Hebrew – since Lord Beaconsfield. To him it was in public affairs, the 'tide which led on to fortune.' With a bitterness unsurpassed, he had been denounced by Daniel O'Connell as a lineal descendant of the thief on the cross. But now his time had come, and he was not the man to permit it to pass unimproved. For the first time, it seems, he conceived the idea of placing himself at the head of a great party, and thus become the chief defender of the landed aristocracy. The way was plain. He was to transcend all others in effective denunciation of Sir Robert Peel, and surpass all others in zeal. His ability was equal to the situation, and the world knows the result of his ambition. I watched him narrowly when I saw him in the House of Commons, but I saw and heard nothing there that foreshadowed the immense space he at last came to fill in the mind of his country and the world. He had nothing of the grace and warmth of Peel in debate, and his speeches were better in print than when listened to – yet when he spoke, all eyes were fixed, and all ears attent. Despite all his ability and power, however, as the defender of the landed interests in England, his cause was already lost. The increasing power of the anti-corn-law league – the burden of the tax upon bread, the cry of distress coming from famine-stricken Ireland, and the adhesion of Peel to the views of Cobden and Bright, made the repeal of the corn laws speedy and certain.

The repeal of the union between England and Ireland was not so fortunate. It is still, under one name or another, the cherished hope and aspiration of her sons. It stands little better or stronger than it did six-and-thirty years ago, when its greatest advocate, Daniel O'Connell, welcomed me to Ireland, and to 'Conciliation Hall', and where I first had a specimen of his truly wondrous eloquence. Until I heard this man, I had thought that the story of his oratory and power were greatly exaggerated. I did not see how a man could speak to twenty or thirty thousand people at one time, and be heard by any considerable number of them; but the mystery was solved when I saw his vast person, and heard his musical voice. His eloquence came down upon the vast assembly like a summer thunder-shower upon a dusty road. He could stir the multitude, at will, to a tempest of wrath, or reduce it to the silence with which a mother leaves the cradle-side of her sleeping babe. Such tenderness – such pathos – such world-embracing love! and, on the other hand, such indignation – such fiery and thunderous denunciation, and such wit and humour, I never heard surpassed, if equalled, at home or abroad. He held Ireland within the grasp of his strong hand, and could lead it whithersoever he would, for Ireland believed in him and loved him, as she has loved and believed in no leader since. In Dublin, when he had been absent from that city a few weeks, I saw him followed through Sackville Street by a multitude of little boys and girls, shouting in loving accents: 'There goes Dan! there goes Dan!' while he looked at the ragged and shoeless crowd with the kindly air of a loving parent returning to his gleeful children. He was called 'The Liberator', and not without cause; for, though he failed to effect the repeal of the union between England and Ireland, he fought out the battle of Catholic emancipation, and was clearly the friend of liberty the world over. In introducing me to an immense audience in Conciliation Hall, he playfully called me the 'Black O'Connell of the United States'; nor did he let the occasion pass without his usual word of denunciation of our slave system. O. A. Brownson had then recently become a Catholic, and taking advantage of his new Catholic audience, in Brownson's *Review*, had charged O'Connell with attacking American institutions. In reply, Mr O'Connell said: 'I am charged with attacking American institutions, as slavery is called; I am not ashamed of this attack. My sympathy is not confined to the narrow limits of my own green Ireland; my spirit walks abroad upon sea and land, and wherever there is oppression, I hate the oppressor, and wherever the tyrant rears his head, I will deal my bolts upon it; and wherever there is sorrow and suffering, there is my spirit to succour and relieve.' No transatlantic statesman bore a testimony more marked and telling against the crime and curse of slavery, than did Daniel O'Connell. He would shake the hand of no slave-holder, nor allow himself to be introduced to one, if he knew him to be such. When the friends of repeal in the Southern States sent him money with which to carry on his work, he, with ineffable scorn, refused the bribe, and sent back what he considered the blood-stained offering, saying he would 'never purchase the freedom of Ireland with the price of slaves'.

It was not long after my seeing Mr O'Connell that his health broke down, and his career ended in death. I felt that a great champion of freedom had fallen, and that the cause of the American slave, not less than the cause of his country, had met with a great loss. All the more was this felt, when I saw the kind of men who came to the front when the voice of O'Connell was no longer heard in Ireland. He was succeeded by the Duffys, Mitchells, Meagher and others – men who loved liberty for themselves and their country, but were utterly destitute of sympathy with the cause of liberty in countries other than their own. One of the first utterances of John Mitchell on reaching the United States, from his exile and bondage, was a wish for a 'slave plantation, well stocked with slaves'.

Besides hearing Cobden, Bright, Peel, Disraeli, O'Connell, Lord John Russell and other Parliamentary debaters, it was my good fortune to hear Lord Brougham when nearly at his best. He was then a little over sixty, and that for a British statesman is not considered old; and in his case there were thirty years of life still before him. He struck me as the most wonderful speaker of them all. How he was ever reported I cannot imagine. Listening to him, was like standing near the track of a railway train, drawn by a locomotive at the rate of forty miles an hour. You were riveted to the spot, charmed with the sublime spectacle of speed and power, but could give no description of the carriages, nor of the passengers at the windows. There was so much to see and hear, and so little time left the beholder and hearer to note particulars, that when this strange man sat down, you felt like one who had hastily passed through the wildering wonders of a world's exhibition. On the occasion of my listening to him, his speech was on the postal relations of England with the outside world, and he seemed to have a perfect knowledge of the postal arrangements of every nation in Europe, and, indeed, in the whole universe. He possessed the great advantage, so valuable to a Parliamentary debater, of being able to make all interruptions serve the purposes of his thought and speech, and carried on a dialogue with several persons without interrupting the rapid current of his reasoning. I had more curiosity to hear this man than any other in England, and he more than fulfilled my expectations.

While in England, I saw few literary celebrities, except William and Mary Howitt, and Sir John Bowering. I was invited to breakfast by the latter in company with Wm Lloyd Garrison, and spent a delightful morning with him, chiefly as a listener to their conversation. Sir John was a poet, a statesman, and a diplomat, and had represented England as minister to China. He was full of interesting information, and had a charming way of imparting his knowledge. The conversation was about slavery, and about China, and as my knowledge was very slender about the 'Flowery Kingdom', and its people, I was greatly interested in Sir John's description of the ideas and manners prevailing among them. According to him, the doctrine of substitution was carried so far in that country that men sometimes procured others to suffer even the penalty of death in their stead. Justice seemed not intent upon the punishment of the actual criminal, if only somebody was punished when the law was violated.

William and Mary Howitt were among the kindliest people I ever met. Their interest in America, and their well-known testimonies against slavery, made me feel much at home with them at their house in that part of London known as Clapham. Whilst stopping there, I met the Swedish poet and author – Hans Christian Andersen. He, like myself, was a guest, spending a few days. I saw but little of him, though under the same roof. He was singular in his appearance, and equally singular in his silence. His mind seemed to me all the while turned inwardly. He walked about the beautiful garden as one might in a dream. The Howitts had translated his works into English, and could of course address him in his own language. Possibly his bad English and my destitution of Swedish, may account for the fact of our mutual silence, and yet I observed he was much the same towards everyone. Mr and Mrs Howitt were indefatigable writers. Two more industrious and kind-hearted people did not breathe. With all their literary work, they always had time to devote to strangers, and to all benevolent efforts, to ameliorate the condition of the poor and needy. Quakers though they were, they took deep interest in the Hutchinsons – Judson, John, Asa, and Abby, who were much at their house during my stay there. Mrs Howitt not inaptly styled them a 'Band of young apostles'. They sang for the oppressed and the poor – for liberty and humanity.

Whilst in Edinburgh, so famous for its beauty, its educational institutions, its literary men, and its history, I had a very intense desire gratified – and that was to see and converse with George Combe, the eminent mental philosopher, and author of *Combe's Constitution of Man*, a book which had been placed in my hands a few years before by Dr Pelig Clark, of Rhode Island, the reading of which had relieved my path of many shadows. In company with George Thompson, James N. Buffum, and William L. Garrison, I had the honour to be invited by Mr Combe to breakfast, and the occasion was one of the most delightful I met in dear old Scotland. Of course in the presence of such men, my part was a very subordinate one. I was a listener. Mr Combe did the most of the talking, and did it so well, that nobody felt like interposing a word, except so far as to draw him on. He discussed the corn laws, and the proposal to reduce the hours of labour. He looked at all political and social questions through his peculiar mental science. His manner was remarkably quiet, and he spoke as not expecting opposition to his views. Phrenology explained everything to him, from the finite to the infinite. I look back to the morning spent with this singularly clear-headed man with much satisfaction.

It would detain the reader too long, and make this volume too large, to tell of the many kindnesses shown me while abroad, or even to mention all the great and noteworthy persons who gave me a friendly hand and a cordial welcome; but there is one other, now long gone to his rest, of whom a few words must be spoken, and that one was Thomas Clarkson – the last of the noble line of Englishmen who inaugurated the anti-slavery movement for England and the civilised world – the life-long friend and co-worker with Granville Sharpe, William Wilberforce, Thomas Fowell Buxton and other leaders in that great reform which has nearly put an end to slavery in all parts of the globe. As in the case of George Combe, I went to see Mr Clarkson in company with Messrs Garrison and Thompson. They had by note advised him of our coming, and had received one in reply, bidding us welcome. We found the venerable object of our visit seated at a table, where he had been busily writing a letter to America against slavery; for, though in his eighty-seventh year, he continued to write. When we were presented to him, he rose to receive us. The scene was impressive. It was the meeting of two centuries. Garrison, Thompson and myself were young men. After shaking hands with my two distinguished friends, and giving them welcome, he took one of my hands in both of his, and, in a tremulous voice, said God bless you, Frederick Douglass! I have given sixty years of my life to the emancipation of your people, and if I had sixty years more they should all be given to the same cause.' Our stay was short with this great-hearted old man. He was feeble, and our presence greatly excited him, and we left the house with something of the feeling with which friends take final leave of a beloved friend at the edge of the grave.

Some notion may be formed of the difference in my feelings and circumstances while abroad, from an extract from one of a series letters addressed by me to Mr Garrison, and published in the *Liberator*. It was written on the 1st day of January 1846.

MY DEAR FRIEND GARRISON – Up to this time, I have given no direct expression of the views, feelings and opinions which I have formed respecting the character and condition of people of this land. I have refrained thus purposely. I wish to speak advisedly, and, in order to do this, I have waited till, I trust, experience has brought my opinion to an intelligent maturity. I have been thus careful, not because I think what I say will have much effect in shaping the opinions of the world, but because what influence I may possess, whether little or much, I wish to go in the right direction, and according to truth. I hardly need say that in speaking of Ireland, I shall be influenced by no prejudice in favour of America. I think my circumstances all forbid that. I have no end to serve, no creed to uphold, no government to defend; and as to nation, I belong to none. I have no protection at home, or resting-place abroad. The land of my birth welcomes me to her shores only as a slave, and spurns with contempt the idea of treating me differently; so that I am an outcast from the society of my childhood, and an outlaw in the land of my birth. 'I am a stranger with thee and a sojourner, as all my fathers were.' That men should be patriotic, is to me perfectly natural; and as a philosophical fact, I am able to give it an intellectual recognition. But no further can I go. If ever I had any patriotism, or any capacity for the feeling, it was whipped out of me long since by the lash of the American soul-drivers. In thinking of America, I sometimes find myself admiring her bright blue sky, her grand old woods, her fertile fields, her beautiful rivers, her mighty lakes, and star-crowned mountains. But my rapture is soon checked – my joy is soon turned to mourning. When I remember that all is cursed with the infernal spirit of slave-holding, robbery, and wrong; when I remember that with the waters of her noblest rivers, the tears of my brethren are borne to the ocean, disregarded and forgotten, and that her most fertile fields drink daily of the warm blood of my outraged sisters, I am filled with unutterable loathing, and led to reproach myself that anything could fall from my lips in praise of such a land. America will not allow her children to love her. She seems bent on compelling those who would be her warmest friends, to be her worst enemies. May God give her repentance before it is too late, is the ardent prayer of my heart. I will continue to pray, labour, and wait, believing that she cannot always be insensible to the dictates of justice, or deaf to the voice of humanity. My opportunities for learning the character and condition of the people of this land have been very great. I have travelled from the Hill of Howth to the Giant's Causeway, and from the Giant's Causeway to Cape Clear. During these travels I have met with much in the character and condition of the people to approve, and much to condemn; much that has thrilled me with pleasure, and much that has filled me with pain. I will not, in this letter, attempt to give any description of those scenes which give me pain. This I will do hereafter. I have said enough, and more than your subscribers will be disposed to read at one time, of the bright side of the picture. I can truly say I have spent some of the happiest days of my life since landing in this country. I seem to have undergone a transformation. I live a new life. The warm and generous co-operation extended to me by the friends of my despised race; the prompt and liberal manner with which the Press has rendered me its aid; the glorious enthusiasm with which thousands have flocked to hear the cruel wrongs of my downtrodden and long-enslaved fellow countrymen portrayed; the deep sympathy for the slave, and the strong abhorrence of the slave-holder everywhere evinced; the cordiality with which members and ministers of various religious bodies, and of various shades of religious opinion have embraced me and lent me their aid; the kind hospitality constantly proffered me by persons of the highest rank in society; the spirit of freedom that seems to animate all with whom I come in contact, and the entire absence of everything that looks like prejudice against me, on account of the colour of my skin, contrasts so strongly with my long and bitter experiences in the United States, that I look with wonder and amazement on the transition. In the Southern part of the United states, I was a slave – thought of and spoken of as property; in the language of *law*, 'held, taken, reputed, and adjudged to be a chattel in the hands of my owners and possessors, and their executors, administrators, and assigns, to all intents, constructions, and purposes, whatsoever.' (Brev. Digest., 224.) In the Northern states, a fugitive slave, liable to be hunted at any moment like a felon, and to be hurled into the terrible jaws of slavery – doomed by an inveterate prejudice against colour, to insult and outrage on every hand – Massachusetts out of the question – denied the privileges and courtesies common to others in the use of the most humble means of conveyance – shut out from the cabins on steamboats, refused admission to respectable hotels, caricatured, scorned, scoffed, mocked, and maltreated with impunity by anyone – no matter how black his heart so long as he was a white skin. But now behold the change! Eleven days and a half gone, and I have crossed three thousand miles of perilous deep. Instead of a democratic government, I am under a monarchical government. Instead of the bright, blue sky of America, I am covered with the soft, grey fog of the Emerald Isle. I breathe, and lo! the chattel becomes a man! I gaze around in vain for one who will question my equal humanity, claim me as a slave, or offer me an insult. I employ a cab – I am seated beside white people – I reach the hotel – I enter the same door – I am shown into the same parlour – I dine at the same table – and no one is offended. No delicate nose grows deformed in my presence. I find no difficulty here in obtaining admission into any place of worship, instruction, or amusement, on equal terms, with people as white as any I ever saw in the United States. I meet nothing to remind me of my complexion. I find myself regarded and treated at every turn with the kindness and deference paid to white people. When I go to church I am met by no upturned nose and scornful lip, to tell me – 'We don't allow niggers in here.'

I remember about two years ago there was in Boston, near the south-west corner of Boston Common, a menagerie. I had long desired to see such a collection as I understood was being exhibited there. Never having had an opportunity while a slave, I resolved to seize this, and as I approached the entrance to gain admission, I was told by the door-keeper, in a harsh and contemptuous tone, 'We don't allow niggers in here.' I also remember attending a revival meeting in the Revd Henry Jackson's meeting-house, at New Bedford, and going up the broad aisle for a seat, I was met by a good deacon, who told me, in a pious tone, 'We don't allow niggers in here.' Soon after my arrival in New Bedford, from the South, I had a strong desire to attend the Lyceum, but was told, 'They don't allow niggers there.' While passing from New York to Boston on the steamer Massachusetts, on the night of the 9th of December 1848, when chilled almost through with the cold, I went into the cabin to get a little warm. I was soon touched upon the shoulder, and told, 'We don't allow niggers in here.' A week or two before leaving the United States, I had a meeting appointed at Weymouth, the house of that glorious band of true abolitionists – the Weston family and others. On attempting to take a seat in the omnibus to that place, I was told by the driver – and I never shall forget his fiendish hate – 'I don't allow niggers in here.' Thank heaven for the respite I now enjoy! I had been in Dublin but a few days when a gentleman of great respectability kindly offered to conduct me through all the public buildings of that beautiful city, and soon afterwards I was invited by the Lord Mayor to dine with him. What a pity there was not some democratic Christian at the door of his splendid mansion to bark out at my approach, 'They don't allow niggers in here!' The truth is, the people here know nothing of the republican negro-hate prevalent in our glorious land. They measure and esteem men according to their moral and intellectual worth, and not according to the colour of their skin. Whatever may be said of the aristocracies here, there is none based on the colour of a man's skin. This species of aristocracy belongs pre-eminently to 'the land of the free, and the home of the brave'. I have never found it abroad in any but Americans. It sticks to them wherever they go. They find it almost as hard to get rid of as to get rid of their skins.

The second day after my arrival in Liverpool, in company with my friend Buffum, and several other friends, I went to Eaton Hall, the residence of the Marquis of Westminster, one of the most splendid buildings in England. On approaching the door, I found several of our American passengers who came out with us in the *Cambria*, waiting for admission, as but one party was allowed in the house at a time. We all had to wait till the company within came out, and of all the faces expressive of chagrin, those of the Americans were pre-eminent. They looked as sour as vinegar, and as bitter as gall, when they found I was to be admitted on equal terms with themselves. When the door was opened, I walked in on a footing with my white fellow-citizens, and, from all I could see, I had as much attention paid me by the servants who showed us through the house, as any with a paler skin. As I walked through the building, the statuary did not fall down, the pictures did not leap from their places, the doors did not refuse to open, and the servants did not say, '*We don't allow niggers in here.*'

My time and labours while abroad were divided between England, Ireland, Scotland, and Wales. Upon this experience alone I might fill a volume. Amongst the few incidents which space will permit me to mention, and one which attracted much attention and provoked much discussion in America, was a brief statement made by me in the World's Temperance Convention, held in Covent Garden Theatre, London, August 7, 1846. The United States was largely represented in this convention by eminent divines, mostly doctors of divinity. They had come to England for the double purpose of attending the World's Evangelical Alliance, and the World's Temperance Convention. In the former these ministers were endeavouring to procure endorsement for the Christian character of slave-holders; and, naturally enough, they were adverse to the exposure of slave-holding practices. It was not pleasant to them to see one of the slaves running at large in England, and telling the other side of the story. The Revd Samuel Hanson Cox, D.D., of Brooklyn, N. Y., was especially disturbed at my presence and speech in the Temperance Convention. I will give here, first, the reverend gentleman's version of the occasion in a letter from him as it appeared in the New York *Evangelist*, the organ of his denomination. After a description of the place, Covent Garden Theatre, and the sneakers, he says:

They all advocated the same cause, showed a glorious unity of thought and feeling, and the effect was constantly raised – the moral scene was superb and glorious – when Frederick Douglass, the coloured abolition agitator and ultraist, came to the platform, and so spake, *à la mode*, as to ruin the influence of almost all that preceded! He lugged in anti-slavery, or abolition, no doubt prompted to it by some of the politic ones, who can use him to do what they would not themselves adventure to do in person. He is supposed to have been well paid for the abomination.

What a perversion, an abuse, an iniquity against the law of reciprocal righteousness, to call thousands together, and get them, some certain ones, to seem conspicuous and devoted for one sole and grand object, and then all at once, with obliquity, open an avalanche on them for some imputed evil or monstrosity, for which, whatever be the wound or injury inflicted, they were both too fatigued and hurried with surprise, and too straightened for time to be properly prepared. I say it is a streak of meanness! It is abominable! On this occasion Mr Douglass allowed himself to denounce America and all its temperance societies together, as a grinding community of the enemies of his people; said evil, with no alloy of good, concerning the whole of us; was perfectly indiscriminate in his severities; talked of the American delegates, and to them, as if he had been our schoolmaster, and we his docile and devoted pupils; and launched his revengeful missiles at our country without one palliative, and as if not a Christian or a true anti-slavery man lived in the whole of the United States. The fact is, the man has been petted, and flattered, and used, and paid by certain abolitionists, not unknown to us, of the *ne plus ultra* stamp, till he forgets himself; and, though he may gratify his own impulses, and those of old Adam in others, yet sure I am that all this is just the way to ruin his own influence, to defeat his own object, and to do mischief – not good – to the very cause he professes to love. With the single exception of one cold-hearted parricide, whose character I abhor, and whom I will not name, and who has, I fear, no feeling of true patriotism or piety within him, all the delegates from our country were together wounded and indignant. No wonder at it. I write freely. It was not done in a corner. It was inspired, I believe, from beneath, and not from above. It was adapted to rekindle on both sides of the Atlantic the flames of national exasperation and war. And this is the game which Mr Frederick Douglass and his silly patrons are playing in England and in Scotland, and wherever they can find 'some mischief still for idle hands to do'. I came here his sympathising friend; I am such no more, as I know him. My own opinion is increasing that this spirit must be exorcised out of England and America before any substantial good can be effected for the cause of the slave. It is adapted only to make bad worse, and to inflame the passions of indignant millions to an incurable resentment. None but an ignoramus or a madman could think that this way was that of the inspired apostles of the son of God. It may gratify the feelings of a self-deceived and malignant few, but it will do no good in any direction – least of all to the poor slave! It is short-sighted, impulsive, partisan, reckless, and tending only to sanguinary ends. None of this with men of sense and principle.

We all wanted to reply, but it was too late; the whole theatre seemed taken with the spirit of the Ephesian uproar; they were furious and boisterous in the extreme, and Mr Kirk could hardly obtain a moment, though many were desirous in his behalf to say a few words, as he did, very calmly and properly, that the cause of temperance was not at all responsible for slavery, and had no connection with it.

Now, to show the reader what ground there was for this tirade from the pen of this eminent divine, and how easily Americans parted with their candour and self-possession when slavery was mentioned adversely, I will give here the head and front of my offence. Let it be borne in mind that this was a world's convention of the friends of temperance. It was not an American or a white man's convention, but one composed of men of all nations and races; and as such, the convention had the right to know all about the temperance cause in every part of the world, and especially to know what hindrances were interposed in any part of the world, to its progress. I was perfectly in order in speaking precisely as I did. I was neither an 'intruder', nor 'out of order'. I had been invited and advertised to speak by the same committee that invited Doctors Beecher, Cox, Patton, Kirk, Marsh and others, and my speech was perfectly within the limits of good order, as the following report will show:

MR CHAIRMAN – LADIES AND GENTLEMEN – I am not a delegate to this convention. Those who would have been most likely to elect me as a delegate could not, because they are tonight held in abject slavery in the United States. Sir, I regret that I cannot fully unite with the American delegates in their patriotic eulogies of

America, and American temperance societies. I cannot do so for this good reason: there are at this moment three millions of the American population, by slavery and prejudice, placed entirely beyond the pale of American temperance societies. The three million slaves are completely excluded by slavery, and four hundred thousand free coloured people are almost as completely excluded by an inveterate prejudice against them, on account of their colour. [Cries of shame! shame!]

I do not say these things to wound the feelings of the American delegates. I simply mention them in their presence and before this audience, that, seeing how you regard this hatred and neglect of the coloured people, they may be inclined on their return home to enlarge the field of their temperance operations, and embrace within the scope of their influence, my long-neglected race. [Great cheering, and some confusion on the platform.] Sir, to give you some idea of the difficulties and obstacles in the way of the temperance reformation of the coloured population in the United States, allow me to state a few facts.

About the year 1840, a few intelligent, sober, and benevolent coloured gentlemen in Philadelphia, being acquainted with the appalling ravages of intemperance among a numerous class of coloured people in that city, and, finding themselves neglected and excluded from white societies, organised societies among themselves, appointed committees, sent out agents, built temperance halls, and were earnestly and successfully rescuing many from the fangs of intemperance.

The cause went nobly on till August 1, 1842, the day when England gave liberty to eight hundred thousand souls in the West Indies. The coloured temperance societies selected this day to march in procession through the city, in the hope that such a demonstration would have the effect of bringing others into their ranks. They formed their procession, unfurled their teetotal banners, and proceeded to the accomplishment of their purpose. It was a delightful sight. But, sir, they had not proceeded down two streets before they were brutally assailed by a ruthless mob; their banner was torn down, and trampled in the dust, their ranks broken up, their persons beaten and pelted with stones and brickbats. One of their churches was burned to the ground, and their best temperance hall utterly demolished. ['Shame! shame! shame!' from the audience – great confusion, and cries of 'Sit down' from the American delegates on the platform.]

In the midst of this commotion, the chairman tapped me on the shoulder, and, whispering, informed me that the fifteen minutes allotted to each speaker had expired; whereupon the vast audience simultaneously shouted: 'Don't interrupt!' 'Don't dictate!' 'Go on!' 'Go on!' 'Douglass!' 'Douglass!' This continued several minutes, when I proceeded as follows: 'Kind friends, I beg to assure you that the chairman has not in the slightest degree sought to alter any sentiment which I am anxious to express on this occasion. He was simply reminding me that the time allotted for me to speak had expired. I do not wish to occupy one moment more than is allotted to other speakers. Thanking your for your kind indulgence, I will take my seat.' Proceeding to do so again, there were cries of 'Go on!' 'Go on!' with which I complied for a few minutes, but without saying anything more that particularly related to the coloured people of America. I did not allow the letter of Dr Cox to go unanswered through the American journals, but promptly exposed its unfairness. That letter is too long for insertion here. A part of it was published in the *Evangelist*, and in many other papers, both in America and in England. Our eminent divine made no rejoinder, and his silence was regarded at the time as an admission of defeat.

Another interesting circumstance connected with my visit to England, was the position of the Free Church of Scotland with the great Doctors Chalmers, Cunningham, and Candlish at its head. That church had settled for itself the question which was frequently asked by the opponents of abolition at home – '*What have we to do with slavery?*' by accepting contributions from slave-holders; i.e., receiving the price of blood into its treasury, with which to build churches and pay ministers for preaching the gospel; and worse than this, when honest John Murray of Bowlein Bay, with William Smeal, Andrew Paton, Frederick Card, and other sterling anti-slavery men in Glasgow, denounced the transaction as disgraceful, and shocking to the religious sentiment of Scotland, this church, through its leading divines, instead of repenting and seeking to amend the *mistake* into which it had fallen, caused that mistake to become a flagrant sin by undertaking to defend, in the name of God and the Bible, the principle not only of taking the money of slave-dealers to build churches and thus extend the gospel, but of holding fellowship with the traffickers in human flesh. This, the reader will see, brought up the whole question of slavery, and opened the way to its full discussion. I have never seen a people more deeply moved than were the people of Scotland on this very question. Public meeting succeeded public meeting, speech after speech, pamphlet after pamphlet, editorial after editorial, sermon after sermon, lashed the conscientious Scotch people into a perfect *furore*. 'SEND BACK THE MONEY!' was indignantly shouted from Greenock to Edinburgh, and from Edinburgh to Aberdeen. George Thompson of London, Henry C. Wright, J. N. Buffum and myself from America were, of course, on the anti-slavery side, and Chalmers, Cunningham and Cavendish, on the other. Dr Cunningham was the most powerful debater on the slavery side of the question, Mr Thompson the ablest on the anti-slavery side. A scene occurred between these two men, a parallel to which I think I have never witnessed before or since. It was caused by a single exclamation on the part of Mr Thompson, and was on this wise:

The general assembly of the Free Church was in progress at Cannon Mills, Edinburgh. The building would hold twenty-five hundred persons, and on this occasion was densely packed, notice having been given that Doctors Cunningham and Candlish would speak that day in defence of the relations of the Free Church of Scotland to slavery in America. Messrs Thompson, Buffum, myself and a few other anti-slavery friends attended, but sat at such distance and in such position as not to be observed from the platform. The excitement was intense, having been greatly increased by a series of meetings held by myself and friends, in the most splendid hall in that most beautiful city, just previous to this meeting of the general assembly. 'SEND BACK THE MONEY!' in large capitals, stared from every street corner; 'SEND BACK THE MONEY!' adorned the broad flags of the pavement; 'SEND BACK THE MONEY!' was the chorus of the popular street-song; 'SEND BACK THE MONEY!' was the heading of leading editorials in the daily newspapers. This day, at Cannon Mills, the great doctors of the church were to give an answer to this loud and stern demand. Men of all parties and sects were most eager to hear. Something great was expected. The occasion was great, the men were great, and great speeches were expected from them.

In addition to the outward pressure there was wavering within. The conscience of the church itself was not at ease. A dissatisfaction with the position of the church touching slavery was sensibly manifest among the members, and something must be done to counteract this untoward influence. The great Dr Chalmers was in feeble health at the time, so his most potent eloquence could not now be summoned to Cannon Mills, as formerly. He whose voice had been so powerful as to rend asunder and dash down the granite walls of the Established Church of Scotland, and to lead a host in solemn procession from it as from a doomed city, was now old and enfeebled. Besides, he had said his word on this very question, and it had not silenced the clamour without nor stilled the anxious heavings within. The occasion was momentous, and felt to be so. The church was in a perilous condition. A change of some sort must take place, or she must go to pieces. To stand where she did was impossible. The whole weight of the matter fell on Cunningham and Candlish. No shoulders in the church were broader than theirs; and I must say, badly as I detested the principles laid down and defended by them, I was compelled to acknowledge the vast mental endowments of the men.

Cunningham rose, and his rising was the signal for tumultuous applause. It may be said that this was scarcely in keeping with the solemnity of the occasion, but to me it served to increase its grandeur and gravity. The applause, though tumultuous, was not joyous. It seemed to me, as it thundered up from the vast audience, like the fall of an immense shaft, flung from shoulders already galled by its crushing weight. It was like saying 'Doctor, we have borne this burden long enough, and willingly fling it upon you. Since it was you who brought it upon us, take it now and do what you will with it, for we are too weary to bear it.'

The Doctor proceeded with his speech – abounding in logic, learning, and eloquence, and apparently bearing down all opposition; but at the moment – the fatal moment – when he was just bringing all his arguments to a point – that point being that 'neither Jesus Christ nor His holy apostles regarded slave-holding as a sin' – George Thompson, in a clear, sonorous, but rebuking voice, broke the deep stillness of the audience, exclaiming 'HEAR! HEAR! HEAR!' The effect of this simple and common exclamation is almost incredible. It was as if a granite wall had been suddenly flung up against the advancing current of a mighty river. For a moment speaker and audience were brought to a dead silence. Both the Doctor and his hearers seemed appalled by the audacity, as well as the fitness of the rebuke. At length a shout went up to the cry of 'Put him out!' Happily no one attempted to execute this cowardly order, and the discourse went on; but not as before. The exclamation of Thompson must have re-echoed a thousand times in the memory of the Doctor, who, during the remainder of his speech, was utterly unable to recover from the blow. The deed was done, however; the pillars of the church – *the proud Free Church of Scotland* – were committed, and the humility of repentance was absent. The Free Church held on to the blood-stained money, and continued to justify itself in its position.

One good result followed the conduct of the Free Church: it

furnished an occasion for making the people thoroughly acquainted with the character of slavery, and for arraying against it the moral and religious sentiment of that country; therefore, while we did not procure the sending back of the money, we were amply justified, by the good which really did result from our labours.

I must add one word in regard to the Evangelical Alliance. this was an attempt to form a union of all Evangelical Christians throughout the world, and which held its first session in London, in the year 1846, at the time of the World's Temperance Convention there. Some sixty or seventy ministers from America attended this convention, the object of some of them being to weave a worldwide garment with which to clothe evangelical slave-holders; and in this they partially succeeded. But the question of slavery was too large a question to be finally disposed of by the Evangelical Alliance, and from its judgement we appealed to the judgement of the people of Great Britain, with the happiest effect – this effort of our countrymen to shield the character of slave-holders serving to open a way to the British ear for anti-slavery discussion.

I may mention here an incident somewhat amusing and instructive, as it serves to illustrate how easily Americans could set aside their notoriously inveterate prejudice against colour, when it stood in the way of their wishes, or when in an atmosphere which made their prejudice unpopular and un-Christian.

At the entrance to the House of Commons I had one day been conversing for a few moments with Lord Morpeth, and just as I was parting from him I felt an emphatic push against my arm, and, looking around, I saw at my elbow the Revd Dr Kirk of Boston. 'Introduce me to Lord Morpeth,' he said. 'Certainly,' said I, and introduced him; not without remembering, however, that the amiable Doctor would scarcely have asked such a favour of a coloured man at home.

The object of my labours in Great Britain was the concentration of the moral and religious sentiment of its people against American slavery. To this end, I visited and lectured in nearly all the large towns and cities in the United Kingdom, and enjoyed many favourable opportunities for observation and information. I should like to write a book on those countries, if for nothing else, to make grateful mention of the many dear friends whose benevolent actions towards me are ineffaceably stamped upon my memory, and warmly treasured in my heart. To these friends, I owe my freedom in the United States.

Mrs Ellen Richardson, an excellent member of the society of friends, assisted by her sister-in-law, Mrs Henry Richardson, a lady devoted to every good word and work – the friend of the Indian and the African, conceived the plan of raising a fund to effect my ransom from slavery. They corresponded with Hon. Walter Forward of Pennsylvania, and through him, ascertained that Captain Auld would take one hundred and fifty pounds sterling for me; and this sum they promptly raised, and paid for my liberation; placing the papers of my manumission in my hands, before they would tolerate the idea of my return to my native land. To this commercial transaction, to this blood-money, I owe my immunity from the operation of the Fugitive-Slave Law of 1798, and also from that of 1850. The whole affair speaks for itself, and needs no comment now that slavery has ceased to exist in the United States, and is not likely ever again to be revived.

Some of my uncompromising anti-slavery friends in America failed to see the wisdom of this commercial transaction, and were not pleased that I consented to it, even by my silence. They thought it a violation of anti-slavery principles, conceding the right of property in man, and a wasteful expenditure of money. For myself, viewing it simply in the light of a ransom, or as money extorted by a robber, and my liberty being of more value to me than one hundred and fifty pounds sterling, I could not see either a violation of the laws of morality or of economy. It is true, I was not in the possession of my claimants, and could have remained in England, for my friends would have generously assisted me in establishing myself there. To this I could not consent. I felt it my duty to labour and suffer with my oppressed people in my native land. Considering all the circumstances, the Fugitive-Slave Bill included, I think now as then, that the very best thing was done in letting Master Hugh have the money, and thus leaving me free to return to my appropriate field of labour. Had I been a private person, with no relations or duties other than those of a personal and family nature, I should not have consented to the payment of so large a sum, for the privilege of living securely under our glorious republican (?) form of government. I could have lived elsewhere, or perhaps might have been unobserved even in the United States; but I had become somewhat notorious and withal quite as unpopular in some directions as notorious, and I was therefore, much exposed to arrest and capture.*

* The following is a copy of these curious papers, both of my transfer from Thomas to Hugh Auld, and from Hugh to myself –

Know all men, by these presents: That I, Thomas Auld of Talbot county and state of Maryland, for, and in consideration of the sum of one hundred dollars, current money, to be paid by Hugh Auld, of the city of Baltimore, in the said state, at and before the sealing and delivery of these presents, the receipt

Having remained abroad nearly two years, and being about to return to America, not as I left it – a slave – but a freeman, prominent friends of the cause of emancipation intimated their intention to present me with a testimonial, both on grounds of personal regard for me, and also of the cause to which they were so ardently devoted. How such a project would have succeeded I do not know, but many reasons led me to prefer that my friends should simply give me the means of obtaining a printing press and materials, to enable me to start a paper, advocating the interests of my enslaved and oppressed people. I told them that perhaps the greatest hindrance to the adoption of abolition

---

whereof, I, the said Thomas Auld, do hereby acknowledge; having granted, bargained, and sold, and by these presents do grant, bargain and sell unto the said Hugh Auld, his executors, administrators, and assigns, ONE NEGRO MAN, by the name of FREDERICK BAILY – or DOUGLASS as he calls himself – he is now about twenty-eight years of age – to have and to hold the said negro man for life. And I, the said Thomas Auld, for myself, my heirs, my executors, and administrators, all and singular, the said FREDERICK BAILY *alias* DOUGLASS unto the said Hugh Auld, his executors and administrators, and against all and every other person or persons whatsoever, shall and will warrant and forever defend by these presents. In witness whereof, I set my hand and seal, this thirteenth day of November, eighteen hundred and forty six (1846).

THOMAS AULD

Signed, sealed, and delivered in the presence of Wrighton Jones, John. C. Lear.

The authenticity of this bill of sale is attested by N. Harrington, a justice of the peace of the State of Maryland, and for the county of Talbot, dated same day as above.

To all whom it may concern: Be it known that I, Hugh Auld, of the city of Baltimore, in Baltimore county in the State of Maryland, for divers good causes and considerations, me thereunto moving, have released from slavery, liberated, manumitted, and set free, and by these presents do hereby release from slavery, liberate, manumit, and set free, MY NEGRO MAN, named FREDERICK BAILY, otherwise called DOUGLASS, being of the age of twenty-eight years, or thereabouts, and able to work and gain a sufficient livelihood and maintenance; and him the said negro man, named FREDERICK DOUGLASS, I do declare to be henceforth free, manumitted, and discharged from all manner of servitude to me, my executors and administrators forever.

In witness whereof, I, the said Hugh Auld, have hereunto set my hand and seal the fifth of December, in the year one thousand eight hundred and forty six.

HUGH AULD

Sealed and delivered in presence of T. Hanson Belt, James N. S. T. Wright.

principles by the people of the United States was the low estimate everywhere in that country placed upon the negro as a man; that because of his assumed natural inferiority, people reconciled themselves to his enslavement and oppression, as being inevitable if not desirable. The grand thing to be done, therefore, was to change this estimation, by disproving his inferiority and demonstrating his capacity for a more exalted civilisation than slavery and prejudice had assigned him. In my judgement, a tolerably well-conducted press in the hands of persons of the despised race, would, by calling out and making them acquainted with their own latent powers, by enkindling their hope of a future, and developing their moral force, prove a most powerful means of removing prejudice and awakening an interest in them. At that time there was not a single newspaper regularly published by the coloured people in the country, though many attempts had been made to establish such, and had from one cause or another failed. These views I laid before my friends. The result was, that nearly two thousand five hundred dollars were speedily raised towards my establishing such a paper as I had indicated. For this prompt and generous assistance, rendered upon my bare suggestion, without any personal effort on my part, I shall never cease to feel deeply grateful, and the thought of fulfilling the expectations of the dear friends who had given me this evidence of their confidence, was an abiding inspiration for persevering exertion.

Proposing to leave England, and turning my face towards America in the spring of 1847, I was painfully reminded of the kind of life which awaited me on my arrival. For the first time in the many months spent abroad, I met with proscription on account of my colour. While in London I had purchased a ticket, and secured a berth, for returning home in the *Cambria* – the steamer in which I had come from thence – and paid therefore the round sum of forty pounds, nineteen shillings sterling. This was first cabin fare; but on going on board I found that the Liverpool agent had ordered my berth to be given to another, and forbidden my entering the saloon. It was rather hard after having enjoyed for so long a time equal social privileges, after dining with persons of great literary, social, political, and religious eminence, and never, during the whole time, having met with a single word, look, or gesture, which gave the slightest reason to think my colour was an offence to anybody – now to be cooped up in the stern of the *Cambria*, and denied the right to enter the saloon, lest my presence should disturb some democratic fellow-passenger. The reader can easily imagine what must have been my feelings under such an indignity.

This contemptible conduct met with stern rebuke from the British Press. The London *Times*, and other leading journals throughout the United Kingdom, held up the outrage to unmitigated condemnation. So good an opportunity for calling out British sentiment on the subject had not before occurred, and it was fully embraced. The result was, that Mr Cunard came out with a letter expressive of his regret, and promising that the like indignity should never occur again on his steamers; which promise, I believe, has been faithfully kept.

CHAPTER VII

Triumphs and Trials

New experiences – Painful disagreement of opinion with old friends – Final decision to publish my paper in Rochester – Its fortunes – Change in my own views regarding the Constitution of the United States – Fidelity to conviction – Loss of old friends – Support of new ones – Loss of house, etc., by fire – Triumphs and trials – Underground railroad – Incidents

Prepared as I was to meet with many trials and perplexities on reaching home, one of which I little dreamed was awaiting me. My plans for future usefulness, as indicated in the last chapter, were all settled, and in imagination I already saw myself wielding my pen as well as my voice in the great work of renovating the public mind, and building up a public sentiment, which should send slavery to the grave, and restore to 'liberty and the pursuit of happiness' the people with whom I had suffered.

My friends in Boston had been informed of what I was intending, and I expected to find them favourably disposed towards my cherished enterprise. In this I was mistaken. They had many reasons against it. First, no such paper was needed; secondly, it would interfere with my usefulness as a lecturer; thirdly, I was better fitted to speak than to write; fourthly, the paper could not succeed. This opposition from a quarter so highly esteemed, and to which I had been accustomed to look for advice and direction, caused me not only to hesitate, but inclined me to abandon the undertaking. All previous attempts to establish such a journal having failed, I feared lest I should but add another to the list, and thus contribute another proof of the mental deficiencies of my race. Very much that was said of me in respect to my imperfect literary attainments, I felt to be most painfully true. The unsuccessful projectors of all former attempts had been my superiors in point of education, and if *they* had failed how could I hope for success? Yet I did hope for success, and persisted in the undertaking, encouraged by my English friends to go forward.

I can easily pardon those who saw in my persistence, an unwarrantable ambition and presumption. I was but nine years escaped from slavery. In many phases of mental experience I was but nine years old. That one under such circumstances should aspire to establish a printing press, surrounded by an educated people, might well be considered unpractical if not ambitious. My American friends looked at me with astonishment. 'A wood-sawyer' offering himself to the public as an editor! A slave, brought up in the depths of ignorance, assuming to instruct the highly civilised people of the North in the principles of liberty, justice, and humanity! The thing looked absurd. Nevertheless I persevered. I felt that the want of education, great as it was, could be overcome by study, and that wisdom would come by experience; and further, what was perhaps the most controlling consideration, I thought that an intelligent public, knowing my early history, would easily pardon the many deficiencies which I well knew my paper must exhibit. The most distressing part of it all, was the offence which I saw I must give my friends of the old anti-slavery organisation, by what seemed to them a reckless disregard of their opinion and advice. I am not sure that I was not under the influence of something like a slavish adoration of these good people, and I laboured hard to convince them that my way of thinking about the matter was the right one, but without success.

From motives of peace, instead of issuing my paper in Boston, among New England friends, I went to Rochester, N.Y., among strangers, where the local circulation of my paper – THE NORTH STAR – would not interfere with that of the *Liberator*, or the *Anti-Slave Standard*; for I was then a faithful disciple of Wm Lloyd Garrison, and fully committed to his doctrine touching the pro-slavery character of the Constitution of the United States, also the *non-voting principle*, of which he was the known and distinguished advocate. With him, I held it to be the first duty of the non-slave-holding States to dissolve the union with the slave-holding States, and hence my cry, like his, was 'No union with slave-holders'. With these views I came into western

New York, and during the first four years of my labours there, I advocated them with pen and tongue, to the best of my ability. After a time, a careful reconsideration of the subject convinced me that there was no necessity for dissolving the 'union between the Northern and Southern States'; that to seek this dissolution was no part of my duty as an abolitionist; that to abstain from voting was to refuse to exercise a legitimate and powerful means for abolishing slavery; and that the Constitution of the United States not only contained no guarantees in favour of slavery, but on the contrary, was in its letter and spirit an anti-slavery instrument, demanding the abolition of slavery as a condition of its own existence, as the supreme law of the land.

This radical change in my opinions produced a corresponding change in my action. To those with whom I had been in agreement and in sympathy, I came to be in opposition. What they held to be a great and important truth, I now looked upon as a dangerous error. A very natural, but to me a very painful thing, now happened. Those who could not see any honest reasons for changing their views, as I had done, could not easily see any such reasons for my change, and the common punishment of apostates was mine.

My first opinions were naturally derived and honestly entertained. Brought directly, when I escaped from slavery, into contact with abolitionists who regarded the Constitution as a slave-holding instrument, and finding their views supported by the united and entire history of every department of the Government, it is not strange that I assumed the Constitution to be just what these friends made it seem to be. I was bound not only by their superior knowledge to take their opinions in respect to this subject, as the true ones, but also because I had no means of showing their unsoundness. But for the responsibility of conducting a public journal, and the necessity imposed upon me of meeting opposite views from abolitionists outside of New England, I should in all probability have remained firm in my disunion views. My new circumstances compelled me to re-think the whole subject, and study with some care not only the just and proper rules of legal interpretation, but the origin, design, nature, rights, powers, and duties of civil governments, and also the relations which human beings sustain to it. By such a course of thought and reading I was conducted to the conclusion that the Constitution of the United States – inaugurated 'to form a more perfect union, establish justice, ensure domestic tranquillity, provide for the common defence, promote the general welfare, and secure the blessings of liberty' – could not well have been designed at the same time to maintain and perpetuate a system of rapine and murder, like slavery, especially as not one word can be found in the Constitution to authorise such a belief. Then, again, if the declared purposes of an instrument are to govern the meaning of all its parts and details, as they clearly should, the Constitution of our country is our warrant for the abolition of slavery in every State of the Union. It would require much time and space to set forth the arguments which demonstrated to my mind the unconstitutionality of slavery; but being convinced of the fact, and duty was plain upon this point in the further conduct of my paper. *The North Star* was a large sheet, published weekly, at a cost of $80 per week, and, an average circulation of 3,000 subscribers. There were many times, when in my experience as editor and publisher, I was very hard pressed for money, but by one means or another I succeeded so well as to keep my pecuniary engagements, and to keep my anti-slavery banner steadily flying during all the conflict from the autumn of 1847 till the union of the States was assured, and emancipation was a fact accomplished. I had friends abroad as well as at home who helped me liberally. I can never be too grateful to the Revd Russell Lunt Carpenter and to Mrs Carpenter, for the moral and material aid they tendered me through all the vicissitudes of my paper enterprise. But to no one person was I more indebted for substantial assistance than to Mrs Julia Griffiths Crofts. She came to my relief when my paper had nearly absorbed all my means, and was heavily in debt, and when I had mortgaged my house to raise money to meet current expenses; and by her energetic and effective management, in a single year enabled me to extend the circulation of my paper from 2,000 to 4,000 copies, pay off the debts and lift the mortgage from my house. Her industry was equal to her devotion. She seemed to rise with every emergency, and her resources appeared inexhaustible. I shall never cease to remember with sincere gratitude the assistance rendered me by this noble lady, and I mention her here in the desire in some humble measure to 'give honour to whom honour is due'. During the first three or four years my paper was published under the name of *The North Star*. It was subsequently changed to *Frederick Douglass' Paper* in order to distinguish it from the many papers with *Stars* in their titles. There were *North Stars*, *Morning Stars*, *Evening Stars*, and I know not how many other stars in the newspaper firmament, and some confusion arose naturally enough in distinguishing between them; for this reason, and also because some of these stars were older than my star I felt that mine, not theirs, ought to be the one to 'go out'.

Of course there were moral forces operating against me in Rochester, as well as material ones. There were those who regarded the publication of a 'Negro paper' in that beautiful city as a blemish and a misfortune. The New York *Herald*, true to the spirit of the times, counselled the people of the place to throw my printing press into Lake Ontario, and to banish me to Canada; and while they were not quite prepared for this violence, it was plain that many of them did not well relish my presence amongst them. This feeling, however, wore away gradually, as the people knew more of me and my works. I lectured every Sunday evening during an entire winter in the beautiful Corinthian Hall, then owned by Wm R. Reynolds, Esq., who though he was not an abolitionist, was a lover of fair-play, and was willing to allow me to be heard. If in these lectures I did not make abolitionists, I did succeed in making a tolerant and moral atmosphere in Rochester; so much so, indeed, that I came to feel as much at home there as I had ever done in the most friendly parts of New England. I had been at work there with my paper but a few years before coloured travellers told me that they felt the influence of my labours when they came within fifty miles. I did not rely alone upon what I could do by the paper, but would write all day, then take a train to Victor, Farmington, Canandaigua, Geneva, Waterloo, Batavia or Buffalo or elsewhere and speak in the evening, returning home afterwards or early in the morning, to be again at my desk writing or mailing papers. There were times when I almost thought my Boston friends were right in dissuading me from my newspaper project. But looking back to those nights and days of toil and thought, compelled often to do work for which I had no educational preparation, I have come to think that, under the circumstances it was the best school possible for me. It obliged me to think and read, it taught me to express my thoughts clearly, and was perhaps better than any other course I could have adopted. Besides, it made it necessary for me to lean upon myself, and not upon the heads of our anti-slavery church; to be a principal, and not an agent. I had an audience to speak to every week, and must say something worth their hearing, or cease to speak altogether. There is nothing like the lash and sting of necessity to make a man work, and my paper furnished this motive power. More than one gentleman from the South, when stopping at Niagara, came to see me, that they might know for themselves if I could indeed write, having, as they said, believed it impossible that an uneducated fugitive slave could write the articles attributed to me. I found it hard to get credit in some quarters either for what I wrote or what I said. While there was nothing very profound or learned in either, the low estimate of Negro possibilities induced the belief that both my editorials and my speeches were written by white persons. I doubt if this scepticism does not still linger in the minds of some of my democratic fellow-citizens.

The 2nd of June 1872 brought me a very grievous loss. My house in Rochester was burned to the ground, and among other things of value, twelve volumes of my paper, covering the period from 1848 to 1860, was devoured by the flames. I have never been able to replace them, and the loss is immeasurable. Only a few weeks before, I had been invited to send these bound volumes to the library of Harvard University, where they would have been preserved in a fire-proof building, and the result of my procrastination attests the wisdom of more than one proverb. Outside the years embraced in the late tremendous war, there has been no period, more pregnant with great events, or better suited to call out the best mental and moral energies of men, than that covered by these lost volumes. If I have at any time said or written that which is worth remembering or repeating, I must have said such things between the years 1848 and 1860, and my paper was a chronicle of most of what I said during that time. Within that space we had the great Free-Soil Convention at Buffalo, the nomination of Martin Van Buren, the Fugitive-Slave Law, the 7th March Speech by Daniel Webster, the Dred Scott decision, the repeal of the Missouri Compromise, the Kansas Nebraska Bill, the border war in Kansas, the John Brown raid upon Harper's Ferry, and a part of the War against the Rebellion, with much else, well calculated to fire the souls of men having one spark of Liberty and Patriotism within them. I have only fragments now, of all the work accomplished during these twelve years, and must cover this chasm, as best I can, from memory and the incidental items which I am able to glean from various sources. Two volumes of the *North Star* have been kindly supplied me, by my friend, Marshall Pierce, of Saco, Me. He had these carefully preserved and bound in one cover and sent to me in Washington. He was one of the most systematically careful men of all my anti-slavery friends, for I doubt if another entire volume of the paper exists.

One important branch of my anti-slavery work in Rochester, in addition to that of speaking and writing against slavery, must not be forgotten or omitted. My position gave me the chance of hitting that old enemy some telling blows, in another direction than these. I was on the southern border of Lake Ontario, and the Queen's Dominions were right over the way – and my prominence as an abolitionist, and as the editor of an anti-slavery paper, naturally made me the station master and conductor of the underground railroad passing through this goodly city. Secrecy and concealment were necessary conditions to the successful operation of this railroad, and hence its prefix 'underground'. My agency was all the more exciting and interesting, because not altogether free from danger. I could take no step in it without exposing myself to fine and imprisonment, for these were the penalties imposed by the Fugitive-Slave Law, for feeding, harbouring, or otherwise assisting a slave to escape from his master; but in face of this fact, I can say, I never did more congenial, attractive, fascinating, and satisfactory work. True, as a means of destroying slavery, it was like an attempt to bail out the ocean with a teaspoon, but the thought that there was *one* less slave, and one more freeman – having myself been a slave, and a fugitive slave – brought to my heart unspeakable joy. On one occasion I had eleven fugitives at the same time under my roof, and it was necessary for them to remain with me, until I could collect sufficient money to get them on to Canada. It was the largest number I ever had at any one time, and I had some difficulty in providing so many with food and shelter, but as may well be imagined, they were not very fastidious in either direction, and were well content with very plain food, and a strip of carpet on the floor for a bed, or a place on the straw in the barn loft.

The underground railroad had many branches; but that one with which I was connected had its main stations in Baltimore, Wilmington, Philadelphia, New York, Albany, Syracuse, Rochester, and St Catharines, Canada. It is not necessary to tell who were the principal agents in Baltimore, Thomas Garrett was the agent in Wilmington; Melloe McKim, William Still, Robert Purvis, Edward M. Davis and others did the work in Philadelphia; David Ruggles, Isaac T. Hooper, Napolian and others, in New York City; the Misses Mott and Stephen Myers, were forwarders from Albany; Revds Samuel J. May and J. W. Loguen, were the agents in Syracuse; and J. P. Morris and myself received and dispatched passengers from Rochester to Canada, where they were received by the Revd Hiram Wilson. When a party arrived in Rochester, it was the business of Mr Morris and myself to raise funds with which to pay their passages to St Catharines, and it is due to truth to state, that we seldom called in vain upon whig or democrat for help. Men were better than their theology, and truer to humanity, than to their politics, or their offices.

On one occasion while a slave-master was in the office of a United States commissioner, procuring the papers necessary for the arrest and rendition of three young men who had escaped from Maryland, one of whom was under my roof at the time, another at Farmington, and the other at work on the farm of Asa Anthony just a little outside the city limits, the law partner of the commissioner, then a distinguished democrat, sought me out, and told me what was going on in his office, and urged me by all means to get these young men out of the way of their pursuers and claimants. Of course no time was to be lost. A swift horseman was dispatched to Farmington, eighteen miles distant, another to Asa Anthony's farm about three miles, and another to my house on the south side of the city, and before the papers could be served, all three of the young men were on the free waves of Lake Ontario, bound to Canada. In writing to their old master, they had dated their letter at Rochester, though they had taken the precaution to send it to Canada to be mailed, but this blunder in the date had betrayed their whereabouts, so that the hunters were at once on their tracks.

So numerous were the fugitives passing through Rochester, that I was obliged at last to appeal to my British friends for the means of sending them on their way, and when Mr and Mrs Carpenter and Mrs Crofts took the matter in hand, I had never any further trouble in that respect. When slavery was abolished I wrote to Mrs Carpenter, congratulating her that she was relieved of the work of raising funds for such purposes, and the characteristic reply of that lady was that she had been very glad to do what she had done, and had no wish for relief.

My pathway was not entirely free from thorns in Rochester, and the wounds and pains inflicted by them were perhaps much less easily born, because of my exemption from such annoyances while in England. Men can in time become accustomed to almost anything, even to being insulted and ostracised, but such treatment comes hard at first, and when to some extent unlooked for. The vulgar prejudice against colour, so common to Americans, met me in several disagreeable forms. A seminary for young ladies and misses, under the auspices of Miss Tracy, was near my house in Alexander Street, and desirous of having my daughter educated like the daughters of other men, I applied to Miss Tracy for her admission to her school. All seemed fair, and the child was duly sent to Tracy Seminary, and I went about my business happy in the thought that she was in the way of a refined and Christian education. Several weeks elapsed before I knew how completely I was mistaken. The little girl came home to me one day and told me she was lonely in that school; that she was in fact kept in solitary confinement; that she was not allowed to be in the room with the other girls, nor to go into the yard when they went out; that she was kept in a room by herself and not permitted to be seen nor heard by the others. No man with the feeling of a parent could be less than moved by such a revelation and I confess that I was shocked, grieved, and indignant. I went at once to Miss Tracy to ascertain if what I had heard was true, and was coolly told it was, and the miserable plea was offered that it would have injured her school if she had done otherwise. I told her she should have told me so at the beginning, but I did not believe that any girl in the school would be opposed to the presence of my daughter, and that I should be glad to have the question submitted to them. She consented to this, and to the credit of the young ladies, not one made objection. Not satisfied with this verdict of the natural and uncorrupted sense of justice and humanity of these young ladies, Miss Tracy insisted that the parents must be consulted, and if one of them objected she should not admit my child to the same apartment and privileges of the other pupils. One parent only had the cruelty to object, and he was Mr Horatio G. Warner, a democratic editor, and upon his adverse conclusion, my daughter was excluded from Tracy Seminary. Of course Miss Tracy was a devout Christian lady after the fashion of the time and locality, in good and regular standing in the church.

My troubles attending the education of my children were not to end here. They were not allowed in the public school in the district in which I lived, owned property, and paid taxes, but were compelled, if they went to a public school, to go over to the other side of the city, to an inferior coloured school. I hardly need say that I was not prepared to submit tamely to this proscription, any more than I had been to submit to slavery, so I had them taught at home for a while, by Miss Thayer. Meanwhile I went to the people with the question and created considerable agitation. I sought and obtained a hearing before the Board of Education, and after repeated efforts with voice and pen, the doors of the public schools were opened and coloured children were permitted to attend them in common with others.

There were barriers erected against coloured people in most other places of instruction and amusements in the city, and until I went there, they were imposed without any apparent sense of injustice or wrong, and submitted to in silence; but, one by one, they have gradually been removed, and coloured people now enter freely all places of public resort without hindrance or observation, This change has not been wholly effected by me. From the first, I was cheered on and supported in my demands for equal rights by such respectable citizens as Isaac Post, Wm Hallowell, Samuel D. Porter, Wm C. Bloss, Benj. Fish, Asa

Anthony, and may other good and true men of Rochester.

Notwithstanding what I have said of the adverse feeling exhibited by some of its citizens at my selection of Rochester as the place to establish my paper, and the trouble in educational matters just referred to, that selection was in many respects very fortunate. The city was, and still is, the centre of a various, intelligent, enterprising, liberal, and growing population. The surrounding country is remarkable for its fertility; and the city itself possesses one of the finest water-powers in the world. It is on the line of the New York Central railroad – a line that with its connections, spans the whole country. Its people were industrious and in comfortable circumstances; not so rich as to be indifferent to the claims of humanity, and not so poor as to be unable to help any good cause which commanded the approval of their judgement.

The ground had been measurably prepared for me by the labours of others – notably by the Hon. Myron Holley, whose monument of enduring marble now stands in the beautiful cemetery at Mount Hope, upon an eminence befitting his noble character. I know of no place in the Union where I could have been located at the time with less resistance, or received a larger measure of sympathy and co-operation; and I now look back upon my life and labours there with unalloyed satisfaction, and having spent a quarter of a century among its people, I shall always feel more at home there than anywhere else in the United States.

CHAPTER VIII

John Brown and Mrs Stowe

My first meeting with Captain John Brown – The Free-Soil Movement – Coloured Convention – *Uncle Tom's Cabin* – Industrial school for coloured people – Letter to Mrs H. B. Stowe

About the time I began my enterprise in Rochester, I chanced to spend a night and a day under the roof of a man whose character and conversation, and whose objects and aims in life made a very deep impression upon my mind and heart. His name had been mentioned to me by several prominent coloured men, among whom were the Revd Henry Highland Garnet and J. W. Loguen. In speaking of him their voices would drop to a whisper, and what they said of him made me very eager to see and know him. Fortunately I was invited to see him in his own house. At the time to which I now refer, this man was a respectable merchant in a populous and thriving city, and our first place of meeting was at his store. This was a substantial brick building, in a prominent, busy street. A glance at the interior, as well as at the massive walls without, gave me the impression that the owner must be a man of considerable wealth. From this store I was conducted to his house, where I was kindly received as an expected guest. My welcome was all I could have asked. Every member of the family, young and old, seemed glad to see me, and I was made much at home in a very little while. I was, however, a little disappointed with the appearance of the house and with its location. After seeing the fine store, I was prepared to see a fine residence, in an eligible locality, but this conclusion was completely dispelled by actual observation. In fact, the house was neither commodious nor elegant, nor its situation desirable, It was a small wooden building, in a back street, in a neighbourhood chiefly occupied by labouring men and mechanics; respectable enough to be sure, but, not quite the place, I thought, where one would look for the residence of a flourishing and successful merchant. Plain as was the outside of this man's house, the inside was plainer. Its furniture would have satisfied a Spartan. It would take longer to tell what was not in this house than what was in it. There was an air of plainness about it which almost suggested destitution. My first meal passed under the misnomer of tea, though there was nothing about it resembling the usual significance of that term. It consisted of beef soup, cabbage, and potatoes; a meal such as a man might relish after following the plough all day, or performing a forced march of a dozen miles over a rough road in frosty weather. Innocent of paint, veneering, varnish, or table-cloth, the table announced itself unmistakably of pine and of the plainest workmanship. There was no hired help visible. The mother, daughters, and sons did the serving, and did it well. They were evidently used to it, and had no thought of any impropriety or degradation in being their own servants. It is said that a house in some measure reflects the character of its occupants; this one certainly did. In it there were no disguises, no illusions, no make believes. Everything implied stern truth, solid purpose, and rigid economy. I was not long in company with the master of this house before I discovered that he was indeed the master of it, and was likely to become mine too if I stayed long enough with him. He fulfilled St Paul's idea of the head of the family. His wife believed in him, and his children observed him with reverence. Whenever he spoke his words commanded earnest atten-tion. His arguments, which I ventured at some points to oppose, seemed to convince all; his appeals touched all, and his will impressed all. Certainly I never felt myself in the presence of a stronger religious influence than while in this man's house.

In person he was lean, strong, and sinewy, of the best New England mould, built for times of trouble, fitted to grapple with the flintiest hardships. Clad in plain American woollen, shod in boots of cowhide leather, and wearing a cravat of the same substantial material, under six feet high, less than 150 pounds in weight, aged about fifty, he presented a figure, straight and symmetrical as a mountain pine. His bearing was singularly impressive. His head was not large, but compact and high. His hair was coarse, strong, slightly grey and closely trimmed, and grew low on his forehead. His face was smoothly shaved, and revealed a strong square mouth, supported by a broad and prominent chin. His eyes were bluish grey, and in conversation they were full of light and fire. When in the street, he moved with a long, springing racehorse step, absorbed by his own reflections, neither seeking nor shunning observation. Such was the man, whose name I had heard in whispers, such was the spirit of his house and family, such was the house in which he lived, and such was Captain John Brown, whose name has now passed into history, as one of the most marked characters, and greatest heroes known to American fame.

After the strong meal already described, Captain Brown cautiously approached the subject which he wished to bring to my attention; for he seemed to apprehend opposition to his views. He denounced slavery in look and language fierce and bitter, thought that slave-holders had forfeited their right to live, that the slaves had the right to gain their liberty in any way they could, did not believe that moral suasion would ever liberate the slave, or that political action would abolish the system. He said that he had long had a plan which could accomplish this end, and he had invited me to his house to lay that plan before me. He said he had been for some time looking for coloured men to whom he could safely reveal his secret, and at times he had almost despaired of finding such men, but that now he was encouraged, for he saw heads of such, rising up in all directions. He had observed my course at home and abroad, and he wanted my co-operation. His plan as it then lay in his mind, had much to commend it. It did not, as some suppose, contemplate a general rising among the slaves, and a general slaughter of the slave-masters. An insurrection he thought would only defeat the object, but his plan did contemplate the creating of an armed force, which should act in the very heart of the South. He was not averse to the shedding of blood, and thought the practice of carrying arms would be a good one for the coloured people to adopt, as it would give them a sense of their manhood. No people, he said, could have self-respect, or be respected, who would not fight for their freedom. He called my attention to a map of the United States, and pointed out to me the far-reaching Alleghanies, which stretch away from the borders of New York, into the Southern States. 'These mountains,' he said, 'are the basis of my plan. God has given the strength of the hills to freedom, they were placed here for the emancipation of the negro race; they are full of natural forts, where one man for defence will be equal to a hundred for attack; they are full also of good hiding places, where large numbers of brave men could be concealed, and baffle and elude pursuit for a long time. I know these mountains well, and could take a body of men into them and keep them there, despite all the efforts of Virginia to dislodge them. The true object to be sought is first of all to destroy the money value of slave property; and that can only be done by rendering such property insecure. My plan then is to take at first about twenty-five picked men, and begin on a small scale; supply them with arms and ammunition, post them in squads of fives on a line of twenty-five miles, the most persuasive and judicious of whom shall go down to the fields from time to time, as opportunity offers, and induce the slaves to join them, seeking and selecting the most restless and daring.'

He saw that in this part of the work the utmost care must be used to avoid treachery and disclosure. Only the most conscientious and skilful should be sent on this perilous duty; with care and enterprise he thought he could soon gather a force of one hundred hardy men, men who would be content to lead the free and adventurous life in which he proposed to train them; when these were properly drilled, and each man had found the place for which he was best suited, they would begin work in earnest; they would run off the slaves in large numbers, retain the brave and strong ones in the mountains, and send the weak and timid to the North by the underground railroad; his operations would be enlarged with increasing numbers, and would not be con-fined to one locality.

When I asked him how he would support these men, he said emphatically, he would subsist them upon the enemy. Slavery was a state of war, and the slave had a right to anything necessary to his freedom. But, said I, 'Suppose you succeed in running off a few slaves, and thus impress the Virginia slave-holders with a sense of insecurity in their slaves, the effect will be only to make them sell their slaves further South.' 'That,' said he, 'will be first what I want to do; then I would follow them up. If we could drive slavery out of *one county*, it would be a great gain; it would weaken the system throughout the State.' 'But they would employ bloodhounds to hunt you out of the mountains.' 'That they might attempt,' said he, 'but the chances are, we should whip them, and when we should have whipped one squad, they would be careful how they pursued.' 'But you might be surrounded and cut off from your provisions or means of subsistence.' He thought that could not be done so that they could not cut their way out; but even if the worst came, he could but be killed; and he had no better use for his life than to lay it down in the cause of the slave. When I suggested that we might convert the slave-holders, he became much excited, and said that could never be – 'he knew their proud hearts, and that they would never be induced to give up their slaves, until they felt a big stick about their heads'. He observed, that I might have noticed the simple manner in which he lived, adding that he had adopted this method in order to save money to carry out his purposes. This was said in no boastful tone, for he felt that he had delayed already too long, and had no room to boast either his zeal or his self-denial. Had some men made such display of rigid virtue, I should have rejected it, as affected, false, and hypocritical, but in John Brown, I felt it to be real as iron or granite. From this night spent with John Brown in Springfield, Mass., 1847, while I continued to write and speak against slavery, I became all the same less hopeful of its peaceful abolition. My utterances became more and more tinged by the colour of this man's strong impressions. Speaking at an anti-slavery convention in Salem, Ohio, I expressed the apprehension that slavery could only be destroyed by bloodshed, when I was suddenly and sharply interrupted by my good old friend, Sojourner Truth, with the question, 'Frederick, is God dead?' 'No,' I answered, 'and because God is not dead slavery can only end in blood.' My quaint old sister was of the Garrison school of non-resistants, and was shocked at my sanguinary doctrine, but she too became an advocate of the sword, when the war for the maintenance of the Union was declared.

In 1848 it was my privilege to attend, and in some measure, to participate in, the famous Free-Soil Convention held in Buffalo, New York. It was a vast and variegated assemblage, composed of persons from all sections of the North, and may be said to have formed a new departure in the history of forces organised to resist the growing and aggressive demands of slavery and the slave power. Until this Buffalo convention, anti-slavery agencies had been mainly directed to the work of changing public sentiment, by exposing through the press and on the platform, the nature of the slave system. Anti-slavery thus far had only been sheet lightning; the Buffalo convention sought to make it a thunderbolt. It is true the Liberty party, a political organisation, had been in existence since 1840, when it cast seven thousand votes for James G. Birney, a former slave-holder, but who, in obedience to an enlightened conscience, had nobly emancipated his slaves, and was now devoting his time and talents to the overthrow of slavery. It is true that this little party of brave men had increased their numbers at one time to sixty thousand voters. It, however, had now apparently reached its culminating point, and was no longer able to attract to itself and combine all the available elements of the North, capable of being marshalled against the growing and aggressive measures and aims of the slave power. There were many in the old Whig party known as conscience Whigs; and in the Democratic party known as Barnburners and Free Democratic, who were anti-slavery in sentiment and utterly opposed to the extension of the slave system to territory hitherto uncursed by its presence; but who, nevertheless, were not willing to join the Liberty party. It was held to be deficient in numbers, and wanting in prestige. Its fate was the fate of all pioneers. The work it had been required to perform had exposed it to assaults from all sides, and it wore on its front the ugly marks of conflict. It was unpopular from its very fidelity to the cause of liberty and justice. No wonder that some of its members, such as Gerrit Smith, William Goodell, Beriah Green, and Julius Lemoyne refused to quit the old for the new. They felt that the Free-Soil party was a step backward, a lowering of the standard, that the people should come to them, not they to the people. The party which had been good enough for them ought to be good enough for all others. Events, however, over-ruled this reasoning. The conviction became general that the time had come for a new organisation, which should embrace all who were in any manner opposed to slavery and the slave power, and this Buffalo Free-Soil Convention was the result of that conviction. It is easy to say that this or that measure would have been wiser and better than the one adopted. But any measure is vindicated by its necessity and its results. It was impossible for the mountain to go to Mahomet, or for the Free-Soil element to go to the old Liberty party, so the latter went to the former. 'All is well that ends well.' This Buffalo convention of Free-Soilers, however low was their standard, did lay the foundation of a grand superstructure. It was a powerful link in the chain of events by which the slave system has been abolished, the slave emancipated, and the country saved from dismemberment.

It is nothing against the actors in this new movement that they did not see the end from the beginning; that they did not at first take the high ground that further on in the conflict their successors felt themselves called upon to take; or that their Free-Soil party, like the old Liberty party, was ultimately required to step aside and make room for the great Republican party. In all this, and more, it illustrates the experience of reform in all ages, and conforms to the laws of human progress – measures change, principles never.

I was not the only coloured man well known to the country who was present at this convention. Samuel Ringold Ward, Henry Highland Garnet, Charles L. Remond and Henry Bibb were there, and made speeches which were received with surprise and gratification by the thousands there assembled. As a coloured man I felt greatly encouraged and strengthened in my cause while listening to these men – in the presence of the ablest men of the Caucasian race. Mr Ward especially attracted attention that convention. As an orator and thinker he was vastly superior, I thought, to any of us, and being perfectly black and of unmixed African descent, the splendours of his intellect went directly to the glory of his race. In depth of thought, fluency of speech, readiness of wit, logical exactness, and general intelligence, Samuel R. Ward has left no successor among the coloured men amongst us, and it was a sad day for our cause when he was laid low in the soil of a foreign country.

After the Free-Soil party, with 'Free Soil', 'Free Labour', 'Free States', 'Free Speech' and 'Free Men' on its banners, had defeated the almost permanently victorious Democratic party under the leadership of so able and popular a standard-bearer as General Lewis Cass, Mr Calhoun, and other Southern statesman were more than ever alarmed at the rapid increase of anti-slavery feeling in the North, and devoted their energies, more and more, to the work of devising means to stay the torrents and tie up the storm. They were not ignorant of whereunto this sentiment would grow if unsubjected and unextinguished. Hence they became fierce and furious in debate, and more extravagant than ever in their demands for additional safeguards to their system of robbery and murder. Assuming that the Constitution guaranteed their rights of property in their fellow men, they held it to be in open violation of the constitution for any American citizen in any part of the United States to speak, write, or act, against this right. But this shallow logic they plainly saw could do them no good unless they could obtain further safeguards for slavery. In order to effect this, the idea was suggested of so changing the constitution that there should be two instead of one President of the United States – one from the North and the other from the South – and that no measure should become a law without the assent of both. But this device was so utterly impracticable that it soon dropped out of sight, and it is mentioned here only to show the desperation of slave-holders to prop up their system of barbarism, against which the sentiment of the North was being directed with destructive skill and effect. They clamoured for more slave States, more power in the Senate and House of Representatives, and insisted upon the suppression of free speech. At the end of two years, in 1850, when Clay and Calhoun, two of the ablest leaders the South ever had, were still in the Senate, we had an attempt at a settlement of differences between the North and South which our legislators meant to be final. What those measures were I need not here enumerate, except to say that chief among them was the 'Fugitive-Slave Bill', framed by James M. Mason of Virginia, and supported by Daniel Webster of Massachusetts; a bill, undoubtedly more designed to involve the North in complicity with slavery and deaden its moral sentiment, than to procure the return of fugitives to their so-called owners. For a time this design did not altogether fail. Letters, speeches and pamphlets literally rained down upon the people of the North, reminding them of their constitutional duty to hunt down and return to bondage runaway slaves. In this the preachers were not much behind the press and the politicians, especially that class of preachers known as Doctors of Divinity. A long list of these came forward with their Bibles to show that neither Christ nor His holy apostles objected to returning fugitives to slavery. Now, that this evil day is past, a sight of those sermons would, I doubt not, bring the red blush of shame to the cheeks of many.

Living as I then did in Rochester, on the borders of Canada, I was compelled to see the terribly distressing effects of this cruel enactment. Fugitive slaves, who had lived for many years safely and securely in western New York and elsewhere, some of whom had by industry and economy saved money and bought little homes for themselves and their children, were suddenly alarmed, and compelled to flee to Canada for safety as from an enemy's land – a doomed city – and take up a dismal march to a new abode, empty-handed, among strangers. My old friend Ward, of whom I have just now spoken, found it necessary to give up the contest and flee to Canada, and thousands followed his example. Bishop Daniel A. Payne, of the African Methodist Episcopal Church, came to me about this time to consult me as to whether it was best to stand our ground or flee to Canada. I told him I could not desert my post until I saw I could not hold it, adding that I did not wish to leave while Garnet and Ward remained. 'Why,' said he, 'Ward, Ward, he is already gone. I saw him crossing from Detroit to Windsor.' I asked him if he was going to stay, and he answered, 'Yes; we are whipped, we are whipped! and we might as well retreat in order.' This was indeed a stunning blow. This man had power to do more to defeat this inhuman enactment than any other coloured man in the land, for no other could bring such brain power to bear against it. I felt like a besieged city at the news that its defenders had fallen at its gates.

The hardships imposed by this atrocious and shameless law were cruel and shocking, and yet only a few of all the fugitives of the Northern States were returned to slavery under its infamously wicked provisions. As a means of recapturing their runaway property in human flesh the law was an utter failure. Its efficiency was destroyed by its enormity. Its chief effect was to produce alarm and terror among the class subject to its operation, and this it did most effectually and distressingly. Even coloured people who had been free all their lives felt themselves very insecure in their freedom, for under this law, the oaths of any two villains were sufficient to consign a free man to slavery for life. While the law was a terror to the free, it was a still greater terror to the escaped bondman. To him there was no peace. Asleep or awake, at work or at rest, in church or market, he was liable to surprise and capture. By the law the judge got ten dollars a head for all he could consign to slavery, and only five dollars apiece for any which he might adjudge free. Although I was now myself free, I was not without apprehension. My purchase was of doubtful validity, having been bought when out of the possession of my owner, and when he must take what was given or take nothing. It was a question, whether my claimant could be stopped by such a sale, from asserting certain or supposable equitable rights in my body and soul. From rumours that reached me my house was guarded by my friends several nights, when kidnappers, had they come, would have got anything but a cool reception, for there would have been 'blows to take as well as blows to give'. Happily this reign of terror did not continue long. Despite the efforts of Daniel Webster and Millard Fillmore and our Doctors of Divinity, the law fell rapidly into disrepute. The rescue of Shadrack, resulting in the death of one of the kidnappers, in Boston, the cases of Simms and Anthony Burns, in the same place, created the deepest feeling against the law and its upholders. But the thing which more than all else destroyed the Fugitive-Slave Law was the resistance made to it by the fugitives themselves. A decided check was given to the execution of the law at Christiana, Penn., where three coloured men, being pursued by Mr Gorsuch and his son, slew the father, wounded the son, drove away the officers, and made their escape to my house in Rochester. The work of getting these men safely into Canada was a delicate one. They were not only fugitives from slavery but charged with murder, and officers were in pursuit of them. There was no time for delay. I could not look upon them as murderers. To me, they were heroic defenders of the just rights of man against man-stealers and murderers. So I fed them, and sheltered them in my house. Had they been pursued then and there, my home would have been stained with blood, for these men who had already tasted blood were well armed and prepared to sell their lives at the expense of the lives and limbs of their probable assailants. What they had already done at Christiana, and the cool determination which showed very plainly, especially in Parker, for that was the name of the leader, left no doubt on my mind that their courage was genuine and that their deeds would equal their words. The situation was critical and dangerous. The telegraph had that day announced their deeds at Christiana, their escape, and that the mountains of Pennsylvania were being searched for the murderers.

These men had reached me simultaneously with this news in the New York papers. Immediately after the occurrence at Christiana, they, instead of going into the mountains, were placed on a train which brought them to Rochester. They were thus almost in advance of the lightning, and much in advance of probable pursuit, unless the telegraph had already raised agents here. The hours they spent at my house were therefore hours of anxiety as well as activity. I dispatched my friend Miss Julia Griffiths to the landing three miles away on the Genesee River to ascertain if a steamer would leave that night for any port in Canada, and remained at home myself to guard my tired, dust-covered, and sleeping guests, for they had been harassed and travelling for two days and nights, and needed rest. Happily for us the suspense was not long, for it turned out, that that very night a steamer was to leave for Toronto, Canada.

This fact, however, did not end my anxiety. There was danger that between my house and the landing or at the landing itself we might meet with trouble. Indeed the landing was the place where trouble was likely to occur, if at all. As patiently as I could, I waited for the shades of night to come on, and then put the men in my 'Democrat carriage', and started for the landing on the Genesee. It was an exciting ride, and somewhat speedy withal. We reached the boat at least fifteen minutes before the time of its departure, and that without remark or molestation. But those fifteen minutes seemed much longer than usual. I remained on board till the order to haul in the gangway was given; I shook hands with my friends, received from Parker the revolver that fell from the hand of Gorsuch when he died, presented now as a token of gratitude and a memento of the battle for Liberty at Christiana, and I returned to my home with a sense of relief which I cannot stop here to describe. This affair, at Christiana, and the Jerry Rescue of Syracuse, inflicted fatal wounds on the Fugitive-Slave Bill. It became thereafter almost a dead letter, for slave-holders found that not only did it fail to put them in possession of their slaves, but that the attempt to enforce it brought odium upon themselves and weakened the slave system.

In the midst of these fugitive-slave troubles came the book known as *Uncle Tom's Cabin*, a work of marvellous depth and power. Nothing could have better suited the moral and humane requirements of the hour. Its effect was amazing, instantaneous, and universal. No book on the subject of slavery had so generally and favourably touched the American heart. It combined all the power and pathos of preceding publications of the kind, and was hailed by many as an inspired production. Mrs Stowe at once became an object of interest and admiration. She made fortune and fame at home, and awakened a deep interest abroad. Eminent parsons in England roused to anti-slavery enthusiasm by her *Uncle Tom's Cabin*, invited her to visit that country, and promised to give her a testimonial. Mrs Stowe accepted the invitation and the proffered testimonial. Before sailing for England, however, she invited me from Rochester, N.Y., to spend a day at her house in Andover, Mass. Delighted with an opportunity to become personally acquainted with the gifted authoress, I lost no time in making my way to Andover. I was received at her home with genuine cordiality. There was no contradiction between the authoress and her book. Mrs Stowe appeared in conversation equally as well as she appeared in her writings. She made to me a nice little speech in announcing her object in sending for me. 'I have invited you here, she said, 'because I wish to confer with you as to what can be done with the free coloured people of the country. I am going to England, and expect to have a considerable sum of money placed in my hands, and I intend to use it in some way, for the permanent improvement of the free coloured people, and especially for that class which has become free by their own exertions. In what way I can do this most successfully is the subject I wish to talk with you about. In any event I desire to have some monument raised after *Uncle Tom's Cabin*, which shall show that it produced more than transient influence.' She said several plans had been suggested, among others an educational institution pure and simple, but that she thought favourably of the establishment of an industrial school; and she desired me to express my views as to what I thought would be the best plan to help the free coloured people. I was not slow to tell Mrs Stowe all I knew and had thought on the subject. As to a purely educational institution, I agreed with her that it did not meet our necessities. I argued against expending money in that way. I was also opposed to an ordinary industrial school where pupils should merely earn the means of obtaining an education in books. There were such schools, already. What I thought of as best was rather a series of workshops, where coloured people could learn some of the handicrafts, learn to work in iron, wood, and leather, and where a plain English education could also be taught. I argued that the want of money was the root of all evil to the coloured people. They were shut out from all lucrative employments and compelled to be merely barbers, waiters, coachmen and the like, at wages so low that they could lay up little or nothing. Their poverty kept them ignorant, and their ignorance kept them degraded. We needed more to learn how to make a good living, than to learn Latin and Greek. After listening to me at considerable length, she was good enough to tell me that she favoured my views, and would devote the money she expected to receive abroad to meeting the want I had described as the most important; by establishing an institution in which coloured youth should learn trades as well as to read, write, and count. When about to leave Andover, Mrs Stowe asked me to put my views on the subject in the form of a letter, so that she could take it to England with her and show it to her friends there, that they might see to what their contributions were to be devoted. I acceded to her request, and wrote her the following letter for the purpose named –

Rochester, March 8, 1853

MY DEAR MRS STOWE – You kindly informed me, when at your house a fortnight ago, that you designed to do something which would permanently contribute to the improvement and elevation of the free coloured people in the United States. You especially expressed interest in such of this class as had become free by their own exertions, and desired most of all to be of service to them. In what manner and by what means you can assist this class most successfully, is the subject upon which you have done me the honour to ask my opinion . . . I assert then that *poverty*, *ignorance* and *degradation* are the combined evils; or in other words, these constitute the social disease of the free coloured people of the United States.

To deliver them from this triple malady, is to improve and elevate them, by which I mean, simply to put them on an equal footing with their white fellow countrymen in the sacred right to '*Life, Liberty*, and the pursuit of happiness'. I am for no fancied or artificial elevation, but only ask fair play. How shall this be obtained? I answer, first, not by establishing for our use high schools and colleges. Such institutions are, in my judgement, beyond our immediate occasions and are not adapted to our present most pressing wants. High schools and colleges are excellent institutions, and will in due season be greatly subservient to our progress; but they are the result, as well as they are the demand of a point of progress, which we as a people have not yet attained. Accustomed as we have been, to the rougher and harder modes of living, and of gaining a livelihood, we cannot, and we ought not to hope that in a single leap from our low condition, we can reach that of *Ministers, Lawyers, Doctors, Editors, Merchants*, etc. These will doubtless be attained by us; but this will only be, when we have patiently and laboriously, and I may add successfully, mastered and passed through the intermediate gradations of agriculture and the mechanical arts. Besides, there are – and perhaps this is a better reason for my view of the case – numerous institutions of learning in this country, already thrown open to coloured youth. To my thinking, there are quite as many facilities now afforded to the coloured people, as they can spare the time from the sterner duties of life, to avail themselves of. In their present condition of poverty, they cannot spare their sons and daughters two or three years at boarding-schools or colleges, to say nothing of finding the means to sustain them while at such institutions. I take it, therefore, that we are well provided for in this respect; and that it may be fairly inferred from the fact, that the facilities for our education, so far as schools and colleges in the Free States are concerned, will increase quite in proportion with our future wants. Colleges have been open to coloured youth in this country during the last dozen years. Yet few comparatively, have acquired a classical education; and even this few have found themselves educated far above a living condition, there being no methods by which they could turn their learning to account. Several of this latter class have entered the ministry; but you need not be told that an educated people is needed to sustain an educated ministry. There must be a certain amount of cultivation among the people, to sustain such a ministry. At present we have not that cultivation amongst us; and therefore, we value in the preacher, strong lungs, rather than high learning. I do not say, that educated ministers are not needed amongst us, far from it! I wish there were more of them! but to increase their number, is *not* the largest benefit you can bestow upon us.

We have two or three coloured lawyers in this country; and I rejoice in the fact; for it affords very gratifying evidence of our progress. Yet it must be confessed, that in point of success, our lawyers are as great failures as our ministers, White people will not employ them to the obvious embarrassment of their causes, and the blacks, taking their *cue* from the whites, have not sufficient confidence in their abilities to employ them. Hence educated coloured men, among the coloured people, are at a very great discount. It would seem that education and emigration go together with us, for as soon as a man rises amongst us, capable, by his genius and learning, to do us great service, just so soon he finds that he can serve himself better by going elsewhere. In proof of this, I might instance the Russwurms, the Garnets, the Wards, the Crummells and others, all men of superior ability and attainments, and capable of removing mountains of prejudice against their race, by their simple presence in the country; but these gentlemen, finding themselves embarrassed here by the peculiar disadvantages to which I have referred, disadvantages in part growing out of their education, being repelled by ignorance on the one hand, and prejudice on the other, and having no taste to continue a contest against such odds, they have sought more congenial climes, where they can live more peaceable and quiet lives. I regret their election, but I cannot blame them; for with an equal amount of education and the hard lot which was theirs, I might follow their example ...

There is little reason to hope that any considerable number of the free coloured people will ever be induced to leave this country, even if such a thing were desirable. This black man – *un*like the Indian – loves civilisation. He does not make very great progress in civilisation himself but he likes to be in the midst of it, and prefers to share its most galling evils, to encountering barbarism. Then the love of the country, the dread of isolation, the lack of adventurous spirit, and the thought of seeming to desert their 'brethren in bonds', are a powerful check upon all schemes of colonisation, which look to the removal of the coloured people, without the slaves. The truth is, dear madam, we are *here*, and here we are likely to remain. Individuals emigrate – nations never. We have grown up with this republic, and I see nothing in her character, or even in the character of the American people as yet, which compels the belief that we must leave the United States. If then, we are to remain here, the question for the wise and good is precisely that you have submitted to me – namely: What can be done to improve the condition of the free people of colour in the United States? The plan which I humbly submit in answer to this enquiry – and in the hope that it may find favour with you, and with the many friends of humanity who honour, love, and co-operate with you – is the establishment in Rochester, N.Y., or in some other part of the United States equally favourable to such an enterprise, of an INDUSTRIAL COLLEGE in which shall be taught several important branches of the mechanical arts. This college to be opened to coloured youth. I will pass over the details of such an institution as I propose ... Never having had a day's schooling in all my life I may not be expected to map out the details of a plan so comprehensive as that involved in the idea of a college. I repeat, then, I leave the organisation and administration to the superior wisdom of yourself and the friends who second your noble efforts. The argument in favour of an industrial college – a college to be conducted by the best men – and the best workmen which the mechanical arts can afford; a college where coloured youth can be instructed to use their hands, as well as their heads; where they can be put into possession of the means of getting a living whether their lot in after life may be cast among civilised or uncivilised men; whether they choose to stay here, or prefer to return to the land of their fathers – is briefly this: Prejudice against the free coloured people in the United States has shown itself nowhere so invincible as among mechanics. The farmer and the professional man cherish no feeling so bitter as that cherished by these. The latter would starve us out of the country entirely. At this moment I can more easily get my son into a lawyer's office to learn law than I can into a blacksmith's shop to blow the bellows and to wield the sledge-hammer. Denied the means of learning useful trades we are pressed into the narrowest limits to obtain a livelihood. In times past we have been the hewers of wood and the drawers of water for American society, and we once enjoyed a monopoly in menial enjoyments, but this is so no longer. Even these enjoyments are rapidly passing away out of our hands. The fact is – every day begins with the lesson, and ends with the lesson – that coloured men must learn trades; and must find new employment; new modes of usefulness to society, or that they must decay under the pressing wants to which their condition is rapidly bringing them.

We must become mechanics; we must build as well as live in houses; we must make as well as use furniture; we must construct bridges as well as pass over them, before we can properly live or be respected by our fellow men. We need mechanics as well as ministers. We need workers in iron, clay, and leather. We have orators, authors, and other professional men, but these reach only a certain class, and get respect for our race in certain select circles. To live here as we ought we must fasten ourselves to our country-men through their everyday cardinal wants. We must not only be able to *black* boots, but to *make* them. At present we are unknown in the Northern States as mechanics. We give no proof of genius or skill at the county, State, or national fairs. We are unknown at any of the great exhibitions of the industry of our fellow-citizens, and being unknown we are unconsidered.

The fact that we make no show of our ability is held conclusive of our inability to make any, hence all the indifference and contempt with which incapacity is regarded, fall upon us, and that too, when we have had no means of disproving the infamous opinion of our natural inferiority. I have during the last dozen years denied before the Americans that we are an inferior race; but this has been done by arguments based upon admitted principles rather than by the presentation of facts. Now, firmly believing, as I do, that there are skill, invention, power, industry, and real mechanical genius, among the coloured people, which will bear favourable testimony for them, and which only need the means to develop them, I am decidedly in favour of the establishment of such a college as I have mentioned. The benefits of such an institution would not be confined to the Northern States, nor to the free coloured people. They would extend over the whole Union. The slave not less than the freeman would be benefited by such an institution. It must be confessed that the most powerful argument now used by the Southern slave-holder, and the one most soothing to his conscience, is that derived from the low condition of the free coloured people of the North. I have long felt that too little attention has been given by our truest friends in this country to removing this stumbling block out of the way of the slave's liberation.

The most telling, the most killing refutation of slavery, is the presentation of an industrious, enterprising, thrifty, and intelligent free black population. Such a population I believe would rise in the Northern States under the fostering care of such a college as that supposed.

To show that we are capable of becoming mechanics I might adduce any amount of testimony; but dear madam, I need not ring the changes on such a proposition. There is no question in the mind of any unprejudiced person that the negro is capable of making a good mechanic. Indeed, even those who cherish the bitterest feelings towards us have admitted that the apprehension that negroes might be employed in their stead, dictated the policy of excluding them from trades altogether. But I will not dwell upon this point as I fear I have already trespassed too long upon your precious time, and written more than I ought to expect you to read. Allow me to say in conclusion, that I believe every intelligent coloured man in America will approve and rejoice at the establishment of some such institution as that now suggested. There are many respectable coloured men, fathers of large families, having boys nearly grown up, whose minds are tossed by day and by night with the anxious enquiry, 'What shall I do with my boy?' Such an institution would meet the wants of such persons. Then, too, the establishment of such an institution would be in character with the eminently practical philanthropy of your transatlantic friends. America could scarcely object to it as an attempt to agitate the public mind on the subject of slavery, or to *dissolve the Union*. It could not be tortured into a cause for hard words by the American people, but the noble and good of all classes would see in the effort an excellent motive, a benevolent object, temperately, wisely, and practically manifested.

Wishing, you, dear madam, renewed health, a pleasant passage, and safe return to your native land.

I am most truly, your grateful friend,

FREDERICK DOUGLASS
Mrs H. B. Stowe

I was not only requested to write the foregoing letter for the purpose indicated, but I was also asked, with admirable foresight, to see and ascertain, as far as possible, the views of the free coloured people themselves in respect to the proposed measure for their benefit. This I was able to do in July 1853, at the largest and most enlightened coloured convention that, up to that time, had ever assembled in the country. This convention warmly approved the plan of a manual labour school, as already described, and expressed high appreciation of the wisdom and benevolence of Mrs Stowe. This convention was held in Rochester, N.Y., and will long be remembered there for the surprise and gratification it caused our friends in that city. They were not looking for such an exhibition of enlightened zeal and ability as were there displayed in speeches, addresses, and resolutions; and in the conduct of the business for which it had assembled. Its proceedings attracted widespread attention at home and abroad.

While Mrs Stowe was abroad, she was attacked by the pro-slavery press of the United States so persistently and vigorously, for receiving money for her own private use, that the Revd Henry Ward Beecher felt called upon to notice and reply to them in the columns of the New York *Independent*, of which he was then the editor. He denied that Mrs Stowe was gathering British gold for herself; and referred her assailants to me, if they would learn what she intended to do with the money. In answer to her maligners, I denounced their accusations as groundless, and assured the public through the columns of my paper, that the testimonial then being raised in England by Mrs Stowe, would be sacredly devoted to the establishment of an industrial school for coloured youth. This announcement was circulated by other journals, and the attacks ceased. Nobody could well object to such an application of money, received from any source, at home or abroad. After her return to this country, I called again on Mrs Stowe, and was much disappointed to learn from her that she had reconsidered her plan for the industrial school. I have never been able to see any force in the reasons for this change. It is enough, however, to say that they were sufficient for her, and that she no doubt acted conscientiously, though her change of purpose was a great disappointment, and placed me in an awkward position before the coloured people of this country, as well as to friends abroad, to whom I had given assurances that the money would be appropriated in the manner I have described.

CHAPTER IX

Increasing Demands of the Slave Power

Increased demands of slavery – War in Kansas – John Brown's raid – His capture and execution – My escape to England from the United States marshals

Notwithstanding the natural tendency of the human mind to weary of an old story, and to turn away from chronic abuses for which it sees no remedy, the anti-slavery agitation for thirty long years – from 1830 to 1860 – was sustained with ever increasing intensity and power. This was not entirely due to the extraordinary zeal and ability of the anti-slavery agitators themselves; for with all their admitted ardour and eloquence, they could have done very little without the aid rendered them unwittingly, by the aggressive character of slavery itself. It was in the nature of the system never to rest in obscurity, although that condition was in a high degree essential to its security. It was for ever forcing itself into prominence. Unconscious, apparently, of its own deformity, it omitted no occasion for inviting disgust by seeking approval and admiration. It was noisiest when it should have been most silent, and unobtrusive. One of its defenders, when asked what would satisfy him as a slave-holder, said, 'he never would be satisfied until he could call the roll of his slaves in the shadow of Bunker Hill monument'. Every effort made to put down agitation only served to impart to it new strength and vigour. Of this class was the 'gag rule', attempted and partially enforced in Congress – the attempted suppression of the right of petition – the mob-ocratic demonstrations against the exercise of free speech – the display of pistols, bludgeons, and plantation manners in the Congress of the nation – the demand, shamelessly made by our Government upon England, for the return of slaves who had won their liberty by their valour on the high seas – the bill for the recapture of runaway slaves – the annexation of Texas for the avowed purpose of increasing the number of slave States, and thus increasing the power of slavery in the union – the war with Mexico – the fillibustering expeditions against Cuba and Central America – the cold-blooded decision of Chief Justice Taney in the Dred Scott case, wherein he states, as it were, a historical fact, that 'negroes are deemed to have no rights which white men are bound to respect' – the perfidious repeal of the Missouri compromise, when all its advantages to the South had been gained and appropriated, and when nothing had been gained by the North – the armed and bloody attempt to force slavery upon the virgin soil of Kansas – the efforts of both of the great political parties to drive from place and power every man suspected of ideas and principles hostile to slavery – the rude attacks made upon Giddings, Hale, Chase, Wilson, Wm H. Seward and Charles Sumner – the effort to degrade these brave men, and drive them from positions of prominence – the summary manner in which Virginia hanged John Brown; in a word, whatever was done or attempted, with a view to the support and security of slavery, only served as fuel to the fire, and heated the furnace of agitation to a higher degree than any before attained. This was true up to the moment when the nation found it necessary to gird on the sword for the salvation of the country and the destruction of slavery.

At no time during all the ten years preceding the war, was the public mind at rest. Mr Clay's compromise measures in 1850, whereby all the troubles of the country about slavery were to be 'in the deep bosom of the ocean buried', was hardly dry on the pages of the statute book before the whole land was rocked with rumoured agitation, and for one, I did my best, by pen and voice, and by ceaseless activity to keep it alive and vigorous. Later on, in 1854, we had the Missouri compromise, which removed the only grand legal barrier against the spread of slavery over all the territory of the United States. From this time there was no pause, no repose. Everybody, however dull, could see that this was a phase of the slavery question which was not to be slighted or ignored. The people of the North had been accustomed to ask, in a tone of cruel indifference, 'What have we to do with slavery?' and now no laboured speech was required in answer. Slave-holding aggression settled this question for us. The presence of slavery in a territory would certainly exclude the sons and daughters of the Free States more effectually than statutes or yellow fever. Those who cared nothing for the slave, and were willing to tolerate slavery inside the slave States, were nevertheless not quite prepared to find themselves and their children excluded from the common inheritance of the nation. It is not surprising therefore, that the public mind of the North was easily kept intensely alive on this subject, nor that in 1856 an alarming expression of feeling on this point was seen in the large vote given for John C. Fremont and William L. Dayton for President and Vice-President of the United States. Until this last uprising of the North against the slave power the anti-slavery movement was largely retained in the hands of the original abolitionists, whose most prominent leaders have already been mentioned elsewhere in this volume. After 1856 a mightier arm and a more numerous host was raised against it: the agitation becoming broader and deeper. The times at this point illustrated the principle of tension and compression, action and reaction. The more open, flagrant, and impudent the slave power, the more firmly it was confronted by the rising anti-slavery spirit of the North. No one act did more to rouse the North to a comprehension of the infernal and barbarous spirit of slavery and its determination to 'rule or ruin', than the cowardly and brutal assault made in the American Senate upon Charles Sumner, by Preston S. Brooks, a member of Congress from South Carolina. Shocking and scandalous as was this attack, the spirit in which the deed was received and commended by the community, was still more disgraceful. Southern ladies even applauded the armed bully for his murderous assault upon an unarmed Northern senator, because of words spoken in debate! This, more than all else, told the thoughtful people of the North the kind of civilisation to which they were linked, and how plainly it foreshadowed a conflict on a larger scale.

As a measure of agitation, the repeal of the Missouri Compromise alluded to, was perhaps the most effective. It was that which brought Abraham Lincoln into prominence, and into conflict with Stephen A. Douglas – who was the author of that measure – and compelled the Western States to take a deeper interest than they ever had done before in the whole question. Pregnant words were now spoken on the side of freedom, words which went straight to the heart of the nation. It was

Mr Lincoln who told the American people at this crisis that the 'Union could not long endure half slave and half free; that they must be all one or the other, and that the public mind could find no resting place but in the belief in the ultimate extinction of slavery.' These were not the words of an abolitionist – branded a fanatic, and carried away by an enthusiastic devotion to the negro – but the calm, cool, deliberate utterance of a statesman, comprehensive enough to take in the welfare of the whole country. No wonder that the friends of freedom saw in this plain man of Illinois the proper standard-bearer of all the moral and political forces which could be united and wielded against the slave power. In a few simple words he had embodied the thought of the loyal nation, and indicated the character fit to lead and guide the country amid perils present and to come.

The South was not far behind the North in recognising Abraham Lincoln as the natural leader of the rising political sentiment of the country against slavery; and it was equally quick in its efforts to counteract and destroy his influence. Its papers teemed with the bitterest invectives against the 'backwoodsman of Illinois', the 'flat-boatman', the 'rail-splitter', the 'third-rate lawyer', and much else and worse.

Preceding the repeal of the Missouri Compromise, I gave at the anniversary of the American Anti-Slavery Society in New York, the following picture of the state of the anti-slavery conflict as it then existed.

It is evident that there is in this country a purely slavery party, a party which exists for no other earthly purpose but to promote the interest of slavery. It is known by no particular name, and has assumed no definite shape, but its branches reach far and wide in Church and State. This shapeless and nameless party is not intangible in other and more important respects. It has a fixed, definite, and comprehensive policy towards the whole free coloured population of the United States. I understand that policy to comprehend: first, the complete suppression of all anti-slavery discussion; second, the expulsion of the entire free coloured people of the United States; third, the nationalisation of slavery; fourth, guarantees for the endless perpetuation of slavery and its extension over Mexico and Central America. Sir, these objects are forcibly presented to us in the stern logic of passing events, and in all the facts that have been before us during the last three years. The country has been and is dividing on these grand issues. Old party ties are broken. Like is finding its like on both sides of these issues, and the great battle is at hand. For the present the best representation of the slavery party is the Democratic party. Its great head for the present is President Pierce, whose boast it was before his election, that his whole life had been consistent with the interests of slavery – that he is above reproach on that score. In his inaugural address he reassures the South on this point, so that there shall be no misapprehension. Well, the head of the slave power being in power, it is natural that the pro-slavery elements should cluster around his administration, and that is rapidly being done. The stringent protectionist and the free-trader strike hands. The supporters of Fillmore are becoming the supporters of Pierce. Silver Grey Whigs shake hands with Hunker Democrats, the former only differing from the latter in name. They are in fact of one heart and one mind, and the union is natural and perhaps inevitable. Pilate and Herod made friends. The keystone to the arch of this grand union of forces of the slave party is the so-called Compromise of 1860. In that measure we have all the objects of our slave-holding policy specified. It is, sir, favourable to this view of the situation, that the Whig party and the Democratic party bent lower, sunk deeper, and strained harder in their conventions, preparatory to the late Presidential election to meet the demands of slavery. Never did parties come before the Northern people with propositions of such undisguised contempt for the moral sentiment and religious ideas of that people. They dared to ask them to unite with them in a war upon free speech, upon conscience, and to drive the Almighty presence from the councils of the nation. Resting their platforms upon the Fugitive-Slave Bill they have boldly asked this people for political power to execute its horrible and hell-black provisions. The history of that election reveals with great clearness, the extent to which slavery has 'shot its leprous distilment' through the life blood of the nation. The party most thoroughly opposed to the cause of justice and humanity triumphed, while the party only suspected of leaning toward those principles was overwhelmingly defeated, and some say annihilated. But here is a still more important fact, which still better discloses the designs of the slave power. It is a fact full of meaning, that no sooner did the Democratic party come into power than a system of legislation was presented to all the legislatures of the Northern States designed to put those States in harmony with the Fugitive-Slave Law, and with the malignant spirit evinced by the national government towards the free coloured inhabitants of the country. The whole movement on the part of the States bears unmistakable evidence of having one origin, of emanating from one head and urged forward by one power. It was simultaneous, uniform and general, and looked only to one end. It was intended to put thorns under foot already bleeding; to crush a people already bowed down; to enslave a people already but half free; in a word, it was intended and well calculated to discourage, dishearten, and if possible to drive the whole free coloured people out of the country. In looking at the black law then recently enacted in the State of Illinois one is struck dumb by its enormity. It would seem that the men who passed that law, had not only successfully banished from their minds all sense of justice, but all sense of shame as well: these law codes propose to sell the bodies and souls of the blacks to provide the means of intelligence and refinement for the whites; to rob every black stranger who ventures among them to increase their educational fund.

While this kind of legislation is going on in the States a pro-slavery political board of health is being established at Washington. Senators Hale, Chase, and Sumner are robbed of their senatorial rights and dignity as representatives of sovereign States, because they have refused to be inoculated with the pro-slavery virus of the times. Among the services which a senator is expected to perform, are many that can only be done efficiently as members of important committees, and the slave power in the Senate in saying to these honourable senators, you shall not serve on the committees of this body, took the responsibility of insulting and robbing the States which had sent them there. It is an attempt at Washington to decide for the States who the States shall send to the Senate. Sir, it strikes me that this aggression on the part of the slave power did not meet at the hands of the proscribed and insulted senators the rebuke which they had a right to expect from them. It seems to me that a great opportunity was lost, that the great principle of senatorial equality was left undefended at a time when its vindication was sternly demanded. But it is not to the purpose of my present statement to criticise the conduct of friends. Such should be left to the discretion of anti-slavery men in Congress. Charges of recreancy should never be made but on the most sufficient grounds. For of all places in the world where an anti-slavery man needs the confidence and encouragement of his friends, I take Washington – the citadel of slavery – to be that place.

Let attention now be called to the social influences operating and co-operating with the slave power at the time, designed to promote all its malign objects. We see here the black man attacked in his most vital interests: prejudice and hate are systematically excited against him. The wrath of other labourers is stirred up against him. The Irish, who at home readily sympathise with the oppressed everywhere, are instantly taught when they step upon our soil to hate and despise the negro. They are taught to believe that he eats the bread that belongs to them. The cruel lie is told them, that we deprive them of labour and receive the money which would otherwise make its way into their pockets. Sir, the Irish-American will find out his mistake one day. He will find that in assuming our avocation, he has also assumed our degradation. But for the present we are the sufferers. Our old employments, by which we have been accustomed to gain a livelihood are gradually slipping from our hands; every hour sees us elbowed out of some employment to make room for some newly-arrived emigrant from the Emerald Isle, whose hunger and colour entitle him to special favour. These white men are becoming house-servants, cooks, stewards, waiters, and flunkies. For aught I see they adjust themselves to their stations with all proper humility. If they cannot rise to the dignity of white men, they show that they can fall to the degradation of black men. But now, sir, look once more! While the coloured people are thus elbowed out of employment; while a ceaseless enmity in the Irish is excited against us; while State after State enacts laws against us; while we are being hunted down like wild beasts, while we are oppressed with the sense of increasing insecurity, the American Colonisation Society, with hypocrisy written on its brow, comes to the front, awakens new life, and vigorously presses its scheme for our expatriation upon the attention of the American people. Papers have been started in the North and the South to promote this long cherished object – to get rid of the negro, who is presumed to be a standing menace to slavery. Each of these papers is adapted to the latitude in which it is published, but each and all are united in calling upon the Government for appropriations to enable the Colonisation Society to send us out of the country by steam. Evidently this society looks upon our extremity as their opportunity, and whenever the elements are stirred against us, they are stimulated to unusual activity. They do not deplore our misfortunes, but rather rejoice in them, since they prove that the two races cannot flourish on the same soil. But, sir, I must hasten. I have thus briefly given my view of one aspect of the present position and future prospects of the coloured people of the United States. And what I have said is far from encouraging to my afflicted people. I have seen the cloud gather upon the sable brows of some who hear me. I confess the case looks bad enough. Sir, I am not a hopeful man. I think I am apt to undercalculate the benefits of the future. Yet, sir, in this seemingly desperate case, I do not despair for my people. There is a bright side to almost every picture, and ours is no exception to the general rule. If the influences against us are strong, those for us are also strong. To the enquiry, will our enemies prevail in the execution of their designs – in my God, and in my soul, I believe they *will not*. Let us look at the first object sought for by the slavery party of the country, viz., the suppression of the anti-slavery discussion. They desire to suppress discussion on this subject, with a view to the peace of the slave-holder and the security of slavery. Now, sir, neither the principle nor the subordinate objects, here declared, can be at all gained by the slave power, and for this reason: it involves the proposition to padlock the lips of the whites, in order to secure the fetters on the limbs of the blacks. The right of speech, precious and priceless, *cannot – will not –* be surrendered to slavery. Its suppression is asked for, as I have said, to give peace and security to slave-holders. Sir, that thing cannot be done. God has interposed an insuperable obstacle to any such result. 'There can be *no peace*, saith my God, to the wicked.' Suppose it were possible to put down this discussion, what would it avail the guilty slave-holder, pillowed as he is upon the heaving bosoms of ruined souls? He could not have a peaceful spirit. If every anti-slavery tongue in the nation were silent – every anti-slavery organisation dissolved – every anti-slavery periodical, paper, pamphlet, book, or what not, searched out, burned to ashes, and their ashes given to the four winds of heaven, still, still the slave-holder could have *no peace*. In every pulsation of the heart, in every throb of his life, in every glance of his eye, in the breeze that soothes, and in the thunder that startles, would be waked up an accuser, whose cause is 'thou art verily guilty concerning thy brother'.

This is no fancy sketch of the times indicated. The situation during all the administration of President Pierce was only less threatening and stormy than that under the administration of James Buchanan. One sowed, the other reaped. One was the wind, the other was the whirlwind. Intoxicated by their success in repealing the Missouri compromise – in divesting the native-born coloured man of American citizenship – in harnessing both the Whig and Democratic parties to the car of slavery, and in holding continued possession of the national government, the propagandists of slavery threw off all disguises, abandoned all semblance of moderation, and very naturally and inevitably proceeded under Mr Buchanan, to avail themselves of all the advantages of their victories Having legislated out of existence the great national wall, erected in the better days of the Republic, against the spread of slavery, and against the increase of its power – having blotted out all distinction, as they thought, between freedom and slavery in the law, theretofore, governing the territories of the United States, and having left the whole question of the legislation or prohibition of slavery to be decided by the people of a territory, the next thing in order was to fill up the territory of Kansas – the one likely to be first organised – with a people friendly to slavery, and to keep out all such as were opposed to making that territory a Free State. Here was an open invitation to a fierce and bitter strife; and the history of the times shows how promptly that invitation was accepted by both classes to which it was given, and the scenes of lawless violence and blood that followed.

All advantages were at first on the side of those who were for making Kansas a slave State. The moral force of the repeal of the Missouri Compromise was with them; the strength of the triumphant Democratic party was with them; the power and patronage of the Federal government was with them; the various governors, sent out under the territorial government, were with them; and, above all, the proximity of the territory to the slave State of Missouri favoured them and all their designs. Those who opposed the making Kansas a slave State, for the most part were far away from the battle-ground, residing chiefly in New England, more than a thousand miles from the eastern border of the territory, and their direct way of entering it was through a country violently hostile to them. With such odds against them, and only an idea – though a grand one – to support them, it will ever be a wonder that they succeeded in making Kansas a Free State. It is not my purpose to write particularly of this or of any other phase of the conflict with slavery, but simply to indicate the nature of the struggle, and the successive steps leading to the final result. The important point to me, as one desiring to see the slave power crippled, slavery limited and abolished, was the effect of this Kansas battle upon the moral sentiment of the North: how it made abolitionists before they themselves became aware of it, and how it rekindled the zeal, stimulated the activity, and strengthened the faith of our old anti-slavery forces. 'Draw on me for £200 per month while the conflict lasts,' said the great-hearted Gerritt Smith. George L. Stearns poured out his thousands, and anti-slavery men of smaller means were proportionally liberal. H. W. Beecher shouted the right word at the head of a mighty column; Sumner in the Senate spoke as no man had ever spoken there before. Lewis Tappan representing one class of the old opponents of slavery, and William L. Garrison the other, lost sight of their former differences, and bent all their energies to the freedom of Kansas. But these and others were merely generators of anti-slavery force. The men who *went* to Kansas with the purpose of making it a Free State, were the heroes and martyrs. One of the leaders in this holy crusade for freedom, with whom I was brought into near relations, was John Brown, whose person, house, and purposes I have already described. This brave old man and his sons were amongst the first to hear and heed the trumpet of freedom calling them to battle. What they did and suffered, what they sought and gained, and by what means, are matters of history, and need not be repeated here.

When it became evident, as it soon did, that the war for and against slavery in Kansas was not to be decided by the peaceful means of words and ballots, but swords and bullets were to be employed on both sides, Captain John Brown felt that now, after long years of waiting, his hour had come; and never did man meet the perilous requirements of any occasion more cheerfully, courageously, and disinterestedly than he. I met him often during this struggle, and saw deeper into his soul than when I met him in Springfield seven or eight years before, and all I saw of him gave me a more favourable impression of the man, and inspired me with a higher respect for his character. In his repeated visits to the East to obtain necessary arms and supplies, he often did me the honour of spending hours and days with me at Rochester. On more than one occasion I got up meetings and solicited aid to be used by him for the cause, and I may say without boasting that my efforts in this respect were not entirely fruitless. Deeply interested as 'Ossawatamie Brown' was in Kansas he never lost sight of what he called his greater work – the liberation of all the slaves in the United States. But for the then present he saw his way to the great end through Kansas. It would be a grateful task to tell of his exploits in the border struggle, how he met persecution with persecution, war with war, strategy with strategy, assassination and house-burning with signal and terrible retaliation, till even the blood-thirsty propagandists of slavery were compelled to cry for quarter. The horrors wrought by his iron hand cannot be contemplated without a shudder, but it is the shudder which one feels at the execution of a murderer. The amputation of a limb is a severe trial to feeling, but necessity is a full justification of it to reason. To call out a murderer at midnight, and without note or warning, judge or jury, run him through with a sword, was a terrible remedy for a terrible malady. The question was not merely which class should prevail in Kansas, but whether free-state men should live there at all. The border ruffians from Missouri had openly declared their purpose not only to make Kansas a slave State, but that they would make it impossible for free-state men to live there. They burned their towns, burned their farm-houses, and by assassination spread terror among them until many of the free-state settlers were compelled to escape for their lives. John Brown was therefore the logical result of slave-holding persecutions. Until the lives of tyrants and murderers shall become more precious in the sight of men than justice and liberty, John Brown will need no defender. In dealing with the ferocious enemies of the free-state cause in Kansas he not only showed boundless courage but eminent military skill. With men so few and odds against him so great, few captains ever surpassed him in achievements, some of which seem too disproportionate for belief, and yet no voice has called them in question. With only eight men he met, fought, whipped, and captured Henry Clay Pate with twenty-five well-armed and well-mounted men. In this battle he selected his ground so wisely, handled his men so skilfully, and attacked his enemies so vigorously, that they could neither run nor fight, and were therefore compelled to surrender to a force less than one-third their own. With just thirty men on another memorable occasion he met and vanquished 400 Missourians under the command of General Read. These men had come into the territory under an oath never to return to their homes in Missouri till they had stamped out the last vestige of the free-state spirit in Kansas. But a brush with old Brown instantly took this high conceit out of them, and they were glad to get home upon any terms, without stopping to stipulate. With less than 100 men to defend the town of Lawrence, he offered to lead them and give battle to 1,400 men on the banks of the Waukerusia river, and was much vexed when his offer was refused by General Jim Lane and others, to whom the defence of the place was committed. Before leaving Kansas he went into the border of Missouri, and liberated a dozen slaves in a single night, and despite of slave laws and marshals, he brought these people through half a dozen States and landed them safe in Canada. The successful efforts of the North in making Kansas a Free State, despite all the sophistical doctrines and the sanguinary measures of the South to make it a slave State, exercised a potent influence upon subsequent political forces and events in the then near future. It is interesting to note the facility with which the statesmanship of a section of the country adapted its convictions to changed conditions. When it was found that the doctrine of popular sovereignty – first I think invented by General Cass, and afterwards adopted by Stephen A. Douglas – failed to make Kansas a slave State, and could not be safely trusted in other emergencies, Southern statesmen promptly abandoned and reprobated that doctrine, and took what they considered firmer ground. They lost faith in the rights, powers, and wisdom of the people, and took refuge in the Constitution. Henceforth the favourite doctrine of the South was that the people of a territory had no voice in the matter of slavery whatever; that the Constitution of the United States, of its own force and effect, carried slavery safely into any territory of the United States and protected the system there until it ceased to be a territory and became a State. The practical operation of this doctrine would be to make all the future new States slave-holding States, for slavery once planted and nursed for years in a territory would easily strengthen itself against the evil day and defy eradication. This doctrine was in some sense supported by Chief Justice Taney, in the infamous Dred Scott decision. This new ground, however, was destined to bring misfortune to its inventors, for it divided for a time the Democratic party, one faction of it going with John C. Breckenridge and the other espousing the cause of Stephen A. Douglass; the one held firmly to the doctrine that the United States Constitution, without any legislation, territorial, national, or otherwise, by its own, force and effect, carried slavery into all the territories of the United States; the other held that the people of a territory had the right to admit slavery or reject slavery, as in their judgement they might deem best. Now, while this war of words – this conflict of doctrines – was in progress, the portentous shadow of a stupendous civil war became more and more visible. Bitter complaints were raised by the slave-holders that they were about to be despoiled of their proper share in territory won by a common valour, or bought by a common treasure. The North, on the other hand, or rather a large and growing party at the North, insisted that the complaint was unreasonable and ground-less; that nothing properly considered as property was excluded or meant to be excluded from the territories; that Southern men could settle in any territory of the United States with some kinds of property, and on the same footing and with the same protection as citizens of the North; that men and women are not property in the same sense as houses, lands, horses, sheep, and swine are property, and that the fathers of the Republic neither intended the extension nor the perpetuity of slavery; that liberty is national, and slavery is sectional. From 1856 to 1860 the whole land rocked with this great controversy. When the explosive force of this controversy had already weakened the bolts of the American Union; when the agitation of the public mind was at its topmost height; when the two sections were at their extreme points of difference; when comprehending the perilous situation, such statesmen of the North as William H. Seward sought to allay the rising storm by soft persuasive speech, and when all hope of compromise had nearly vanished, as if to banish even the last glimmer of hope for peace between the sections, John Brown came upon the scene. On the night of the 16th of October 1859, there appeared near the confluence of the Potomac and Shenandoah rivers, a party of nineteen men – fourteen white and five coloured. They were not only armed themselves, but they brought with them a large supply of arms for such persons as might join them. These men invaded the town of Harper's Ferry, disarmed the watchman, took possession of the arsenal, rifle factory, armoury, and other Government property at that place, arrested and made prisoners of nearly all the prominent citizens in the neighbourhood, collected about fifty slaves, put bayonets into the hands of such as were able and willing to fight for their liberty, killed three men, proclaimed general emancipation, held the ground more than thirty hours, were subsequently overpowered and nearly all killed, wounded, or captured by a body of United States troops under command of Colonel Robert E. Lee, since famous as the rebel General Lee. Three out of the nineteen invaders were captured while fighting, and one of them was Captain John Brown – the man who originated, planned, and commanded the expedition. At the time of his capture Captain Brown was supposed to be mortally wounded, as he had several ugly gashes and bayonet wounds on his head and body, and apprehending that he might speedily die, or that he might be rescued by his friends, and thus the opportunity to make him a signal example of slave-holding vengeance, would be lost, his captors hurried him to Charlestown, ten miles further within the border of Virginia, placed him in prison strongly guarded by troops, and before his wounds were healed he was brought into court.

[The preliminary examination of Brown took place at Charlestown,

Virginia. He protested against the unfairness of being so hastily charged, and denounced the whole proceedings as a mockery of justice. His conviction was a foregone conclusion, as the conviction of any man must be, who is taken in the very act of breaking the laws. He had challenged the strength of Virginia, and indeed of all the Southern States, and of the Federation itself. He had defied ordinances which he knew to exist, and roused the passions and fears of men. It was not to be expected that the slave-owners would show him any mercy. They had power on their side, and legal right; and, however great one's admiration of the motives which influenced this man, it is impossible not to see that a slave-insurrection, had it been really brought about, would have proved the most disastrous method of settling the great difficulty that could possibly have been devised. Brown was warmly supported by the Abolitionists; but, even in the North, more temperate politicians deplored the error he had committed, and saw that there was no reasonable hope of his being spared. The case was handed over to the grand jury, and the trial took place on the 27th of October. The prisoner requested time to prepare his defence, the assistance of counsel from the Free States, and liberty of communicating with the other prisoners; but most of these demands were refused, and the trial was pushed on with cruel and indecent haste. Virginia was frightened and vindictive, and, as an excuse for not granting any delay, it was urged that the women of the State were harassed by alarm and anxiety as long as their husbands were away from home, and that the jurymen desired to return to them. When Brown was brought into court, he was so weak, owing to the wounds he had received, that he could not stand upon his feet, but lay full-length upon a bed; yet the fears of his enemies were even then predominant. The Governor of Virginia, Mr Wise, is stated to have remarked at Richmond, before the members of the Legislature, that Brown was a murderer, and ought to be hanged. As it was one of the prerogatives of the Governor to grant pardons, after convictions which might appear to him not strictly in accordance with justice, it was a monstrous outrage on propriety to give utterance to such an opinion while the case was yet awaiting trial. But the remark was only of a piece with the whole procedure. The prisoner was, indeed, furnished with counsel by the court; but the gentlemen to whom the duty of defending him was assigned, had no time for preparing their speeches, for calling witnesses, or for examining the law of the case. He was supplied with no list of witnesses, for the prosecution, nor had he any knowledge of who they were to be, until they were produced in court. Brown himself had sent for counsel to the

Northern States; but on arriving, they were so exhausted by their long and hurried journey that they asked for a short delay, which was denied them. All this while, the prisoner lay on his pallet, sick, feverish, and half-conscious, knowing little of the methods by which his conviction was to be secured, but feeling certain from the first that conviction was inevitable A verdict of guilty, on the 31st of October, was followed by sentence of death, and the execution was fixed for the 2nd of December. The decision was appealed against, but ultimately confirmed. On hearing the verdict and the sentence of the judge, Brown said, 'Gentlemen, make an end of slavery, or slavery will make an end of you.' It was an utterance in the spirit of prophecy.

As the fatal day approached, the feeling of apprehension on the part of the Virginians became still more intense. Governor Wise ordered out a large military force, to overawe any attempt at rescue that might be made. It was also proposed to establish martial law; but this was not done. Brown expressed entire resignation to his fate, and money was liberally contributed in the Northern and Western States to support his family. At eleven o'clock on the morning of the 2nd of December, the prisoner was brought out of gaol. Before leaving, he bade adieu to his fellow-prisoners, and was very affectionate to all excepting his principal assistant, a man named Cook, whom he charged with having deceived and misled him respecting the support he was to receive from the slaves. Brown, it appears, had been led to believe that they were ripe for insurrection; but, whether from fear, or from actual disinclination, this seems not to have been the case. Cook denied the charge, but otherwise said very little. When asked whether he was ready, Brown replied, 'I am always ready,' and it was the simple truth. His arms were pinioned, and, wearing a black slouched hat, and the same clothes in which he had appeared at the trial, he proceeded to the door, apparently calm and cheerful. As he stepped out into the open air he saw a negro woman with her child in her arms: he paused for a moment, and kissed the infant tenderly. Another black woman exclaimed, 'God bless you, old man! I wish I could help you, but I cannot.' Six companies of infantry, and one troop of horse, were drawn up in front of the gaol; close by was a waggon, containing a coffin. After talking with some persons whom he knew, Brown seated himself in the waggon, and looked at the soldiers gathered about him. The vehicle then moved off, flanked by two files of riflemen in close order. The field where the gallows had been erected was also in full possession of the military. Pickets were stationed at various localities, and the spectators were kept back at the point of the bayonet, to prevent all possibility of a rescue. When Brown had mounted the gallows, and the cap had been put on his head, together with the rope around his neck, the executioner asked him to step forward on to the trap. He replied, 'You must lead me – I cannot see.' All was now ready on the scaffold itself; but, owing to some fear on the part of the authorities, the soldiers were marched and counter-marched, frequently changing their positions as if in the face of an enemy. This lasted ten minutes, and the executioner asked the unfortunate man if he was not tired. 'No,' answered Brown, 'not tired; but don't keep me waiting longer than is necessary.' At length the fatal act was completed; but Brown was a strong man and the pulse did not entirely cease until after thirty-five minutes. His companions were executed in March 1860.

It was a curious feature in the case that the criminal had expressed a desire that no religious ceremony should be performed over his body by 'ministers who consent to or approve of the enslavement of their fellow-creatures'. He said he should prefer to be accompanied to the scaffold by a dozen slave-children and a good old slave-mother, with their appeal to God for blessings on his soul, rather than have all the eloquence of the whole clergy of the commonwealth combined. – Ed.]

His corpse was given up to his woe-stricken widow, and she, assisted by anti-slavery friends, caused it to be borne to North Elba, Essex county, N.Y., and there his dust now reposes amid the silent, solemn, and snowy grandeurs of the Adirondacks. This raid upon Harper's Ferry was as the last straw to the camel's back. What in the tone of Southern sentiment had been fierce before, became furious and uncontrollable now. A scream for vengeance came up from all sections of the slave States, and from great multitudes in the North. All who were supposed to have been any way connected with John Brown were to be hunted down and surrendered to the tender mercies of slave-holding and panic-stricken Virginia, and there to be tried after the fashion of John Brown, and of course to be summarily executed.

On the evening when the news came that John Brown had taken and was then holding the town of Harper's Ferry, it so happened that I was speaking to a large audience in National Hall, Philadelphia. The announcement came upon us with the startling effect of an earthquake. It was something to make the boldest hold his breath. I saw at once that my old friend had attempted what he had long ago resolved to do, and I felt certain that the result must be his capture and destruction. As I expected, the next day brought the news that with two or three men he had fortified and was holding a small engine house, but that he was surrounded by a body of Virginia militia, who thus far had not ventured to capture the insurgents, but that escape was impossible. A few hours later, and word came that Colonel Robert E. Lee, with a Company of United States troops had made a breach in Captain Brown's fort, and had captured him alive, though mortally wounded. His carpet bag had been secured by Governor Wise, and it was found to contain numerous letters and documents which directly implicated Gerritt Smith, Joshua R. Giddings, Samuel G. Howe, Frank P. Sanborn and myself. This intelligence was soon followed by a telegram saying that we were all to be arrested. Knowing that I was then in Philadelphia, stopping with my friend, Thomas J. Dorsey, Mr John Horn, the telegraph operator, came to me and with others urged me to leave the city by the first train, as it was known through the newspapers that I was then in Philadelphia, and officers might even then be on my track. To me there was nothing improbable in all this. My friends for the most part were appalled at the thought of my being arrested then and there, or while on my way across the ferry from Walnut Street wharf to Camden, for there was where I felt sure the arrest would be made, and asked some of them to go so far as this with me merely to see what might occur, but upon one ground or another they all thought it best not to be found in my company at such a time, except dear old Franklin Turner – a true man. The truth is, that in the excitement which prevailed, my friends had reason to fear that the very fact that they were with me would be a sufficient reason for their arrest with me. The delay in the departure of the steamer seemed unusually long to me, for I confess I was seized with a desire to reach a more Northern latitude. My friend Frank did not leave my side till 'all ashore' was ordered and the paddles began to move. I reached New York at night, still under the apprehension of arrest at any moment, but no signs of such event being made, I went at once to the Barclay Street Ferry, took the boat across the river and went direct to Washington Street, Hoboken, the home of Mrs Marks, where I spent the night, and I may add without undue profession of timidity, an *anxious* night. The morning papers brought no relief, for they announced that the Government would spare no pains in ferretting out and bringing to punishment all who were connected with the Harper's Ferry outrage, and that papers as well as persons would be searched for. I was now somewhat uneasy from the fact that sundry letters and a constitution written by John Brown were locked up in my desk in Rochester. In order to prevent these papers from falling into the hands of the government of Virginia, I got my friend Miss Ottilia Assing to write by my dictation the following telegram to B. F. Blackall, the telegraph operator in Rochester, a friend and frequent visitor at my house, who would readily understand the meaning of the dispatch:

> B. F. BLACKALL, Esq. – Tell Lewis – my eldest son – to secure all the important papers in my high desk.

I did not sign my name, and the result showed that I had rightly judged that Mr Blackall would understand and promptly attend to the request. The mark of the chisel with which the desk was opened is still on the drawer, and is one of the traces of the John Brown raid. Having taken measures to secure my papers the trouble was to know just what to do with myself. To stay at Hoboken was out of the question, and to go to Rochester was to all appearance to go into the hands of the hunters, for they would naturally seek me at my home if they sought me at all. I, however, resolved to go home and risk my safety there. I felt sure that once in the city I could not be easily taken from there without a preliminary hearing upon the requisition, and not then, if the people could be made aware of what was in progress. But how to get to Rochester became a serious question. It would not do to go to New York city and take the train, for that city was not less incensed against the John Brown conspirators than many parts of the South. The course hit upon by my friends, Mr Johnson and Miss Assing, was to take me at night in a private conveyance from Hoboken to Paterson, where I could take the Erie railroad for home. This plan was carried out and I reached home in safety, but had been there but a few moments when I was called upon by Samuel D. Porter, Esq., and my neighbour, Lieutenant-Governor Selden, who informed me that the Governor of the State would certainly surrender me on a proper requisition from the Governor of Virginia, and that while the people of Rochester would not permit me to be taken South, yet in order to avoid collision with the Government and consequent bloodshed, they advised me to quit the country, which I did going to Canada. Governor Wise, in the meantime, being advised that I had left Rochester for the State of Michigan, made requisition on the Governor of that State for my surrender to Virginia.

The following letter from Governor Wise to President James Buchanan – which since the war was sent me by B. J. Lossing, the historian – will show by what means the Governor of Virginia meant to get me in his power, and that my apprehensions of arrest were not altogether groundless –

[Confidential]
Richmond, Va., Nov 13, 1859
*To His Excellency, James Buchanon, President of the United States, and
to the Honourable Postmaster-General of the United States*

GENTLEMEN – I have information such as has caused me, upon proper affidavits, to make requisition upon the Executive of Michigan for the delivery up of the person of Frederick Douglass, a negro man, supposed now to be in Michigan, charged with murder, robbery, and inciting servile insurrection in the State of Virginia. My agents for the arrest and reclamation of the person so charged are Benjamin M. Morris and William N. Kelly. The latter has the requisition, and will wait on you to the end of obtaining nominal authority as post-office agents. They need be very secretive in this matter and some pretext for travelling through the dangerous section for the execution of the laws in this behalf, and some protection against obtrusive, unruly, or lawless, violence. If it be proper so to do, will the Postmaster-General be pleased to give to Mr Kelly, for each of these men, a permit and authority to act as detectives for the post office department, without pay, but to pass and repass without question, delay, or hindrance?

Respectfully submitted by your obedient servant,

HENRY H. WISE

There is no reason to doubt that James Buchanan afforded Governor Wise all the aid and co-operation for which he was asked. I have been informed that several United States marshals were in Rochester in search of me within six hours after my departure. I do not know that I can do better at this stage of my story than to insert the following letter, written by me to the Rochester *Democrat and American*:

Canada West, Oct. 31st, 1859
MR EDITOR – I notice that the telegraph makes Mr Cook – one of the unfortunate insurgents at Harper's Ferry, and now a prisoner in the hands of the thing calling itself the Government of Virginia, but which in fact is but an organised conspiracy by one party of the people against another and weaker – denounce me as a coward, and assert that I promised to be present in person at the Harper's Ferry Insurrection. This is certainly a very grave impeachment, whether viewed in its bearings upon friends or upon foes, and you will not

think it strange that I should take a somewhat serious notice of it. Having no acquaintance whatever with Mr Cook, and never having exchanged a word with him about the Harper's Ferry Insurrection, I am disposed to doubt if he could have used the language concerning me, which the wires attribute to him. The lightning when speaking for itself, is among the most direct, reliable, and truthful of things; but when speaking of the terror-stricken slave-holders at Harper's Ferry, it has been made the swiftest of liars. Under its nimble and trembling fingers it magnifies 17 men into 700 and has since filled the columns of the New York *Herald* for days with its interminable contradictions. But assuming that it has told only the simple truth as to the sayings of Mr Cook in this instance, I have this answer to make to my accuser: Mr Cook may be perfectly right in denouncing me as a coward; I have not one word to say in defence or vindication of my character for courage; I have always been more distinguished for running than fighting, and tried by the Harper's-Ferry-Insurrection test, I am most miserably deficient in courage, even more so than Cook, when he deserted his brave old captain and fled to the mountains. To this extent Mr Cook is entirely right, and will meet no contradiction from me, or from anybody else. But wholly, grievously and most unaccountably wrong is Mr Cook when he asserts that I promised to be present in person at the Harper's Ferry Insurrection. Of whatever other imprudence and indiscretion I may have been guilty, I have never made a promise so rash and wild as this. The taking of Harper's Ferry was a measure never encouraged by my word or by my vote. At any time or place, my wisdom or my cowardice, has not only kept me from Harper's Ferry, but has equally kept me from making any promise to go there. I desire to be quite emphatic here, for of all guilty men, he is the guiltiest who lures his fellow men to an undertaking of this sort, under promise of assistance which he afterwards fails to render. I therefore declare that there is no man living, and no man dead, who if living, could truthfully say that I ever promised him, or anybody else, either conditionally, or otherwise, that I would be present in person at the Harper's Ferry Insurrection. My field of labour for the abolition of slavery has not extended to an attack upon the United States Arsenal. In the teeth of the documents already published, and of those which may hereafter be published, I affirm that no man connected with that insurrection, from its noble and heroic leader down, can connect my name with a single broken promise of any sort whatever. So much I deem it proper to say negatively. The time for a full statement of what I know, and of ALL I know, of this desperate but sublimely disinterested effort to emancipate the slaves of Maryland and Virginia from their cruel task-masters, has not yet come, and may never come. In the denial which I have now made, my motive is more a respectful consideration for the opinions of the slave's friends than from my fear of being made an accomplice in the general conspiracy against slavery, when there is a reasonable hope for success. Men who live by robbing their fellow men of their labour and liberty have forfeited their right to know anything of the thoughts, feelings, or purposes of those whom they rob and plunder. They have by the single act of slave-holding, voluntarily placed themselves beyond the laws of justice and honour, and have become only fitted for companionship with thieves and pirates – the common enemies of God and of any mankind. While it shall be considered right to protect oneself against thieves, burglars, robbers, and assassins, and to slay a wild beast in the act of devouring his human prey, it can never be wrong for the imbruted and whip-scarred slaves, or their friends, to hunt, harass, and even strike down the traffickers in human flesh. If anybody is disposed to think less of me on account of this sentiment, or because I may have had a knowledge of what was about to occur, and did not assume the base and detestable character of an informer, he is a man whose good or bad opinion of me may be equally repugnant and despicable.

Entertaining these sentiments, I may be asked why I did not join John Brown – the noble old hero whose one right hand has shaken the foundation of the American Union, and whose ghost will haunt the bedchambers of all the born and unborn slave-holders of Virginia through all generations, filling them with alarm and consternation. My answer to this has already been given – at least impliedly given – 'The tools to those who can use them!' Let every man work for the abolition of slavery in his own way. I would help all and hinder none. My position in regard to the Harper's Ferry Insurrection may be easily inferred from these remarks, and I shall be glad if those papers which have spoken of me in connection with it, would find room for this brief statement. I have no apology for keeping out of the way of those gentlemanly United States Marshals, who are said to have paid Rochester a somewhat protracted visit lately, with a view to an interview with me. A government recognising the validity of the *Dred Scott* decision, at such a time as this is not likely to have any very charitable feelings towards me, and if I am to meet its representatives I prefer to do so at least upon equal terms. If I have committed any offence against society I have done so on the soil of the State of New York, and I should be perfectly willing to be arraigned there before an impartial jury; but I have quite insuperable objections to being caught by the hounds of Mr Buchanan, and '*bagged*' by Governor Wise. For this appears to be the arrangement. Buchanan does the fighting and hunting, and Wise '*bags*' the game. Some reflections may be made upon my leaving on a tour to England just at this time. I have only to say that my going to that country has been rather delayed than hastened by the insurrection at Harper's Ferry. All know that I had intended to leave here in the first week in November.

FREDERICK DOUGLASS

CHAPTER X

The Beginning of the End

My connection with John Brown – To and from England – Presidential contest – Election of Abraham Lincoln

What was my connection with John Brown, and what I knew of his scheme for the capture of Harper's Ferry, I may now proceed to state. From the time of my visit to him at Springfield, Mass., in 1847, our relations were friendly and confidential. I never passed through Springfield without calling on him, and he never came to Rochester without calling on me. He often stopped overnight with me, when we talked over the feasibility of his plan for destroying the value of slave property, and the motive for holding slaves in the border States. That plan, as already intimated elsewhere, was to take twenty or twenty-five discreet and trustworthy men into the mountains of Virginia and Maryland, and station them in squads of five, about five miles apart, on a line of twenty-five miles; each squad to co-operate with all, and all with each. They were to have selected for them, secure and comfortable retreats in the fastnesses of the mountains, where they could easily defend themselves in case of attack. They were to subsist upon the country roundabout. They were to be well armed, but were to avoid battle or violence, unless compelled by pursuit or in self-defence. In that case, they were to make it as costly as possible to the assailing party, whether that party should be soldiers or citizens. He further proposed to have a number of stations from the line of Pennsylvania to the Canada border, where such slaves as he might, through his men, induce to run away, should be supplied with food and shelter, and be forwarded from one station to another till they should reach a place of safety either in Canada or the Northern States. He proposed to add to his force in the mountains any courageous and intelligent fugitives who might be willing to remain and endure the hardships and brave the dangers of this mountain life. These, he thought, if properly selected, on account of their knowledge of the surrounding country, could be made valuable auxiliaries. The work of going into the valley of Virginia and persuading the slaves to flee to the mountains, was to be committed to the most courageous and judicious man connected with each squad.

Hating slavery as I did, and making its abolition the object of my life, I was ready to welcome any new mode of attack upon the slave system which gave any promise of success. I readily saw that this plan could be made very effective in rendering slave property in Maryland and Virginia valueless by rendering it insecure. Men do not like to buy runaway horses, nor to invest their money in a species of property likely to take legs and walk off with itself. In the worst case, too, if the plan should fail, and John Brown should be driven from the mountains, a new fact would be developed by which the nation would be kept awake to the existence of slavery. Hence, I assented to this, John Brown's scheme or plan for running off slaves.

To set this plan in operation, money and men, arms and ammunition, food and clothing, were needed; and these, from the nature of the enterprise, were not easily obtained, and nothing was immediately done. Captain Brown, too, notwithstanding his rigid economy, was poor, and was unable to arm and equip men for the dangerous life he had mapped out. So the work lingered till after the Kansas trouble was over, and freedom was a fact accomplished in that Territory. This left him with arms and men, for the men who had been with him in Kansas, believed in him, and would follow him in any humane but dangerous enterprise he might undertake.

After the close of his Kansas work, Captain Brown came to my house in Rochester, and said he desired to stop with me several weeks; 'But,' he added, 'I will not stay unless you will allow me to pay board.' Knowing that he was no trifler and meant all he said, and desirous of retaining him under my roof, I charged three dollars a week. While here, he spent most of his time in correspondence. He wrote often to George L. Stearns of Boston, Gerrit Smith of Peterboro, N.Y., and many others, and received many letters in return. When he was not writing letters, he was writing and revising a constitution which he meant to put in operation by the men who should go with him into the mountains. He said that to avoid anarchy and confusion, there should be a regularly constituted government, to which each man who came with him should be sworn to honour and support. I have a copy of this constitution in Captain Brown's own handwriting, as prepared by himself at my house.

He called his friends from Chatham, Canada, to come together that he might lay his constitution before them, for their approval and adoption. His whole time and thought were given to this subject. It was the first thing in the morning and last thing at night, till I confess it began to be something of a bore to me. Once in a while, he would say he could, with a few resolute men, capture Harper's Ferry, and supply himself with arms belonging to the government at that place, but he never announced his intention to do so. It was, however, very evidently passing in his mind as a thing he might do. I paid but little attention to such remarks, though I never doubted that he thought just what he said. Soon after his coming to me, he asked me to get for him two smoothly planed boards, upon which he could illustrate, with a pair of dividers, by a drawing, the plan of fortification which he meant to adopt in the mountains.

These forts were to be so arranged as to connect one with the other, by secret passages, so that if one was carried, another could easily be fallen back upon, and be the means of dealing death to the enemy at the very moment when he might think himself victorious. I was less interested in these drawings than my children were, but they showed that the old man had an eye to the means as well as to the end, and was giving his best thought to the work he was about to take in hand.

While at my house, John Brown made the acquaintance of a coloured man, who called himself by different names – sometimes 'Emperor', at other times, 'Shields Green'. He was a fugitive slave, who had made his escape from Charlestown, South Carolina, a State from which a slave found it no easy matter to run away. But Shields Green was not one to shrink from hardships or dangers. He was a man of few words, and his speech was singularly broken; but his courage and self-respect made him quite a dignified character. John Brown saw at once what 'stuff' Green 'was made of', and confided to him his plans and purposes. Green easily believed in Brown, and promised to go with him whenever he should be ready to move. About three weeks before the raid on Harper's Ferry, John Brown wrote to me, informing me that a beginning in his work would soon be made, and that before going forward he wanted to see me, and appointed an old stone quarry near Chambersburg, Penn., as our place of meeting. Mr Kagi, his secretary, would be there, and they wished me to bring any money I could command, and Shields Green along with me. In the same letter, he said that his 'mining tools' and stores were then at Chambersburg, and that he would be there to remove them. I obeyed the old man's summons. Taking Shields, we passed through New York City, where we called upon the Revd James Glocester and his wife, and told them where and for what we were going, and that our old friend needed money. Mrs Glocester gave me ten dollars, and asked me to hand the same to John Brown, with her best wishes.

When I reached Chambersburg, a good deal of surprise was expressed, for I was instantly recognised, that I should come there unannounced, and I was pressed to make a speech to them, with which invitation I readily complied. Meanwhile, I called upon Mr Henry Watson, a simple-minded and warm-hearted man, to whom Captain Brown had imparted the secret of my visit, to show me the road to the appointed rendezvous. Watson was very busy in his barber's shop, but he dropped all and put me on the right track. I approached the old quarry very cautiously, for John Brown was generally well armed, and regarded strangers with suspicion. He was there under the ban of the government, and heavy rewards were offered for his arrest, for offences said to have been committed in Kansas. He was passing under the name of John Smith. As I came near, he regarded me rather suspiciously, but soon recognised me, and received me cordially. He had in his hand when I met him, a fishing tackle, with which he had apparently been fishing in a stream hard by; but I saw no fish, and did not suppose that he cared much for his 'fisherman's luck'. The fishing was simply a disguise, and was certainly a good one. He looked every way like a man of the neighbourhood, and as much at home as any of the farmers around there. His hat was old, and storm-beaten, and his clothing was about the colour of the stone quarry itself – his then present dwelling-place.

His face wore an anxious expression, and he was much worn by thought and exposure. I felt that I was on a dangerous mission, and was as little desirous of discovery as himself, though no reward had been offered for me.

We – Mr Kagi, Captain Brown, Shields Green, and myself, sat down among the rocks and talked over the enterprise which was about to be undertaken. The taking of Harper's Ferry, of which Captain Brown had merely hinted before, was now declared as his settled purpose, and he wanted to know what I thought of it. I at once opposed the measure with all the arguments at my command. To me, such a measure would be fatal to running off slaves, as was the original plan, and fatal to all engaged in doing so. It would be an attack upon the Federal Government, and would array the whole country against us. Captain Brown did most of the talking on the other side of the question. He did not at all object to rousing the nation; it seemed to him that something startling was just what the nation needed. He had completely renounced his old plan, and thought that the capture of Harper's Ferry would serve as notice to the slaves that their friends had come, and as a trumpet, to rally them to his standard. He described the place as to its means of defence, and how impossible it would be to dislodge him if once in possession. Of course, I was no match for him in such matters, but I told him, and these were my words, that all his arguments, and all his descriptions of the place, convinced me that he was going into a perfect steel-trap, and that once in he would never get out alive; that he would be surrounded at once and escape would be impossible. He was not to be shaken by anything I could say, but treated my views respectfully, replying that even if surrounded he would find means for cutting his way out; but that would not be forced upon him; he should have a number of the best citizens of the neighbourhood as his prisoners at the start, and that holding them as hostages, he should be able if worse came to worse, to dictate terms of egress from the town. I looked at him with some astonishment, that he could rest upon a reed so weak and broken, and told him that Virginia would blow him and his hostages sky-high, rather than that he should hold Harper's Ferry an hour. Our talk was long and earnest; we spent the most of Saturday and a part of Sunday in this debate – Brown for Harper's Ferry, and I against it; he for striking a blow which should instantly rouse the country, and I for the policy of gradually and unaccountably drawing off the slaves to the mountains, as at first suggested and proposed by him. When I found that he had fully made up his mind and could not be dissuaded, I turned to Shields Green and told him he heard what Captain Brown had said; his old plan was changed, and that I should return home, and if he wished to go with me he could do so. Captain Brown urged us both to go with him, but I could not do so, and could but feel that he was about to rivet the fetters more firmly than ever on the limbs of the enslaved. In parting he put his arms around me in a manner more than friendly, and said: 'Come with me, Douglass, I will defend you with my life. I want you for a special purpose. When I strike, the bees will begin to swarm, and I shall want you to help hive them.' But my discretion or my cowardice made me proof against the dear old man's eloquence – perhaps it was something of both which determined my course. When about to leave I asked Green what he had decided to do, and was surprised by his coolly saying in his broken way, 'I b'leve I'll go wid de ole man.' Here we separated; they to go to Harper's Ferry, I to Rochester. There has been some difference of opinion as to the propriety of my course in thus leaving my friend. Some have thought that I ought to have gone with him, but I have no reproaches for myself on this point, and since I have been assailed only by coloured men who kept even farther from this brave and heroic man than I did, I shall not trouble myself about their criticisms. They compliment me in assuming that I should perform greater deeds than themselves.

Such then was my connection with John Brown, and it may be asked if this is all, why should I have objected to being sent to Virginia to be tried for the offence charged. The explanation is not difficult. I knew if my enemies could not prove me guilty of the offence of being with John Brown they could prove that I was Frederick Douglass; they could prove that I was in correspondence and conspiracy with Brown against slavery; they could prove that I brought Shields Green, one of the bravest of his soldiers, all the way from Rochester to him at Chambersburg; they could prove that I brought money to aid him, and in what was then the state of the public mind I could not hope to make a jury of Virginia believe I did not go the whole length which he went, or that I was not one of his supporters, and I knew that all Virginia, were I once in her clutches, would say 'let him be hanged'. Before I had left Canada for England, Jeremiah Anderson, one of Brown's men, who was present and took part in the raid but escaped by the mountains, joined me, and he told me that he and Shields Green were sent out on special duty as soon as the capture of the arsenal, etc., was effected. Their business was to bring in the slaves from the surrounding country, and hence they were on the outside when Brown was surrounded. I said to him, 'Why then did not Shields come with you?' 'Well,' he said, 'I told him to come; that we could do nothing more, but he simply said he must go down to de ole man.' Anderson further told me that Captain Brown was careful to keep his plans from his men, and that there was much opposition among them when they found what were the precise movements determined upon; but they were an oath-bound company, and like good soldiers were agreed to follow their captain wherever he might lead.

On the 12th of November 1859, I took passage from Quebec on board the steamer *Scotia*, under the command of Captain Thompson, of the Allan line. My going to England was not at first suggested by my connection with John Brown, but the fact that I was now in danger of arrest on the ground of complicity with him, made what I had intended a pleasure a necessity, for though in Canada, and under British law, it was not impossible that I might be kidnapped and taken to Virginia. England had given me shelter and protection when the slave-hounds were on my track fourteen years before, and her gates were still open to me now that I was pursued in the name of Virginian justice. I could but feel that I was going into exile, perhaps for life. Slavery seemed to be at the very top of its power; the national government, with all its powers and appliances, were in its hands, and it bade fair to wield them for many years to come. Nobody could then see that in the short space of four years this power would be broken and the slave system destroyed. So I started on my voyage with feelings far from cheerful. No one who has not himself been compelled to leave his home and country to go into permanent banishment, can well imagine the state of mind and heart which such a conditioning brings. The voyage out was by the North Passage, and at this season, as usual, it was cold, dark, and stormy. Before quitting the coast of Labrador, we had four degrees below zero. Although I had crossed the Atlantic twice before, I had not experienced such unfriendly weather as during the most of this voyage. Our great ship was dashed about upon the surface of the sea as though she had been the smallest 'dug-out'. It seemed to tax all the seamanship of our captain to keep her in manageable condition; but after battling with the waves on an angry ocean during fourteen long days, I gratefully found myself upon the soil of Great Britain, beyond the reach of Buchanan's power and Virginia's prisons. On reaching Liverpool, I learned that England was nearly as much alive to what had happened at Harper's Ferry as the United States, and I was immediately called upon in different parts of the country to speak on the subject of slavery, and especially to give some account of the men who had thus flung away their lives in a desperate attempt to free the slaves. My own relation to the affair was a subject of much interest, as was the fact of my presence there being in some sense to elude the demands of Governor Wise, who having learned that I was not in Michigan, but *was* on a British steamer bound for England, publicly declared that 'could he overtake that vessel, he would take me from her deck at any cost.'

While in England, and wishing to visit France, I wrote to Mr George M. Dallas, the American minister at the British court, to obtain a passport. The attempt upon the life of Napoleon III about that time, and the suspicion that the conspiracy against him had been hatched in England, made the French government very strict in the enforcement of its passport system. I might possibly have been permitted to visit that country without a certificate of my citizenship, but wishing to leave nothing to chance, I applied to the only competent authority; but, true to the traditions of the Democratic party – true to the slave-holding policy of his country – true to the decision of the United States Supreme Court, and true, perhaps, to the petty meanness of his own nature, Mr George M. Dallas, the Democratic American minister, refused to grant me a passport, on the ground that I was not a citizen of the United States. I did not beg or remonstrate with this dignitary further, but simply addressed a note to the French minister in London, asking for a permit to visit France, and that paper came without delay. I mention this, not to belittle the civilisation of my native country, but as a part of the story of my life. I could have born this denial with more serenity, could I have foreseen what has since happened, but, under the circumstances, it was a galling disappointment.

I had at this time been about six months out of the United States. My time had been chiefly occupied in speaking on slavery, and other subjects, in different parts of England and Scotland, meeting and enjoying the while the society of many of the kind friends whose acquaintance I had made during my visit to those countries fourteen years before. Much of the excitement caused by the Harper's Ferry Insurrection had subsided, both at home and abroad, and I should have now gratified a long-cherished desire to visit France, and avail myself, for that purpose, of the permit so promptly and civilly given by the French minister, had not news reached me from home of the death of my beloved daughter Annie, the light and life of my house. Deeply distressed by this bereavement, and acting upon the impulse of the moment, regardless of the peril, I at once resolved to return home, and took the first outgoing steamer for Portland, Maine. After a rough passage of seventeen days, I reached home by way of Canada, and remained in my house nearly a month before the knowledge got abroad that I was again in America. Great changes had now taken place in the public mind touching the John Brown Raid. Virginia had satisfied her thirst for blood. She had executed all the raiders who had fallen into her hands. She had not given Captain Brown the benefit of a reasonable doubt, but hurried him to the scaffold in panic-stricken haste. She had made herself ridiculous by her fright, and despisable by her fury. Emerson's prediction that Brown's gallows would become like the Cross, was already being fulfilled. The old hero, in the trial hour, had behaved so grandly that men regarded him not as a murderer, but as a martyr. All over the North men were singing the John Brown song. His body was in the dust, but his soul was marching on. His defeat was already assuming the form and pressure of victory, and his death was giving new life and power to the principles of justice and liberty. He had spoken great words in the face of death and the champions of slavery. He had quailed before neither. What he had lost by the sword, he had more than gained by the truth. Had he wavered, had he retreated or apologised, the case had been different. He did not even ask that the cup of death might pass from him. To his own soul he was right, and neither 'principalities nor powers, life nor death, things present nor things to come', could shake his dauntless spirit, or move him from his ground. He may not have stooped on his way to the gallows to kiss a little coloured child, as it is reported he did, but the act would have been in keeping with the tender heart, as well as with the heroic spirit of the man. Those who looked for confession heard only the voice of rebuke and warning.

Early after the insurrection at Harper's Ferry, an investigating committee was appointed by Congress, and a 'drag-net' was spread all over the country, in the hope of inculpating many distinguished persons. They had imprisoned Thaddeus Hyatt, who denied their right to interrogate him, and had called many witnesses before them, as if the judicial power of the nation had been confided to their committee, and not the Supreme Court of the United States. But Captain Brown implicated nobody. Upon his own head he invited all the bolts of slave-holding vengeance. He said that he, and he alone, was responsible for all that had happened. He had many friends, but no instigators. In all their efforts this committee signally failed, and soon after my arrival home, they gave up the search, and asked to be discharged, not having half fulfilled the duty for which they were appointed.

I have never been able to account satisfactorily for the sudden abandonment of this investigation on any other ground than that the men engaged in it expected soon to be in rebellion themselves, and that, not a rebellion for liberty like that of John Brown, but a rebellion for slavery; and that they saw that by using their senatorial power in search of rebels they might be whetting a knife for their own throats. At any rate the country was soon relieved of the congressional drag-net, and was now engaged in the heat and turmoil of a presidential canvass – a canvass which had no parallel, involving as it did the question of peace or war, the integrity or the dismemberment of the Republic; and I may add, the maintenance or destruction of slavery. In some of the Southern States the people were already organising and arming to be ready for an apprehended contest, and with this work on their hands they had no time to spare for those they had wished to convict as instigators of the raid, however desirous they might have been to do so under other circumstances, for they had parted with none of their hate. As showing their feeling towards me, I may state, that a coloured man appeared about this time in Knoxville, Ten., and was beset by a furious crowd with knives and bludgeons, because he was supposed to be Fred Douglass. But, however perilous it would have been for me to have shown myself in any Southern State, there was no especial danger for me in the North.

Though disappointed in my tour on the Continent, and called home by one of the saddest events that can afflict the domestic circle, my presence here was fortunate, since it enabled me to participate in the most important and memorable presidential canvass ever witnessed in the United States, and to labour for the election of a man who in the order of events was destined to do a greater service to his country and to mankind, than any man who had gone before him in the presidential office. It is something to couple one's name with great occasions, and it was a great thing to me to be permitted to bear some humble part in this, the greatest that had thus far come to the American people. It was a great thing to achieve American independence when we numbered three millions, but it was a greater thing to save the country from dismemberment and ruin when it numbered thirty millions. He alone of all our Presidents was to have the opportunity to destroy slavery, and to lift into manhood millions of his countrymen hitherto held as chattels and numbered with the beasts of the field.

The presidential canvass of 1860 was three sided, and each side had its distinctive doctrine as to the question of slavery and slavery extension. We had three candidates in the field. Stephen A. Douglas was the standard-bearer of what may be called the Western faction of the old divided Democratic party, and John a. Breckenridge was the standard-bearer of the Southern or slave-holding faction of that party. Abraham Lincoln represented the then young, growing, and united

Republican party. The lines between these parties and candidates were about as distinctly and clearly drawn as political lines are capable of being drawn. The name of Douglas stood for territorial sovereignty, or in other words, for the right of the people of a territory to admit or exclude, to establish or abolish, slavery, as to them might seem best. The doctrine of Breckenridge was that slave-holders were entitled to carry their slaves into any territory of the United States and to hold them there, with or without the consent of the people of the territory; that the Constitution of its own force carried slavery, and protected it, into any territory open for settlement in the United States. To both these parties, factions, and doctrines, Abraham Lincoln and the Republican party stood opposed. They held that the Federal Government had the right and the power to exclude slavery from the territories of the United States, and that that right and power ought to be exercised to the extent of confining slavery inside the slave States, with a view to its ultimate extinction. The position of Mr Douglas gave him a splendid pretext for the display of a species of oratory of which he was a distinguished master. He alone of the three candidates took the stump, as the preacher of popular sovereignty, called in derision at the time 'Squatter' sovereignty. This doctrine, if not the times, gave him a chance to play fast and loose, and blow hot and cold, as occasion might require. In the South and among slave-holders he could say, 'My great principle of popular sovereignty does not and was not intended by me to prevent the extension of slavery; on the contrary, it gives you the right to take your slaves into the territories and secure legislation legalising slavery; it denies to the Federal Government all right of interference against you, and hence is eminently favourable to your interests.' When among people known to be indifferent, he could say, 'I do not care whether slavery is voted up or voted down in the territory,' but when addressing the known opponents of the extension of slavery, he could say that the people of the territories were in no danger of having slavery forced upon them since they could keep it out by adverse legislation. Had he made these representations before railroads, electric wires, phonography, and newspapers had become the powerful auxiliaries they have done, Mr Douglas might have gained many votes, but they were of little avail now. The South was too sagacious to leave slavery to the chance of defeat in a fair vote by the people of a territory. Of all property, none could less afford to take such a risk, for no property can require more strongly favouring conditions for its existence. Not only the intelligence of the slave, but the instincts of humanity, must be barred by positive law, hence

Breckenridge and his friends erected the flinty walls of the Constitution and the Supreme Court for the protection of slavery at the outset. Against both Douglas and Breckenridge, Abraham Lincoln proposed his grand historic doctrine of the power and duty of the National Government to prevent the spread and perpetuity of slavery. Into this contest I threw myself, with firmer faith and more ardent hope than ever before, and what I could do by pen or voice was done with a will. The most remarkable and memorable feature of this canvass, was that it was prosecuted under the portentous shadow of a threat. Leading public men of the South had with the vehemence of fiery purpose, given it out in advance that in case of their failure to elect their candidate – Mr C. Breckenridge – they would proceed to take the slave-holding States out of the Union, and that in no event whatever would they submit to the rule of Abraham Lincoln. To many of the peace-loving friends of the Union, this was a fearful announcement, and it doubtless cost the Republican candidate many votes. By many others, however, it was deemed a mere bravado – sound and fury signifying nothing. With a third class its effect was very different. They were tired of the rule-or-ruin intimidation adopted by the South, and felt then, if never before, that they had quailed before it too often and too long. It came as an insult and a challenge in one, and imperatively called upon them for independence, self-assertion, and resentment. Had Southern men puzzled their brains to find the most effective means to array against slavery and slave-holding manners the solid opposition of the North, they could not have hit upon any expedient better suited to that end, than was this threat. It was not only unfair, but insolent, and more like an address to cowardly slaves than to independent freemen; it had in it the meanness of the horse-jockey, who, on entering a race, proposes, if beaten, to run off with the stakes. In all my speeches made during this canvass, I did not fail to take advantage of this Southern bluster and bullying.

As I have said, this Southern threat lost many votes, but it gained more than would have covered the loss. It frightened the timid, but stimulated the brave; and the result was – the triumphant election of Abraham Lincoln.

Then came the question, what will the South do about it? Will she eat her bold words, and submit to the verdict of the people, or proceed to the execution of the programme she had marked out for herself prior to the election? The enquiry was an anxious one, and the blood of the North stood still, waiting for the response. It had not to wait long, for the trumpet of war was soon sounded, and the tramp of armed men was heard in that region. During all the winter of 1860 notes of preparation for a tremendous conflict came to us from that quarter on every wind. Still the warning was not taken. Few of the North could really believe that this insolent display of arms would end in anything more substantial than dust and smoke.

The shameful and shocking course of President Buchanan and his Cabinet towards this rising rebellion against the Government which each and all of them had solemnly sworn to 'support, defend and maintain' – that the treasury was emptied, that the army was scattered, that our ships of war were sent out of the way, that our forts and arsenals in the South were weakened and crippled – purposely left an easy prey to the prospective insurgents – that one after another the States were allowed to secede, that these rebel measures were largely encouraged by the doctrine of Mr Buchanan, that he found no power in the constitution to coerce a State, are all matters of history, and need only the briefest mention here.

To arrest this tide of secession and revolution which was sweeping over the South, the Southern papers, which still had some dread of the consequences likely to ensue from the course marked out before the election, proposed as a means for promoting conciliation and satisfaction, that 'each Northern State, through her legislature, or in convention assembled, should repeal all laws passed for the injury of the constitutional rights of the South – meaning thereby, all laws passed for the protection of personal liberty; that they should pass laws for the easy and prompt execution of the Fugitive-Slave Law; that they should pass other laws imposing penalties on all malefactors who should hereafter assist or encourage the escape of fugitive slaves; also, laws declaring and protecting the right of slave-holders to travel and sojourn in Northern States, accompanied by their slaves; also, that they should instruct their representatives and senators in Congress, to repeal the law prohibiting the sale of slaves in the district of Columbia, and pass laws sufficient for the full protection of slave property in the territories of the Union.'

It may, indeed, be well regretted that there was a class of men in the North willing to patch up a peace with this rampant spirit of disunion, by compliance with these offensive, scandalous, and humiliating terms; and to do so without any guarantee that the South would then be pacified; rather with the certainty, learned by past experience, that it would by no means promote this end. I confess to a feeling allied to satisfaction at the prospect of a conflict between the North and the South. Standing outside the pale of American humanity, denied citizenship, unable to call the land of my birth my country, and adjudged by the Supreme Court of the United States to have no rights which white men were bound to respect, and longing for the end of the bondage of my people, I was ready for any political upheaval which should bring about a change in the existing condition of things. Whether the war of words would or would not end in blows was for a time a matter of doubt; and when it became certain that the South was wholly in earnest, and meant at all hazards to execute its threats of disruption, a visible change in the sentiments of the North was apparent.

The reaction from the glorious assertion of freedom and independence on the part of the North in the triumphant election of Abraham Lincoln, was a painful and humiliating development of its weakness. It seemed as if all that had been gained in the canvass was about to be surrendered to the vanquished; that the South, though beaten at the polls, was to be victorious and have everything its own way in the final result. During all the intervening months, from November to the ensuing March, the drift of Northern sentiment was towards compromise. To smooth the way for this, most of the Northern legislatures repealed their personal liberty bills, as they were supposed to embarrass the surrender of fugitive slaves to their claimants. The feeling everywhere seemed to be that something must be done to convince the South that the election of Mr Lincoln meant no harm to slavery or the slave power, that the North was sound on the question of the right of the master to hold and hunt his slave as long as he pleased, and that even the right to hold slaves in the Territories should be submitted to the Supreme Court, which would probably decide in favour of the most extravagant demands of the slave States. The Northern Press took a more conservative tone towards the slavery propagandists, and a corresponding tone of bitterness towards anti-slavery men and measures. It came to be a no uncommon thing to hear men denouncing South Carolina and Massachusetts in the same breath, and in the same measure of disapproval. The old pro-slavery spirit which, in 1835, mobbed anti-slavery prayer-meetings, and dragged William Lloyd Garrison through the streets of Boston with a halter about his neck, was revived. From Massachusetts to Missouri, anti-slavery meetings were ruthlessly assailed and broken up. With others, I was roughly handled by a mob headed by one of the wealthiest men of that city, in Tremont Temple, Boston. The talk was that the blood of some abolitionist must be shed to appease the wrath of the offended South, and to restore peaceful relations between the two sections of the country. A howling mob followed Wendell Phillips for three days whenever he appeared on the pavements of his native city, because of his ability and prominence in the propagation of anti-slavery opinions.

While this humiliating reaction was going on in the North, various devices were suggested and pressed at Washington, to bring about peace and reconciliation. Committees were appointed to listen to Southern grievances, and, if possible, devise means of redress for such as might be alleged. Some of these peace propositions would have been shocking to the last degree to the moral sense of the North, had not fear for the safety of the Union overwhelmed all moral conviction. Such men as William H. Seward, Charles Francis Adams, Henry B. Anthony, Joshua R. Giddings and others – men whose courage had been equal to all other emergencies – bent before this Southern storm, and were ready to purchase peace at any price. Those who had stimulated the courage of the North before the election, and had shouted 'Who's afraid?' were now shaking in their shoes with apprehension and dread. One was for passing laws in the Northern States for the better protection of slave-hunters, and for the greater efficiency of the Fugitive-Slave Bill. Another was for enacting laws to punish the invasion of the slave states, and others were for so altering the Constitution of the United States that the Federal Government should never abolish slavery while any one State should object to such a measure. Everything that could be demanded by insatiable pride and selfishness on the part of the slave-holding South, or could be surrendered by abject fear and servility on the part of the North, had able and eloquent advocates.

Happily for the cause of human freedom, and for the final unity of the American nation, the South was mad, and would listen to no concessions. They would neither accept the terms offered, nor offer others to be accepted. They had made up their minds that under a given contingency they would secede from the Union and thus dismember the Republic. That contingency had happened, and they should execute their threat. Mr Ireson, of Georgia, expressed the ruling sentiment of his section when he told the Northern peacemakers that if the people of the South were given a blank sheet of paper upon which to write their own terms on which they would remain in the Union, they would not stay. They had come to hate everything which had the prefix 'Free' – free soil, free states, free territories, free schools, free speech, and freedom generally, and they would have no more such prefixes. This haughty, unreasonable, and unreasoning attitude of the imperious South saved the slave and saved the nation. Had the South accepted our concessions and remained in the Union the slave power would in all probability have continued to rule; the North would have become utterly demoralised; the hands on the dial-plate of American civilisation would have been reversed, and the slave would have been dragging his hateful chains today wherever the American flag floats to the breeze. Those who may wish to see to what depths of humility and self-abasement a noble people can be brought under the sentiment of fear, will find no chapter of history more instructive than that which treats of the events in official circles in Washington during the space between the months of November 1859 and March 1860.

CHAPTER XI

Secession and War

Recruiting of the 54th and 55th Coloured Regiments – Visit to President Lincoln and Secretary Stanton – Promised a commission as Adjutant General to General Thomas – Disappointment

The cowardly and disgraceful reaction, from a courageous and manly assertion of right principles, as described in the foregoing pages, continued surprisingly long after secession and war were commenced. The patience and forbearance of the loyal people of the North were amazing. Speaking of this feature of the situation in Corinthian Hall, Rochester, at the time, I said –

We, the people of the North, are a charitable people, and in the excess of this feeling we were disposed to put the very best construction upon the strange behaviour of our Southern brethren. We hoped that all would yet go well. We thought that South Carolina might secede; it was entirely like her to do so. She had talked extravagantly about going out of the Union, and it was natural that she should do something extravagant and startling if for nothing else, to make a show of consistency. Georgia, too, we thought might possibly secede. But strangely enough we thought and felt quite sure that these twin rebellious states would stand alone and unsupported in infamy and impotency; that they would soon tire of their isolation, repent of their folly, and come back to their places in the Union. Traitors withdrew from the Cabinet, from the House of Representatives, and from the Senate, and hastened to their several States to 'fire the Southern heart', and to fan the hot flames of treason at home. Still we doubted if anything serious would come of it. We treated it as a bubble on the wave – a nine days' wonder. Calm and thoughtful men ourselves, we relied upon the sober second thought of the Southern people. Even the capture of a fort, a shot at one of our ships – an insult to the national flag – caused only a momentary feeling of indignation and resentment. We could not but believe that there existed in the South a latent and powerful Union sentiment which would assert itself at last. Though loyal soldiers had been fired upon in the streets of Baltimore though loyal blood had stained the pavements, of that beautiful city, and the National Government was warned to send no troops through Baltimore to the defence of the National Capital, we could not be made to believe that the border States would plunge madly into the bloody vortex of rebellion.

But this confidence, patience, and forbearance could not last for ever. Those blissful illusions of hope were in a measure dispelled when the batteries of Charlestown harbour were opened upon the starving garrison at Fort Sumpter. For the moment the Northern lamb was transformed into a lion, and his roar was terrible. But he only showed his teeth, and clearly had no wish to use them. We preferred to fight with dollars and not daggers. 'The fewer battles the better', was the hopeful motto at Washington. 'Peace in sixty days', was held out by the astute Secretary of State. In fact, there was at the North no disposition to fight; no spirit of hate; no comprehension of the stupendous character and dimensions of the rebellion, and no proper appreciation of its inherent wickedness. Treason had shot its poisonous roots deeper, and had spread its death-dealing branches further than any Northern calculation had covered. Thus while rebels were waging a barbarous war, marshalling savage Indians to join them in slaughter; while rifled cannon balls were battering down the walls of our forts, and the iron-clad hand of monarchical power was being involved to assist in the destruction of our government and the dismemberment of our country; while a tremendous rebel ram was sinking our fleet and threatening the cities of our coast, we were still dreaming of peace. This infatuation, this blindness to the significance of passing events can only be accounted for by the rapid passage of these events, and by the fact of the habitual leniency and good-will cherished by the North towards the South. Our very lack of preparation for the conflict disposed us to look for some other way than the way of blood out of the difficulty. Treason had largely infected both army and navy. Floyd had scattered our arms, Cobb had depleted our treasury, and Buchanan had poisoned the political thought of the times by his doctrines of anti-coercion. It was in such a condition of things as this that Abraham Lincoln, compelled from fear of assassination to enter the capital in disguise, was inaugurated and issued his proclamation for the 'repossession of the forts, places, and property which had been seized from the Union', and his call upon the militia of the several States to the number of 75,000 men – a paper which showed how little even he comprehended the work then before the loyal nation. It was perhaps better for the country and for mankind that the good man could not know the end from the beginning. Had he foreseen the thousands who must sink into bloody graves; the mountains of debt to be laid on the breast of the nation; the terrible hardships and sufferings involved in the contest; and his own death by an assassin's hand, he too might have adopted the weak sentiment of those who said 'erring sisters, depart in peace'.

From the first, I, for one, saw in this war the end of slavery; and truth requires me to say that my interest in the success of the North was largely due to this belief. True it is that this faith was many times shaken by passing events, but never destroyed. When Secretary Seward instructed our ministers to say to the Governments to which they were accredited, that, 'terminate however it might, the status of no class of the people of the United States would be changed by the rebellion – that the slaves would be slaves still, and that the masters would be masters still'– when General McClellan and General Butler warned the slaves in advance that if any attempt was made by them to gain their freedom, it would be suppressed with an iron hand – when the Government persistently refused to employ coloured troops – when the emancipation proclamation of General John C. Freemont in Missouri was withdrawn – when slaves were being returned from our lines to their masters – when Union soldiers were stationed about the farm houses of Virginia to guard and protect the master in holding his slaves – when Union soldiers made themselves more active in kicking coloured men out of their camps than in shooting rebels – when even Mr Lincoln could tell the poor negro that 'he was the cause of the war', I still believed, and spoke as I believed, all over the North, that the mission of the war was the liberation of the slave, as well as the salvation of the Union; and hence from the first I reproached the North that they fought the rebels with only one hand, when they might strike effectually with two – that they fought with their soft white hand while they kept their black iron hand chained and helpless behind them – that they fought the effect while they protected the cause, and that the Union cause would never prosper till the war assumed an anti-slavery attitude, and the negro was enlisted on the loyal side. In every way possible, in the columns of my paper and on the platform, by letters to friends, at home and abroad, I did all that I could to impress this conviction upon the country. But nations seldom listen to advice from individuals, however reasonable. They are taught less by theories than by facts and events. There was much that could be said against making the war an abolition war – much that seemed wise and patriotic. 'Make the war an abolition war,' we were told, 'and you drive the border States into the rebellion, and thus add power to the enemy, and increase the number you will have to meet on the battlefield. You will exasperate and intensify Southern feeling, making it more desperate, and put far away the day of peace between the two sections.' 'Employ the arm of the negro, and the loyal men of the North will throw down their arms and go home.' 'This is the white man's country, and the white man's war.' 'It would inflict an intolerable wound upon the pride and spirit of white soldiers of the Union, to see the negro in the United States uniform. Besides, if you make the negro a soldier, you cannot depend on his courage: a crack of his old master's whip would send him scampering in terror from the field.' And so it was, that custom, pride, prejudice, and the old-time respect for Southern feeling, held back the Government from an anti-slavery policy, and from arming the negro. Meanwhile the rebellion availed itself of the negro most effectively. He was not only the stomach of the rebellion, by supplying its commissary department, but he built its forts, and dug its entrenchments, and performed other duties of its camp, which left the rebel soldier more free to fight the loyal army than he could otherwise have been. It was the cotton and corn of the negro that made the rebellion sack stand on end, and caused a continuance of the war. 'Destroy these', was the burden of all my utterances during this part of the struggle, 'and you cripple and destroy the rebellion.' It is surprising how long and bitterly the Government resisted and rejected this view of the situation. The abolition heart of the North ached over the delay, and uttered its bitter complaints, but the administration remained blind and dumb. Bull's Run, Ball's Bluff, Big Bethel, Fredericksburg, and the Peninsula disasters were the only teachers whose authority was of sufficient importance to excite the attention or respect of our rulers, and they were even slow in being taught by these. An important point was gained, however, when General B. F. Butler, at Fortress Monroe, announced the policy of treating the slaves as 'contrabands', to be made useful to the Union cause, and was sustained therein at Washington, and sentiments of a similar nature were expressed on the floor of Congress by Hon. A. G. Riddle of Ohio. A grand accession was made to this view of the case when the Hon. Simon Cameron, then Secretary of War, gave it his earnest support, and General David Hunter put the measure into practical operation in South Carolina. General Phelps from Vermont, in command at Carrollton, La., also advocated the same plan, though under discouragements which cost him his command. And many and grievous disasters on flood and field were needed to educate the loyal nation and President Lincoln up to the realisation of the necessity, not to say justice, of this position, and many devices, intermediate steps, and makeshifts were suggested to smooth the way for the ultimate policy of freeing the slave, and arming the freedman.

When at last the truth began to dawn upon the administration, that the negro might be made useful to loyalty, as well as to treason, to the Union as well as to the Confederacy, it then considered in what way it could employ him, which would in the least shock and offend the popular prejudice against him. He was already in the army as a waiter, and in that capacity there was no objection to him, and so it was thought that as this was the case, the feeling which tolerated him as a waiter would not seriously object if he should be admitted to the army as a labourer, especially as no one cared to have a monopoly of digging and toiling in trenches under a Southern sun. This was the first step in employing negroes in the United States service. The second step was to give them a peculiar costume which should distinguish them from soldiers, and yet mark them as a part of the loyal force. As the eyes of the loyal administration still further opened, it was proposed to give these labourers something better than spades and shovels with which to defend themselves in cases of emergency.

Still later it was proposed to make them soldiers, but soldiers without the blue uniform – soldiers with a mark upon them to show that they were inferior to other soldiers; soldiers with a badge of degradation upon them. However, once in the army as a labourer, once there with a red shirt on his back and a pistol in his belt, the negro was not long in appearing on the field as a soldier. But still he was not to be a soldier in the sense, and on an equal footing, with white soldiers. It was given out that he was not to be employed in the open field with white troops, under the inspiration of doing battle and winning victories for the Union cause, and in the face and teeth of his old masters; but that he should be made to garrison forts in yellow fever and otherwise unhealthy localities of the South, to save the health of white soldiers, and in order to keep up the distinction further, the black soldiers were to have only half the wages of the white soldiers, and were to be commanded entirely by white commissioned officers. While of course I was deeply pained and saddened by the estimate thus put upon my race, and grieved at the slowness of heart which marked the conduct of the loyal government, I was not discouraged, and urged every man who could to enlist; to get an eagle on his button, a musket on his shoulder, and the star-spangled banner over his head. Hence, as soon as Governor Andrew of Massachusetts received permission from Mr Lincoln to raise two coloured regiments, the 54th and 55th, I wrote the following address to the coloured citizens of the North. It appeared in my paper, then being published in Rochester, and was copied in the leading journals –

MEN OF COLOUR, TO ARMS

When first the rebel cannon shattered the walls of Sumpter and drove away its starving garrison, I predicted that the war then and there inaugurated would not be fought out entirely by white men. Every month's experience during these dreary years has confirmed that opinion. A war undertaken and brazenly carried on for the perpetual enslavement of coloured men, calls logically and loudly for coloured men to help and suppress it. Only a moderate share of sagacity was needed to see that the arm of the slave was the best defence against the arm of the slave-holder. Hence with every reverse to the national arms, with every exulting shout of victory raised by the slave-holding rebels, I have implored the imperilled nation to unchain against her foes, her powerful black hand. Slowly and reluctantly that appeal is beginning to be heeded. Stop not now to complain that it was not heeded sooner. It may or it may not have been best that it should not. This is not the time to discuss that question. Leave it to the future. When the war is over, the country saved, peace established, and the black man's rights secured, as they will be, history with an impartial hand, will dispose of that and sundry other questions. Action! Action! not criticism, is the plain duty of this hour. Words are now useful only as they stimulate to blows. The office of speech now is only to point out when, where, and how to strike to the best advantage. There is no time to delay. The tide is at its flood that leads on to fortune. From East to West, from North to South, the sky is written all over NOW OR NEVER. Liberty won by white men would lose half its lustre. 'Who would be free, themselves must strike the blow.' 'Better even die free, than to live slaves.' This is the sentiment of every brave coloured man amongst us. There are weak and cowardly men in all nations. We have them amongst us. They tell you this is the 'white man's war'; that you will be no 'better off after than before the war'; that the getting of you into the army is to 'sacrifice you on the first opportunity'. Believe them not; cowards themselves, they do not wish to have their cowardice shamed by your brave example. Leave them to their timidity, or to whatever motive may hold them back I have not thought lightly of the words I am now addressing you. The counsel I give comes of close observation of the great struggle now in progress, and of the deep conviction that this is your hour and mine. In good earnest then, and after the best deliberation, I now for the first time during this war, feel at liberty to call and counsel you to arms. By every consideration which binds you to your enslaved fellow-countrymen, and the peace and welfare of your country; by every aspiration which you cherish for the freedom and equality of yourselves and your children; by all the ties of blood and identity which makes us one with the brave black men now fighting our battles in Louisiana and South Carolina, I urge you to fly to arms and smite with death the power that would bury the Government and your liberty in the same hopeless grave. I wish I could tell you that the State of New York calls you to this high honour. For the moment her constituted authorities are silent on the subject. They will speak by and by, and doubtless on the right side; but we are not compelled to wait for her. We can get at the throat of treason and slavery through the State of Massachusetts. She was first in the War of Independence; first to break the chains of her slaves; first to make the black man equal before the law; first to admit coloured children to her common schools, and she was first to answer with her blood the alarm cry of the nation, when its capital was menaced by rebels. You know her patriotic governor, and you know Charles Sumner. I need not add more.

Massachusetts now welcomes you to arms as soldiers. She has but a small coloured population from which to recruit. She has full leave of the general government to send one regiment to the war, and she has undertaken to do it. Go quickly and help fill up the first coloured regiment from the North. I am authorised to assure you that you will receive the same wages, the same rations the same equipments, the same protection, the same treatment, and the same bounty, secured to white soldiers. You will be led by able and skilful officers, men who will take especial pride in your efficiency and success. They will be quick to accord to you all the honour you shall merit by your valour, and see that your rights and feelings are respected by other soldiers. I have assured myself on these points, and can speak with authority. More than twenty years of unswerving devotion to our common cause may give me some humble claim to be trusted at this momentous crisis. I will not argue. To do so implies hesitation and doubt, and you do not hesitate. You do not doubt. The day dawns; the morning star is bright upon the horizon! The iron gate of our prison stands half open. One gallant rush from the North will fling it wide open, while four millions of our brothers and sisters shall march out into liberty. The chance is now given you to end in a day the bondage of centuries, and to rise in one bound from social degradation to the plane of common equality with all other varieties of men. Remember Denmark Vesey of Charlestown; remember Nathaniel Turner of South Hampton; remember Shields Green and Copeland, who followed noble John Brown, and fell as glorious martyrs for the cause of the slave. Remember that in a contest with oppression, the Almighty has no attribute which can take sides with oppressors. The case is before you. This is our golden opportunity. Let us accept it, and for ever wipe out the dark reproaches unsparingly hurled against us by our enemies. Let us win for ourselves the gratitude of our country, and the best blessings of our posterity through all time. The nucleus of this first regiment is now in camp at Readville, a short distance from Boston. I will undertake to forward to Boston all persons adjudged fit to be mustered into the regiment who shall apply to me at any time within the next two weeks.

Rochester, March 2, 1863

Immediately after authority had been given by President Lincoln to Governor John A. Andrew of Massachusetts to raise and equip two regiments of coloured men for the war, I received a letter from George L. Stearns, of Boston, a noble worker for freedom in Kansas, and a warm friend of John Brown, earnestly entreating me to assist in raising the required number of men. It was presumed that by my labours in the anti-slavery cause, I had gained some influence with the coloured men of the country, and that they would listen to me in this emergency; which supposition, I am happy to say, was supported by the results. There were fewer coloured people in Massachusetts then than now, and it was necessary in order to make up the full quota of these regiments, to recruit for them in other Northern States. The nominal conditions on which coloured men were asked to enlist, were not satisfactory to me or them; but assurances from Governor Andrew that they would in the end be made just and equal, together with my faith in the logic of events, and my conviction that the wise thing to do, was for the coloured man to get into the army by any door open to him, no matter how narrow, made me accept with alacrity the work to which I was invited. The raising of these two regiments – the 54th and 55th – and their splendid behaviour in South and North Carolina was the beginning of great things for the coloured people of the whole country; and not the least satisfaction I now have in contemplating my humble part in raising them, is the fact that my two sons, Charles and Lewis, were the two first in the State of New York to enlist in them. The 54th was not long in the field before it proved itself gallant and strong, worthy to rank with the most courageous of its white companions in arms. Its assault upon Fort Wagner, in which it was so fearfully cut to pieces, and lost nearly half its officers, including its beloved and trusted commander, Colonel Shaw, at once gave it a name and a fame throughout the country. In that terrible battle, under the wing of night, more cavils in respect of the quality of negro manhood were set at rest than could have been during a century of ordinary life and observation. After that assault we heard no more of sending negroes to garrison forts and arsenals, to fight miasma, yellow fever, and small-pox. Talk of his ability to meet the foe in the open field, and of his equal fitness with the white man to stop a bullet, then began to prevail. From this time, and the fact ought to be remembered, the coloured troops were called upon to occupy positions which required the courage, steadiness, and endurance of veterans, and even their enemies were obliged to admit that they proved themselves worthy of the confidence reposed in them. After the 54th and 55th Massachusetts coloured regiments were placed in the field, and one of them had distinguished itself with so much credit in the hour of trial, the desire to send more such troops to the front became pretty general. Pennsylvania proposed to raise ten regiments. I was again called upon by my friend Mr Stearns to assist in raising these regiments, and I set about the work with full purpose of heart, using every argument of which I was capable, to persuade every coloured man able to bear arms to rally around the flag, and help to save the country and save the race. It was during this time that the attitude of the Government at Washington caused me deep sadness and discouragement, and forced me in a measure to suspend my efforts in that direction. I had assured coloured men that once in the Union Army they would be put upon an equal footing with other soldiers; that they would be paid, promoted, and exchanged as prisoners of war, Jeff Davis' threat that they would be treated as felons to the contrary notwithstanding. But thus far, the Government had not kept its promise, nor the promise made for it. The following letter which I find published in my paper of the same date will show the course I felt it my duty to take under the circumstances –

Rochester, August 1st, 1863
Major George L. Stearns

My Dear Sir – Having declined to attend the meeting to promote enlistments, appointed for me at Pittsburgh, in present circumstances, I owe you a word of explanation. I have hitherto deemed it a duty, as it certainly has been a pleasure, to co-operate with you in the work of raising coloured troops in the Free States to fight the battles of the Republic against slave-holding rebels and traitors. Upon the first call you gave me to this work I responded with alacrity. I saw, or thought I saw a ray of light, brightening the future of my whole race as well as that of our war-troubled country, in arousing coloured men to fight for the nation's life. I continue to believe in the black man's arm, and still have some hope in the integrity of our rulers. Nevertheless I must for the present leave to others the work of persuading coloured men to join the Union Army. I owe it to my long-abused People, and especially to those already in the army, to expose their wrongs and plead their cause. I cannot do that in connection with recruiting. When I plead for recruits I want to do it with all my heart, without qualification. I cannot do that now. The impression settles upon me that coloured men have much over-rated the enlightenment, justice, and generosity of our rulers at Washington. In my humble way I have contributed somewhat to that false estimate. You know that when the idea of raising coloured troops was first suggested, the special duty to be assigned them, was the garrisoning of forts and arsenals in certain warm, unhealthy, and miasmetic localities in the South. They were thought to be better adapted to that service than white troops. White troops trained to war, brave and daring, were to take fortifications, and the blacks were to hold them from falling again into the hands of the rebels. Three advantages were to arise out of this wise division of labour: 1st, The spirit and pride of white troops was not to waste itself in dull monotonous inactivity in fort life; their arms were to be kept bright by constant use. 2nd, The health of white troops was to be preserved. 3rd, Black troops were to have the advantage of sound military training and to be otherwise useful at the same time that they should be tolerably secure from capture by the rebels, who early avowed their determination to enslave and slaughter them in defiance of the laws of war. Two out of the three advantages were to accrue to the white troops. Thus far, however, I believe that no such duty as holding fortifications has been committed to coloured troops. They have done far other and more important work than holding fortifications. I have no special complaint to make at this point, and I simply mention it to strengthen the statement, that from the beginning of this business it was the confident belief among both the coloured and white friends of coloured enlistments that President Lincoln as commander-in-chief of the army and navy, would certainly see to it that his coloured troops should be so handled and disposed of as to be but little exposed to capture by the rebels, and that, if so exposed, as they have repeatedly been from the first, the President possesses both the disposition and the means for compelling the rebels to respect the rights of such as might fall into their hands. The piratical proclamation of Jefferson Davis, announcing slavery and assassination to coloured prisoners was before the country and the world. But men had faith in Mr Lincoln and his advisers. He was silent to be sure, but charity suggested that being a man of action rather than words he only waited for a case in which he should be required to act. This faith in the man enabled us to speak with warmth and effect in urging enlistments among coloured men. That faith, my dear sir, is now nearly gone. Various occasions have arisen during the last six months for the exercise of his power in behalf of the coloured men in his service, But no word comes to us from the War Department, sternly assuring the rebel chief that inquisition shall yet be made for innocent blood. No word of retaliation when a black man is slain by a rebel in cold blood. No word was said when free men from Massachusetts were caught and sold into slavery in Texas. No word is said when brave black men who, according to the testimony of both friend and foe, fought like heroes to plant the star-spangled banner on the blazing parapets of Fort Wagner, and in doing so were captured, some mutilated and killed, and others sold into slavery. The same crushing silence reigns over this scandalous outrage as over that of the slaughtered teamsters at Murfreesboro; the same as over that at Milliken's Bend and Vicksburg. I am free to say, my dear sir, that the case looks as if the confiding coloured soldiers had been betrayed into bloody hands by the Government in whose defence they were heroically fighting. I know what you will say to this: you will say 'wait a little longer, and after all, the best way to have justice done to your people is to get them into the army as fast as you can'. You may be right in this; my argument has been the same, but have we not already waited, and have we not already shown the highest qualities of soldiers, and on this account deserve the protection of the Government for which we are fighting? Can any case stronger than that before Charlestown ever arise? If the President is ever to demand justice and humanity, for black soldiers, is not this the time for him to do it? How many 54th's must be out to pieces, its mutilated prisoners killed, and its living prisoners sold into slavery, to be tortured to death by inches, before Mr Lincoln shall say, 'Hold, enough!'

You know the 54th. To you, more than to any man, belongs the credit of raising that regiment. Think of its noble and brave officers literally hacked to pieces, while many of its rank and file have been sold into slavery worse than death, and pardon me, if I hesitate about assisting in raising a fourth regiment until the President shall give the same protection to them as to white soldiers.

With warm and sincere regards,

FREDERICK DOUGLASS

Since writing the foregoing letter, which we have now put upon record, we have received assurances from Major Stearns that the Government of the United States is already taking measures which will secure the captured coloured soldiers at Charlestown and elsewhere the same protection against slavery and cruelty extended to white soldiers. What ought to have been done at the beginning,

comes late, but it comes. The poor coloured soldiers have purchased interference dearly. It really seems that nothing of justice,
liberty, or humanity can come to us except through tears and blood.

THE BLACK MAN AT THE WHITE HOUSE

My efforts to secure just and fair treatment for the coloured soldiers did
not stop at letters and speeches. At the suggestion of my friend, Major
Stearns, to whom the foregoing letter was addressed, I was induced to
go to Washington and lay the complaints of my people before President
Lincoln and the Secretary of War; and to urge upon them such action
as should secure to the coloured troops then fighting for the country a
reasonable degree of fair play. I need not say that at the time I
undertook this mission it required much more nerve than a similar one
would require now. The distance then between the black man and the
white American citizen, was immeasurable. I was an ex-slave, identified
with a despised race; and yet I was to meet the most exalted person in
this great Republic. It was altogether an unwelcome duty, and one from
which I would gladly have been excused. I could not know what kind of
a reception would be accorded me. I might be told to go home and
mind my own business and leave such questions as I had come to discuss
to be managed by the men wisely chosen by the American people to
deal with them, or I might be refused an interview altogether. Nevertheless, I felt bound to go; and my acquaintance with Senators Charles
Sumner, Henry Wilson, Samuel Pomeroy, Secretary Salmon, P. Chase,
Secretary William H. Seward and Assistant Secretary of War Charles A.
Dana encouraged me to hope at least for a civil reception. My
confidence was fully justified in the result. I shall never forget my first
interview with this great man. I was accompanied to the executive
mansion and introduced to President Lincoln by Senator Pomeroy.
The room in which he received visitors was the one now used by the
president's secretaries. I entered it with a moderate estimate of my own
consequence, and yet there I was to talk with, and even to advise, the
head man of a great nation. Happily for me, there was no vain pomp
and ceremony about him. I was never more quickly or more completely
put at ease in the presence of a great man, than in that of Abraham
Lincoln. He was seated, when I entered, in a low armchair, with his feet
extended on the floor, surrounded by a large number of documents, and
several busy secretaries. The room bore the marks of business, and the
persons in it, the President included, appeared to be much over-worked
and tired. Long lines of care were already deeply written on Mr

Lincoln's brow, and his strong face, full of earnestness, lighted up as soon as my name was mentioned. As I approached and was introduced to him, he rose and extended his hand, and bade me welcome. I at once felt myself in the presence of an honest man – one whom I could love, honour, and trust without reserve or doubt. Proceeding to tell him who I was, and what I was doing, he promptly, but kindly, stopped me, saying: 'I know who you are, Mr Douglass; Mr Seward has told me all about you. Sit down. I am glad to see you.' I then told him the object of my visit: that I was assisting to raise coloured troops; that several months before I had been very successful in getting men to enlist, but that now it was not easy to induce the coloured men to enter the service, because there was a feeling among them that the Government did not deal fairly with them in several respects. Mr Lincoln asked me to state particulars. I replied that there were three particulars which I wished to bring to his attention. First, that coloured soldiers ought to receive the same wages as those paid to white soldiers. Second, that coloured soldiers ought to receive the same protection when taken prisoners, and be exchanged as readily, and on the same terms, as any other prisoners, and if Jefferson Davis should shoot or hang coloured soldiers in cold blood, the United States Government should retaliate in kind and degree without delay upon Confederate prisoners in its hands. Third, when coloured soldiers, seeking the 'bubble-reputation at the cannon's mouth', performed great and uncommon service on the battlefield, they should be rewarded by distinction and promotion, precisely as white soldiers are rewarded for like services.

Mr Lincoln listened with patience and silence to all I had to say. He was serious and even troubled by what I had said, and by what he had evidently thought himself before upon the same points. He impressed me with the solid gravity of his character, by his silent listening, not less than by his earnest reply to my words.

He began by saying that the employment of coloured troops at all was a great gain to the coloured people; that the measure could not have been successfully adopted at the beginning of the war; that the wisdom of making coloured men soldiers was still doubted; that their enlistment was a serious offence to popular prejudice; that they had larger motives for being soldiers than white men; that they ought to be willing to enter the service upon any conditions; that the fact that they were not to receive the same pay as white soldiers, seemed a necessary concession to smooth the way to their employment at all as soldiers; but that ultimately they would receive the same. On the second point, in respect to equal protection, he said the case was more difficult.

Retaliation was a terrible remedy, and one which it was very difficult to apply; one which if once begun, there was no telling where it would end; that if he could get hold of the confederate soldiers who had been guilty of treating coloured soldiers as felons, he could easily retaliate, but the thought of hanging men for a crime perpetrated by others, was revolting to his feelings. He thought that the rebels themselves would stop such barbarous warfare, and less evil would be done if retaliation were not resorted to. That I had already received information that coloured soldiers were being treated as prisoners of war. In all this I saw the tender heart of the man rather than the stern warrior and commander-in chief of the American army and navy, and while I could not agree with him, I could not but respect his humane spirit.

On the third point he appeared to have less difficulty, though he did not absolutely commit himself. He simply said that he would sign any commission to coloured soldiers whom his Secretary of War should commend to him. Though I was not entirely satisfied with his views, I was so well satisfied with the man and with the educating tendency of the conflict, that I determined to go on with the recruiting.

From the President, I went to see Secretary Stanton. The manner of no two men could be more widely different. I was introduced by Assistant Secretary Dana, whom I had known many years before at Brook Farm, Mass., and afterwards as managing editor of the New York *Tribune*. Every line in Mr Stanton's face told me that my communication with him must be brief, clear, and to the point; that he might turn his back upon me as a bore at any moment; that politeness was not one of his weaknesses. His first glance was that of a man who says, 'Well, what do you want? I have no time to waste upon you or anybody else, and I shall waste none. Speak quick, or I shall leave you.' The man and the place seemed alike busy. Seeing I had no time to lose, I hastily went over the ground I had gone over with President Lincoln. As I ended, I was surprised by seeing a changed man before me. Contempt and suspicion, and brusqueness, had all disappeared from his face and manner, and for a few minutes he made the best defence that I had then heard from anybody of the treatment of coloured soldiers by the Government. I was not satisfied, yet I left in the full belief that the true course to the black man's freedom and citizenship was over the battlefield, and that my business was to get every black man I could into the Union armies. Both the President and Secretary of War assured me that justice would ultimately be done to my race, and I gave full faith and credit to their promise. On assuring Mr Stanton of my willingness to take a commission, he said he would make me assistant adjutant to

General Thomas, who was then recruiting and organising troops in the Mississippi Valley. He asked me how soon I could be ready. I told him in two weeks, and that my commission might be sent me to Rochester. For some reason, however, my commission never came. The Government, I fear, was still clinging to the idea that positions of honour in the service should be occupied by white men, and that it would not do to inaugurate just then the policy of perfect equality. I wrote to the department for my commission, but was simply told to report to General Thomas. This was so different from what I expected, and from what I had been promised, that I wrote to Secretary Stanton that I would report to General Thomas on receipt of my commission, but it did not come, and I did not go to the Mississippi Valley as I had fondly hoped. I knew too much of camp life and the value of shoulder straps in the army to go into the service without some visible mark of my rank. I have no doubt that Mr Stanton, in the moment of our meeting, meant all he said, but thinking the matter over, he felt that the time had not then come for a step so radical and aggressive. Meanwhile, my three sons were in the service; Lewis and Charles, as already named, in the Massachusetts regiments, and Frederick recruiting coloured troops in the Mississippi Valley.

CHAPTER XII

Hope for the Nation

The first of January 1863, was a memorable day in the progress of American liberty and civilisation. It was the turning-point in the conflict between freedom and slavery. A death-blow was then given to the slave-holding rebellion. Until then the Federal arm had been more than tolerant to that relic of barbarism. It had defended it inside the Slave States; it had countermanded the emancipation policy of John C. Fremont in Missouri; it had returned slaves to their so-called owners; and had threatened that any attempt on the part of the slaves to gain their freedom by insurrection, or otherwise, would be put down with an iron hand; it had even refused to allow the Hutchinson family to sing their anti-slavery songs in the camps of the army of the Potomac; it had surrounded the houses of slave-holders with bayonets for their protection; and through its Secretary of War, William H. Seward, had given notice to the world that, 'however the war for the Union might terminate, no change would be made in the relation of master and slave'. Upon this pro-slavery platform the war against the rebellion had been waged during more than two years. It had not been a war of conquest, but rather a war of conciliation. McClellan, in command of the army, had been trying, apparently, to put down the rebellion without hurting the rebels, certainly without hurting slavery, and the Government had seemed to co-operate with him in both respects. Charles Sumner, William Lloyd Garrison, Wendell Phillips, Gerrit Smith and the whole anti-slavery phalanx at the North had denounced this policy, and had besought Mr Lincoln to adopt an opposite one, but in vain. Generals in the field, and councils in the Cabinet, had persisted in advancing this policy through defeats and disasters, even to the verge of ruin. We fought the rebellion, but not its cause. The key to the situation was the four million of slaves; yet the slave who loved us, was hated, and the slave-holder who hated us, was loved. We kissed the hand that smote us, and spurned the hand that helped us. When the means of victory were before us – within our grasp – we went in search of the means of defeat. And now, on this 1st day of January 1863, the formal and solemn announcement was made that thereafter the Government would be found on the side of emancipation. This proclamation changed everything. It gave a new direction to the councils of the Cabinet, and to the conduct of the national arms. I shall leave to the statesman, the philosopher, and historian, the more comprehensive discussion of this document, and only tell how it touched me, and those in like condition with me at the time. I was in Boston, and its reception there may indicate the importance attached to it elsewhere. An immense assembly convened in Tremont Temple to await the first flash of the electric wires announcing the 'new departure'. Two years of war prosecuted in the interests of slavery, had made free speech possible in Boston, and we now met together to receive and celebrate the first utterance of the long-hoped-for proclamation, *if* it came, and if it did *not* come, to speak our minds freely; for, in view of the past, it was by no means certain that it would come. The occasion, therefore, was one of both hope and fear. Our ship was on the open sea, tossed by a terrible storm; wave after wave was passing over us, and every hour was fraught with increasing peril. Whether we should survive or perish, depended in large measure upon the coming of this proclamation. At least so we felt. Although the conditions on which Mr Lincoln had promised to withhold it, had not been complied with, yet, from many considerations, there was room to doubt and fear. Mr Lincoln was known to be a man of tender heart, and boundless patience; no man could tell to what length he might go, or might refrain from going in the direction of peace and reconciliation. Hitherto, he had not shown himself a man of heroic measures, and, properly enough, this step belonged to that class. It must be the end of all compromises with slavery – a declaration that thereafter the war was to be conducted on a new principle, with a new aim. It would be a full and fair assertion that the Government would neither trifle, nor be trifled with any longer. But would it come? On the side of doubt, it was said that Mr Lincoln's kindly nature might cause him to relent at the last moment; that Mrs Lincoln, coming from an old slave-holding family, would influence him to delay, and give the slave-holders one other chance.* Every moment of waiting chilled our hopes, and strengthened our fears. A line of messengers was established between the telegraph office and the platform of Tremont Temple, and the time was occupied with brief speeches from Hon. Thomas Russell of Plymouth, Miss Anna J. Dickinson (a lady of marvellous eloquence), Revd Mr Grimes, J. Sella Martin, William Wells Brown and myself. But speaking or listening to speeches was not the thing for which the people had come together. The time for argument was passed. It was not logic, but the trump of jubilee, which everybody wanted to hear. We were waiting and listening as for a bolt from the sky, which should rend the fetters of four million of slaves; we were watching, as it were, by the dim light of the stars, for the dawn of a new day; we were longing for the answer to the agonising prayers of centuries. Remembering those in bonds as bound with them, we wanted to join in the shout for freedom, and in the anthem of the redeemed.

Eight, nine, ten o'clock came and went, and still no word. A visible shadow seemed falling on the expecting throng, which the confident

---

* I have reason to know that this supposition did Mrs Lincoln great injustice.

utterances of the speakers sought in vain to dispel. At last, when patience was well-nigh exhausted, and suspense was becoming agony, a man – I think it was Judge Russell – with hasty step advanced through the crowd, and with a face fairly illuminated with the news he bore, exclaimed in tones that thrilled all hearts, 'It is coming!' 'It is on the wires!' The effect of this announcement was startling beyond description, and the scene was wild and grand. Joy and gladness exhausted all forms of expression from shouts of praise, to sobs and tears. My old friend Rue, a coloured preacher, a man of wonderful vocal power, expressed the heartfelt emotion of the hour, when he led all voices in the anthem, 'Sound the loud timbrel o'er Egypt's dark sea, Jehovah hath triumphed, his people are free.' About twelve o'clock, seeing there was no disposition to retire from the hall, which must be vacated, my friend Grimes – of blessed memory – rose and moved that the meeting adjourn to the Twelfth Baptist Church, of which he was pastor, and soon that church was packed from doors to pulpit, and this meeting did not break up till near the dawn of day. It was one of the most affecting and thrilling occasions I ever witnessed, and a worthy celebration of the first step on the part of the nation in its departure from the thraldom of ages.

There was evidently no disposition on the part of this meeting to criticise the proclamation; nor was there with anyone at first. At the moment we saw only its anti-slavery side. But further and more critical examination showed it to be extremely defective. It was not a proclamation of 'liberty throughout all the land, unto all the inhabitants thereof', such as we had hoped it would be; but was one marked by discrimination and reservations. Its operation was confined within certain geographical and military lines. It only abolished slavery where it did not exist, and left it intact where it did exist. It was a measure apparently inspired by the law motive of military necessity, and by so far as it was so, it would become inoperative and useless when military necessity should cease. There was much said in this line, and much that was narrow and erroneous. For my own part, I took the proclamation, first and last, for a little more than it purported; and saw in its spirit, a life and power far beyond its letter. Its meaning to me was the entire abolition of slavery, wherever the evil could be reached by the Federal arm, and I saw that its moral power would extend much further. It was in my estimation an immense gain to have the war for the Union committed to the extinction of slavery, even from a military necessity. It is not a bad thing to have individuals or nations do right though they do so from selfish motives. I approved the one-spur wisdom of 'Paddy' who thought if he could get one side of his horse to go, he could trust the speed of the other side.

The effect of the proclamation abroad was highly beneficial to the loyal cause. Disinterested parties could now see in it a benevolent character. It was no longer a mere strife for territory and dominion, but a contest of civilisation against barbarism.

The Proclamation itself was like Mr Lincoln throughout. It was framed with a view to the least harm and the most good possible in the circumstances, and with especial consideration of the latter. It was thoughtful, cautious, and well guarded at all points. While he hated slavery, and really desired its destruction, he always proceeded against it in a manner the least likely to shock or drive from him any who were truly in sympathy with the preservation of the Union, but who were not friendly to emancipation. For this he kept up the distinction between loyal and disloyal slave-holders, and discriminated in favour of the one, as against the other. In a word, in all that he did, or attempted, he made it manifest that the one great and all commanding object with him, was the peace and preservation of the Union, and that this was the motive and main spring of all his measures. His wisdom and moderation at this point were for a season useful to the loyal cause in the border States, but it may be fairly questioned, whether it did not chill the Union ardour of the loyal people of the North in some degree, and diminish, rather than increase, the sum of our power against the rebellion: for moderate, cautious and guarded as was this proclamation, it created a howl of indignation and wrath amongst the rebels and their allies. The old cry was raised by the copperhead organs of 'an abolition war', and a pretext was thus found for an excuse for refusing to enlist, and for marshalling all the negro prejudice of the North on the rebel side. Men could say they were willing to fight for the Union, but that they were not willing to fight for the freedom of the negroes; and thus it was made difficult to procure enlistments or to enforce the draft. This was especially true of New York, where there was a large Irish population. The attempt to enforce the draft in that city was met by mobs, riot, and bloodshed. There is perhaps no darker chapter in the whole history of the war, than this cowardly and bloody uprising in July 1863. For three days and nights New York was in the hands of a ferocious mob, and there was not sufficient power in the government of the Country or of the City itself, to stay the hands of violence, and the effusion of blood. Though this mob was nominally against the draft which had been ordered, it poured out its fiercest wrath upon the coloured people and their friends. It spared neither age nor sex; it hanged negroes simply because they were negroes; it murdered women in their homes, and burned their homes over their heads; it dashed out the brains of young children against the lamp posts; it burned the coloured orphan asylum, a noble charity on the corner of Fifth Avenue, and scarce allowing time for the helpless two hundred children to make good their escape, plundered the building of every valuable piece of furniture; and coloured men, women, and children were forced to seek concealment in cellars or garrets, or wheresoever else it could be found, until this high carnival of crime and reign of terror should pass away.

In connection with Geo. L. Stearns, Thomas Webster and Colonel Wagner, I had been at Camp William Penn, Philadelphia, assisting in the work of filling up the coloured regiments, and was on my way home from there, just as these events were transpiring in New York. I was met by a friend at Newark, who informed me of this condition of things. I, however, pressed on my way to the Chambers Street station of the Hudson River Railroad in safety, the mob being in the upper part of the city, fortunately for me, for not only my colour, but my known activity in procuring enlistments would have made me especially obnoxious to its murderous spirit. This was not the first time I had been in imminent peril in New York city. My arrival there, after my escape from slavery, was full of danger. My passage through its borders after the attack of John Brown on Harper's Ferry was scarcely less safe. I had encountered Isaiah Rynders and his gang of ruffians in the old Broadway Tabernacle at our anti-slavery anniversary meeting, and I knew something of the crazy temper of such crowds; but this anti-draft – anti-negro mob was something more and something worse – it was a part of the rebel force, without the rebel uniform, but with all its deadly hate; it was the fire of the enemy opened in the rear of the loyal army. Such men as Franklin Pierce and Horatio Seymour had done much in their utterances to encourage resistance to the drafts. Seymour was then Governor of the State of New York, and while the mob was doing its deadly work he addressed them as 'My friends', telling them to desist then, while he could arrange at Washington to have the draft arrested. Had Governor Seymour been loyal to his country, and to his country's cause, in this her moment of need, he would have burned his tongue with a red hot iron sooner than allow it to call these thugs, thieves, and murderers his 'friends'.

My interviews with President Lincoln and his able Secretary, before narrated, greatly increased my confidence in the anti-slavery integrity of the Government, although I confess I was greatly disappointed at my failure to receive the commission promised me by Secretary Stanton. I, however, faithfully believed, and loudly proclaimed my belief, that the rebellion would be suppressed, the Union preserved, the slaves emancipated, and the coloured soldiers would in the end have justice done them. This confidence was immeasurably strengthened when I saw General George B. McClellan relieved from the command of the army of the Potomac, and General U. S. Grant placed at its head, and in command of all the armies of the United States. My confidence in General Grant was not entirely due to the brilliant military successes achieved by him, but there was a moral as well as military basis for my faith in him. He had shown his single mindedness and superiority to popular prejudice by his prompt co-operation with President Lincoln in his policy of employing coloured troops, and his order commanding his soldiers to treat such troops with due respect. In this way he proved himself to be not only a wise general, but a great man – one who could adjust himself to new conditions, and adopt the lessons taught by the events of the hour. This quality in General Grant was and is made all the more conspicuous and striking in contrast with his West Point education and his former political associations; for neither West Point nor the Democratic party have been good schools in which to learn justice and fair play to the negro.

It was when General Grant was fighting his way through the Wilderness to Richmond, on the 'line' he meant to pursue 'if it took all summer', and every reverse to his arms was made the occasion for a fresh demand for peace without emancipation, that President Lincoln did me the honour to invite me to the Executive Mansion for a conference on the situation. I need not say I went most gladly. The main subject on which he wished to confer with me was as to the means most desirable to be employed outside the army to induce the slaves in the rebel States to come within the Federal lines. The increasing opposition to the war, in the North, and the mad cry against it, because it was being made an abolition war, alarmed Mr Lincoln, and made him apprehensive that a peace might be forced upon him which would leave still in slavery all who had not come within our lines. What he wanted was to make his proclamation as effective as possible in the event of such a peace. He said in a regretful tone, 'The slaves are not coming so rapidly and so numerously to us as I hoped.' I replied that the slave-holders knew how to keep such things from their slaves, and probably very few knew of his proclamation, 'Well,' he said, 'I want you to set about devising some means for making them acquainted with it, and for bringing them into our lines.' He spoke with great earnestness and much solicitude, and seemed troubled by the attitude of Mr Greeley, and the growing impatience there was being manifested through the North at the war. He said he was being accused of protracting the war beyond its legitimate object, and of failing to make peace, when he might have done so to advantage. He was afraid of what might come of all these complaints, but was persuaded that no solid and lasting peace could come, short of absolute submission on the part of the rebels, and he was not for giving them rest by futile conferences at Niagara Falls, or elsewhere, with unauthorised persons. He saw the danger of premature peace, and, like a thoughtful and sagacious man as he was, he wished to provide means of rendering such consummation as harmless as possible. I was the more impressed by this benevolent consideration because he before said, in answer to the peace clamour, that his object was to *save the Union*, and to do so with or without slavery. What he said on this day showed a deeper moral conviction against slavery than I had even seen before in anything spoken or written by him. I listened with the deepest interest and profoundest satisfaction, and, at his suggestion, agreed to undertake the organising a band of scouts, composed of coloured men, whose business should be somewhat after the original plan of John Brown, to go into the rebel States, beyond the lines of our armies, and carry the news of emancipation, and urge the slaves to come within our boundaries.

This plan, however, was very soon rendered unnecessary by the success of the war in the Wilderness and elsewhere, and by its termination in the complete abolition of slavery.

I refer to this conversation because I think it is evidence conclusive on Mr Lincoln's part that the proclamation, so far as least as he was concerned, was not effected merely as a 'necessity'.

An incident occurred during this interview which illustrates the character of this great man, though the mention of it may savour a little of vanity on my part. While in conversation with him his secretary twice announced 'Governor Buckingham of Connecticut': one of the noblest and most patriotic of the loyal Governors. Mr Lincoln said, 'Tell Governor Buckingham to wait, for I want to have a long talk with my friend Frederick Douglass.' I interposed, and begged him to see the Governor at once, as I could wait; but no, he persisted he wanted to talk with me, and Governor Buckingham could wait. This was probably the first time in the history of this Republic when its chief magistrate found occasion or disposition to exercise such an act of impartiality between persons so widely different in their positions and supposed claims upon his attention. From the manner of the Governor, when he was finally admitted, I inferred that he was as well satisfied with what Mr Lincoln had done, or had omitted to do, as I was.

I have often said elsewhere what I wish to repeat here, that Mr Lincoln was not only a great President, but a GREAT MAN – too great to be small in anything. In his company I was never in any way reminded of my humble origin, or of my unpopular colour. While I am, as it may seem, bragging of the kind consideration which I have reason to believe that Mr Lincoln entertained towards me, I may mention one thing more. At the door of my friend John A. Gray, where I was stopping in Washington, I found, one afternoon, the carriage of Secretary Dole, and a messenger from President Lincoln with an invitation for me to take tea with him at the Soldiers' Home, where he then passed his nights, riding out after the business of the day was over at the Executive Mansion. Unfortunately, I had an engagement to speak that evening, and having made it one of the rules of my conduct in life never to break an engagement, if possible to keep it, I felt obliged to decline the honour. I have often regretted that I did not make this an exception to my general rule. Could I have known that no such opportunity would come to me again, I should have justified myself in disappointing a large audience for the sake of such a visit with Abraham Lincoln.

It is due perhaps to myself to say here that I did not take Mr Lincoln's attentions as due to my merits or personal qualities. While I have no doubt that Messrs Seaward and Chase had spoken well of me to him, and the fact of my having been a slave, and gained my freedom, and of having picked up some sort of an education, and being in some sense 'self-made man', and having made myself useful as an advocate of the claims of my people, gave me favour in his eyes; yet I am quite sure that the main thing which gave me consideration with him was my well-known relation to the coloured people of the Republic, and especially the help which that relation enabled me to give to the work of suppressing the rebellion and of placing the Union on a firmer basis than it ever had or could have sustained in the days of slavery.

So long as there was any hope whatsoever of the success of rebellion, there was of course a corresponding fear that a new lease of life would be granted to slavery. The proclamation of Fremont in Missouri, the letter of Phelps in the Department of the Gulf, the enlistment of coloured troops by General Hunter, the 'Contraband' letter of General B. F. Butler, the soldierly qualities surprisingly displayed by coloured soldiers in the terrific battles of Port Hudson, Vicksburg, Morris Island, and elsewhere, the Emancipation Proclamation by Abraham

Lincoln had given slavery many and deadly wounds, yet it was in fact only wounded and crippled, not disabled and killed. With this condition of national affairs came the summer of 1864, and with it the revived Democratic party, with the story in its mouth that the war was a failure, and with General George B. McClellan, the greatest failure of the war, as its candidate for the Presidency. It is needless to say that the success of such a party, on such a platform, with such a candidate at such a time, would have been a fatal calamity. All that had been done towards suppressing the rebellion and abolishing slavery would have proved of no avail, and the final settlement between the two sections of the Republic, touching slavery and the right of secession, would have been left to tear and rend the country again at no distant future.

It was said that this Democratic party, which, under Mr Buchanan, had betrayed the Government into the hands of secession and treason; was the only party which could restore the country to peace and union. No doubt it would have 'patched up' a peace, but it would have been a peace more to be dreaded than war. So at least I felt and worked. When we were thus asked to exchange Abraham Lincoln for McClellan – a successful Union President for an unsuccessful Union General – a party earnestly endeavouring to save the Union, torn and rent by a gigantic rebellion, I thought with Mr Lincoln, that it was not wise to 'swap horses while crossing a stream'. Regarding, as I did, the continuance of the war to the complete suppression of the rebellion, and the retention in office of President Lincoln as essential to the total destruction of slavery, I certainly exerted myself to the uttermost, in my small way, to secure his re-election. This most important object was not attained, however, by speeches, letters, or other electioneering appliances. The staggering blows dealt upon the rebellion that year by the armies under Grant and Sherman, and his own great character, ground all opposition to dust, and made his election sure, even before the question reached the polls. Since William the Silent, who was the soul of the mighty war for religious liberty against Spain and the Spanish inquisition, no leader of men has been loved and trusted in such generous measure as Abraham Lincoln. His election silenced, in a good degree, the discontent felt at the length of the war, and the complaints of its being an Abolition war. Every victory of our arms, on flood and field, was a rebuke to McClellan and the Democratic party, and an endorsement of Abraham Lincoln for President, and his new policy. It was my good fortune to be present at his inauguration in March, and to hear on that occasion his remarkable inaugural address. On the night previous I took tea with Chief Justice Chase, and assisted his beloved daughter, Mrs

Sprague, in placing over her honoured father's shoulders the new robe, then being made, in which he was to administer the oath of office to the re-elected President. There was a dignity and grandeur about the Chief Justice which marked him as one born great. He had known me in early anti-slavery days, and had conquered his race-prejudice, if he ever had any; at any rate, he had welcomed me to his home and his table, when to do so was a strange thing in Washington; and the fact was by no means an insignificant one.

The inauguration, like the election, was a most important event. Four years before, after Mr Lincoln's first election, the pro-slavery spirit determined against his inauguration, and it no doubt would have accomplished its purpose had he attempted to pass openly and recognised through Baltimore. There was murder in the air then, and there was murder in the air now. His first inauguration arrested the fall of the Republic, and the second was to restore it to enduring foundations. At the time of the second inauguration the rebellion was apparently vigorous, defiant, and formidable; but in reality weak, dejected, and desperate. It had reached that verge of madness when it had called upon the negro for help to fight against the freedom which he so longed to find, for the bondage he would escape – against Lincoln the Emancipator for Davis the enslaver. But desperation discards logic as well as law, and the South was desperate. Sherman was marching to the sea, and Virginia with its rebel capital was in the firm grip of Ulysses S. Grant. To those who knew the situation it was evident that unless some startling change was made the confederacy had but a short time to live, and that time full of misery. This condition of things made the air at Washington dark and lowering. The friends of the Confederate cause here were neither few nor insignificant. They were among the rich and influential. A wink or a nod from such men might unchain the hand of violence and set order and law at defiance. To those who saw beneath the surface it was clearly perceived that there was danger abroad; and as the procession passed down Pennsylvania Avenue, I for one felt an instinctive apprehension that at any moment a shot from some assassin in the crowd might end the glittering pageant, and throw the country into the depths of anarchy. I did not then know, what has since become history, that the plot was already formed and its execution contemplated for that very day, which though several weeks delayed, at last accomplished its deadly work. Reaching the Capitol, I took my place in the crowd where I could see the Presidential procession as it came upon the east portico, and where I could hear and see all that took place. There was no such throng as that which celebrated the inauguration of

President Garfield, nor that of President Rutherford B. Hayes. The whole proceeding was wonderfully quiet, earnest, and solemn. From the oath, as administered by Chief Justice Chase, to the brief but weighty address delivered by Mr Lincoln, there was a leaden stillness about the crowd. The address sounded more like a sermon than a state paper. In the fewest words possible it referred to the condition of the country four years before, on his first accession to the presidency – to the causes of the war, and the reasons on both sides for which it had been waged. 'Neither party,' he said, 'expected for the war the magnitude or the duration which it had already attained. Neither anticipated that the cause of the conflict might cease with or even before the conflict itself should cease. Each looked for an easier triumph, and a result less fundamental and astounding.' Then in a few short sentences, admitting the conviction that slavery had been the 'offence which, in the providence of God, must needs come, and the war as the woe due to those by whom the offence came', he asked if there can be 'discerned in this, any departure from those Divine attributes which the believers in a loving God always ascribe to Him? Fondly do we hope,' he continued, 'fervently do we pray that this mighty scourge of war may speedily pass away. Yet if God wills that it continue until all the wealth piled by the bondman's two hundred and fifty years of unrequited toil shall be sunk, and until every drop of blood drawn with the lash shall be paid by another drawn with the sword, as was said three thousand years ago, so still it must be said, "The judgements of the Lord are true and righteous altogether."

'With malice towards none, with charity for all, with firmness in the right, as God gives us to see the right, let us strive to finish the work we are in, and bind up the nation's wounds, to care for him who shall have borne the battle, and for his widow and his orphans, to do all which may achieve and cherish a just and lasting peace among ourselves and with all nations.'

I know not how many times, and before how many people I have quoted these solemn words of our martyred President; they struck me at the time, and have seemed to me ever since to contain more vital substance than I have ever seen compressed into a space so narrow; yet on this memorable occasion when I clapped my hands in gladness and thanksgiving at their utterance, I saw in the faces of many about me expressions of widely different emotion.

On this inauguration day, while waiting for the opening of the ceremonies, I made a discovery in regard to the Vice President – Andrew Johnson. There are moments in the lives of most men, when the doors of their souls are open, and unconsciously to themselves, their true characters may be read by the observant eye. It was at such an instant I caught a glimpse of the real nature of this man, which all subsequent developments proved true. I was standing in the crowd by the side of Mrs Thomas J. Dorsey, when Mr Lincoln touched Mr Johnson, and pointed me out to him. The first expression which came to his face, and which I think was the true index of his heart, was one of bitter contempt and aversion. Seeing that I observed him, he tried to assume a more friendly appearance; but it was too late; it was useless to close the door when all within had been seen. His first glance was the frown of the man, the second was the bland and sickly smile of the demagogue. I turned to Mrs Dorsey and said, 'Whatever Andrew Johnson may be, he certainly is no friend of our race.'

No stronger contrast could well be presented between two men than between President Lincoln and Vice-President Johnson on this day. Mr Lincoln was like one who was treading the hard and thorny path of duty and self-denial; Mr Johnson was like one just from a drunken debauch. The face of the one was full of manly humility, although at the topmost height of power and pride, the other was full of pomp and swaggering vanity. The fact was though it was yet early in the day, Mr Johnson was drunk.

In the evening of the day of the inauguration, another new experience awaited me. The usual reception was given at the executive mansion, and though no coloured persons had ever ventured to present themselves on such occasions, it seemed, now that freedom had become the law of the Republic, now that coloured men were on the battlefield mingling their blood with that of white men in one common effort to save the country, it was not too great an assumption for a coloured man to offer his congratulations to the President with those of other citizens. I decided to go, and sought in vain for someone of my own colour to accompany me. It is never an agreeable experience to go where there can be any doubt of welcome, and my coloured friends had too often realised discomfiture from this cause to be willing to subject themselves to such unhappiness; they wished me to go, as my New England coloured friends, in the long ago, liked very well to have me take passage on the first-class cars and be hauled out and pounded by rough-handed brakesmen, to make way for them. It was plain, then, that someone must lead the way, and that if the coloured man would have his rights, he must take them; and now, though it was plainly quite the thing for me to attend President Lincoln's reception, 'they all with one accord began to make excuse'. It was finally arranged that

Mrs Dorsey should bear me company, so together we joined in the grand procession of citizens from all parts of the country, and moved slowly towards the executive mansion. I had for some time looked upon myself as a man, but now in this multitude of the elite of the land, I felt myself a man among men. I regret to be obliged to say, however, that this comfortable assurance was not of long duration, for on reaching the door, two policemen stationed there took me rudely by the arm and ordered me to stand back, for their directions were to admit no persons of my colour. The reader need not be told that this was a disagreeable set-back. But once in the battle, I did not think it well to submit to repulse. I told the officers I was quite sure there must be some mistake, for no such order could have emanated from President Lincoln; and if he knew I was at the door he would desire my admission. They then, to put an end to the parley, as I suppose, for we were obstructing the doorway, and were not easily pushed aside, assumed an air of politeness, and offered to conduct me in. We followed their lead, and soon found ourselves walking some planks out of a window, which had been arranged as a temporary passage for the exit of visitors. We halted as soon as we saw the trick, and I said to the officers: 'You have deceived me. I shall not go out of this building till I have seen President Lincoln.' At this moment a gentleman who was passing in, recognised me, and I said to him: 'Be so kind as to say to Mr Lincoln that Frederick Douglass is detained by officers at the door.' It was not long before Mrs Dorsey and I walked into the spacious East Room, amid a scene of elegance such as in this country I had never witnessed before. Like a mountain pine high above all others, Mr Lincoln stood, in his grand simplicity, and *home-like beauty*. Recognising me, even before I reached him, he exclaimed, so that all around could hear him, 'Here comes my friend Douglass.' Taking me by the hand, he said, 'I am glad to see you. I saw you in the crowd today, listening to my inaugural address; how did you like it?' I said, 'Mr Lincoln, I must not detain you with my poor opinion, when there are thousands waiting to shake hands with you.' 'No, no,' he said, 'you must stop a little, Douglass; there is no man in the country whose opinion I value more than yours. I want to know what you think of it?' I replied, 'Mr Lincoln, that was a sacred effort.' 'I am glad you liked it!' he said, and I passed on, feeling that any man, however distinguished, might well regard himself honoured by such expressions, from such a man.

It came out that the officers at the White House had received no orders from Mr Lincoln, or from anyone else. They were simply complying with an old custom, the outgrowth of slavery, as dogs will sometimes rub their necks, long after their collars are removed, thinking they are still there. My coloured friends were well pleased with what had seemed to them a doubtful experiment, and I believe were encouraged by its success to follow my example. I have found in my experience that the way to break down an unreasonable custom, is to contradict it in practice. To be sure in pursuing this course I have had to contend not merely with the white race, but with the black. The one has condemned me for my presumption in daring to associate with them, and the other for pushing myself where they take it for granted I am not wanted. I am pained to think that the latter objection springs largely from a consciousness of inferiority, for as colours alone can have nothing against each other, and the conditions of human association are founded upon character rather than colour, character depending upon mind and morals, there can be nothing blameworthy in people thus equal, meeting each other on the plane of civil or social rights.

A series of important events followed soon after the second inauguration of Mr Lincoln, conspicuous amongst which was the fall of Richmond. The strongest endeavour, and the best generalship of the rebellion was employed to hold that place, and when it fell, the pride, prestige, and power of the rebellion fell with it, never to rise again. The news of this great event found me again in Boston. The enthusiasm of that loyal city cannot be easily described. As usual, when anything touches the great heart of Boston, Faneuil Hall became vocal and eloquent. This Hall is an immense building, and its history is correspondingly great. It has been the theatre of much patriotic declamation from the days of the 'Revolution' and before; as it has, since my day, been the scene where the strongest efforts of the most popular orators of Massachusetts have been made. Here Webster the great 'expounder' addressed the 'sea of upturned faces'. Here Choate, the wonderful Boston barrister, by his weird, electric eloquence, enchained his thousands; here Everett charmed with his classic periods the flower of Boston aristocracy; and here, too, Charles Sumner, Horace Mann, John A. Andrew, and Wendell Phillips, the last superior to most, and equal to any, have for forty years spoken their great words for justice, liberty, and humanity, sometimes in the calm and sunshine of unruffled peace, but oftener in the tempest and whirlwind of mob-ocratic violence. It was here that Mr Phillips made his famous speech in denunciation of the murder of Elijah P. Lovejoy in 1887, which changed the whole current of his life and made him pre-eminently the leader of anti-slavery thought in New England. Here too Theodore

Parker, whose early death not only Boston, but the lovers of liberty throughout the world, still mourn, gave utterance to his deep and life-giving thoughts in words of fullness and power. But I set out to speak of the meeting, which was held there in celebration of the fall of Richmond, for it was a meeting as remarkable for its composition, as for its occasion. Among the speakers by whom it was addressed, and who gave voice to the patriotic sentiments which filled and overflowed each loyal heart, were the Hon. Henry Wilson, and the Hon. Robert C. Winthrop. It would be difficult to find two public men more distinctly opposite than these. If anyone may properly boast an aristocratic descent, or if there be any value or worth in that boast, Robert C. Winthrop may without undue presumption, avail himself of it. He was born in the midst of wealth and luxury, and never felt the flint of hardship or the grip of poverty. Just the opposite to this was the experience of Henry Wilson. The son of common people, wealth and education had done little for him; but he had in him a true heart, with a world of common sense; and these with industry, good habits, and perseverance, had carried him further and lifted him higher, than the brilliant man with whom he formed such a striking contrast. Winthrop, before the war, like many others of his class, had sided largely with the demands of the slave power, had abandoned many of his old Whig friends when they went for the Free Soil and Free Men in 1848, and had gone into the Democratic party.

When the war broke out he was found to be too good to be a rebel sympathiser, and he became as Wilson also did – a power in the Union cause. I regret that I had imagined him capable of taking sides, or seeming to do so with the enemies of the Republic in the hour of its peril. For, when the Union needed him, and all others, as the slave-holding rebellion was raising its defiant head – as when that head was in the dust and ashes of defeat – the beloved Winthrop, the proud representative of what Daniel Webster once called the 'solid men of Boston', showed that he was not prepared to sacrifice his patriotism to party. He made the loyal cause his own. Its 'gates, like those of Heaven, stood open night and day', and he showed no reluctance to enter in. Regiment after regiment, brigade after brigade, passed over Boston Common to endure the perils and hardships of war; Governor Andrew poured out his soul, and exhausted his wonderful powers of speech in patriotic words to the brave departing sons of old Massachusetts, and, as was fitting, burning words of loyal devotion fell from the lips of Winthrop also, and did their part in nerving those young soldiers going forth to lay down their lives for the life of the Republic. In large public meetings his voice was eloquently raised in the advocacy of the cause of the Union, and he did much to rally his countrymen around the Government when every effort was needed to crush the slave-holders' rebellion. And now, in the last quarter of the eleventh hour, when the day's work was nearly done, faithful to the end, Robert C. Winthrop was seen standing upon the same platform with the veteran Henry Wilson. He was there in all his native grace and dignity, elegantly and aristocratically clothed, his whole bearing marking his social sphere as widely different from that of many present. It will hereafter be remembered with pride by those who bear his honoured name when he is no longer among the living, that he was found on the right side, and in the right place – in old Faneuil Hall – side by side with plain Henry Wilson – the shoemaker senator. But this was not the only contrast on that platform on that day. It was my strange fortune to follow Mr Winthrop on this interesting occasion. I remembered him as the guest of John H. Clifford of New Bedford, afterwards Governor of Massachusetts, when twenty-five years before, I had been only a few months from slavery – I was behind his chair as waiter, and was even then charmed by his elegant conversation – and now after this lapse of time, I found myself no longer behind the chair of this princely man, but announced to succeed him in the order of speakers, before that brilliant audience. I was not insensible to the contrast in our history and positions, and was curious to observe if it effected him, and how. To his credit, I am happy to say, he bore himself grandly throughout. His speech was fully up to the enthusiasm of the hour, and the great audience greeted his utterances with merited applause. I need not speak of the speeches of Henry Wilson and others, nor of my own. The meeting was in every way a remarkable expression of popular feeling, created by a great and important event.

After the fall of Richmond, the collapse of the rebellion was not long delayed, though it did not perish without adding to its long list of atrocities, one which sent a thrill of horror throughout the civilised world, in the assassination of Abraham Lincoln: a man so amiable, so kind, humane, and honest, that one is at a loss to know how he could have had an enemy on earth. The details of his 'taking off' are too familiar to be more than mentioned here. The assassination of James Abraham Garfield has made us all too painfully familiar with the shock and sensation produced by the hell-black crime, to make any descrip-tion necessary. The curious will note, that the Christian name of both men is the same, and that both were remarkable for their kind qualities, and for having risen by their own energies from among the people, and that both were victims of assassins at the beginning of a presidential term.

Mr Lincoln had reason to look forward to a peaceful and happy term of office. To all appearance, we were on the eve of a restoration of the Union, and a solid and lasting peace. He had served one term as President of the Disunited States, he was now for the first time to be President of the United States. Heavy had been his burden, hard had been his toil, bitter had been his trials, and terrible had been his anxiety; but the future seemed now bright and full of hope. Richmond had fallen, Grant had General Lee and the army of Virginia firmly in his clutch; Sherman had fought and found his way from the banks of the great river to the shores of the sea, leaving the two ends of the rebellion squirming and twisting in agony, like the severed parts of a serpent, doomed to inevitable death; and now there was but a little time longer for the good President to bear his burden, and be the target of reproach. His accusers, in whose opinion he was always too fast or too slow, too weak or too strong, too conciliatory or too aggressive, would soon become his admirers; it was soon to be seen that he had conducted the affairs of the nation with singular wisdom, and with absolute fidelity to the great trust confided to him. A country, redeemed and regenerated from the foulest crime against human nature that ever saw the sun! What a bright vision of peace, prosperity, and happiness must have come to that tired and overworked brain, and weary spirit. Men used to talk of his jokes, and he no doubt indulged in them, but I seemed never to have the faculty of calling them to the surface. I saw him oftener than many who have reported him, but I never saw any levity in him. He always impressed me as a strong, earnest man, having no time or disposition to trifle; grappling the work he had in hand with all his might. The expression of his face was a blending of suffering with patience and fortitude. Men called him homely, and homely he was; but it was manifestly a human homeliness, for there was nothing of the tiger or other wild animal about him. His eyes had in them the tenderness of motherhood, and his mouth and other features the highest perfection of a genuine manhood. His picture, by Marshall, now before me in my study, corresponds well with the impression I have of him. But, alas! what are all good and great qualities; what are human hopes and human happiness to the revengeful hand of an assassin? What are sweet dreams of peace; what are visions of the future? A simple leaden bullet, and a few grains of powder, in the shortest limit of time, are sufficient to blast and ruin all that is precious in human existence, not alone of the murdered, but of the murderer. I write this in the deep gloom flung over my spirit by the cruel, wanton, and cold-blooded assassination of Abraham Garfield, as well as that of Abraham Lincoln.

I was in Rochester, N.Y., where I then resided, when news of the death of Mr Lincoln was received. Our citizens, not knowing what else to do in the agony of the hour, betook themselves to the City Hall. Though all hearts ached for utterance, few felt like speaking. We were stunned and overwhelmed by a crime and calamity hitherto unknown to our country and our government. The hour was hardly one for speech, for no speech could rise to the level of feeling. Doctor Robinson, then of Rochester University, but now of Brown University, Providence, R.I, was prevailed upon to take the stand, and made one of the most touching and eloquent speeches I ever heard. At the close of his address, I was called upon, and spoke out of the fullness of my heart, and, happily, I gave expression to so much of the soul of the people present, that my voice was several times utterly silenced by the sympathetic tumult of the great audience. I had resided long in Rochester, and had made many speeches there which had more or less touched the hearts of my hearers, but never till this day was I brought into such close accord with them. We shared in common a terrible calamity, and this 'touch of nature' made us more than countrymen, it made us 'kin'.

CHAPTER XIII

Vast Changes

Satisfaction and anxiety – New fields of labour opening –
Lyceums and colleges soliciting addresses – Literary
attractions – Pecuniary gain – Still pleading for human rights –
President Andy Johnson – Coloured delegation – Their reply to
him – National Loyalist Convention, 1866, and its procession –
Not wanted – Meeting with an old friend – Joy and surprise –
The old master's welcome, and Miss Amanda's friendship –
Enfranchisement discussed – Its accomplishment – The negro a
citizen

When the war for the union was substantially ended, and peace had
dawned upon the land, as was the case almost immediately after the
tragic death of President Lincoln; when the gigantic system of American slavery which had defied the march of time, resisted all the appeals
and arguments of the abolitionists, and the humane testimonies of
good men of every generation during two hundred and fifty years, was
finally abolished and for ever prohibited by the organic law of the land;
a strange and, perhaps, perverse feeling came over me. My great and
exceeding joy over these stupendous achievements, especially over the
abolition of slavery – which had been the deepest desire and the great
labour of my life – was slightly tinged with a feeling of sadness.

I felt I had reached the end of the noblest and best part of my life; my
School was broken up, my church disbanded, and the beloved congregation dispersed, never to come together again. The anti-slavery
platform had performed its work, and my voice was no longer needed.
'Othello's occupation was gone.' The great happiness of meeting with
my fellow-workers was now to be among the things of memory. Then,
too, some thought of my personal future came in. Like Daniel
Webster, when asked by his friends to leave John Tyler's Cabinet, I
naturally enquired: 'Where shall I go?' I was still in the midst of my
years, and had something of life before me, and as the minister, urged

by my old friend George Bradburn to preach anti-slavery, when to do so was unpopular, said, 'It is necessary for ministers to live,' I felt it was necessary for me to live, and to live honestly. But where should I go, and what should I do? I could not now take hold of life as I did when I first landed in New Bedford, twenty-five years before; I could not go to the wharf of either Gideon or George Howland, to Richmond's brass foundry, or Richeton's candle and oil works, load and unload vessels, or even ask Governor Clifford for a place as a servant. Rolling oil casks and shovelling coal were all well enough when I was younger, immediately after getting out of slavery. Doing this was a step up, rather than a step down; but all these avocations had had their day for me, and I had had my day for them. My public life and labours had unfitted me for the pursuits of my earlier years, and yet had not prepared me for more congenial and higher employment. Outside the question of slavery, my thoughts had not been much directed, and I could hardly hope to make myself useful in any other cause than that to which I had given the best twenty-five years of my life. A man in the situation I found myself, has not only to divest himself of the old, which is never easily done, but to adjust himself to the new, which is still more difficult. Delivering lectures under various names, John B. Gough says, 'whatever may be the title, my lecture is always on Temperance'; and such is apt to be the case with any man who has devoted his time and thoughts to one subject for any considerable length of time. But what should I do? was the question. I had a few thousand dollars – a great convenience, and one not generally so highly prized by my people as it ought to be – saved from the sale of 'my bondage and my freedom', and the proceeds of my lectures at home and abroad. With this sum I thought of following the noble example of my old friends Stephen and Abby Kelley Foster, purchase a little farm and settle myself down to earn an honest living by tilling the soil. My children were all grown up, and ought to be able to take care of themselves. This question, however, was soon decided for me. I had after all acquired – a very unusual thing – a little more knowledge and aptitude fitting me for the new condition of things than I knew, and had a deeper hold upon public attention than I had supposed. Invitations began to pour in upon me from colleges, Lyceums, and literary societies, offering me one hundred, and even two hundred dollars for a single lecture.

I had some time before, prepared a lecture on 'Self-made Men', and also one upon Ethnology, with a special reference to Africa. The latter had cost me much labour, though as I now look back upon it, it was a very defective production. I wrote it at the instance of my friend

Doctor M. B. Anderson, President of Rochester University, himself a distinguished Ethnologist, a deep thinker and scholar. I had been invited by one of the literary societies of Western Reserve College – then at Hudson, but recently removed to Cleveland, Ohio – to address it on Commencement Day; and never having spoken on such an occasion, never, indeed, having been inside of a schoolhouse for the purpose of an education, I hesitated about accepting the invitation, and finally called upon Prof. Henry Wayland, son of the great Doctor Wayland of Brown University, and on Doctor Anderson, and asked their advice whether I ought to accept. Both gentlemen advised me to do so. They knew me, and evidently thought well of my ability. But the puzzling question now was, what shall I say if I go there? It won't do to give them an old-fashioned anti-slavery discourse. I learned afterwards that such a discourse was precisely what they needed, though not what they wished; for the faculty, including the President, was in great distress because I, a coloured man, had been invited, and because of the reproach this circumstance might bring upon the College. But what shall I talk about? became the difficult question. I finally hit upon the one before mentioned. I had read, when in England a few years before, with great interest, parts of Doctor Pritchard's *Natural History of Man*, a large volume marvellously calm and philosophical in its discussion of the Science of the origin of the races, and was thus in the line of my then convictions. I sought this valuable book at once in our bookstores, but could not obtain it anywhere in this country. I sent to England, where I paid the sum of seven and a half dollars for it. In addition to this valuable work, President Anderson kindly gave me a little book entitled *Man and his Migrations*, by Dr R. G. Latham, and loaned me the large work of Dr Morton, the famous archaeologist, and that of Messrs Nott and Glidden, the latter written evidently to degrade the negro and support the then prevalent Calhoun doctrine of the rightfulness of slavery. With these books, and occasional suggestions from Dr Anderson and Professor Wayland, I set about preparing my Commencement address. For many days and nights I toiled, and succeeded at last in getting something together in due form. Written orations had not been in my line. I had usually depended upon my unsystematised knowledge, and the inspiration of the hour and the occasion; but I had now got the 'scholar bee in my bonnet', and supposed that inasmuch as I was to speak to college professors and students, I must at least, make a show of some familiarity with letters. It proved, as to its immediate effect, a great mistake; for my carefully studied and written address, full of learned quotations, fell dead at my feet, while a few remarks I made extemporaneously at collation were enthusiastically received. Nevertheless, the reading and labour expended were of much value to me. They were needed steps preparatory to the work upon which I was about to enter. If they failed at the beginning, they helped to success in the end. My lecture on 'The Races of Men' was seldom called for, but that on 'Self-made Men' was in great demand, especially through the West. I found that the success of a lecturer depends more upon the quality of his stock in store, than the amount. My friend, Wendell Phillips – for such I esteem him – who has said more cheering words to me, and in vindication of my race, than any man now living, has delivered his famous lecture on the 'Lost Arts' during the last forty years; and I doubt if among all his lectures, and he has many, there is one in such requisition as this. When Daniel O'Connell was asked why he did not make a new speech, he playfully replied, that 'It would take Ireland twenty years to learn his old ones.' Upon some such consideration as this, I adhered pretty closely to my old lecture on 'Self-made Men', retouching and shading it a little from time to time as occasion seemed to require.

Here, then, was a new vocation before me, full of advantages, mentally and pecuniarily. When in the employment of the American Anti-Slavery Society, my salary was about four hundred and fifty dollars a year, and I felt I was well paid for my services; but I could now make from fifty to a hundred dollars a night, and have the satisfaction, too, that I was in some small measure helping to lift my race into consideration: for no man who lives at all, lives unto himself; he either helps or hinders all who are in anywise connected with him. I never rise to speak before an American audience without something of the feeling that my failure or success will bring blame or benefit to my whole race. But my activities were not now confined entirely to lectures before Lyceums. Though slavery was abolished, the wrongs of my people were not ended. Though they were not slaves they were not yet quite free. No man can be truly free, whose liberty is dependent upon the thought, feeling, and action of others; and who has himself no means in his own hands for guarding, protecting, defending, and maintaining that liberty. Yet the negro, after his emancipation, was precisely in this state of destitution. The law, on the side of freedom, is of great advantage only where there is power to make that law respected. I know no class of my fellow men, however just, enlightened, and humane, which can be wisely and safely trusted absolutely with the liberties of any other class. Protestants are excellent people, but it would not be wise for Catholics to depend entirely upon them to look after their rights and interests. Catholics are a pretty good sort of people – though there is a soul-shuddering history behind them – yet no enlightened Protestant would commit his liberty to their care and keeping. And yet the Government had left the freedmen in a worse condition than either of these. It felt that it had done enough for them. It had made them free, and henceforth they must make their own way in the world, or as the slang phrase has it, 'Root, pig, or die'; yet they had none of the conditions for self-preservation or self-protection. They were free from the individual master, but the slaves of society. They had neither property, money, nor friends. They were free from the old plantation, but they had nothing but the dusty road under their feet. They were free from the old quarter that once gave them shelter, but slaves to the rains of summer and the frosts of winter. They were in a word, literally turned loose, naked, hungry, and destitute to the open sky. The first feeling towards them by the old master classes, was full of bitterness and wrath. They resented their emancipation as an act of hostility towards themselves, and since they could not punish the emancipator, they felt like punishing the objects which that act had emancipated. Hence they drove them off the old plantation, and told them they were no longer wanted there. They not only hated them because they had been freed as a punishment to them, but because they felt that they had been robbed of their labour. An element of still greater bitterness came into their hearts: the freedmen had been the friends of the Government, and many of them had borne arms against their masters during the war. The thought of paying cash for labour that they could formerly extort by the lash did not in anywise improve their disposition to the emancipated slaves, or improve their own condition. Now, since poverty has, and can have no chance against wealth, the landless against the land owner, the ignorant against the intelligent, the freedmen were powerless. They had nothing left them but a slavery-distorted and diseased body, and lame and twisted limbs with which to fight the battle of life. I, therefore, soon found that the negro had still a cause, and that he needed my voice and pen with others to plead for it. The American Anti-Slavery Society, under the lead of Mr Garrison, had disbanded, its newspapers were discontinued, its agents were withdrawn from the field, and all systematic efforts by abolitionists were abandoned. Many of the society, Mr Phillips and myself amongst the number, differed from Mr Garrison as to the wisdom of this course. I felt that the work of the Society was not done, that it had not fulfilled its mission, which was not merely to emancipate, but to elevate the enslaved class; but against Mr Garrison's leadership, and amid the surprise and joy occasioned by the emancipation, it was impossible to keep the association alive; and the cause of the freedmen was left mainly to individual effort, and to hastily extemporised societies of ephemeral character, brought together under benevolent impulse, but having no history behind them, and being new to the work, they were not as effective for good as the old society would have been, had it followed up its work and kept its old instrumentalities in operation.

From the first I saw no chance of bettering the condition of the freedman, until he should cease to be merely a freedman, and should become a citizen. I insisted that there Was no safety for him, nor for anybody else in America, outside the American Government: that to guard, protect, and maintain his liberty, the freedman should have the ballot; that the liberties of the American people were dependent upon the Ballot-box, the Jury-box and the Cartridge-box, that without these no class of people could live and flourish in this country; and this was now the word for the hour with me, and the word to which the people of the North willingly listened when I spoke. Hence, regarding as I did, the elective franchise as the one great power by which all civil rights are obtained, enjoyed, and maintained under our form of government, and the one without which freedom to any class is delusive if not impossible, I set myself to work with whatever force and energy I possessed to secure this power for the recently emancipated millions.

The demand for the ballot was such a vast advance upon the former objects proclaimed by the friends of the coloured race, that it startled and struck men as preposterous and wholly inadmissible. Anti-slavery men themselves were not united as to the wisdom of such demand. Mr Garrison himself, though foremost for the abolition of slavery, was not yet quite ready to join this advanced movement. In this respect he was in the rear of Mr Phillips; who saw not only the justice, but the wisdom and necessity of the measure. To his credit it may be said, that he gave the full strength of his character and eloquence to its adoption. While Mr Garrison thought it too much to ask, Mr Phillips thought it too little. While the one thought it might be postponed to the future, the other thought it ought to be done at once. But Mr Garrison was not a man to lag far in the rear of truth and right, and he soon came to see with the rest of us that the ballot was essential to the freedom of the freemen. A man's head will not long remain wrong, when his heart is right. The applause awarded to Mr Garrison by the Conservatives, for his moderation both in respect of his views on this question, and the disbandment of the American Anti-Slavery Society must have disturbed him. He was at any rate soon found on the right side of the suffrage question.

The enfranchisement of the freedmen was resisted on many grounds, but mainly these two: first the tendency of the measure to bring the freedmen into conflict with the old master class, and the white people of the South generally. Secondly, their unfitness, by reason of their ignorance, servility, and degradation, to exercise so great a power as the ballot, over the destinies of this great nation.

These reasons against the measure, which were supposed to be unanswerable, were in some senses the most powerful arguments in its favour. The argument that the possession of the suffrage would be likely to bring the negro into conflict with the old master-class of the South, had its main force in the admission that the interests of the two classes antagonised each other and that the maintenance of the one would prove inimical to the other. It resolved itself into this, if the negro had the means of protecting his civil rights, those who had formerly denied him these rights would be offended and would make war upon him. Experience has shown, in a measure, the correctness of this position. The old master was offended to find the negro whom he lately possessed the right to enslave and flog to toil, casting a ballot equal to his own; and he resorted to all sorts of meanness, violence, and crime to dispossess him of the enjoyment of this point of equality. In this respect the exercise of the right of suffrage by the negro has been attended with the evil, which the opponents of the measure predicted, and they could say 'I told you so,' but immeasurably and intolerably greater would have been the evil consequences resulting from the denial to one class, of this natural means of protection, and granting it to the other, and the hostile class. It would have been, to have committed the lamb to the care of the wolf – the arming of one class and disarming the other – protecting one interest, and destroying the other – making the rich strong, and the poor weak – the white man a tyrant, and the black man a slave. The very fact, therefore, that the old master-classes of the South felt that their interests were opposed to those of the freedmen, instead of being a reason against their enfranchisement, was the most powerful one in its favour. Until it shall be safe to leave the lamb in the hold of the lion, the labourer in the power of the capitalist, the poor in the hands of the rich, it will not be safe to leave a newly emancipated people completely in the power of their former masters, especially when such masters have not ceased to be such from enlightened moral convictions, but by irresistible force. Then on the part of the Government itself, had it denied this great right to the freedmen, it would have been another proof that 'Republics are ungrateful.' It would have been rewarding its enemies, and punishing its friends – embracing its foes, and spurning its allies – setting a premium on treason, and degrading loyalty. As to the second point, viz.: the negro's ignorance and degradation, there was no disputing either. It was the nature of slavery, from whose depths he had arisen, to make him so, and it would have kept him so. It was the policy of the system to keep him both ignorant and degraded, the better and more safely to defraud him of his hard earnings; and this argument never staggered me. The ballot in the hands of the negro was necessary to open the door of the schoolhouse, and to unlock the treasures of knowledge to him. Granting all that was said of his ignorance, I used to say, 'If the negro knows enough to fight for his country, he knows enough to vote; if he knows enough to pay taxes for the support of the Government, he knows enough to vote; if he knows as much when sober, as an Irishman knows when drunk, he knows enough to vote.'

And now, while I am not blind to the evils which have thus far attended the enfranchisement of the coloured people, I hold that the evils from which we escaped, and the good we have derived from that act, amply vindicate its wisdom. The evils it brought are in their nature temporary, and the good is permanent. The one is comparatively small, the other absolutely great. The young child has staggered on to his little legs, and he has sometimes fallen and hurt his head in the fall, but then he has learned to walk. The boy in the water came near drowning, but then he has learned to swim. Great changes in the relations of mankind can never come, without evils analagous to those which have attended the emancipation and enfranchisement of the coloured people of the United States. I am less amazed at these evils, than by the rapidity with which they are subsiding, and not more astonished at the facility with which the former slave has become a free man, than at the rapid adjustment of the master-class to the new situation.

Unlike the movement for the abolition of slavery, the success of the effort for the enfranchisement of the freedmen was not long delayed. It is another illustration of how one advance in pursuance of a right principle, prepares and makes easy the way to another. The way of transgression is a bottomless pit, one step in that direction invites the next, and the end is never reached; and it is the same with the path of righteous obedience. Two hundred years ago, the pious Dr Godwin dared affirm that it was 'not a sin to baptise a negro', and won for him the rite of baptism. It was a small concession to his manhood; but it was strongly resisted by the slave-holders of Jamaica, and Virginia. In this they were logical in their argument, but they were not logical in their object. They saw plainly, that to concede the negro's right to baptism was to receive him into the Christian Church, and make him a brother in Christ; and hence they opposed the first step sternly and bitterly. So long as they could keep him beyond the circle of human brotherhood, they could scourge him to toil, as a beast of burden, with a good Christian conscience, and without reproach. 'What!' said they, 'baptise a negro? preposterous!' Nevertheless the negro was baptised and admitted to church fellowship; and though for a long time his soul belonged to God, his body to his master, and he, poor fellow, had nothing left for himself, he is at last not only baptised, but emancipated and enfranchised.

In this achievement, an interview with President Andrew Johnson, on the 7th of February 1866, by a delegation consisting of George T. Downing, Lewis H. Douglass, Wm E. Matthews, John Jones, John F. Cook, Joseph E. Otis, A. W. Ross, William Whipper, John M. Brown, Alexander Dunlop and myself, will take its place in history as one of the first steps. What was said on that occasion brought the whole question, virtually, before the American people. Until that interview, the country was not fully aware of the intentions and policy of President Johnson on the subject of reconstruction, especially in respect of the newly emancipated class of the South. After having heard the brief addresses made to him by Mr Downing and myself, he occupied at least three-quarters of an hour in what seemed a set speech, and refused to listen to any reply on our part, although solicited to grant a few moments for that purpose. Seeing the advantage that Mr Johnson would have over us in getting his speech paraded before the country in the morning papers, the members of the delegation met on the evening of that day, and instructed me to prepare a brief reply which should go out to the country simultaneously with the President's speech to us. Since this reply indicates the points of difference between the President and ourselves, I produce it here as a part of the history of the times, it being concurred in by all the members of the delegation.

Both the speech and the reply were commented upon very extensively.

MR PRESIDENT: In consideration of a delicate sense of propriety, as well as your own repeated intimations of indisposition to discuss, or listen to a reply to the views and opinions you were pleased to express to us in your elaborate speech today, the undersigned would respectfully take this method of replying thereto. Believing as we do that the views and opinions you expressed in that address are entirely unsound and prejudicial to the highest interests of our race well as our country at large, we cannot do other than expose the same, and, as far may be in our power, arrest their dangerous influence. It is not necessary at this time to call attention to more than two or three features of your remarkable address:

1. The first point to which we feel especially bound to take exception, is your attempt to found a policy opposed to our enfranchisement, upon the alleged ground of an existing hostility on the part of the former slaves toward the poor white people of the South. We admit the existence of this hostility, and hold that it is entirely reciprocal. But you obviously commit an error by drawing an argument from an incident of slavery, and making it a basis for a policy adapted to a state of freedom. The hostility between the whites and blacks of the South is easily explained. It has its root and sap in the relation of slavery, and was incited on both sides by the cunning of the slave-masters. Those masters secured their ascendancy over both the poor whites and blacks by putting enmity between them.

They divided both to conquer each. There was no earthly reason why the blacks should not hate and dread the poor whites when in a state of slavery, for it was from this class that their masters received their slave catchers, slave-drivers, and overseers. They were the men called in upon all occasions by the masters, whenever any fiendish outrage was to be committed upon the slave. Now, sir, you cannot but perceive that the cause of this hatred removed, the effect must be removed also. Slavery is abolished. The cause of this antagonism is removed, and you must see that it is altogether illogical, and 'putting new wine into old bottles', to legislate from slave-holding and slave-driving premises, for a people whom you have repeatedly declared your purpose to maintain in freedom.

2. Besides, even if it were true, as you allege, that the hostility of the blacks towards the poor whites must necessarily project itself into a state of freedom, and that this enmity between the two races is even more intense in a state of freedom than in a state of slavery, in the name of Heaven, we reverently ask you how you can, in view of your professed desire to promote the welfare of the black man, deprive him of all means of defence, and clothe him whom you regard as his enemy in the panoply of political power? Can it be that you recommend a policy which would arm the strong and cast down the defenceless? Can you, by any possibility of reasoning,

regard this as just, fair or wise?

Experience proves that those are most abused who can be abused with the greatest impunity. Men are whipped oftenest who are whipped easiest. Peace between races is not to be secured by degrading one race and exalting another, by giving power to one race and withholding it from another, but, by maintaining a state of equal justice between all classes. First pure, then peaceable.

3. On the colonisation theory you were pleased to broach, very much could be said. It is impossible to suppose, in view of the usefulness of the black man in time of peace as a labourer in the South, and in time of war as a soldier in the North, and the growing respect for his rights among the people, and his increasing adaptation to a high state of civilisation in his native land, there can ever come a time when he can be removed from this country without a terrible shook to its prosperity and peace. Besides, the worst enemy of a nation could not cast upon its fair name a greater infamy than to admit that negroes could be tolerated among them in a state of the most degrading slavery and oppression, and must be cast away, driven into exile, for no other cause than having been freed from their chains.

Washington, February 7th, 1866

From this time onward, the question of suffrage for the freedmen, was not allowed to rest. The rapidity with which it gained strength, was something quite marvellous and surprising even to its advocates. Senator Charles Sumner soon took up the subject in the Senate and treated it in his usually able and exhaustive manner. It was a great treat to listen to his argument, running through two days, abounding as it did, in eloquence, learning, and conclusive reasoning. A committee of the Senate had reported a proposition giving to the States lately in rebellion in so many words complete option as to the enfranchisement of their coloured citizens; only coupling with that proposition the condition, that to such States as chose to enfranchise such citizens, the basis of their representation in Congress should be proportionately increased; or, in other words, only three-fifths of the coloured citizens should be counted in the basis of representation in States where coloured citizens were not allowed to vote, while in the States granting suffrage to coloured citizens, the entire coloured people should be counted in the basis of representation. Against this proposition, myself and associates addressed to the Senate of the United States the following memorial:

To the honourable the Senate of the United States

The undersigned, being a delegation representing the coloured people of several states, and now sojourning in Washington, charged with the duty to look after the best interests of the recently emancipated, would most respectfully, but earnestly, pray your honourable body to favour no amendment of the Constitution of the United States which would grant any one or all of the States of this Union to disfranchise any class of citizens on the ground of race or colour, for any consideration whatever. They would further respectfully represent that Constitution as adopted by the fathers of the Republic in 1789, evidently contemplated the result which has now happened, to wit, the abolition of slavery. The men who framed it, and those who adopted it, framed and adopted it for the people, and the whole people – coloured men being at that time legal voters in most of the States. In that instrument, as it now stands, there is not a sentence nor a syllable conveying any shadow of right or authority by which any State may make colour or race a disqualification for the exercise of the right of suffrage; and the undersigned will regard as a real calamity the introduction of any words, expressly or by implication, giving any State or States such power; and we respectfully submit that if the amendment now pending before your honourable body shall be adopted, it will enable any State to deprive any class of citizens of the elective franchise, notwithstanding it was obviously framed with a view to affect the question of negro suffrage only.

For these, and other reasons, the undersigned respectfully pray that the amendment to the Constitution, recently passed by the House, and now before your body, be not adopted. And as in duty bound, etc.

It was the opinion of Senator Wm Pitt Fessenden, Senator Henry Wilson, and many others, that the measure here memorialised against, would, if incorporated into the Constitution, certainly bring about the enfranchisement of the whole coloured population of the South. It was held by them to be an inducement to the States to make suffrage universal, since the basis of representation would be enlarged or contracted, according as suffrage should be extended or limited; but the judgement of these leaders was not the judgement of Senator Sumner, Senator Wade, Yates, Howe, and others, or of the coloured people. Yet, weak as this measure was, it encountered the united opposition of Democratic senators. On that side, the Hon. Thomas H. Hendricks of Indiana, took the lead in appealing to popular prejudice against the negro. He contended that among other objectionable and insufferable results that would flow from its adoption would be, that a negro would ultimately be a member of the United States Senate. I never shall forget the ineffable scorn and indignation with which Mr Hendricks deplored the possibility of such an event. In less, however, than a decade from that debate, Senators Revels and Bruce, both coloured men, have fulfilled the startling prophecy of the Indiana senator. It was not, however, by the half-way measure, which he was opposing for its radicalism, but by the fourteenth and fifteenth amendments, that these gentlemen reached their honourable positions.

In defeating the option proposed to be given to the States, to extend or deny suffrage to their coloured population, much credit is due to the delegation already named as visiting President Johnson. That delegation made it their business to personally see and urge upon leading Republican statesmen the wisdom and duty of impartial suffrage. Day after day, Mr Downing and myself saw and conversed with those members of the Senate, whose advocacy of the suffrage would be likely to ensure its success.

The second marked step in effecting the enfranchisement of the negro, was made at the National Loyalist Convention, held at Philadelphia in September 1866. This body was composed of delegates from the South, North and West. Its object was to diffuse clear views of the situation of affairs in the South, and to indicate the principles deemed advisable by it to be observed in the reconstruction of society in the Southern States.

This Convention was, as its history shows, numerously attended by the ablest and most influential men from all sections of the country, and its deliberations participated in, by them.

The policy foreshadowed by Andrew Johnson, who, by the grace of the assassin's bullet, was then in Abraham Lincoln's seat, a policy based upon the idea that the rebel States were never out of the Union, and hence had forfeited no rights which his pardon could not restore – gave importance to this Convention, more than anything which was then occurring in the South; for through the treachery of this bold, bad man, we seemed then about to lose nearly all that had been gained by the war.

I was residing in Rochester at the time, and was duly elected as a delegate from that city to attend this Convention. The honour was a surprise and a gratification to me. It was unprecedented for a city of over sixty thousand white citizens and only about two hundred coloured residents, to elect a coloured man to represent them in a national political convention, and the announcement of it gave a shock to the country, of no inconsiderable violence. Many Republicans, with every feeling of respect for me personally were unable to see the wisdom of such a course. They dreaded the clamour of social equality and amalgamation which would be raised against the party, in consequence of this startling innovation. They, dear fellows, found it much more agreeable to talk of the principles of liberty as glittering generalities, than to reduce those principles to practice.

When the train on which I was going to the convention reached Harrisburgh, it met and was attached to another from the West, crowded with Western and Southern delegates on the way to the Convention, and among them were several loyal Governors, chief among whom was the loyal Governor of Indiana, Oliver P. Morton, a man of Websterian mould in all that appertained to mental power. When my presence became known to these gentlemen, a consultation was immediately held among them, upon the question as to what it was best to do with me. It seems strange now, in view of all the progress which has been made, that such a question could arise. But the circumstances of the times made me the Jonah of the Republican ship, and responsible for the contrary winds and misbehaving weather. Before we reached Lancaster, on our eastward bound trip, I was duly waited upon by a committee of my brother delegates, which had been appointed by other honourable delegates, to represent to me the undesirableness of my attendance upon the National Loyalist Convention. The spokesman of these sub-delegates was a gentleman from New Orleans, with a very French name, which has now escaped me, but which I wish I could recall, that I might credit him with a high degree of politeness and the gift of eloquence. He began by telling me that he knew my history and my works, that he entertained a very high respect for me, that both himself and the gentlemen who sent him, as well as those who accompanied him, regarded me with admiration; that there was not among them the remotest objection to sitting in the Convention with me, but their personal wishes in the matter they felt should be set aside for the sake of our common cause; that whether I should or should not go into the Convention was purely a matter of expediency; that I must know that there was a very strong and bitter prejudice against my race in the North as well as in the South; and that the cry of social and political equality would not fail to be raised against the Republican party if I should attend this Loyal National Convention. He insisted that it was a time for the sacrifice of my own personal feeling, for the good of the Republican cause; that there were several districts in the State of Indiana so evenly balanced that a very slight circumstance would be likely to turn the scale against us, and defeat our Congressional candidates, and thus leave Congress without a two-thirds vote to control the headstrong and treacherous man then in the presidential chair. It was urged that this was a terrible responsibility for me or any other man to take.

I listened very attentively to this address, uttering no word during its delivery; but when it was finished, I said to the speaker and the committee, with all the emphasis I could throw into my voice and manner: 'Gentlemen, with all respect, you might as well ask me to put a loaded pistol to my head and blow my brains out, as to ask me to keep out of this Convention, to which I have been duly elected. Then, gentlemen, what would you gain by this exclusion? Would not the charge of cowardice, certain to be brought against you, prove more damaging than that of amalgamation? Would you not be branded all over the land as dastardly hypocrites, professing principles which you have no wish or intention of carrying out? As a mere matter of policy or expediency, you will be wise to let me in. Everybody knows that I have been duly elected as a delegate by the city of Rochester. The fact has been broadly announced and commented upon all over the country. If I am not admitted, the public will ask, "Where is Douglass? Why is he not seen in the convention?" And you would find that enquiry more difficult to answer than any charge brought against you for favouring political or social equality; but, ignoring the question of policy altogether, and looking at it as one of right and wrong, I am bound to go into that Convention; not to do so, would contradict the principle and practice of my life.' With this answer, the committee retired from the car in which I was seated, and did not again approach me on the subject; but I saw plainly enough then, as well as on the morning when the Loyalist procession was to march through the streets of Philadelphia, that while I was not to be formally excluded, I was to be ignored by the Convention.

I was the ugly and deformed child of the family, and to be kept out of sight as much as possible while there was company in the house. Especially was it the purpose to offer me no inducement to be present in the ranks of the procession of its members and friends, which was to start from Independence Hall on the first morning of its meeting.

In good season, however, I was present at this grand starting point. My reception there confirmed my impression as to the policy intended to be pursued towards me. Few of the many I knew were prepared to give me a cordial recognition, and among these few I may mention General Benj. F. Butler, who, whatever others may say of him, has always shown a courage equal to his convictions. Almost everybody else on the ground whom I met seemed to be ashamed or afraid of me. On the previous night I had been warned that I should not be allowed to walk through the city in the procession; fears had been expressed that my presence in it would so shock the prejudices of the people in Philadelphia, as to cause the procession to be mobbed.

The members of the Convention were to walk two abreast, and as I was the only coloured member of the Convention, the question was, as to who of my brother members would consent to walk with me? The answer was not long in coming. There was one *man* present who was broad enough to take in the whole situation, and brave enough to meet the duty of the hour; one who was neither afraid nor ashamed to own me as a man and a brother; one man of the purest Caucasian type, a poet and a scholar, brilliant as a writer, eloquent as a speaker, and holding a high and influential position – the editor of a weekly journal having the largest circulation of any weekly paper in the city or State of New York – and that man was *Mr Theodore Tilton*. He came to me in my isolation, seized me by the hand in a most brotherly way, and proposed to walk with me in the procession.

I have been in many awkward and disagreeable positions in my life, when the presence of a friend would have been highly valued, but I think I never appreciated an act of courage and generous sentiment more highly than I did in this brave young man, when we marched through the streets of Philadelphia on this memorable day.

Well! what came of all these dark forebodings of timid men? How was my presence regarded by the populace, and what effect did it produce? I will tell you. The fears of our loyal Governors, who wished me excluded, to propitiate the favour of the crowd, met with a signal reproof, their apprehensions were shown to be groundless, and they were compelled, as many of them confessed to me afterwards, to own themselves entirely mistaken. The people were more enlightened, and had made more progress than their leaders had supposed. An act for which those leaders expected to be pelted with stones, only brought to them unmeasured applause. Along the whole line of march my presence was cheered repeatedly and enthusiastically. I was myself utterly surprised by the heartiness and unanimity of the popular approval. We were marching through a city remarkable for the depth and bitterness of its hatred of the abolition movement; a city whose populace had mobbed anti-slavery meetings, burned temperance halls and churches owned by coloured people, and burned down Pennsylvania Hall because it had opened its doors to people of different colours upon terms of equality. But now the children of those who had committed these outrages and follies were applauding the very principles which their fathers had condemned. After the demonstrations of this first day, I found myself a welcome member of the Convention, and cordial greeting took the place of cold aversion. The victory was short, signal, and complete.

During the passage of the procession, as we were marching through Chesnut Street, an incident occurred which excited some interest in the crowd, and was noticed by the Press at the time, and may perhaps be properly related here as a part of the story of my eventful life. It was my meeting Mrs Amanda Sears, the daughter of my old mistress, Miss Lucretia Auld, the same Lucretia to whom I was indebted for so many acts of kindness when under the rough treatment of Aunt Katy, on the 'old plantation home' of Colonel Edward Lloyd. Mrs Sears now resided in Baltimore, and as I saw her at the corner of Ninth and Chesnut Streets, I hastily ran to her, and expressed my surprise and joy at meeting her, 'But what brought you to Philadelphia at this time?' I asked. She replied, with animated voice and countenance, 'I heard you were to be here, and I came to see you walk in this procession.' The dear lady, with her two children, had been following us for hours. Here was the daughter of the owner of a slave, following with enthusiasm that slave now a free man, and listening with joy to the plaudits he received as he marched along through the crowded streets of the great city. And here I may relate another circumstance which should have found place earlier in; this story, which will further explain the feeling subsisting between Mrs Sears and myself.

Seven years prior to our meeting, as just described, I delivered a lecture in National Hall, Philadelphia, and at its close a gentle man approached me and said, 'Mr Douglass, do you know that your once mistress has been listening to you tonight?' I replied that I did not, nor was I inclined to believe it. The fact was, that I had four or five times before had a similar statement made to me by different individuals in different States, and this made me sceptical in this instance. The next morning, however, I received a note from a Mr Wm Needles, very elegantly written, which stated that she who was Amanda Auld, daughter of Thomas and Lucretia Auld, and granddaughter to my old master, Captain Aaron Anthony, was now married to Mr John L. Sears, a coal merchant in West Philadelphia. The street and number of Mr Sear's office was given, so that I might, by seeing him, assure myself of the facts in the case, and perhaps learn something of the relatives whom I left in slavery. This note, with the intimation given me the night before, convinced me there was something in it, and I resolved to know the truth. I had now been out of slavery twenty years, and no word had come to me from my sisters, or my brother Perry, or my grandmother. My separation had been as complete as if I had been an inhabitant of another planet. A law of Maryland at that time visited with heavy fine and imprisonment any coloured person who should come into the State; so I could not go to them any more than they could come to me.

Eager to know if my kinsfolk still lived, and what was their condition, I made my way to the office of Mr Sears, found him in, and handed him the note I had received from Mr Needles, and asked him to be so kind as to read it and tell me if the facts were as there stated. After reading the note, he said it was true, but he must decline any conversation with me, since not to do so would be a sacrifice to the feelings of his father-in-law. I deeply regretted his decision, and spoke of my long separation from my relations, appealing to him to give me some information concerning them. I saw that my words were not without their effect. Presently he said, 'You publish a newspaper, I believe?' 'I do,' I said, 'but if that is your objection to speaking to me, no word shall go into its columns of our conversation.' To make a long story short, we had then quite a long conversation, during which Mr Sears said that in my 'Narrative' I had done his father-in-law injustice, for he was really a kind-hearted man, and a good master. I replied that there must be two sides to the relation of master and slave, and what was deemed kind and just to the one was the opposite to the other. Mr Sears was not disposed to be unreasonable, and the longer we talked the nearer we came together. I finally asked permission to see Mrs Sears, the little girl of seven or eight years when I left the Eastern Shore of Maryland. This request was a little too much for him at first, and he put me off by saying she was a mere child when I last saw her, and she was now the mother of a large family of children, and I would not know her. He could tell me everything about my people as well as she. I pressed my suit, however, insisting that I could select Miss Amanda out of a thousand other ladies, my recollection of her was so perfect, and begged him to test my memory at this point. After much parley of this nature, he at length consented to my wishes, giving me the number of his house and name of the street, with permission to call at 8 o'clock p.m. on the next day. I left him, delighted, and prompt to the hour was ready for my visit. I dressed myself in my best, and hired the finest carriage I could get to take me, partly because of the distance, and partly to make the contrast between the slave and the free man as striking as possible. Mr Sears had been equally thoughtful. He had invited to his house a number of friends to witness the meeting between Mrs Sears and myself.

I was somewhat disconcerted when I was ushered into the large parlour occupied by about thirty ladies and gentlemen, to all of whom I was a perfect stranger. I saw the design to test my memory by making it difficult for me to guess which of the company was 'Miss Amanda'. In her girlhood, she was small and slender, and hence a thin and delicately formed lady was seated in a rocking chair, near the centre of the room, with a little girl by her side. The device was good, but it did not succeed. Glancing around the room, I saw in an instant the lady who was a` child twenty-five years before, and the wife and mother now. Satisfied of this, I said, 'Mr Sears, if you will allow me, I will select Miss Amanda from this company.' I started towards her, and she, seeing that I recognised her, bounded to me with joy in every feature, and expressed her great happiness at seeing me. All thought of slavery, colour, or what might seem to be long to the dignity of her position vanished, and the meeting was as the meeting of friends long separated, yet still present in each other's memory and affection.

Amanda made haste to tell me that she agreed with me about slavery, and that she had freed all her slaves as they had become of age. She brought her children to me, and I took them in my arms, with sensations which I could not, if I would, stop here to describe. One explanation of the feeling of this lady towards me was, that her mother, who died when she was yet a tender child, had been briefly described by me in a little 'Narrative of my Life', published many years before our meeting, and when I could have had no motive but the highest for what I said of her. She had read my story, and learned something of the amiable qualities of her mother through me. She also recollected that as I had had trials as a slave, she had had her trials under the care of a stepmother, and that when she was harshly spoken to by her father's second wife, she could always read in my dark face the sympathy of one who had often received kind words from the lips of her beloved mother. Mrs Sears died three years ago in Baltimore, but she did not depart without calling me to her bedside, that I might tell her as much as I could about her mother, whom she was firm in the faith that she should meet in another, and a better world. She especially wished me to describe to her the personal appearance of her mother, and desired to know if any of her own children then present resembled her. I told her that the young lady standing in the corner of the room was the image of her mother in form and features. She looked at her daughter and said, 'Her name is Lucretia – after my mother.' After telling me that her life had been a happy one, and thanking me for coming to see her on her deathbed, she said she was ready to die. We parted to meet no more in life. The interview touched me deeply, and was, I could not help thinking, a strange one – another proof that 'Truth is often stranger than Fiction.'

If any reader of this part of my life shall see in it the evidence of a want of manly resentment for wrongs inflicted upon myself and race by slavery, and by the ancestors of this lady, so it must be. No man can be stronger than nature, one touch of which, we are told, makes all the world akin. I esteem myself a good, persistent hater of injustice and oppression, but my resentment ceases when they cease, and I have no heart to visit upon children the sins of their fathers.

It will be noticed, when I first met Mr Sears in Philadelphia, he declined to talk with me, on the ground that I had been unjust to Captain Auld, his father-in-law. Soon after that meeting, Captain Auld had occasion to go to Philadelphia, and, as usual, went straight to the house of his son-in-law, and had hardly finished the ordinary salutations, when he said: 'Sears, I see by the papers that Frederick has recently been in Philadelphia. Did you go to hear him?' 'Yes, sir,' was the reply. After asking something more about my lecture, he said, 'Well, Sears, did Frederick come to see you?' 'Yes, sir,' said Sears. 'Well, how did you receive him?' Mr Sears then told him all about my visit, and had the satisfaction of hearing the old man say that he had done right in giving me welcome to the house. This last fact I have from the Revd J. D. Long, who, with his wife, was one of the party invited to meet me at the house of Mr Sears, on the occasion of my visit to Mrs Sears.

But I must now return from this digression, and further relate my experience in the Loyalist National Convention, and how from that time there was an impetus given to the enfranchisement of the freedmen, which culminated in the fifteenth amendment to the Constitution of the United States. From the first, the members of the Convention were divided in their views of the proper measures of reconstruction, and this division was in some sense sectional. The men from the far South, strangely enough, were quite radical, while those from the border States were mostly conservative, and, unhappily, these last had control of the Convention from the first. A Kentucky gentleman was made President, and its other officers were for the most part Kentuckians, and all opposed to coloured suffrage in sentiment.

There was a 'whole heap' – to use a Kentucky phrase – 'of halfness' in that State during the war for the Union, and there was much more there after the war. The Maryland delegates, with the exception of the Hon. John L. Thomas, were in sympathy with Kentucky. Those from Virginia, except the Hon. John Miner Botts, were unwilling to entertain the question. The result was, that the Convention was broken square in two. The Kentucky President declared it adjourned, and left the chair against the earnest protests of the fields of manhood suffrage.

But the friends of this measure were not to be out-generalled and suppressed in this way, and instantly reorganising, elected John M. Botts of Virginia, President, discussed and passed resolutions in favour of enfranchising the freedmen, and thus placed the question before the country in such a manner that it could not be ignored. The delegates from the Southern States were quite in earnest, and bore themselves grandly in support of the measure; but the chief speakers and advocates of suffrage on that occasion were Mr Theodore Tilton and Miss Anna E. Dickinson. Of course, on such a question, I could not be expected to be silent. I was called forward, and responded with all the energy of my soul, for I looked upon suffrage to the negro, as the only measure which could prevent him from being thrust back into slavery.

From this time onward the question of suffrage had no rest. The rapidity with which it gained strength was more than surprising to me.

In addition to the justice of the measure, it was soon commended by events as a political necessity. As in the case of the abolition of slavery, the white people of the rebellious States have themselves to thank for its adoption. Had they accepted, with moderate grace, the decision of the court to which they appealed, and the liberal conditions of peace offered to them, and united heartily with the National Government in its efforts to reconstruct their shattered institutions, instead of sullenly refusing as they did, their counsel and their votes to that end, they might easily have defeated the argument based upon necessity for the measure. As it was, the question was speedily taken out of the hands of coloured delegations and mere individual efforts, and became a part of the policy of the Republican party; and President U. S. Grant, with his characteristic nerve and clear perception of justice, promptly recommended the great amendment to the Constitution, by which coloured men are today invested with complete citizenship – the right to vote, and to be voted for, in the American Republic.

CHAPTER XIV

Living and Learning

Inducements to a political career – Objections – A newspaper enterprise – The *New National Era* – Its abandonment – The Freedmen's Savings and Trust Company – Sad experience – Vindication

The adoption of the fourteenth and fifteenth amendments, and their incorporation into the Constitution of the United States, opened a very tempting field to my ambition, and one to which I should have probably yielded, had I been a younger man. I was earnestly urged by many of my respected fellow-citizens, both coloured and white, and from all sections of the country, to take up my abode in some one of the many districts of the South, where there was a large coloured vote, and get myself elected, as they were sure I easily could do, to a seat in Congress – possibly in the Senate. That I did not yield to this temptation was not entirely due to my age; for the idea did not square well with my better judgement and sense of propriety. The thought of going to live among a people in order to gain their votes and acquire official honours, was repugnant to my self-respect, and I had not lived long enough in the political atmosphere of Washington to have this sentiment sufficiently blunted to make me indifferent to its suggestions. I do not deny that the arguments of my friends had some weight in them, and from their standpoint it was all right; but I was better known to myself than to them. I had small faith in my aptitude as a politician, and could not hope to cope with rival aspirants. My life and labours in the North had in a measure unfitted me for such work, and I could not readily have adapted myself to the peculiar oratory found to be most effective with the newly enfranchised class. In the New England and Northern atmosphere I had acquired a style of speaking which in the South would have been considered tame and spiritless; and, consequently, he who 'could tear a passion to tatters and split the ear of groundlings', had far better chance of success with the masses there, than one so little boisterous as myself.

Upon the whole, I have never regretted that I did not enter the arena of Congressional honours to which I was invited.

Outside of mere personal considerations, I saw, or thought I saw, that in the nature of the case the sceptre of power had passed from the old slave and rebellious States, to the free and loyal States, and that hereafter, at least for some time to come, the loyal North, with its advanced civilisation, must dictate the policy and control the destiny of the Republic. I had an audience ready made in the free States: one which the labours of thirty years had prepared for me, and before this audience the freedmen of the South needed an advocate as much as they needed a member of Congress. I think in this I was right; for thus far our coloured members of Congress have not largely made themselves felt in the legislation of the country; and I have little reason to think I could have done any better than they.

I was not, however, to remain long in my retired home in Rochester, where I had planted my trees and was reposing under their shadows. An effort was being made about this time to establish a large weekly newspaper in the city of Washington, which should be devoted to the defence and enlightenment of the newly emancipated and enfranchised people; and I was urged by such men as George T. Downing, J. H. Hawes, J. Sella Martin, and others, to become its editor-in-chief. My sixteen years' experience as editor and publisher of my own paper, and the knowledge of the toil and anxiety which such a relation to a public journal must impose, caused me much reluctance and hesitation; nevertheless, I yielded to the wishes of my friends and counsellors, went to Washington, threw myself into the work, hoping to be able to lift up a standard at the National Capital, for my people, which should cheer and strengthen them in the work of their own improvement and elevation.

I was not long connected with this enterprise before I discovered my mistake. The co-operation so liberally promised, and the support which had been assured, were not very largely realised. By a series of circumstances, a little bewildering as I now look back upon them, I found myself alone, under the mental and pecuniary burden involved in the prosecution of the enterprise. I had been misled by loud talk of a grand incorporated publishing company, in which I should have shares if I wished, and in any case a fixed salary for my services; and after all these fair-seeming conditions, I had not been connected with the paper one year before its affairs had been so managed by the agent appointed by this invisible company or corporate body, as to compel me to bear the burden alone, and to become the sole owner of the printing establishment. Having become publicly associated with the enterprise, I was unwilling to have it prove a failure, and had allowed it to become in debt to me, both for money loaned, and for services, and at last it seemed wise that I should purchase the whole concern, which I did, and turned it over to my sons Lewis and Frederik, who were practical printers, and who, after a few years, were compelled to discontinue its publication. This paper was the *New National Era*, to the columns of which the coloured people are indebted for some of the best things ever uttered in behalf of their cause; for, aside from its editorials and selections, many of the ablest coloured men of the country made it the medium through which to convey their thoughts to the public. A misadventure though it was, which cost me from nine to ten thousand dollars, over it I have no tears to shed. The journal was valuable while it lasted, and the experiment was full of instruction to me, which has to some extent been heeded, for I have kept well out of newspaper undertakings since.

Someone has said that 'experience is the best teacher'. Unfortunately the wisdom acquired in one experience seems not to serve for another and new one; at any rate, my first lesson at the National Capital, bought rather dearly as it was, did not preclude the necessity of a second whetstone to sharpen my wits in this my new home and new surroundings. It is not altogether without a feeling of humiliation that I must narrate my connection with the Freedmen's Savings and Trust Company.

This was an institution designed to furnish a place of security and profit for the hard earnings of the coloured people, especially of the South. Though its title was the Freedmen's Savings and Trust Company, it was known generally as the Freedmen's Bank. According to its managers it was to be this and something more. There was something missionary in its composition, and it dealt largely in exhortations as well as promises. The men connected with its management were generally church members, and reputed eminent for their piety. Some of its agents had been preachers of the 'Word'. Their aim was now to instil into the minds of the untutored Africans lessons of sobriety, wisdom, and economy, and to show them how to rise in the world. Circulars, tracts, and other papers were scattered like snowflakes in winter by this benevolent institution among the sable millions, and they were told to 'look' to the Freedmen's Bank and 'live'. Branches were established in all the Southern States, and as a result, money flowed into its vaults to the amount of millions. With the usual effect of sudden wealth, the managers felt like making a little display of their prosperity. They accordingly erected one of the most costly and splendid buildings of the time on one of the most desirable and expensive sites in the National Capital, finished on the inside with black walnut, and furnished with marble counters and all the modern improvements. The magnificent dimensions of the building bore testimony to its flourishing condition. In passing it in the street I often peeped into its spacious windows, and looked down the row of its gentlemanly and elegantly-dressed coloured clerks, with their pens behind their ears and button-hole bouquets in their coat-fronts, and felt my very eyes enriched. It was a sight I had never expected to see. I was amazed with the facility with which they counted the money; they threw off the thousands with the dexterity, if not the accuracy, of old and experienced clerks. The whole thing was beautiful. I had read of this Bank when I lived in Rochester, and had indeed been solicited to become one of its trustees, and had reluctantly consented to do so; but when I came to Washington and saw its magnificent brown stone front, its towering height, and its perfect appointments, and the fine display it made in the transaction of its business, I felt like the Queen of Sheba when she saw the riches of Solomon, 'the half had not been told me'.

After settling myself down in Washington in the office of the *New Era*, I could, and did occasionally, attend the meetings of the Board of Trustees, and had the pleasure of listening to the rapid reports of the condition of the institution, which were generally of a most encouraging character. My confidence in the integrity and wisdom of the management was such that at one time I had entrusted to its vaults about twelve thousand dollars. It seemed fitting to me to cast in my lot with my brother freedmen, and help to build up an institution which represented their thrift and economy to such striking advantage; for the more millions accumulated there, I thought, the more consideration and respect would be shown to the coloured people of the whole country.

About four months before this splendid institution was compelled to close its doors in the starved and deluded faces of its depositors, and while I was assured by its President and by its Actuary of its sound condition, I was solicited by some of its trustees to allow them to use my name in the board as a candidate for its Presidency. So I awoke one morning to find myself seated in a comfortable armchair, with gold spectacles on my nose, and to hear myself addressed as President of the Freedmen's Bank. I could not help reflecting on the contrast between Frederick the slave boy, running about at Colonel Lloyd's with only a tow linen shirt to cover him, and Frederick – President of a Bank counting its assets by millions. I had heard of golden dreams, but such dreams had no comparison with this reality. And yet this seeming reality was scarcely more substantial than a dream. My term of service on this golden height covered only the brief space of three months, and these three months were divided into two parts, during the first part of which I was quietly employed in an effort to find out the real condition of the Bank and its numerous branches. This was no easy task. On paper, and from the representations of its management, its assets amounted to three millions of dollars, and its liabilities were about equal to its assets. With such a showing I was encouraged in the belief that by curtailing expenses, doing away with non-paying branches, which policy the trustees had now adopted, we could be carried safely through the financial distress then upon the country. So confident was I of this, that in order to meet what was said to be a temporary emergency, I was induced to loan the Bank ten thousand dollars of my own money, to be held by it until it could realise on a part of its abundant securities. This money, though it was repaid, was not done so promptly as under the supposed circumstances I thought it should be, and these circumstances increased my fears lest the chasm was not so easily bridged as the Actuary of the institution had assured me it could be. The more I observed and learned, the more my confidence diminished. I found that those trustees who wished to issue cards and publish addresses professing the utmost confidence in the Bank, had themselves not one dollar deposited there. Some of them, while strongly assuring me of its soundness had withdrawn their money and opened accounts elsewhere. Gradually I discovered that the Bank had sustained heavy losses at the South through dishonest agents, that there was a discrepancy on the books of forty thousand dollars, for which no account could be given, that instead of our assets being equal to our liabilities we could not in all likelihoods of the case pay seventy-two cents on the dollar. There was an air of mystery, too, about the spacious and elegant apartments of the Bank building which greatly troubled me, and which I have only been able to explain to myself on the supposition that the *employees*, from the Actuary and the Inspector down to the messengers, were, perhaps, naturally, anxious to hold their places, and consequently have the business continued. I am not a violent advocate of the doctrine of the total depravity of human nature, I am inclined, on the whole, to believe it a tolerably good nature, yet instances do occur which oblige me to concede that men can and do act from mere personal and selfish motives. In this case, at any rate, it seemed not unreasonable to conclude that the finely dressed young gentlemen, adorned with pens and bouquets, the most fashionable and genteel of all our coloured youth, stationed behind those marble counters, should desire to retain their places as long as there was money in the vaults to pay them their salaries.

Standing on the platform of this large and complicated establishment, with its thirty-four branches, extending from New Orleans to Philadelphia, its machinery in full operation, its correspondence carried on in cipher, its Actuary dashing in and out of the Bank with an air of pressing business, if not of bewilderment, I found the path of enquiry I was pursuing an exceedingly difficult one. I knew there had been very lately several runs on the Bank, and that there had been a heavy draft made upon its reserve fund, but I did not know, what I should have been told before being allowed to enter upon the duties of my office, that this reserve, which the bank by its charter was required to keep, had been entirely exhausted, and that hence there was nothing left to meet any future emergency. Not to make too long a story, I was, in six weeks after my election as President of this Bank, convinced that it was no longer a safe custodian of the hard earnings of my confiding people. This conclusion once reached, I could not hesitate as to my duty in the premises, and this was, to save as much as possible of the assets held by the Bank for the benefit of the depositors; and to prevent their being further squandered in keeping up appearances, and in paying the salaries of myself and other officers in the bank. Fortunately, Congress, from which we held our charter, was then in session, and its committees on finance were in daily session. I felt it my duty to make known as speedily as possible to the Hon. John Sherman, chairman of the Senate committee on finance, and to Senator Scott of Pennsylvania, also of the same committee, that I regarded the institution as insolvent and irrecoverable, and that I could no longer ask my people to deposit their money in it. This representation to the finance committee subjected me to very bitter opposition on the part of the officers of the Bank. Its Actuary, Mr Stickney, immediately summoned some of the trustees, a dozen or so of them, to go before the finance committee and make a counter statement to that made by me; and this they did. Some of them who had assisted me by giving me facts showing the insolvency of the bank, now made haste to contradict that conclusion, and to assure the committee that it was abundantly able to weather the financial storm, and pay dollar for dollar to its depositors if allowed to go on.

I was not exactly thunderstruck, but I was much amazed by this contradiction. I, however, adhered to my statement that the bank ought to stop. The Finance Committee substantially agreed with me, and in a few weeks so legislated as to bring this imposing banking business to a close by appointing three commissioners to take charge of its affairs.

This is a fair and unvarnished narration of my connection with the Freedmen's Savings and Trust Company, otherwise known as the Freedmen's Savings Bank, a connection which has brought upon my head an amount of abuse and detraction greater than any encountered in any other part of my life.

Before leaving the subject, I ought in justice to myself, to state that when I found that the affairs of the Bank were to be closed up, I did not, as I might easily have done, and as others did, make myself a preferred creditor and take my money out of the Bank, but on the contrary, I determined to take my chances with other depositors, and left my money, to the amount of two thousand dollars, to be divided with the assets among the creditors of the bank. And now, after seven years have been allowed for the value of the securities to appreciate, and the loss of interests on the deposits for that length of time, the depositors may deem themselves fortunate if they receive sixty cents on the dollar of what they placed in the care of this fine savings institution.

It is also due to myself to state, especially since I have seen myself accused of bringing the Freedmen's Bank into ruin, and squandering in senseless loans on bad security the hard-earned moneys of my race, that all the loans ever made by the Bank were made prior to my connection with it as its President. Not a dollar, not a dime of its millions were loaned by me, or with my approval. The fact is, and all investigation shows it, that I was married to a corpse. The fine building was there, with its marble counters and black walnut finishings, the affable and agile clerks, and the discreet and comely coloured cashier; but the LIFE, which was the money, was gone, and I found that I had been placed there with the hope that by 'some drugs, some charms, some conjuration, or some mighty magic', I would bring it back.

When I became connected with the Bank I had a tolerably fair name for honest dealing; I had expended in the publication of my paper in Rochester, thousands of dollars annually, and had often to depend upon my credit to bridge over immediate wants, but no man, there or elsewhere, can say I ever wronged him out of a cent; and I could, today, with the confidence of the converted tax collector, offer 'to restore fourfold to any from whom I have unjustly taken aught'. I say this, not for the benefit of those who know me, but for the thousands of my own race who hear of me mostly through the malicious and envious assaults of unscrupulous aspirants, who vainly fancy that they lift themselves into consideration by wanton attacks upon the characters of men who receive a larger share of respect and esteem than themselves.

CHAPTER XV

'Weighed in the Balance'

The most of my story is now before the reader. Whatever of good or ill the future may have in store for me, the past at least is secure. As I review the last decade up to the present writing, I am impressed with a sense of completeness; a sort of rounding up of the arch to the point where the key stone may be inserted, the scaffolding removed, and the work, with all its perfections or faults, left to speak for itself. This decade, from 1871 to 1881, has been crowded, if time is capable of being thus described, with incidents and events which may well enough be accounted remarkable. To me they certainly appear strange, if not wonderful. My early life not only gave no visible promise, but no hint of such experience. On the contrary, that life seemed to render it, in part at least, impossible. In addition to what is narrated in the foregoing chapter, I have to speak of my mission to Santo Domingo, my appointment as a member of the council for the government of the District of Columbia; my election as elector at large for the State of New York; my invitation to speak at the monument of the unknown loyal dead, at Arlington, on Decoration Day; my address on the unveiling of the Lincoln monument, at Lincoln Park, Washington; my appointment to bring the electoral vote from New York to the National Capital; my invitation to speak near the statue of Abraham Lincoln, Madison Square, New York; my accompanying the body of Vice-President Wilson from Washington to Boston; my conversations with Senator Sumner and President Grant; my welcome to the receptions of Secretary Hamilton Fish; my appointment by President R. B. Hayes to the office of Marshal of the District of Columbia; my visit to Thomas Auld, the man who claimed me as his slave, and from whom I was purchased by my English friends; and my visit to Lloyd's plantation, the home of my childhood, after an absence of fifty-six years; my appointment by President James A. Garfield to the office of Recorder of Deeds of the District of Columbia, are some of the matters which belong to this decade, and may come into the chapter I am now about to write.

Those who knew of my more than friendly relations with the Hon. Charles Sumner, and of his determined opposition to the annexation of Santo Domingo to the United States, were surprised to find me earnestly taking sides with General Grant upon that question. Some of my white friends, and a few of those of my own colour – who, unfortunately, allow themselves to look at public questions more through the medium of feeling than of reason, and who follow the line of what is grateful to their friends rather than what is consistent with their own Convictions – thought my course was an ungrateful return for the eminent services of the Massachusetts senator. I am free to say that, had I been guided only by the promptings of my heart, I should, in this controversy, have followed the lead of Charles Sumner. He was not only the most clear-sighted, brave, and uncompromising friend of my race who had ever stood upon the floor of the Senate, but was to me a loved, honoured, and precious personal friend; a man possessing the exalted and matured intellect of a statesman, with the pure and artless heart of a child. Upon any issue, as between him and others, when the right seemed in anywise doubtful, I should have followed his counsel and advice. But the annexation of Santo Domingo, to my understanding, did not seem to be any such question. The reasons in its favour were many and obvious; and those against it, as I thought, were easily answered. To Mr Sumner, annexation was a measure to extinguish a coloured nation, and to do so by dishonourable means and for selfish motives. To me it meant the alliance of a weak and defenceless people, having few or none of the attributes of a nation, torn and rent by internal feuds, unable to maintain order at home, or command respect abroad, to a government which would give it peace, stability, prosperity, and civilisation, and make it helpful to both countries. To favour annexation at the time when Santo Domingo asked for a place in our Union, was a very different thing from what it was when Cuba and Central America were sought by filibustering expeditions. When the slave power bore rule, and a spirit of injustice and oppression animated and controlled every part of our Government, I was for limiting our dominion to the smallest possible margin; but since liberty and equality have become the law of our land, I am for extending our dominion whenever and wherever such extension can peaceably and honourably, and with the approval and desire of all the parties concerned, be accomplished. Santo Domingo wanted to come under our Government upon the terms thus described; and for more reasons than I can stop here to give, I then believed, and do now believe, it would have been wise to have received her into our sisterhood of States.

The idea that annexation meant degradation to a coloured nation was altogether fanciful; there was no more dishonour to Santo Domingo in making her a State of the American Union, than in making Kansas, Nebraska, or any other territory such a State. It was giving to a part the strength of the whole, and lifting what must be despised for its isolation into an organisation and relationship which would compel consideration and respect.

Though I differed from Mr Sumner in respect to this measure, and although I told him I thought he was unjust to President Grant, it never disturbed our friendship. After his great speech against annexation, which occupied six hours in its delivery, and in which he arraigned the President in a most bitter and fierce manner, being at the White House one day, I was asked by President Grant what I 'now thought of my friend Mr Sumner'? I replied that I believed Mr Sumner sincerely thought, that in opposing annexation, he was defending the cause of the coloured race as he always had done, but that I thought he was mistaken. I saw my reply was not very satisfactory, and said 'What do you, Mr President, think of Senator Sumner?' He answered, with some feeling, 'I think he is mad.'

The difference in opinion on this question between these two great men was the cause of bitter personal estrangement, and one which I intensely regretted. The truth is, that neither was entirely just to the other, because neither saw the other in his true character; and having once fallen asunder, the occasion never came when they could be brought together.

Variance between great men finds no healing influence in the atmosphere of Washington. Interested parties are ever ready to fan the flame of animosity and magnify the grounds of hostility in order to gain the favour of one or the other. This is perhaps true in some degree in every community; but it is especially so of the National Capital, and this for the reason that there is ever a large class of people here dependent upon the influence and favour of powerful public men for their daily bread.

My selection to visit Santo Domingo with the commission sent thither, was another point indicating the difference between the OLD TIME and the NEW. It placed me on the deck of an American man-of-war, manned by one hundred marines and five hundred men-of-wars-men, under the national flag, which I could now call mine, in common with other American citizens, and gave me a place not in the forecastle, among the hands, nor in the caboose with the cooks, but in the captain's saloon, and in the society of gentlemen, scientists, and statesmen. It would be a pleasing task to narrate the varied experiences and the distinguished persons encountered in this Santo Domingo tour, but the material is too boundless for the limits of these pages. I can only say, it was highly interesting and instructive. The conversations at the captain's table, at which I had the honour of a seat, were usually led by Messrs Wade, Howe, and White – the three commissioners; and by Mr Hurlburt of the *New York World*; the last-named gentleman impressed me as one remarkable for knowledge and refinement, in which he was no whit behind Messrs Howe and White. As for the Hon. Benj. F. Wade, he was there, as everywhere, abundant in knowledge and experience, fully able to take care of himself in the discussion of any subject in which he chose to take a part. In a circle so brilliant, it is no affectation of modesty to say I was for the most part a listener and a learner. The commander of our good ship on this voyage, Captain Temple, now promoted to the position of Commodore, was a very imposing man, and deported himself with much dignity towards us all. For his treatment of me I am especially grateful. A son of the United States navy as he was – a department of our service considerably distinguished for its aristocratic tendencies – I expected to find something a little forbidding in his manner; but I am bound to say that in this I was agreeably disappointed. Both the commander and the officers under him bore themselves in a friendly manner towards me during all the voyage, and this is saying a great thing for them, for the spectacle presented by a coloured man seated at the captain's table was not only unusual, but had never before occurred in the history of the United States navy. If during this voyage there was anything to complain of, it was not in the men in authority, or in the conduct of the thirty gentlemen who went out as the honoured guests of the expedition, but in the coloured waiters. My presence and position seemed to trouble them from its incomprehensibility; and they did not know exactly how to deport themselves towards me. Possibly they may have detected in me something of the same sort in respect to themselves; at any rate we seemed awkwardly related to each other during several weeks of the voyage. In their eyes I was Fred Douglass suddenly, and possibly undeservedly, lifted above them. The fact that I was coloured and they were coloured had so long made us equal, that the contradiction now presented was too much for them. After all, I have no blame for Sam and Garrett. They were trained in the school of servility to believe that white men alone were entitled to be waited upon by coloured men; and the lesson taught by my presence on the *Tennessee* was not to be learned upon the instant, without thought and experience. I refer to the matter simply as an incident quite commonly met with in the lives of coloured men who, by their own exertions or otherwise, have happened to occupy positions of respectability and honour. While the rank and file of our race quote with much vehemence the doctrine of human equality, they are often among the first to deny and denounce it in practice. Of course this is true only of the more ignorant. Intelligence is a great leveller here as elsewhere. It sees plainly the real worth of men and things, and is not easily imposed upon by the dressed-up emptiness of human pride.

With a coloured man as conductor on a sleeping car, the last to have his bed made up at night, and the last to have his boots blacked in the morning, and the last to be served in any way, is the coloured passenger. This conduct is the homage which the black man pays to the white man's prejudice, whose wishes, like a well-trained servant, he is taught to anticipate and obey. Time, education, and circumstances are rapidly destroying these mere colour distinctions, and men will be valued in this country as well as in others, for what they are, and for what they can do.

My appointment at the hands of President Grant to a seat in the council – by way of eminence sometimes called the Upper House of the territorial legislature of the District of Columbia – at the time it was made, must be taken as a signal evidence of his high sense of justice, fairness, and impartiality. The coloured people of the district constituted then, as now, about one-third of the whole population. They were given by General Grant, three members of this legislative council – a representation more proportionate than any that has existed since the Government has passed into the hands of commissioners, for they have all been white men.

It has sometimes been asked why I am called 'Honourable'. My appointment to this council must explain this, as it explains the impartiality of General Grant, though I fear it will hardly sustain this prodigious handle to my name, as well as it does the former part of this proposition. The members of this district council were required to be appointed by the President, with the advice and consent of the United States Senate. This is the ground, and only ground that I know of, upon which anybody has claimed this title for me. I do not pretend that the foundation is a very good one, but as I have generally allowed people to call me what they pleased, and as there is nothing necessarily dishonourable in this, I have never taken the pains to dispute its application and propriety; and yet I confess that I am never so spoken of without feeling a trifle uncomfortable – about as much so as when I am called, as I sometimes am, the *Revd* Frederick Douglass. My stay in this legislative body was of short duration. My vocation abroad left me little time to study the many matters of local legislation; hence my resignation, and the appointment of my son Lewis to fill out my term.

I have thus far told my story without copious quotations from my letters, speeches, or other writings, and shall not depart from this rule in what remains to be told, except to insert here my speech, delivered at Arlington, near the monument to the 'Unknown Loyal Dead', on Decoration Day, 1871. It was delivered under impressive circumstances, in presence of President Grant, his Cabinet, and a great multitude of distinguished people, and expresses, as I think, the true view which should be taken of the great conflict between slavery and freedom to which it refers.

FRIENDS AND FELLOW CITIZENS: Tarry here for a moment. My words shall be few and simple. The solemn rites of this hour and place call for no lengthened speech. There is in the very air of this resting ground of the unknown dead a silent, subtle, and an all-pervading eloquence, far more touching, impressive, and thrilling, than living lips have ever uttered. Into the measureless depths of every loyal soul it is now whispering lessons of all that is precious, priceless, holiest, and most enduring in human existence.

Dark and sad will be the hour to this nation when it forgets to pay grateful homage to its greatest benefactors. The offering we bring today is due alike to the patriot soldiers dead and their noble comrades who still live; for whether living or dead, whether in time or eternity, the loyal soldiers who imperilled all for country and freedom are one and inseparable.

Those unknown heroes whose whitened bones have been piously gathered here, and whose green graves we now strew with sweet and beautiful flowers, choice emblems alike of pure hearts and brave spirits, reached in their glorious career that last highest point of nobleness beyond which human power cannot go. They died for their country.

No loftier tribute can be paid to the most illustrious of all the benefactors of mankind than we pay to these unrecognised soldiers, when we write above their graves this shining epitaph.

When the dark and vengeful spirit of slavery, always ambitious, preferring to rule in hell to serving in heaven, fired the Southern heart and stirred all the malign elements of discord; when our great Republic, the hope of freedom and self-government throughout the world, had reached the point of supreme peril; when the Union of these States was torn and rent asunder at the centre, and the armies of a gigantic rebellion came forth with broad blades and bloody hands to destroy the very foundation of American society, the unknown braves who flung themselves into the yawning chasm, where cannon roared and bullets whistled, fought and fell. They died for their country.

We are sometimes asked, in the name of patriotism, to forget the merits of this fearful struggle, and to remember with equal admiration those who struck at the nation's life and those who struck to save it – those who fought for slavery, and those who fought for liberty and justice.

I am no minister of malice. I would not strike the fallen. I would not repel the repentant, but may my 'right hand forget her cunning, and my tongue cleave to the roof of my mouth', if I forget the difference between the parties to that terrible, protracted, and bloody conflict.

If we ought to forget a war which has filled our land with widows and orphans, which has made stumps of men in the very flower of their youth; sent them on the journey of life armless, legless, maimed and mutilated; which has piled up a debt heavier than a mountain of gold – swept uncounted thousands of men into bloody graves, and planted agony by a million hearthstones; I say if this war is to be forgotten, I ask in the name of all things sacred what shall men remember?

The essence and significance of our devotions here today are not to be found in the fact that the men whose remains fill these graves were brave in battle. If we met simply to show our sense of bravery, we should find enough to kindle admiration on both sides. In the raging storm of fire and blood, in the fierce torrent of shot and shell, of sword and bayonet, whether on foot or on horse, unflinching courage marked the rebel not less than the loyal soldier.

But we are not here to applaud manly courage, save as it has been displayed in a noble cause. We must never forget that victory to the rebellion meant death to the Republic. We must never forget that the loyal soldiers who rest beneath this sod flung themselves between the nation and the nation's destroyers. If today we have a country not boiling in an agony of blood like France; if now we have a united country, no longer cursed by the hell-black system of human bondage; if the American name is no longer a by-word and a hissing to the mocking earth; if the star-spangled banner floats only over free American citizens in every quarter of the land, and our country has before it a long and glorious career of justice, liberty, and civilisation, we are indebted to the unselfish devotion of the noble army who rest in these honoured graves all around us.

In the month of April 1872, I had the honour to attend and preside over a National Convention of coloured citizens, held in New Orleans. It was a critical period in the history of the Republican party, as well us in that of the country. Eminent men who had hitherto been looked upon as the pillars of Republicanism had become dissatisfied with President Grant's administration, and determined to defeat his nomination for a second term. The leaders in this unfortunate revolt were Messrs Trumbull, Schurz, Greeley and Sumner. Mr Schurz had already succeeded in destroying the Republican party in the State of Missouri, and it seemed to be his ambition to be the founder of a new party, and to him, more than to any other man, belongs the credit of what was once known as the Liberal Republican party which made Horace Greeley its standard bearer in the campaign of that year.

At the time of the Convention in New Orleans the elements of this new combination were just coming together. The division in the Republican ranks seemed to be growing deeper and broader every day. The coloured people of the country were much affected by the threatened disruption, and their leaders were much divided as to the side upon which they should give their voice and their votes. The names of Greeley and Sumner, on account of their long and earnest advocacy of justice and liberty to the blacks, had powerful attractions for the newly enfranchised class; and there was in this Convention at New Orleans, naturally enough, a strong disposition to fraternise with the new party and follow the lead of their old friends. Against this policy I exerted whatever influence I possessed, and, I think, succeeded in holding back that Convention from what I felt sure then would have been a fatal political blunder, and time has proved the correctness of that position. My speech on taking the chair on that occasion was telegraphed from New Orleans in full to the New York *Herald*, and the keynote of it was that there was no path out of the Republican party that did not lead directly into the Democratic party – away from our friends and directly to our enemies. Happily this Convention pretty largely agreed with me, and its members have not since regretted that agreement.

From this Convention onward, until the nomination and election of Grant and Wilson, I was actively engaged on the stump, a part of the time in Virginia with the Hon. Henry Wilson, in North Carolina with John M. Longston and John H. Smyth, and in the State of Maine with Senator Hamlin, General B. F. Butler, General Woodford and the Hon. James G. Blaine.

Since 1879 I have been regularly what my old friend Parker Pillsbury would call a 'field-hand' in every important political campaign, and at each National Convention have sided with what has been called the stalwart element of the Republican party. It was in the Grant Presidential campaign that New York took an advanced step in the renunciation of a timid policy. The Republicans of that State not having the fear of popular prejudice before their eyes placed my name as an Elector at large at the head of their Presidential ticket. Considering the deep-rooted sentiment of the masses against negroes, the noise and tumult likely to be raised, especially among our adopted citizens of Irish descent, this was a bold and manly proceeding, and one for which the Republican of the State of New York deserve the gratitude of every coloured citizen of the Republic, for it was a blow at popular prejudice, in a quarter where it was capable of making the strongest resistance. The result proved not only the justice and generosity of the measure, but its wisdom. The Republicans carried the State by majority of fifty thousand over the heads of the Liberal Republican and the Democratic parties combined.

Equally significant of the turn now taken in the political sentiment of the country, was the action of the Republican Electoral College at its meeting in Albany, when it committed to my custody the sealed-up electoral vote of the great State of New York, and commissioned me to bring that vote to the National Capital. Only a few years before, any coloured man was forbidden by law to carry a United States mail bag from one post office to another. He was not allowed to touch the sacred leather, though locked in 'triple steel'; but now, not a mail bag, but a document which was to decide the Presidential questions with all its momentous interests, was committed to the hands of one of this despised class; and around him, in the execution of his trust, was thrown all the safeguards provided by the Constitution and the laws of the land. Though I worked hard and long, to secure the nomination and the election of General Grant in 1872, I neither received nor sought office under him. He was my choice upon grounds altogether free from selfish or personal considerations. I supported him because he had done, and would do, all he could to save, not only the country from ruin, but the emancipated class from oppression and ultimate destruction; and because Mr Greeley, with the Democratic party behind him, would not have the power, even if he had the disposition, to afford us the needed protection which our peculiar condition required. I could easily have secured the appointment as Minister to Haiti, but preferred to urge the claims of my friend, Ebenezer Bassett, a gentleman and a scholar, and a man well fitted by his good sense and amiable qualities to fill the position with credit to himself and his country. It is with a certain degree of pride that I am able to say that my opinion of the wisdom of sending Mr Bassett to Haiti has been fully justified by the creditable manner in which, for eight years, he discharged the difficult duties of that position; for I have the assurance of the Hon. Hamilton Fish, Secretary of State of the United States, that Mr Bassett was a good Minister. In so many words, the ex-Secretary told me, that he 'wished that one-half of his Ministers abroad performed their duties as well as Mr Bassett'. To those who know the Hon. Hamilton Fish, this compliment will not be deemed slight, for few men are less given to exaggeration and are more scrupulously exact in the observance of law, and in the use of language, than is that gentleman. While speaking in this strain of complacency in reference to Mr Bassett, I take pleasure also in bearing my testimony, based upon knowledge obtained at the State Department, that Mr John Mercer Langston, the present Minister to Haiti, has acquitted himself with equal wisdom and ability to that of Mr Bassett in the same position. Having known both these gentlemen in their youth, when the one was at Yale, and the other at Oberlin College, and witnessed their efforts to qualify themselves for positions of usefulness, it has afforded me no limited satisfaction to see them rise in the world. Such men increase the faith of all, in the possibilities of their race, and make it easier for those who are to come after them.

The unveiling of the Lincoln Monument in Lincoln Park, Washington, April 14th, 1876, and the part taken by me in the ceremonies of that grand occasion, take rank among the most interesting incidents of my life, since it brought me into mental communication with a greater number of the influential and distinguished men of the country than any I had before known. There were present the President of the United States and his Cabinet, Judges of the Supreme Court, the Senate and House of Representatives, and many thousands of citizens to listen to my address upon the illustrious man in whose memory the coloured people of the United States had, as a mark of their gratitude, erected that impressive monument. Occasions like this have done wonders in the removal of popular prejudice, and in lifting into consideration the coloured race; and I reckon it one of the high privileges of my life, that I was permitted to have a share in this and several other like celebrations.

The following is the substance of the oration delivered by me on the occasion of the unveiling of the freedmen's monument, in memory of Abraham Lincoln, in Lincoln Park, Washington, D.C., April 14, 1876.

FRIENDS AND FELLOW CITIZENS – I warmly congratulate you upon the highly interesting object which has caused you to assemble in such numbers and spirit as you have today. This occasion is in some respects remarkable. Wise and thoughtful men of our race, who shall come after us, and study the lesson of our history in the United States; who shall survey the long and dreary spaces over which we have travelled; who shall count the links in the great chain of events by which we have reached our present position, will make a note of this occasion; they will think of it and speak of it with a sense of manly pride and complacency.

I congratulate you, also, upon the very favourable circumstances in which we meet today. They are high, inspiring, and uncommon. They lend grace, glory, and significance to the object for which we have met. Nowhere else in this great country, with its uncounted towns and cities, unlimited wealth, and immeasurable territory extending from sea to sea, could conditions be found more favourable to the success of this occasion than here.

We stand today at the national centre to perform something like a national act – an act which is to go into history; and we are here where every pulsation of the national heart can be heard, felt, and reciprocated. A thousand wires, fed with thought and winged with lightning, put us in instantaneous communication with the loyal and true men all over this country.

Few facts could better illustrate the vast and wonderful change which has taken place in our condition as a people, than the fact of our assembling here for the purpose we have today. Harmless, beautiful, proper, and praiseworthy as this demonstration is, I cannot forget that no such demonstration would have been tolerated here twenty years ago. The spirit of slavery and barbarism, which still lingers to blight and destroy in some dark and distant parts of our country, would have made our assembling here the signal and excuse for opening upon us all the flood-gates of wrath and violence. That we are here in peace today is a compliment and a credit to American civilisation, and a prophecy of still greater national enlightenment and progress in the future. I refer to the past not in malice, for this is no day for malice; but simply to place more distinctly in front the gratifying and glorious change which has come both to our white fellow-citizens and ourselves, and to congratulate all upon the contrast between now and then; the new dispensation of freedom with its thousand blessings to both races, and the old dispensation of slavery with its ten thousand evils to both races – white and black. In view, then, of the past, the present, and the future, with the long and dark history of our bondage behind us, and with liberty, progress, and enlightenment before us, I again congratulate you upon this auspicious day and hour.

Friends and fellow citizens, the story of our presence here is soon and easily told. We are here in the District of Columbia, here in the city of Washington, the most luminous point of American territory; a city recently transformed and made beautiful in its body and in its spirit; we are here in the place where the ablest and best men of the country are sent to devise the policy, enact the laws, and shape the destiny of the Republic; we are here, with the stately pillars and majestic dome of the Capitol of the nation looking down upon us; we are here, with the broad earth freshly adorned with the foliage and flowers of spring for our church, and all races, colours, and conditions of men for our congregation – in a word, we are here to express, as best we may, by appropriate forms and ceremonies, our grateful sense of the vast, high, and pre-eminent services rendered to ourselves, to our race, to our country, and to the whole world by Abraham Lincoln.

The sentiment that brings us here today is one of the noblest that can stir and thrill the human heart. It has crowned and made glorious the high places of all civilised nations with the grandest and most enduring works of art, designed to illustrate the characters and perpetuate the memories of great public men. It is the sentiment which from year to year adorns with fragrant and beautiful flowers the graves of our loyal, brave, and patriotic soldiers who fell in defence of the Union and liberty. It is the sentiment of gratitude and appreciation, which often, in the presence of many who hear me, has filled yonder heights of Arlington with the eloquence of eulogy and the sublime enthusiasm of poetry and song; a sentiment which can never die while the Republic lives.

For the first time in the history of our people, and in the history of the whole American people, we join in this high worship, and march conspicuously in the line of this time-honoured custom. First things are always interesting, and this is one of our first things. It is the first time that, in this form and manner, we have sought to do honour to an American great man, however deserving and illustrious. I commend the fact to notice; let it be told in every part of the Republic; let men of all parties and opinions hear it; let those who despise us, not less than those who respect us, know that now and here, in the spirit of liberty, loyalty, and gratitude, let it be known everywhere, and by everybody who takes an interest in human progress and in the amelioration of the condition of mankind, that, in the presence and with the approval of the members of the American House of Representatives, reflecting the general sentiment of the country; that in the presence of that august body, the American Senate, representing the highest intelligence and the calmest judgement in the country; in presence of the Supreme Court and Chief-Justice of the United States, to whose decisions we all patriotically bow; in the presence and under the steady eye of the honoured and trusted President of the United States, with the members of his wise and patriotic Cabinet, we, the coloured people, newly emancipated and rejoicing in our blood-bought freedom, near the close of the first century in the life of this Republic, have now and here unveiled, set apart, and dedicated a monument of enduring granite and bronze, in every line, feature, and figure of which the men of this generation may read, and those of after-coming generations may read, something of the exalted character and great works of Abraham Lincoln, the first martyr President of the United States.

Fellow citizens, in what we have said and done today, and in what we may say and do hereafter, we disclaim everything like arrogance and assumption. We claim for ourselves no superior devotion to the character, history, and memory of the illustrious man whose monument we have here dedicated today. We fully comprehend the relation of Abraham Lincoln both to ourselves and to the white people of the United States. Truth is proper and beautiful at all times and in all places, and it is never more proper and beautiful in any case than when speaking of a great public man whose example is likely to be commended for honour and imitation long after his departure to the solemn shades – the silent continents of eternity. It must be admitted, truth compels me to admit, even here in the presence of the monument we have erected to his memory, Abraham Lincoln was not, in the fullest sense of the word, either our man or our model. In his interests, in his associations, in his habits of thought, and in his prejudices, he was a white man.

He was pre-eminently the white man's President, entirely devoted to the welfare of white men. He was ready and willing at any time during the first years of his administration to deny, postpone, and sacrifice the rights of humanity in the coloured people to promote the welfare of the white people of this country. In all his education and feeling he was an American of the Americans. He came into the Presidential chair upon one principle alone, namely, opposition to the extension of slavery. His arguments in furtherance of this policy had their motive and mainspring in his patriotic devotion to the interests of his own race. To protect, defend, and perpetuate slavery in the States where it existed, Abraham Lincoln was not less ready than any other President to draw the sword of the nation. He was ready to execute all the supposed constitutional guarantees of the United States Constitution in favour of the slave system anywhere inside the slave States. He was willing to pursue, recapture, and send back the fugitive slave to his master, and to suppress a slave rising for liberty, though his guilty master were already in arms against the Government. The race to which we belong were not the special objects of his consideration. Knowing this, I concede to you, my white fellow citizens, a pre-eminence in this worship at once full and supreme. First, midst, and last, you and yours were the objects of his deepest affection and his most earnest solicitude. You are the children of Abraham Lincoln. We are at best only his step-children; children by adoption, children by force of circumstances and necessity. To you it especially belongs to sound his praises, to preserve and perpetuate his memory, to multiply his statues, to hang his pictures high upon your walls, and commend his example, for to you he was a great and glorious friend and benefactor. Instead of supplanting you at this altar, we would exhort you to build high his monuments; let them be of the most costly material, of the most cunning workmanship; let their forms be symmetrical, beautiful, and perfect; let their bases be upon solid rooks, and their summits lean against the unchanging, blue, overhanging sky, and let them endure for ever! But while in the abundance of your wealth, and in the fullness of your just and patriotic devotion, you do all this, we entreat you to despise not the humble offering we this day unveil to view; for while Abraham Lincoln saved for you a country, he delivered us from a bondage, one hour of which, according to Jefferson, was worse than ages of the oppression your fathers rose in rebellion to oppose.

Fellow citizens, ours is no new-born zeal and devotion – merely a thing of this moment. The name of Abraham Lincoln was near and dear to our hearts in the darkest and most perilous hours of the Republic. We were no more ashamed of him when shrouded in clouds of darkness, of doubt, and defeat, than when we saw him crowned with victory, honour, and glory. Our faith in him was often taxed and strained to the uttermost, but it never failed. When he tarried long in the mountain; when he strangely told us that we were the cause of the war; when he still more strangely told us to leave the land in which we were born; when he refused to employ our arms in defence of the Union; when, after accepting our services as coloured soldiers, he refused to retaliate our murder and torture as coloured prisoners; when he told us he would save the Union if he could with slavery; when he revoked the Proclamation of Emancipation of General Fremont; when he refused to remove the popular commander of the army of the Potomac, in the days of its inaction and defeat, who was more zealous in his efforts to protect slavery than to suppress rebellion; when we saw all this, and more, we were at times grieved, stunned, and greatly bewildered; but our hearts believed while they ached and bled. Nor was this, even at that time, a blind and unreasoning superstition. Despite the mist and haze that surrounded him; despite the tumult, the hurry, and confusion of the hour, we were able to take a comprehensive view of Abraham Lincoln, and to make reasonable allowance for the circumstances of his position. We saw him, measured him, and estimated him; not by stray utterances to injudicious and tedious delegations, who often tried his patience; not by isolated facts torn from their connection; not by any partial and imperfect glimpses, caught at inopportune moments; but by a broad survey, in the light of the stern logic of great events, and in view of that 'divinity which shapes our ends, rough hew them how we will', we came to the conclusion that the hour and the man of our redemption had somehow met in the person of Abraham Lincoln. It mattered little to us what language he might employ on special occasions; it mattered little to us, when we fully knew him, whether he was swift or slow in his movements; it was enough for us that Abraham Lincoln was at the head of a great movement, and was in living and earnest sympathy with that movement, which, in the nature of things, must go on until slavery should be utterly and for ever abolished in the United States.

When, therefore, it shall be asked what we have to do with the memory of Abraham Lincoln, or what Abraham Lincoln had to do with us, the answer is ready, full, and complete. Though he loved Ceasar less than Rome, though the Union was more to him than our freedom or our future, under his wise and beneficent rule, we saw ourselves gradually lifted from the depths of slavery to the heights of liberty and manhood; under his wise and beneficent rule, and by measures approved and vigorously pressed by him, we saw that the handwriting of ages, in the form of prejudice and proscription, was rapidly fading away from the face of our whole country; under his rule, and in due time, about as soon after all as the country could tolerate the strange spectacle, we saw our brave sons and brothers laying off the rags of bondage, and being clothed all over in the blue uniform of the soldiers of the United States; under his rule we saw two hundred thousand of our dark and dusky people responding to the call of Abraham Lincoln, and with muskets on their shoulders, and eagles on their buttons, timing their high footsteps to liberty and union under the national flag; under his rule we saw the independence of the black republic of Haiti, the special object of slave-holding aversion and horror, fully recognised, and her minister, a coloured gentleman, duly received here in the City of Washington; under his rule we saw the internal slave trade, which so long disgraced the nation, abolished, and slavery abolished in the District of Columbia; under his rule we saw, for the first time, the law enforced against the foreign slave-trade, and the first slave-trader hanged like any other pirate or murderer; under his rule, assisted by the greatest captain of our age, and his inspiration, we saw the Confederate States, based upon the idea that our race must be slaves, and slaves for ever, battered to pieces and scattered to the four winds; under his rule, and in the fullness of time, we saw Abraham Lincoln, after giving the slave-holder three months' grace in which to save their hateful slave system, penning the immortal paper, which, though special in its language, was general in its principles and effect, making slavery for ever impossible in the United States. Though we waited long, we saw all this and more.

Can any coloured man, or any white man, friendly to the freedom of all men, ever forget the night which followed the first day of January, 1868, when the world was to see if Abraham Lincoln would prove to be as good as his word. I shall never forget that memorable night, when in a distant city I waited and watched at a public meeting, with three thousand others not less anxious than myself, for the word of deliverance which we have heard read today. Nor shall I ever forget the outburst of joy and thanksgiving that rent the air when the lightning brought to us the emancipation proclamation. In that happy hour we forgot all delay, and forgot all tardiness, forgot that the President had bribed the rebels to lay down their arms by a promise to withhold the bolt which would smite the slave-system with destruction; and we were thenceforward willing to allow the President all the latitude of time, phraseology, and every honourable device that statesmanship might require for the achievement of a great and beneficent measure of liberty and progress.

Fellow citizens, there is little necessity on this occasion to speak at length and critically of this great and good man, and of his high mission in the world. That ground has been fully occupied and completely covered both here and elsewhere. The whole field of fact and fancy has been gleaned and garnered. Any man can say things that are true of Abraham Lincoln, but no man can say anything that is new of Abraham Lincoln. His personal traits and public acts are better known to the American people than are those of any other man of his age. He was a mystery to no man who saw him and heard him. Though high in position, the humblest could approach him and feel at home in his presence. Though deep, he was transparent; though strong, he was gentle; though decided and pronounced in his convictions, he was tolerant towards those who differed from him, and patient under reproaches. Even those who only knew him through his public utterances obtained a tolerably clear idea of his character and his personality. The image of the man went out with his words, and those who read them, knew him.

I have said that President Lincoln was a white man, and shared the prejudices common to his countrymen towards the coloured race. Looking back to his times and to the condition of his country, we are compelled to admit that this unfriendly feeling on his part may be safely set down as one element of his wonderful success in organising the loyal American people for the tremendous conflict before them, and bringing them safely through that conflict. His great mission was to accomplish two things: first, to save his country from dismemberment and ruin; and second, to free his country from the great crime of slavery. To do one or the other, or both, he must have the earnest sympathy and the powerful co-operation of his loyal fellow-countrymen. Without this primary and essential condition to success, his efforts must have been vain and utterly fruitless. Had he put the abolition of slavery before the salvation of the Union, he would have inevitably driven from him a powerful class of the American people and rendered resistance to rebellion impossible. Viewed from the genuine abolition ground, Mr Lincoln seemed tardy, cold, dull, and indifferent; but measuring him by the sentiment of his country, a sentiment he was bound as a statesman to consult, he was swift, zealous, radical, and determined.

Though Mr Lincoln shared the prejudices of his white fellow-countrymen against the negro, it is hardly necessary to say that in his heart of hearts he loathed and hated slavery.* The man who could say, 'Fondly do we hope, fervently do we pray, that this mighty scourge of war shall soon pass away, yet if God wills it to continue till all the wealth piled by two hundred years of bondage shall have been wasted, and each drop of blood drawn by the lash shall have been paid for by one drawn by the sword, the judgements of the Lord are true and righteous altogether,' gives all needed proof of his feelings on the subject of slavery. He was willing, while the South was loyal, that it should have its pound of flesh, because he thought it was so nominated in the bond; but farther than this no earthly power could make him go.

Fellow citizens, whatever else in the world may be partial, unjust, and uncertain, Time, time, is impartial, just, and certain in its action. In the realm of mind, as well as in the realm of matter, it is a great worker, and often works wonders. The honest and comprehensive statesman, clearly discerning the needs of his country, and earnestly endeavouring to do his whole duty, though covered and blistered with reproaches, may safely leave his course to the silent judgement of time. Few great public men have ever been the victims of fiercer denunciation than Abraham Lincoln was during his administration. He was often wounded in the house of his friends. Reproaches came thick and fast upon him from within and from without, and from opposite quarters. He was assailed by abolitionists; he was assailed by slave-holders; he was assailed by the men who were for peace at any price; he was assailed by those who were for a more vigorous prosecution of the war; he was assailed for not making the war an abolition war; and he was most bitterly assailed for making the war an abolition war.

But now behold the change: the judgement of the present hour is, that taking him for all in all, measuring the tremendous magnitude of the work before him, considering the necessary means to ends, and surveying the end from the beginning, infinite wisdom has seldom sent any man into the world better fitted for his mission than Abraham Lincoln. His birth, his training, and his natural endowments, both mental and physical, were strongly in his favour. Born and reared among the lowly, a stranger to wealth and luxury, compelled to grapple single-handed with the flintiest hardships of life, from tender youth to sturdy manhood, he grew strong in the manly and heroic qualities

* 'I am naturally anti-slavery. If slavery is not wrong, nothing is wrong. I cannot remember when I did so think and feel.' Letter of Mr Lincoln to Mr Hodges, of Kentucky, April 4, 1864.

demanded by the great mission to which he was called by the votes of his countrymen. The hard condition of his early life, which would have depressed and broken down weaker men, only gave greater life, vigour, and buoyancy to the heroic spirit of Abraham Lincoln. He was ready for any kind and quality of work. What other young men dreaded in the shape of toil, he took hold of with the utmost cheerfulness.

> A spade, a rake, a hoe,
>   A pick-axe, or a bill;
> A hook to reap, a scythe to mow,
>   A flail, or what you will.

All day long he could split heavy rails in the woods, and half the night long he could study his English Grammar by the uncertain flare and glare of the light made by a pine-knot. He was at home on the land with his axe, with his maul, with his gluts, and his wedges; and he was equally at home on water, with his oars, with his poles, with his planks and with his boat-hooks. And whether in his flat-boat on the Mississippi river, or at the fireside of his frontier cabin, he was a man of work. A son of toil himself, he was linked in brotherly sympathy with the sons of toil in every loyal part of the Republic. This very fact gave him tremendous power with the American people, and materially contributed, not only to selecting him for the Presidency, but in sustaining his administration of the government.

Upon his inauguration as President of the United States, an office, even when assumed under the most favourable conditions, fitted to tax and strain the largest abilities, Abraham Lincoln was met by a tremendous crisis. He was called upon not merely to administer the government, but to decide, in the face of terrible odds, the fate of the Republic.

A formidable rebellion rose in his path before him; the Union was practically dissolved; his country was torn and rent asunder at the centre. Hostile armies were already organised against the Republic, armed with the munitions of war which the Republic had provided for its own defence. The tremendous question for him to decide was whether his country should survive the crisis and flourish, or be dismembered and perish. His predecessor in office had already decided the question in favour of national dismemberment, by denying to it the right of self-defence and self-preservation – a right which belongs to the meanest insect.

Happily for the country, happily for you and for me, the judgement of James Buchanan, the patrician, was not the judgement of Abraham Lincoln, the plebeian. He brought his strong common sense, sharpened in the school of adversity, to bear upon the question. He did not hesitate, he did not doubt, he did not falter; but at once resolved at whatever peril, at whatever cost, the Union of the States should be preserved. A patriot himself, his faith was strong and unwavering in the patriotism of his countrymen. Timid men said before Mr Lincoln's inauguration, that we had seen the last President of the United States. A voice in influential quarters said, 'Let the Union slide.' Some said that a Union maintained by the sword was worthless. Others said a rebellion of 8,000,000 cannot be suppressed; but in the midst of all this tumult and timidity, and against all this, Abraham Lincoln was clear in his duty, and had an oath in heaven. He calmly and bravely heard the voice of doubt and fear all around him; but he had an oath in heaven, and there was not power enough on earth to make this honest boatman, backwoodsman, and broad-handed splitter of rails to evade or violate that sacred oath. He had not been schooled in the ethics of slavery; his plain life had favoured his love of truth. He had not been taught that treason and perjury were the proof of honour and honesty. His moral training was against his saying one thing when he meant another. The trust which Abraham Lincoln had in himself and in the people was surprising and grand, but it was also enlightened and well-founded. He knew the American people better than they knew themselves, and his truth was based upon this knowledge.

Fellow citizens, the fourteenth day of April 1865, of which this is the eleventh anniversary, is now and will ever remain a memorable day in the annals of this Republic. It was on the evening of this day, while a fierce and sanguinary rebellion was in the last stages of its desolating power; while its armies were broken and scattered before the invincible armies of Grant and Sherman; while a Great nation, torn and rent by war, was already beginning to raise to the skies loud anthems of joy at the dawn of peace, it was startled, amazed, and overwhelmed by the crowning crime of slavery – the assassination of Abraham Lincoln. It was a new crime, a pure act of malice. No purpose of the rebellion was to be served by it. It was the simple gratification of a hell-black spirit of revenge. But it has done good after all. It has filled the country with a deeper abhorrence of slavery and a deeper love for the great liberator.

Had Abraham Lincoln died from any of the numerous ills to which flesh is heir; had he reached that good old age of which his vigorous constitution and his temperate habits gave promise; had he been permitted to see the end of his great work; had the solemn curtain of death come down but gradually – we should still have been smitten with a heavy grief, and treasured his name lovingly. But dying as he did die, by the red hand of violence, killed, assassinated, taken off without warning, not because of personal hate – for no man who knew Abraham Lincoln could hate him – but because of his fidelity to union and liberty, he is doubly dear to us, and his memory will be precious for ever.

Fellow citizens, I end as I began, with congratulations. We have done a good work for our race today. In doing honour to the memory of our friend and liberator, we have been doing highest honours to ourselves and those who come after us; we have been fastening ourselves to a name and fame imperishable and immortal; we have also been defending ourselves from a blighting scandal. When now it shall be said that the coloured man is soulless, that he has no appreciation of benefits or benefactors; when the foul reproach of ingratitude is hurled at us, and it is attempted to scourge us beyond the range of human brotherhood, we may calmly point to the monument we have this day erected to the memory of Abraham Lincoln.

The progress of a nation is sometimes indicated by small things. When Henry Wilson, an honoured Senator and Vice-President of the United States, died in the capital of the nation, it was a significant and telling indication of national advance, that three coloured citizens, Mr Robert Purvis, Mr James Wormley, and myself, were selected with the Senate committee, to accompany his honoured remains from Washington to the grand old commonwealth he loved so well, and whom in turn she had so greatly loved and honoured. It was meet and right that we should be represented in the long procession that met those remains in every State between here and Massachusetts, for Henry Wilson was among the foremost friends of the coloured race in this country, and this was the first time in its history that a coloured man was made a pallbearer at the funeral, as I was in this instance, of a Vice-President of the United States.

An appointment to any important and lucrative office under the United States Government, usually brings its recipient a large measure of praise and congratulation on the one hand, and much abuse and disparagement on the other; and he may think himself singularly fortunate if the censure does not exceed the praise. I need not dwell upon the causes of this extravagance, but I may say there is no office of any value in the country which is not desired and sought by many persons equally meritorious and equally deserving. But as only one person can be appointed to any one office, only one can be pleased, while many are offended, unhappily, resentment follows disappointment, and this resentment often finds expression as disparagement and abuse of the successful man. As in most else I have said, I borrow this reflection from my own experience.

My appointment as United States Marshal of the District of Columbia, was in keeping with the rest of my life, as a freeman. It was an innovation upon long established usage, and opposed to the general current of sentiment in the community. It came upon the people of the District as a gross surprise, and almost a punishment; and provoked something like a scream – I will not say a yell – of popular displeasure. As soon as I was named by President Hayes for the place, efforts were made by members of the bar to defeat my confirmation before the Senate. All sorts of reasons against my appointment, but the true one, were given, and that was withheld more from a sense of shame, than from a sense of justice. The apprehension doubtless was, that if appointed Marshal I should surround myself with coloured deputies, coloured bailiffs, coloured messengers, and pack the jury box with coloured jurors; in a word, Africanise the courts. But the most dreadful thing threatened, was a coloured man at the Executive Mansion in white kid gloves, swallow-tailed coat, patent leather boots, and alabaster cravat, performing the ceremony – a very empty one – of introducing the aristocratic citizens of the republic to the President of the United States. This was something entirely too much to be borne; and men asked themselves in view of it, to what is the world coming, and where will these things stop? Dreadful! Dreadful!

It is creditable to the manliness of the American Senate, that it was moved by none of these things, and that it lost no time in the matter of my confirmation. I learn, and believe my information correct, that foremost among those who supported my confirmation against the objections made to it, was the Hon. Roscoe Conkling of New York. His speech in executive session is said by the senators who heard it, to have been one of the most masterly and eloquent ever delivered on the floor of the Senate; and this too I readily believe, for Mr Conkling possesses the ardour and fire of Henry Clay, the subtlety of Calhoun, and the massive grandeur of Daniel Webster.

The effort to prevent my confirmation having failed, nothing could be done but to wait for some overt act to justify my removal; and for this my *un*friends had not long to wait. In the course of one or two months I was invited by a number of citizens of Baltimore to deliver a lecture in that city, in Douglass Hall – a building named in honour of myself, and devoted to educational purposes. With this invitation I complied, giving the same lecture which I had two years before delivered in the city of Washington, and which was at the time published in full in the newspapers, and very highly commended by them. The subject of the lecture was, 'Our National Capital', and in it I said many complimentary things of the city, which were as true as they were complimentary. I spoke of what it had been in the past, what it was at that time, and what I thought it destined to become in the future; giving it all credit for its good points, and calling attention to some of its ridiculous features. For this I got myself pretty roughly handled. The newspapers worked themselves up to a frenzy of passion, and committees were appointed to procure names to a petition to President Hayes demanding my removal. The tide of popular feeling was so violent, that I deemed it necessary to depart from my usual custom when assailed, so far as to write the following explanatory letter, from which the reader will be able to measure the extent and quality of my offence –

To the Editor of the *Washington Evening Star* – SIR – You were mistaken in representing me as being off on a lecturing tour, and, by implication, neglecting my duties as United States Marshal of the District of Columbia. My absence from Washington during two days was due to an invitation by the managers to be present on the occasion of the inauguration of the International Exhibition in Philadelphia.

In complying with this invitation, I found myself in company with other members of the Government who went thither in obedience to the call of patriotism and civilisation. No one interest of the Marshal's office suffered by my temporary absence, as I had seen to it that those upon whom the duties of the office devolved were honest, capable, industrious, painstaking, and faithful. Mr Deputy Marshal is a man every way qualified for his position, and the citizens of Washington may rest assured that no unfaithful man will be retained in any position under me. Of course I can have nothing to say as to my own fitness for the position I hold. You have a right to say what you please on that point; yet I think it would be only fair and generous to wait for some dereliction of duty on my part before I shall be adjudged as incompetent to fill the place.

You will allow me to say, also, that the attacks upon me on account of the remarks alleged to have been made by me in

Baltimore, strike me as both malicious and silly. Washington is a great city, not a village, nor a hamlet, but the capital of a great nation, and the manners and habits of its various places are proper subjects for presentation and criticism, and I very much mistake if this great city can be thrown into a tempest of passion by any humorous reflections I may take the liberty to utter. The city is too great to be small, and I think it will laugh at the ridiculous attempt to rouse it to a point of furious hostility to me for anything said in my Baltimore lecture.

Had the reporters of that lecture been as careful to note what I said in praise of Washington as what I said, if you please, in disparagement of it, it would have been impossible to awaken any feeling against me in this community for what I said. It is the easiest thing in the world, as all editors know, to pervert the meaning and give a one-sided impression of a whole speech, by simply giving isolated passages from the speech itself, without any qualifying connections. It would hardly be imagined from anything that has appeared here that I had said one word in that lecture in honour of Washington, and yet the lecture itself, as a whole, was decidedly in the interest of the national capital. I am not such a fool as to decry a city in which I have invested my money and made my permanent residence.

After speaking of the power of the sentiment of patriotism I held this language: 'In the spirit of this noble sentiment I would have the American people view the national capital. It is our national centre. It belongs to us; and whether it is mean or majestic, whether arrayed in glory or covered with shame, we cannot but share its character and its destiny. In the remotest section of the Republic, in the most distant parts of the globe, amid the splendours of Europe or the wilds of Africa, we are still held and firmly bound to this common centre. Under the shadow of Bunker's Hill monument, in the peerless eloquence of his diction, I once heard the great Daniel Webster give welcome to all American citizens, assuring them that wherever else they might be strangers, they were all at home there. The same boundless welcome is given to any American citizens by Washington. Elsewhere we may belong to individual States, but here we belong to the whole United States. Elsewhere we may belong to a section, but here we belong to a whole country, and the whole country belongs to us. It is national territory, and the one place where no American is an intruder or a carpet-bagger. The newcomer is not less at home than the old resident. Under its lofty domes and stately pillars, as under the broad blue sky, all races and colours of men stand upon a footing of common equality.

The wealth and magnificence which elsewhere might oppress the humble citizen has an opposite effect here. They are felt to be a part of himself and serve to ennoble him in his own eyes. He is an owner of the marble grandeur which he beholds about him – as much so as any of the forty millions of this great nation. Once in his life every American who can, should visit Washington; not as the Mahommedan goes to Mecca; not as the Catholic to Rome; not as the Hebrew to Jerusalem, nor as the Chinaman to the Flowery kingdom, but in the spirit of enlightened patriotism, knowing the value of free institutions and how to perpetuate and maintain them.

Washington should be contemplated not merely as an assemblage of fine buildings; not merely as the chosen resort of the wealth and fashion of the country; not merely as the honoured place where the statesmen of the nation assemble to shape the policy and frame the laws; not merely as the point at which we are most visibly touched by the outside world, and where the diplomatic skill and talent of the old continent meet and match themselves against those of the new, but as the national flag itself – a glorious symbol of civil and religious liberty, leading the world in the race of social science, civilisation and renown.'

My lecture in Baltimore required more than an hour and a half for its delivery, and every intelligent reader will see the difficulty of doing justice to such a speech when it is abbreviated and compressed into a half or three-quarters of a column. Such abbreviation or condensation has been resorted to in this instance. A few stray sentences, culled out from their connections, would be deprived of much of their harshness if presented in the form and connection in which they were uttered; but I am taking up too much space, and will close with the last paragraph of the lecture as delivered in Baltimore. 'No city in the broad world has a higher or more beneficent mission. Among all the great capitals of the world it is pre-eminently the capital of free institutions. Its fall would be a blow to freedom and progress throughout the world. Let it stand then where it does now stand – where the father of his country planted it, and where it has stood for more than half a century; no longer sandwiched between two slave States; no longer a contradiction to human progress; no longer the hot-bed of slavery and the slave trade; no longer the home of the duellist, the gambler, the assassin; no longer the frantic partisan of one section of the country against the other; no longer anchored to a dark and semi-barbarous past, but a redeemed city, beautiful to the eye and attractive to the heart, a bond of perpetual union, an angel of peace on earth and good will to men, a common ground upon which Americans of all races and colours, all sections North and South, may meet and shake hands, not over a chasm of blood, but over a free, united, and progressive republic.'

I have already alluded to the fact that much of the opposition to my appointment to the office of United States Marshal of the District of Columbia was due to the possibility of my being called to attend President Hayes at the Executive Mansion upon state occasions, and having the honour to introduce the guests on such occasions. I now wish to refer to reproaches liberally showered upon me for holding the office of Marshal while denied this distinguished honour, and to show that the complaint against me at this point is not a well-founded complaint.

1st. Because the office of United States Marshal is distinct, and separate, and complete in itself, and must be accepted or refused upon its own merits. If, when offered to any person, its duties are such as he can properly fulfil, he may very properly accept it; or, if otherwise, he may as properly refuse it.

2nd. Because the duties of the office are clearly and strictly defined in the law by which it was created; and because nowhere among these duties is there any mention or intimation that the Marshal may or shall attend upon the President of the United States at the Executive Mansion on state occasions.

3rd. Because the choice as to who shall have the honour and privilege of such attendance upon the President, belongs exclusively and reasonably to the President himself, and that therefore no one, however distinguished, or in whatever office, has any just cause to complain of the exercise by the President of this right of choice, or because he is not himself chosen.

In view of these propositions, which I hold to be indisputable, I should have presented to the country a most foolish and ridiculous figure had I, as absurdly counselled by some of my coloured friends, resigned the office of Marshal of the District of Columbia, because President Rutherford B. Hayes, for reasons that must have been satisfactory to his judgement, preferred some person other than myself to attend upon him at the Executive Mansion and perform the ceremony of introduction on state occasions. But it was said that this statement did not cover the whole ground; that it·was customary for the United States Marshal of the District of Columbia to perform this social office; and that the usage had come to have almost the force of law. I met this at the time, and I meet it now, by denying the binding force of this custom. No former President has any right or power to make his example the rule for his successor. The custom of inviting the Marshal to do this duty was made by a President, and could be as properly unmade by a President. Besides, the usage is altogether a modern one, and had its origin in peculiar circumstances, and was justified by those circumstances. It was introduced in time of war by President Lincoln, when he made his old law partner and intimate acquaintance Marshal of the District, and was continued by General Grant when he appointed a relative of his, General Sharp, to the same office. But again it was said that President Hayes only departed from this custom because the Marshal in my case was a coloured man. The answer I made to this, and now make to it, is that it is a gratuitous assumption, and entirely begs the question. It may or may not be true that my complexion was the cause of this departure, but no man has any right to assume that position in advance of a plain declaration to that effect by President Hayes himself. Never have I heard from him any such declaration or intimation. In so far as my intercourse with him is concerned, I can say that I at no time discovered in him a feeling of aversion to me on account of my complexion, or on any other account, and, unless I am greatly deceived, I was ever a welcome visitor at the Executive Mansion on state occasions and all others, while Rutherford B. Hayes was President of the United States. I have further to say that I have many times during his administration had the honour to introduce distinguished strangers to him, both of native and foreign birth, and never had reason to feel myself slighted by himself or his amiable wife; and I think he would be a very unreasonable man who could desire for himself, or for any other, a larger measure of respect and consideration than this at the hands of a man and woman occupying the exalted positions of Mr and Mrs Hayes.

I should not do entire justice to the Honourable ex-President if I did not bear additional testimony to his noble and generous spirit. When all Washington was in an uproar, and a wild clamour rent the air for my removal from the office of Marshal on account of the lecture delivered by me in Baltimore, when petitions were flowing in upon him demanding my degradation, he nobly rebuked the mad spirit of persecution by openly declaring his purpose to retain me in my place.

One other word. During the tumult raised against me in consequence of this lecture on the 'National Capital', Mr Columbus
Alexander, one of the old and wealthy citizens of Washington, who
was on my bond for twenty thousand dollars, was repeatedly besought
to withdraw his name, and thus leave me disqualified; but like the
President, both he and my other bondsman, Mr George Hill, junior,
were steadfast and immovable. I was not surprised that Mr Hill stood
bravely by me, for he was a Republican; but I was surprised and
gratified that Mr Alexander, a Democrat, and, I believe, once a slave-
holder, had not only the courage, but the magnanimity to give me fair
play in this fight. What I have said of these gentlemen, can be
extended to very few others in this community, during that period of
excitement, among either the white or coloured citizens, for, with the
exception of Dr Charles B. Purvis, no coloured man in the city uttered
one public word in defence or extenuation of me or of my Baltimore
speech.

This violent hostility kindled against me was singularly evanescent. It
came like a whirlwind, and like a whirlwind departed. I soon saw
nothing of it, either in the courts among the lawyers, or in the streets
among the people; for it was discovered that there was really in my
speech at Baltimore nothing which made me 'worthy of stripes or of
bonds'.

I can say from my experience in the office of United States Marshal
of the District of Columbia, it was in every way agreeable. When it was
an open question whether I should take the office or not, it was
apprehended and predicted if I should accept it in face of the
opposition of the lawyers and judges of the courts, I should be
subjected to numberless suits for damages, and so vexed and worried
that the office would be rendered valueless to me; that it would not
only eat up my salary, but possibly endanger what little I might have
laid up for a rainy day. I have now to report that this apprehension was
in no sense realised. What might have happened had the members of
the District bar been half as malicious and spiteful as they had been
industriously represented as being, or if I had not secured as my
assistant a man so capable, industrious, vigilant, and careful as Mr L. P.
Williams, of course I cannot know. But I am bound to praise the bridge
that carries me safely over it. I think it will ever stand as a witness to my
fitness for the position of Marshal, that I had the wisdom to select for
my assistant a gentlemen so well instructed and competent. I also take
pleasure in bearing testimony to the generosity of Mr Phillips, the
Assistant-Marshal, who preceded Mr Williams in that office, in giving

the new assistant valuable information as to the various duties he would be called upon to perform. I have further to say of my experience in the Marshal's office, that while I have reason to know that the eminent Chief Justice of the District of Columbia and some of his associates were not well pleased with my appointment, I was always treated by them, as well as by the chief clerk of the courts, the Hon. J. R. Meigs, and the subordinates of the latter – with a single exception – with the respect and consideration due to my office. Among the eminent lawyers of the District I believe I had many friends, and there were those of them to whom I could always go with confidence in an emergency for sound advice and direction, and this fact, after all the hostility felt in consequence of my appointment, and revived by my speech at Baltimore, is another proof of the vincibility of all feeling arising out of popular prejudices.

In all my forty years of thought and labour to promote the freedom and welfare of my race, I never found myself more widely and painfully at variance with leading coloured men of the country than when I opposed the effort to set in motion a wholesale exodus of coloured people of the South to the Northern States; and yet I never took a position in which I felt myself better fortified by reason and necessity. It was said of me, that I had deserted to the old master class, and that I was a traitor to my race; that I had run away from slavery myself, and yet I was opposing others in doing the same. When my opponents condescended to argue, they took the ground that the coloured people of the South needed to be brought into contact with the freedom and civilisation of the North: that no emancipated and persecuted people ever had or ever could rise in the presence of the people by whom they had been enslaved, and that the true remedy for the ills which the freedmen were suffering, was to initiate the Israelitish departure from our modern Egypt to a land abounding, if not in 'milk and honey', certainly in pork and hominy.

Influenced, no doubt, by the dazzling prospects held out to them by the advocates of the Exodus movement, thousands of poor, hungry, naked, and destitute coloured people were induced to quit the South amid the frosts and snows of a dreadful winter in search of a better country. I regret to say there was something sinister in this so-called exodus, for it transpired that some of the agents most active in promoting it had an understanding with certain railroad companies, by which they were to receive one dollar per head upon all such passengers. Thousands of these poor people, travelling only so far as they had money to bear their expenses, were dropped on the levees of

St Louis, in the extremest destitution; and their tales of woe were such as to move a heart much less sensitive to human suffering than mine. But while I felt for these poor deluded people, and did what I could to put a stop to their ill-advised and ill-arranged stampede, I also did what I could to assist such of them as were within my reach, who were on their way to this land of promise. Hundreds of these people came to Washington, and at one time there were from two to three hundred lodged here, unable to get further for the want of money. I lost no time in appealing to my friends for the means of assisting them. Conspicuous among these friends was Mrs Elizabeth Thompson of New York city – the lady who, several years ago, made the nation a present of Carpenter's great historical picture of the 'Signing of the Emancipation Proclamation', and who has expended large sums of her money in investigating the causes of yellow-fever, and in endeavours to discover means for preventing its ravages in New Orleans and elsewhere. I found Mrs Thompson consistently alive to the claims of humanity in this, as in other instances, for she sent me, without delay, a draft for two hundred and fifty dollars, and in doing so expressed the wish that I would promptly inform her of any other opportunity of doing good. How little justice was done me by those who accused me of indifference to the welfare of the coloured people of the South on account of my opposition to the so-called exodus will be seen by the following extracts from a paper on that subject laid before the Social Science Congress at Saratoga, when that question was before the country:

Important as manual labour is everywhere, it is nowhere more important and absolutely indispensable to the existence of society than in the more southern of the United States. Machinery may continue to do, as it has done, much of the work of the North, but the work of the South requires bone, sinew, and muscle of the strongest and most enduring kind for its performance. Labour in that section must know no pause. Her soil is pregnant and prolific with life and energy. All the forces of nature within her borders are wonderfully vigorous, persistent, and active. Aided by an almost perpetual summer abundantly supplied with heat and moisture, her soil readily and rapidly covers itself with noxious weeds dense forests, and impenetrable jungles. Only a few years of non-tillage would be needed to give the sunny and fruitful South to the bats and owls of a desolate wilderness. From this condition, shocking for a Southern man to contemplate, it is now seen that nothing less powerful than the naked iron arm of the negro, can save her. For him, as a Southern labourer, there is no competitor or substitute. The thought of filling his place by any other variety of the human family, will be found delusive and utterly impracticable. Neither Chinaman, German, Norwegian, nor Swede, can drive him from the sugar and cotton fields of Louisiana and Mississippi. They would certainly perish in the black bottoms of these states if they could be induced, which they cannot, to try the experiment.

Nature itself, in those States, comes to the rescue of the negro, fights his battles, and enables him to exact conditions from those who would unfairly treat and oppress him. Besides being dependent upon the roughest and flintiest kind of labour, the climate of the South makes such labour uninviting and harshly repulsive to the white man. He dreads it, shrinks from it, and refuses it. He shuns the burning sun of the fields and seeks the shade of the verandas. On the contrary, the negro walks, labours, and sleeps in the sunlight unharmed. The standing apology for slavery was based upon a knowledge of this fact. It was said that the world must have cotton and sugar, and that only the negro could supply this want; and that he could be induced to do it only under the 'beneficent whip' of some bloodthirsty *Legree*. The last part of this argument has been happily disproved by the large crops of these productions since Emancipation; but the first part of it stands firm, unassailed and unassailable.

Even if climate and other natural causes did not protect the negro from all competition of the labour-market of the South, inevitable social causes would probably effect the same result. The slave system of that section has left behind it, as in the nature of the case it must, manners, customs, and conditions to which free white labouring men will be in no haste to submit themselves and their families. They do not emigrate from the free North, where labour is respected, to a lately enslaved South, where labour has been whipped, chained and degraded for centuries. Naturally enough such emigration follows the lines of latitude in which they who compose it were born. Not from South to North, but from East to West 'the Star of Empire takes its way'.

Hence it is seen that the dependence of the planters, land-owners, and old master class of the South upon the negro, however galling and humiliating to Southern pride and power, is nearly complete and perfect. There is only one mode of escape for them, and that mode they will certainly not adopt. It is to take off their own coats, cease to whittle sticks and talk politics at crossroads, and go themselves to work in their broad and sunny fields of cotton and sugar. An invitation to do this is about as harsh and distasteful to all their inclinations as would be an invitation to step down into their graves. With the negro, all this is different. Neither natural, artificial, nor traditional causes stand in the way of the freedman to labour in the South. Neither the heat nor the fever-demon which lurks in her tangled and oozy swamps affright him, and he stands today the admitted author of whatever prosperity, beauty, and civilisation are now possessed by the South, and the admitted arbiter of her destiny.

This, then, is the high vantage ground of the negro; he has labour; the South wants it, and must have it or perish. Since he is free he can now give it or withhold it, use it where he is, or take it elsewhere as he pleases. His labour made him a slave, and his labour can, if he will, make him free, comfortable, and independent. It is more to him than fire, swords, ballot-boxes, or bayonets. It touches the heart of the South through its pocket. This power served him well years ago, when in the bitterest extremity of destitution. But for it, he would have perished when he dropped out of slavery. It saved him then, and it will save him again. Emancipation came to him, surrounded by extremely unfriendly circumstances. It was not the choice or consent of the people among whom he lived, but against their will, and a death struggle on their part to prevent it. His chains were broken in the tempest and whirlwind of civil war. Without food, without shelter, without land, without money, and without friends, he with his children, his sick, his aged and helpless ones, were turned loose and naked to the open sky. The announcement of his freedom was instantly followed by an order from his master to quit his old quarters, and to seek bread thereafter from the hands of those who had given him his freedom. A desperate extremity was thus forced upon him at the outset of his freedom, and the world watched with humane anxiety, to see what would become of him. His peril was imminent. Starvation and death stared him in the face and marked him for their victim.

It will not soon be forgotten that at the close of a five hours' speech by the late Senator Sumner, in which he advocated with unequalled learning and eloquence the enfranchisement of the freedmen, the best argument with which he was met in the Senate, was that legislation at that point would be utterly superfluous; that the negro was rapidly dying out, and must inevitably and speedily disappear and become extinct.

Inhuman and shocking as was this consignment of millions of human beings to extinction, the extremity of the negro, at that date, did not contradict, but favoured the prophecy. The policy of the old master class dictated by passion, pride, and revenge, was then to make the freedom of the negro, a greater calamity to him, if possible, than had been his slavery. But happily, both for the old master class, and for the recently emancipated, there came then, as there will come now, the sober second thought. The old master class then found it had made a great mistake. It had driven away the means of its own support. It had destroyed the hands, and left the mouths. It had starved the negro, and starved itself. Not even to gratify its own anger and resentment could it afford to allow its fields to go uncultivated, and its tables unsupplied with food. Hence the freedman, less from humanity than cupidity, less from choice than necessity, was speedily called back to labour and life.

But now, after fourteen years of service, and fourteen years of separation from the visible presence of slavery, during which he has shown both disposition and ability to supply the labour market of the South, and that he could do so far better as a freedman than he ever did as a slave; that more cotton and sugar could be raised by the same hands, under the inspiration of liberty and hope, than can be raised under the influence of bondage and the whip, he is again, alas! in the deepest trouble; again without a home, out under the open sky, with his wife and little ones. He lines the sunny banks of the Mississipi, fluttering in rags and wretchedness, mournfully imploring hard-hearted steamboat captains to take him on board; while the friends of the emigration movement are diligently soliciting funds all over the North to help him away from his old home to the new Canaan of Kansas.

I am sorry to be obliged to omit the statement which here follows, of the reasons given for the Exodus movement, and my explanation of them, but from want of space I can present such portions of the paper as express most vividly and in fewest words, my position in regard to the question. I go on to say:

Bad as is the condition of the negro today at the South, there was a time when it was flagrantly and incomparably worse. A few years ago he had nothing – he had not even himself. He belonged to somebody else, who could dispose of his person and his labour as he pleased. Now he has himself, his labour, and his right to dispose of one and the other as shall best suit his own happiness. He has more. He has a standing in the supreme law of the land – in the Constitution of the United States – not to be changed or affected by any conjunction of circumstances likely to occur in the immediate or remote future. The Fourteenth Amendment makes him a citizen and the Fifteenth makes him a voter. With power behind him, at work for him, and which cannot be taken from him, the negro of the South may wisely bide his time. The situation of the moment is exceptional and transient. The permanent powers of the Government are all on his side. What though for the moment the hand of violence strike down the negro's rights in the South, those rights will revive, survive, and flourish again. They are not the only people who have been, in a moment of popular passion, maltreated and driven from the polls. The Irish and Dutch have frequently been so treated. Boston, Baltimore, and New York have been the scenes of lawless violence; but those scenes have now disappeared . . . Without abating one jot of our horror and indignation at the outrages committed in some parts of the Southern States against the negro, we cannot but regard the present agitation of an African exodus from the South as ill-timed and in some respects hurtful. We stand today at the beginning of a grand and beneficent reaction. There is a growing recognition of the duty and obligation of the American people to guard, protect, and defend the personal and political rights of all the people of all the States; to uphold the principles upon which rebellion was suppressed, slavery abolished, and the country saved from dismemberment and ruin.

We see and feel today, as we have not seen and felt before, that the time for conciliation and trusting to the honour of the late rebels and slave-holders has passed. The President of the United States, himself, while still liberal, just, and generous toward the South, has yet sounded a halt in that direction and has bravely, firmly, and ably asserted the constitutional authority to maintain the public peace in every State in the Union, and upon every day in the year, and has maintained this ground against all the powers of House and Senate.

We stand at the gateway of a marked and decided change in the statesmanship of our rulers. Every day brings fresh and increasing evidence that we are, and of right ought to be, a nation; that Confederate notions of the nature and powers of our Government ought to have perished in the rebellion which they supported; that they are anachronisms and superstitions and no longer fit to be above ground . . .

At a time like this, so full of hope and courage, it is unfortunate that a cry of despair should be raised in behalf of the coloured people of the South; unfortunate that men are going over the country begging in the name of the poor coloured man of the South, and telling the people that the Government has no power to enforce the Constitution and laws in that section, and that there is no hope for the poor negro but to plant him in the new soil of Kansas or Nebraska.

These men do the coloured people of the South a real damage. They give their enemies an advantage in the argument for their manhood and freedom. They assume their inability to take care of themselves. The country will be told of the hundreds who go to Kansas, but not of the thousands who stay in Mississippi and Louisiana.

It will be told of the destitute who require material aid, but not of the multitude who are bravely sustaining themselves where they are.

In Georgia the negroes are paying taxes upon six millions of dollars; in Louisiana upon forty or fifty millions; and upon unascertained sums elsewhere in the Southern States.

Why should a people who have made such progress in the course of a few years be humiliated and scandalised by exodus agents, begging money to remove them from their homes; especially at a time when every indication favours the position that the wrongs and hardships which they suffer are soon to be redressed?

Besides the objection thus stated, it is manifest that the public and noisy advocacy of a general stampede of the coloured people from the South to the North is necessarily an abandonment of the great and paramount principle of protection to person and property in every State in the Union. It is an evasion of a solemn obligation and duty. The business of this nation is to protect its citizens *where they are*, not to transport them where they will not need protection. The best that can be said of this exodus in this respect is that it is an attempt to climb up some other way; it is an expedient, a half-way measure, and tends to weaken in the public mind a sense of absolute right, power, and duty of the Government, inasmuch as it concedes, by implication at least, that on the soil of the South the law of the land cannot command obedience, the ballot-box cannot be kept pure, peaceable elections cannot be held, the Constitution cannot be enforced, and the lives and liberties of loyal and peaceable citizens cannot be protected. It is a surrender, a premature disheartening surrender, since it would secure freedom and free institutions by migration rather than by protection; by flight rather than by right; by going into a strange land rather than by staying in one's own. It leaves the whole question of equal rights on the soil of the South open and still to be settled, with the moral influence of exodus against us; since it is a confession of the utter impracticability of equal rights and equal protection in any State where those rights may be struck down by violence.

It does not appear that the friends of freedom should spend either time or talent or furtherance of this exodus, as a desirable measure, either for the North or the South. If the people of this country cannot be protected in every State of the Union, the Government of the United States is shorn of its rightful dignity and power, the late rebellion has triumphed, the sovereignty of the nation is an empty name, and the power and authority in individual States greater than the power and authority of the United States ...

The coloured people of the South, just beginning to accumulate a little property, and to lay the foundation of family, should not be in haste to sell that little and be off to the banks of the Mississippi. The habit of roaming from place to place in pursuit of better conditions of existence is never a good one. A man should never leave his home for a new one till he has earnestly endeavoured to make his immediate surroundings accord with his wishes. The time and energy expended in wandering from place to place, if employed in making him a comfortable home where he is, will, in nine cases out of ten, prove the best investment. No people ever did much for themselves or for the world without the sense and inspiration of native land, of a fixed home, of familiar neighbourhood and common associations. The fact of being to the manner born has an elevating power upon the mind and heart of a man. It is a more cheerful thing to be able to say I was born here and know all the people, than to say I am a stranger here and know none of the people.

It cannot be doubted that in so far as this exodus tends to promote restlessness in the coloured people of ·the South, to unsettle their feeling of home, and to sacrifice positive advantages where they are, for fancied ones in Kansas or elsewhere, it is an evil. Some have sold their little homes, their chickens, mules, and pigs at a sacrifice, to follow the exodus. Let it be understood that you are going, and you advertise the fact that your mule has lost half its value; for your staying with him makes half his value. Let the coloured people of Georgia offer their six millions' worth of property for sale, with the purpose to leave Georgia, and they will not realise half its value. Land is not worth much where there are no people to occupy it, and a mule is not worth much where there is no one to drive him.

It may be safely asserted that whether advocated and commended to favour on the ground that it will increase the political power of the Republican party, and thus help to make a solid North against a solid South, or upon the ground that it will increase the power and influence of the coloured people as a political element, and enable them the better to protect their rights, and ensure their moral and social elevation, the exodus will prove a disappointment, a mistake and a failure; because, as to strengthening the Republican party, the emigrants will go only to those States where the Republican party is strong and solid enough already with their votes; and in respect to the other part of the argument, it will fail because it takes coloured voters from a section of the country where they are sufficiently numerous to elect some of their number to places of honour and profit, and places them in a country where their proportion to other classes will be so small as not to be recognised as a political element or entitled to be represented by one of themselves. And further, because go where they will, they must for a time inevitably carry with them poverty, ignorance, and other repulsive incidents, inherited from their former condition as slaves – a circumstance which is about as likely to make votes for Democrats as for Republicans, and to raise up bitter prejudice against them as to raise up friends for them . . .

Plainly enough, the exodus is less harmful as a measure than are the arguments by which it is supported. The one is the result of a feeling of outrage and despair; but the other comes of cool, selfish calculation. One is the result of honest despair, and appeals powerfully to the sympathies of men; the other is an appeal to our selfishness, which shrinks from doing right because the way is difficult.

Not only is the South the best locality for the negro, on the ground of his political powers and possibilities, but it is best for him as a field of labour. He is there, as he is nowhere else, an absolute necessity. He has a monopoly of the labour market. His labour is the only labour which can successfully offer itself for sale in that market. This fact, with a little wisdom and firmness, will enable him to sell his labour there on terms more favourable to himself than he can elsewhere. As there are no competitors or substitutes he can demand living prices with the certainty that the demand will be complied with. Exodus would deprive him of this advantage . . .

The negro, as already intimated, is pre-eminently a Southern man. He is so both in constitution and habits, in body as well as mind. He will not only take with him to the North, Southern modes of labour, but Southern modes of life. The careless and improvident habits of the South cannot be set aside in a generation. If they are adhered to in the North, in the fierce winds and snows of Kansas and Nebraska, the emigration must be large to keep up their numbers . . .

As an assertion of power by a people hitherto held in bitter contempt, as an emphatic and stinging protest against high-handed, greedy, and shameless injustice to the weak and defenceless, as a means of opening the blind eyes of oppressors to their folly and peril, the exodus has done valuable service. Whether it has accomplished all of which it is capable in this direction, for the present, is a question which may well be considered. With a moderate degree of intelligent leadership among the labouring class of the South, properly handling the justice of their cause, and wisely using the exodus example, they can easily exact better terms for their labour than ever before. Exodus is medicine, not food; it is for disease, not health; it is not to be taken from choice, but necessity. In anything like a normal condition of things, the South is the best place for the negro. Nowhere else is there for him a promise of a happier future. Let him stay there if he can, and save both the South and himself to civilisation. While, however, it may be the highest wisdom in the circumstances for the freedmen to stay where they are, no encouragement should be given to any measures of coercion to keep them there. The American people are bound, if they are, or can be bound to anything, to keep the north gate of the South open to black and white and to all the people. 'The time to assert a right,' Webster says, is when it is called in question. If it is attempted by force or fraud to compel the coloured people to stay there, they should by all means go – go quickly, and die if need be in the attempt.

CHAPTER XVI

'Time Makes All Things Even'

Return to the 'old master' – A last interview – Captain Auld's
admission: '. . . had I been in your place, I should have done as
you did' – Speech at Easton – The old gaol there – Invited
to a sail in the revenue cutter *Guthrie* – Hon. J. L. Thomas –
Visit to the old plantation – Home of Colonel Lloyd – Kind
reception and attentions – Familiar scenes – Old memories –
Burial ground – Hospitality – Gracious reception from Mrs
Buchanan – A little girl's floral gift – A promise of 'a good time
coming'– Speech at Harper's Ferry – Storer College – Hon. A. J.
Hunter

The leading incidents to which it is my purpose to call attention and
make prominent in the present chapter, will, I think, address the
imagination of the reader with peculiar and poetic force, and might
well enough be dramatised for the stage They certainly afford another
striking illustration of the trite saying, that 'truth is stranger than
fiction'.

The first of these events occurred four years ago, when, after a
period of more than forty years, I visited and had an interview with
Captain Thomas Auld, at St Michaels, Talbot County, Maryland. It
will be remembered by those who have followed the thread of my
story, that St Michaels was at one time the place of my home, and the
scene of some of my saddest experiences of slave life; and that I left
there, or, rather, was compelled to leave there, because it was believed
that I had written passes for several slaves to enable them to escape
from slavery, and that prominent slave-holders in that neighbourhood
had, for this alleged offence, threatened to shoot me on sight, and to
prevent the execution of this threat, my master had sent me to
Baltimore.

My return, therefore, to this place, in peace, among the same people,
was strange enough of itself, but that I should, when there, be formally
invited by Captain Thomas Auld, then over eighty years old, to come

to the side of his dying bed, evidently with a view to a friendly talk over our past relations, was a fact still more strange, and one which, until its occurrence, I could never have thought possible. To me, Captain Auld had sustained the relation of master – a relation which I had held in extremest abhorrence, and which for forty years, I had denounced in all bitterness of spirit and fierceness of speech. He had struck down my personality, had subjected me to his will, made property of my body and soul, reduced me to a chattel, hired me out to a noted slave-breaker to be worked like a beast and flogged into submission; he had taken my hard earnings, sent me to prison, offered me for sale, broken up my Sunday-school, forbidden me to teach my fellow slaves to read on pain of nine and thirty lashes on my bare back; he had sold my body to his brother Hugh, had pocketed the price of my flesh and blood without any apparent disturbance of his conscience. I, on my part, had travelled through the length and breath of this country and of England, holding up this conduct of his, in common with that of other slave-holders, to the reprobation of all men who would listen to my words. I had made his name and his deeds familiar to the world by my writings in four different languages, yet here we were after four decades once more face to face – he on his bed, aged and tremulous, drawing near the sunset of life, and I, his former slave, United States Marshal of the District of Columbia, holding his hand and in friendly conversation with him, in a sort of final settlement of past differences, preparatory to his stepping into his grave, where all distinctions are at an end, and where the great and small, the slave and his master, are reduced to the same level. Had I been asked in the days of slavery to visit this man, I should have regarded the invitation as one to put fetters on my ankles and handcuffs on my wrists. It would have been an invitation to the auction-block and the slave whip. I had no business with this man under the old *régime* but to keep out of his way. But now that slavery was destroyed, and the slave and the master stood upon equal ground, I was not only willing to meet him, but was very glad to do so. The conditions were favourable for remembrance of all his good deeds, and generous extenuation of all his evil ones. He was to me no longer a slave-holder either in fact or in spirit, and I regarded him as I did myself, a victim of the circumstances of birth, education, law, and custom.

Our courses had been determined for us, not by us. We had both been flung, by powers that did not ask our consent, upon a mighty current of life, which we could neither resist nor control. By this current he was a master, and I a slave; but now our lives were verging towards a point where differences disappear, where even the constancy of hate breaks down, where the clouds of pride, passion, and selfishness vanish before the brightness of infinite light. At such a time, and in such a place, when a man is about closing his eyes on this world and ready to step into the eternal unknown, no word of reproach or bitterness should reach him or fall from his lips; and on this occasion there was to this rule no transgression on either side.

As this visit to Captain Auld had been made the subject of mirth by heartless triflers, and regretted as a weakening of my life-long testimony against slavery, by serious-minded men, and as the report of it, published in the papers immediately after it occurred, was in some respects defective and coloured, it may be proper to state exactly what was said and done at this interview.

It should in the first place be understood that I did not go to St Michaels upon Captain Auld's invitation, but upon that of my coloured friend, Charles Caldwell; but when once there, Captain Auld sent Mr Green, a man in constant attendance upon him during his sickness, to tell me he would be very glad to see me, and wished me to accompany Green to his house, with which request I complied. On reaching the house I was met by Mr Wm H. Bruff, a son-in-law of Captain Auld, and Mrs Louisa Bruff, his daughter, and was conducted by them immediately to the bedroom of Captain Auld. We addressed each other simultaneously, he calling me 'Marshal Douglass', and I, as I had always called him, 'Captain Auld'. Hearing myself called by him 'Marshal Douglass', I instantly broke up the formal nature of the meeting by saying, 'Not *Marshal* but Frederick to you as formerly.' We shook hands cordially, and in the act of doing so, he, having been long stricken with palsy, shed tears as men thus afflicted will do when excited by any deep emotion. The sight of him, the changes which time had wrought in him, his tremulous hands constantly in motion, and all the circumstances of his condition affected me deeply, and for a time choked my voice and made me speechless. We both, however, got the better of our feelings, and conversed freely about the past.

Though broken by age and palsy, the mind of Captain Auld was remarkably clear and strong. After he had become composed I asked him what he thought of my conduct in running away and going to the North. He hesitated a moment as if to properly formulate his reply, and said: 'Frederick, I always knew you were too smart to be a slave, and had I been in your place I should have done as you did.' I said, 'Captain Auld, I am glad to hear you say this. I did not run away from *you*, but from *slavery*; it was not that I loved Caesar less, but Rome more.' I told him I had made a mistake in my narrative, a copy of which

I had sent him, in attributing to him ungrateful and cruel treatment of my grandmother; that I had done so on the supposition that in the division of the property of my old master, Mr Aaron Anthony, my grandmother had fallen to him, and that he had left her in her old age, when she could be no longer of service to him, to pick up her living in solitude with none to help her, or in other words had turned her out to die like an old horse. 'Ah!' he said, 'that was a mistake, I never owned your grandmother; she in the division of the slaves was awarded to my brother-in-law, Andrew Anthony; but,' he added quickly, 'I brought her down here and took care of her as long as she lived.' The fact is, that after writing my narrative describing the condition of my grandmother, Captain Auld's attention being thus called to it, he rescued her from her destitution. I told him that this mistake of mine was corrected as soon as I discovered it, and that I had at no time any wish to do him injustice; that I regarded both of us as victims of a system. 'Oh, I never liked slavery,' he said, 'and I meant to emancipate all of my slaves when they reached the age of twenty-five years.' I told him I had always been curious to know how old I was, that it had been a serious trouble to me not to know when was my birthday. He said he could not tell me that, but he thought I was born in February 1818. This date made me one year younger than I had supposed myself from what was told me by Mistress Lucretia, Captain Auld's former wife, when I left Lloyd's for Baltimore in the spring of 1825; she having then said that I was eight, going on nine. I know that it was in the year 1825 that I went to Baltimore, because it was in that year that Mr James Beacham built a large frigate at the foot of Alliceana Street, for one of the South American Governments. Judging from this, and from certain events which transpired at Colonel Lloyd's, such as a boy, without any knowledge of books, under eight years old, would hardly take cognisance of, I am led to believe that Mrs Lucretia was nearer right as to my age than her husband.

Before I left his bedside, Captain Auld spoke with a cheerful confidence of the great change that awaited him, and felt himself about to depart in peace. Seeing his extreme weakness I did not protract my visit. The whole interview did not last more than twenty minutes, and we parted to meet no more. His death was soon after announced in the papers, and the fact that he had once owned me as a slave was cited as rendering that event noteworthy.

It may not, perhaps, be quite artistic to speak in this connection of another incident of something of the same nature as that which I have just narrated, and yet it quite naturally finds place here; and that is, my visit to the town of Easton, county seat of Talbot County, two years later, to deliver an address in the Court House, for the benefit of some association in that place. This visit was made interesting to me, by the fact that forty-five years before, I had, in company with Henry and John Harris, been dragged to Easton behind horses, with my hands tied, put in gaol, and offered for sale, for the offence of intending to run away from slavery.

It may easily be seen that this visit, after this lapse of time, brought with it feelings and reflections such as only unusual circumstances can awaken. There stood the old gaol, with its whitewashed walls and iron gratings, as when in my youth I heard its heavy locks and bolts clank behind me.

Strange too, Mr Joseph Graham, who was then Sheriff of the County, and who locked me in this gloomy place, was still living, though verging towards eighty, and was one of the gentlemen who now gave me a warm and friendly welcome, and was among my hearers when I delivered my address at the Court House. There too in the same old place stood Solomon Law's Tavern, where once the slave traders were wont to congregate, and where I now took up my abode and was treated with a hospitality and consideration undreamed of as possible by me in the olden time.

When one has advanced far in the journey of life, when he has seen and travelled over much of this great world, and has had many and strange experiences of shadow and sunshine, when long distances of time and space have come between him and his point of departure, it is natural that his thoughts should return to the place of his beginning, and that he should be seized with a strong desire to revisit the scenes of his early recollection, and live over in memory the incidents of his childhood. At least, such for several years had been my thoughts and feelings in respect to Colonel Lloyd's plantation on Wye River, Talbot County, Maryland; for I had never been there since I left it, when eight years old, in 1825.

While slavery continued, of course this very natural desire could not be safely gratified; for my presence among slaves was dangerous to the public peace, and could no more be tolerated than could a wolf among sheep, or fire in a magazine. But now that the results of the war had changed all this, I had for several years determined to return to my old home upon the first opportunity. Speaking of this desire of mine last winter, to the Hon. John L. Thomas, the efficient collector at the port of Baltimore, and a leading Republican of the State of Maryland, he urged me very much to go, and added that he often took a trip to the

Eastern Shore in his revenue cutter *Guthrie* – otherwise known in time of war as the *Ewing* – and would be much pleased to have me accompany him on one of these trips. I expressed some doubt as to how such a visit would be received by the present Colonel Edward Lloyd, now proprietor of the old place, and grandson of Governor Edward Lloyd whom I remembered. Mr Thomas promptly assured me that from his own knowledge I need have no trouble on that score. Mr Lloyd was a liberal minded gentleman, and he had no doubt would take a visit from me very kindly. I was very glad to accept the offer. The opportunity for the trip, however, did not occur till the 12th of June, and on that day, in company with Messrs Thomas, Thompson and Chamberlain, on board the cutter, we started for the contemplated visit. In four hours after leaving Baltimore, we were anchored in the river off the Lloyd estate, and from the deck of our vessel I saw once more the stately chimneys of the grand old mansion which I had last seen from the deck of the *Sally Lloyd* when a boy. I left there as a slave, and returned as a freeman. I left there unknown to the outside world, and returned well known; I left there on a freight boat and returned on a revenue cutter; I left on a vessel belonging to Colonel Edward Lloyd, and returned on one belonging to the United States.

As soon as we had come to anchor, Mr Thomas dispatched a note to Colonel Edward Lloyd, announcing my presence on board his cutter, and inviting him to meet me, informing him it was my desire, if agreeable to him, to revisit my old home. In response to this note, Mr Howard Lloyd, a son of Colonel Lloyd, a young gentleman of very pleasant address, came on board the cutter, and was introduced to the several gentlemen and myself.

He told us that his father was gone to Easton on business, expressed his regret at his absence, hoped he would return before we should leave, and in the meantime received us cordially and invited us ashore, escorted us over the grounds, and gave us as hearty a welcome as we could have wished. I hope I shall be pardoned for speaking of this incident with much complacency. It was one which could happen to but few men, and only once in the life time of any. The span of human life is too short for the repetition of events which occur at the distance of fifty years. That I was deeply moved, and greatly affected by it, can be easily imagined. Here I was, being welcomed and escorted by the great-grandson of Colonel Edward Lloyd – a gentlemen I had known well fifty-six years before, and whose form and features were as vividly depicted on my memory as if I had seen him but yesterday. He was a gentleman of the olden time, elegant in his apparel, dignified in his deportment, a man of few words and of weighty presence; and I can easily conceive that no Governor of the State of Maryland ever commanded a larger measure of respect than did this great-grandfather of the young gentleman now before me. In company with Mr Howard was his little brother Decosa, a bright boy of eight or nine years, disclosing his aristocratic descent in the lineaments of his face, and in all his modest and graceful movements. As I looked at him I could not help the reflections naturally arising from having seen so many generations of the same family on the same estate. I had seen the elder Lloyd, and was now walking around with the youngest member of that name. In respect to the place itself, I was most agreeably surprised to find that time had dealt so gently with it, and that in all its appointments it was so little changed from what it was when I left it, and from what I have elsewhere described it. Very little was missing except the squads of little black children which were once seen in all directions, and the great number of slaves on its fields. Colonel Lloyd's estate comprised twenty-seven thousand acres, and the home-farm seven thousand. In my boyhood sixty men were employed in cultivating the home-farm alone. Now, by the aid of machinery, the work is accomplished by ten men. I found the buildings, which gave it the appearance of a village, nearly all standing, and I was astonished to find that I had carried their appearance and location so accurately in my mind during so many years. There was the long quarter, the quarter on the hill, the dwelling-house of my old master, Aaron Anthony; the overseer's house, once occupied by William Sevier, Austin Gore, James Hopkins and other overseers. In connection with my old master's house was the kitchen where Aunt Katy presided, and where my head had received many a thump from her unfriendly hand. I looked into this kitchen with peculiar interest, and remembered that it was there I last saw my mother. I went round to the window at which Miss Lucretia used to sit with her sewing, and at which I used to sing when hungry, a signal which she well understood, and to which she readily responded with bread. The little closet in which I slept in a bag had been taken into the room; the dirt floor, too, had disappeared under plank. But upon the whole, the house is very much as it was in the olden time. Not far from it was the stable formerly in charge of old Barney. The storehouse at the end of it, of which my master carried the keys, had been removed. The large carriage house, too, which in my boy's days contained two or three fine coaches, several phaetons, gigs, and a large sleigh – for the latter there was seldom any use – was gone. This carriage house was of much interest to me, because Colonel Lloyd sometimes allowed his servants the use of it for festal occasions, and in it there was at such times music and dancing. With these two exceptions, the houses of the estate remained. There was the shoemaker's shop, where Uncle Abe made and mended shoes; and there the blacksmith's shop, where Uncle Tony hammered iron, and the weekly closing of which first taught me to distinguish Sundays from other days. The old barn, too, was there – time-worn, to be sure, but still in good condition – a place of wonderful interest to me in my childhood, for there I often repaired to listen to the chatter and watch the flight of swallows among its lofty beams, and under its ample roof. Time had wrought some changes in the trees and foliage. The Lombardy poplars, in the branches of which the red-winged blackbirds used to congregate and sing, and whose music awakened in my young heart sensations and aspirations deep and undefinable, were gone; but the oaks and elms where young Daniel – the uncle of the present Edward Lloyd – used to divide with me his cakes and biscuits, were there as umbrageous and beautiful as ever. I expressed a wish to Mr Howard to be shown into the family burial ground, and thither we made our way. It is a remarkable spot – the resting place for all the deceased Lloyds for two hundred years, for the family have been in possession of the estate since the settlement of the Maryland colony.

The tombs there reminded one of what may be seen in the grounds of moss-covered churches in England. The very names of those who sleep within the oldest of them are crumbled away and become indecipherable. Everything about it is impressive, and suggestive of the transient character of human life and glory. No one could stand under its weeping willows, amidst its creeping ivy and myrtle, and look through its sombre shadows, without a feeling of unusual solemnity. The first interment I ever witnessed was in this place. It was the great-great-grandmother, brought from Annapolis in a mahogany coffin, and quietly, without ceremony, deposited in this ground.

While here, Mr Howard gathered for me a bouquet of flowers and evergreens from the different graves around us, and which I carefully brought to my home for preservation.

Notable among the tombs were those of Admiral Buchanan, who commanded the *Merrimac* in the action at Hampton Roads with the *Monitor*, March 8, 1862, and that of General Winter of the Confederate army, both sons-in-law of the elder Lloyd. There was also pointed out to me the grave of a Massachusetts man, a Mr Page, a teacher in the family, whom I had often seen and wondered what he could be thinking about as he silently paced up and down the garden walks, always alone, for he associated neither with Captain Anthony, Mr McDermot, nor the overseers. He seemed to be one by himself. I believe he belonged to some place near Greenfield, Massachusetts, and members of his family will perhaps learn for the first time, from these lines, the place of his burial; for I have had intimation that they knew little about him after he once left home.

We then visited the garden, still kept in fine condition, but not as in the days of the elder Lloyd, for then it was tended constantly by Mr McDermot, a scientific gardener, and four experienced hands, and formed, perhaps, the most beautiful feature of the place. From this we were invited to what was called by the slaves the great house – the mansion of the Lloyd's, and were helped to chairs upon its stately veranda, where we could have a full view of its garden, with its broad walks, hedged with box and adorned with fruit trees and flowers of almost every variety. A more tranquil and tranquilising scene I have seldom met in this or any other country.

We were soon invited from this delightful outlook into the large dining-room, with its old-fashioned furniture, its mahogany sideboard, its cut-glass chandeliers, decanters, tumblers and wine glasses, and cordially invited to refresh ourselves with wine of most excellent quality.

To say that our reception was every way gratifying is but a feeble expression of the feeling of each and all of us.

Leaving the great house, my presence became known to the coloured people, some of whom were children of those I had known when a boy. They all seemed delighted to see me, and were pleased when I called over the names of many of the old servants, and pointed out the cabin where Dr Copper, an old slave, used to teach us with a hickory stick in hand, to say the 'Lords Prayer'. After spending a little time with these, we bade goodbye to Mr Howard Lloyd, with many thanks for his kind attentions, and steamed away to St Michaels, a place of which I have already spoken.

The next part of this memorable trip took us to the home of Mrs Buchanan, the widow of Admiral Buchanan, one of the two only living daughters of old Governor Lloyd, and here my reception was as kindly as that received at the great house, where I had often seen her when a slender young lady of eighteen. She is now about seventy-four years old, but marvellously well preserved. She invited me to a seat by her side, introduced me to her grandchildren, conversed with me as freely and with as little embarrassment as if I had been an old acquaintance and occupied an equal station with the most aristocratic of the

Caucasian race. I saw in her much of the quiet dignity as well as the features of her father. I spent an hour or so in conversation with Mrs Buchanan, and when I left, a beautiful little granddaughter of hers, with a pleasant smile on her face, handed me a bouquet of many-coloured flowers. I never accepted such a gift with a sweeter sentiment of gratitude than from the hand of this lovely child. It told me many things, and among them that a new dispensation of justice, kindness, and human brotherhood was dawning not only in.the North, but in the South; that the war, and the slavery that caused the war, were things of the past, and that the rising generation are turning their eyes from the sunset of decayed institutions to the grand possibilities of a glorious future.

The next, and last noteworthy incident in my experience, and one which further and strikingly illustrates the idea with which this chapter sets out, is my visit to Harper's Ferry, on the 30th of May, this year, and my address on John Brown, delivered in that place before Storer College, an Institution established for the education of the children of those whom John Brown endeavoured to liberate. It is only a little more than twenty years ago when the subject of my discourse – as will be seen elsewhere in this volume – made a raid upon Harper's Ferry; when its people, and we may say the whole nation, were filled with astonishment, horror, and indignation at the mention of his name; when the Government of the United States co-operated with the State of Virginia in efforts to arrest and bring to capital punishment all persons in any way connected with John Brown and his enterprise; when United States Marshals visited Rochester and elsewhere in search of me, with a view to my apprehension and execution, for my supposed complicity with Brown; when many prominent citizens of the North were compelled to leave the country to avoid arrest, and men were mobbed, even in Boston, for daring to speak a word in vindication or extenuation of what was considered Brown's stupendous crime; and yet here I was, after two decades, upon the very soil he had stained with blood, among the very people he had startled and outraged, and who, a few years ago, would have hanged me upon the first tree, in open daylight, allowed to deliver an address, not merely defending John Brown, but extolling him as a hero and martyr to the cause of liberty, and doing it with scarcely a murmur of disapprobation. I confess that as I looked out upon the scene before me and the towering heights around me, and remembered the bloody drama there enacted; saw the log house in the distance where John Brown collected his men, saw the little engine house where the brave old Puritan fortified himself against a dozen companies of Virginia Militia, and the place where he was finally captured by United States troops under Colonel Robert E. Lee, I was a little shocked at my own boldness in attempting to deliver an address in such presence, and of the character advertised in advance of my coming. But there was no cause of apprehension. The people of Harper's Ferry have made wondrous progress in their ideas of freedom of thought and speech. The abolition of slavery has not merely emancipated the negro, but liberated the whites; taken the lock from their tongues, and the fetters from their press. On the platform from which I spoke, sat the Hon. Andrew J. Hunter, the prosecuting attorney for the State of Virginia, who conducted the cause of the State against John Brown, that consigned him to the gallows. This man, now well-stricken in years, greeted me cordially, and in conversation with me after the address, bore testimony to the manliness and courage of John Brown, and though he still disapproved of the raid made by him upon Harper's Ferry, he commended me for my address, and gave me a pressing invitation to visit Charlestown, where he lives, and offered to give me some facts which might prove interesting to me, as to the sayings and conduct of Captain Brown while in prison and on trial, up to the time of his execution. I regret that my engagements and duties were such that I could not then and there accept his invitation, for I could not doubt the sincerity with which it was given, or fail to see the value of compliance. Mr Hunter not only congratulated me upon my speech, but at parting, gave me a friendly grip, and added that if Robert E. Lee were alive and present, he knew he would give me his hand also.

This man's presence added much to the interest of the occasion by his frequent interruptions, approving and condemning my sentiments as they were uttered. I only regret that he did not undertake a formal reply to my speech, but this, though invited, he declined to do. It would have given me an opportunity of fortifying certain positions in my address which were perhaps insufficiently defended. Upon the whole, taking the visit to Captain Auld, to Easton with its old gaol, to the home of my old master at Colonel Lloyd's, and this visit to Harper's Ferry, with all their associations, they fulfil the expectation created at the beginning of this chapter.

CHAPTER XVI

Incidents and Events

Hon. Gerrit Smith, and Mr E. C. Delevan – Experiences at
hotels and on steamboats and other modes of travel –
Hon. Edward Marshall – Grace Greenwood – Hon. Moses
Norris – Robert J. Ingersoll – Reflections and conclusions –
Compensations

In escaping from the South, the reader will have observed that I did not
escape from its widespread influence in the North. That influence met
me almost everywhere outside of pronounced anti-slavery circles, and
sometimes even within them. It was in the air, and men breathed it and
were permeated by it, often when they were quite unconscience of its
presence.

I might recount many occasions when I have encountered this
feeling, some painful and melancholy, some ridiculous and amusing. It
has been a part of my mission to expose the absurdity of this spirit of
caste and in some measure help to emancipate men from its control.

Invited to accompany the Hon. Gerrit Smith to dine with Mr E. C.
Delevan, at Albany many years ago, I expressed to Mr Smith, my
awkwardness and embarrassment in the society I was likely to meet
there. 'Ah!' said that good man, 'you must go, Douglass, it is your
mission to break down the walls of separation between the two races.' I
went with Mr Smith, and was soon made at ease by Mr Delevan and
the ladies and gentlemen there. They were among the most refined
and brilliant people I had ever met. I felt somewhat surprised that I
could be so much at ease in such company, but I found it then, as I have
since, that the higher the gradation in intelligence and refinement, the
farther removed are all artificial distinctions, and restraints of mere
caste or colour.

In one of my anti-slavery campaigns in New York, five and thirty
years ago, I had an appointment at Victor, a town in Ontario County. I
was compelled to stop at the hotel. It was the custom at that time, to

seat the guests at a long table running the length of the dining-room. When I entered I was shown a little table in a corner. I knew what it meant, but took my dinner all the same. When I went to the desk to pay my bill, I said, 'Now, landlord, be good enough to tell me just why you gave me my dinner at the little table in the corner by myself?' He was equal to the occasion, and quickly replied: 'Because you see, I wished to give you something better than the others.' The cool reply staggered me, and I gathered up my change, muttering only that I did not want to be treated better than other people, and bade him good-morning.

On an anti-slavery tour through the West, in company with H. Ford Douglas, a young coloured man of fine intellect and much promise, and my old friend John Jones, both now deceased, we stopped at a hotel in Janesville, and were seated by ourselves to take our meals, where all the bar-room loafers of the town could stare at us. Thus seated I took occasion to say, loud enough for the crowd to hear me, that I had just been out to the stable and had made a great discovery. Asked by Mr Jones what my discovery was, I said that I saw there, black horses and white horses eating together from the same trough in peace, from which I inferred that the horses of Janesville were more civilised than its people. The crowd saw the hit, and broke out into a good-natured laugh. We were afterwards entertained at the same table with other guests.

Many years ago, on my way from Cleveland to Buffalo, on one of the Lake steamers, the gong sounded for supper. There was a rough element on board, such as at that time might be found anywhere between Buffalo and Chicago. It was not to be trifled with especially when hungry. At the first sound of the gong there was a furious rush for the table. From prudence, more than from lack of appetite, I waited for the second table, as did several others. At this second table I took a seat far apart from the few gentlemen scattered along its side, but directly opposite a well-dressed, finely-featured man, of the fairest complexion, high forehead, golden hair and light beard. His whole appearance told me he was somebody. I had been seated but a minute or two, when the steward came to me, and roughly ordered me away. I paid no attention to him, but proceeded to take my supper, determined not to leave, unless compelled to do so by superior force, and being young and strong I was not entirely unwilling to risk the consequences of such a contest. A few moments passed, when on each side of my chair, there appeared a stalwart of my own race. I glanced at the gentleman opposite. His brow was knit, his colour changed from white to scarlet, and his eyes were full of fire. I saw the lightning flash, but I could not tell where it would strike. Before my sable brethren could execute their captain's orders, and just as they were about to lay violent hands upon me, a voice from that man of golden hair and fiery eyes resounded like a clap of summer thunder. 'Let the gentleman alone! I am not ashamed to take my tea with Mr Douglass.' His was a voice to be obeyed, and my right to my seat and my supper was no more disputed.

I bowed my acknowledgements to the gentleman, and thanked him for his chivalrous interference; and as modestly as I could, asked him his name. 'I am Edward Marshall, of Kentucky, now of California,' he said. 'Sir, I am very glad to know you, I have just been reading your speech in Congress,' I said. Supper over, we passed several hours in conversation with each other, during which he told me of his political career in California, of his election to Congress, and that he was a Democrat, but had no prejudice against colour. He was then just coming from Kentucky, where he had been in part to see his black mammy, for, said he, 'I was nursed at the breasts of a coloured mother.'

I asked him if he knew my old friend John A. Collins in California. 'Oh, yes,' he replied, 'he is a smart fellow; he ran against me for Congress. I charged him with being an Abolitionist, but he denied it, so I sent off and got the evidence of his having been general agent of the Massachusetts Anti-Slavery Society, and that settled him.'

During the passage, Mr Marshall invited me into the bar-room to take a drink. I excused myself from drinking, but went down with him. There were a number of thirsty-looking individuals standing around, to whom Mr Marshall said, 'Come, boys, take a drink.' When the drinking was over, he threw down upon the counter a twenty-dollar gold piece, at which the bar-keeper made large eyes, and said he could not change it. 'Well, keep it,' said the gallant Marshall, 'it will all be gone before morning.' After this, we naturally fell apart, and he was monopolised by other company; but I shall never fail to bear willing testimony to the generous and manly qualities of this brother of the gifted and eloquent Thomas Marshall of Kentucky.

In 1842 I was sent by the Massachusetts Anti-Slavery Society to hold a Sunday meeting in Pittsfield, N.H., and was given the name of Mr Hilles, a subscriber to the *Liberator*. It was supposed that any man who had the courage to take and read the *Liberator*, edited by Wm Lloyd Garrison, or the *Herald of Freedom*, edited by Nathaniel P. Rodgers, would gladly receive and give food and shelter to any coloured brother labouring in the cause of the slave. As a general rule this was very true.

There were no railroads in New Hampshire in those days, so I reached Pittsfield by stage, glad to be permitted to ride upon the top, for no coloured person could be allowed inside. This was many years before the days of Civil Rights Bills, black Congressmen, coloured United States Marshals, and suchlike.

Arriving at Pittsfield, I was asked by the driver where I would stop. I gave him the name of my subscriber to the *Liberator*. 'That is two miles beyond,' he said. So after landing his other passengers, he took me on to the house of Mr Hilles.

I confess I did not seem a very desirable visitor. The day had been warm and the road dusty. I was covered with dust, and then I was not of the colour fashionable in that neighbourhood, for coloured people were scarce in that part of the old Granite State. I saw in an instant, that though the weather was warm, I was to have a cool reception; but cool or warm, there was no alternative left me but to stay and take what I could get.

Mr Hilles scarcely spoke to me, and from the moment he saw me jump down from the top of the stage, carpet-bag in hand, his face wore a troubled look. His good wife took the matter more philosophically, and evidently thought my presence there for a day or two could do the family no especial harm; but her manner was restrained, silent, and formal, wholly unlike that of anti-slavery ladies I had met in Massachusetts and Rhode Island.

When tea time came, I found that Mr Hilles had lost his appetite, and could not come to the table. I suspected his trouble was colourphobia, and though I regretted his malady, I knew his case was not necessarily dangerous; and I was not without some confidence in my skill and ability in healing diseases of that type. I was, however, so affected by his condition that I could not eat much of the pie and cake before me, and felt so little in harmony with things about me that I was, for me, remarkably reticent during the evening, both before and after the family worship, for Mr Hilles was a pious man.

Sunday morning came, and in due season the hour for meeting. I had arranged a good supply of work for the day. I was to speak four times: at ten o'clock a.m., at one p.m., at five, and again at half-past seven in the evening.

When meeting time came, Mr Hilles brought his fine phaeton to the door, assisted his wife in, and, although there were two vacant seats in his carriage, there was no room in it for me. On driving off from his door, he merely said, addressing me, 'You can find your way to the town hall, I suppose?' 'I suppose I can,' I replied, and started along behind his carriage on the dusty road toward the village. I found the hall, and was very glad to see in my small audience the face of good Mrs Hilles. Her husband was not there but had gone to his church. There was no one to introduce me, and I proceeded with my discourse without introduction. I held my audience till twelve o'clock – noon – and then took the usual recess of Sunday meetings in country towns, to allow the people to take their lunch. No one invited me to lunch, so I remained in the town hall till the audience assembled again, when I spoke till nearly three o'clock, when the people again dispersed and left me as before. By this time I began to be hungry, and seeing a small hotel near, I went into it, and offered to buy a meal; but I was told 'they did not entertain niggers there'. I went back to the old town hall hungry and chilled, for an infant 'New England north-easter' was beginning to chill the air, and a drizzling rain to fall. I saw that my movements were being observed, from the comfortable homes around, with apparently something of the feeling that children might experience in seeing a bear prowling about town. There was a graveyard near the town hall, and attracted thither, I felt some relief in contemplating the resting place of the dead, where there was an end to all distinctions between rich and poor, white and coloured, high and low.

While thus meditating on the vanities of the world and my own loneliness and destitution, and recalling the sublime pathos of the saying of Jesus, 'The foxes have holes, and the birds of the air have nests, but the Son of Man hath not where to lay His head,' I was approached rather hesitatingly by a gentleman, who enquired my name. 'My name is Douglass,' I replied. 'You do not seem to have any place to stay at while in town?' I told him I had not. 'Well,' said he, 'I am no Abolitionist, but if you will go with me I will take care of you.' I thanked him, and turned with him towards his fine residence. On the way I asked him his name. 'Moses Norris,' he said. 'What! the Hon. Moses Norris?' I asked. 'Yes,' he answered. I did not for a moment know what to do, for I had read that this same man had literally dragged the Reverend George Storrs from the pulpit for preaching Abolitionism. I, however, walked along with him and was invited into his house, when I heard the children running and screaming 'Mother, mother, there is a nigger in the house, there's a nigger in the house'; and it was with some difficulty that Mr Norris succeeded in quieting the tumult. I saw that Mrs Norris, too, was much disturbed by my presence, and I thought for a moment of beating a retreat, but the kind assurance of Mr Norris decided me to stay. When quiet was restored, I ventured the experiment of asking Mrs Norris to do me a kindness. I said, 'Mrs Norris, I have taken cold, and am hoarse from speaking, and I have found that nothing relieves me so readily as a little loaf sugar and cold water.' The lady's manner changed, and with her own hands she brought me the water and sugar. I thanked her with genuine earnestness, and from that moment I could see that her prejudices were more than half gone, and that I was more than half welcome at the fireside of this Democratic Senator. I spoke again in the evening, and at the close of the meeting there was quite a contest between Mrs Norris and Mrs Hilles, as to which I should go home with. I considered Mrs Hilles' kindness to me, though her manner had been formal; I knew the cause, and I thought, especially as my carpet-bag was there, I would go with her. So giving Mr and Mrs Norris many thanks, I bade them goodbye, and went home with Mr and Mrs Hilles, where I found the atmosphere wonderously and most agreeably changed. Next day, Mr Hilles took me in the same carriage in which I did not ride on Sunday, to my next appointment, and on the way told me he felt more honoured by having me in it, than he would be if he had the President of the United States. This compliment would have been a little more flattering to my self-esteem, had not John Tyler then occupied the Presidential chair.

In those unhappy days of the Republic, when all presumptions were in favour of slavery, and a coloured man as a slave met less resistance in the use of public conveyances than a coloured man as a freeman, I happened to be in Philadelphia, and was afforded an opportunity to witness this preference. I took a seat in a street car by the side of my friend Mrs Amy Post, of Rochester, New York, who, like myself, had come to Philadelphia to attend an anti-slavery meeting. I had no sooner seated myself when the conductor hastened to remove me from the car. My friend remonstrated, and the amazed conductor said, 'Lady, does he belong to you?' 'He does,' said Mrs Post, and there the matter ended. I was allowed to ride in peace, not because I was a man, and had paid my fare, but because I belonged to somebody. My colour was no longer offensive when it was supposed that I was not a person, but a piece of property.

Another time, in the same city, I took a seat, unobserved, far up in the street car, among the white passengers. All at once I heard the conductor, in an angry tone, order another coloured man, who was modestly standing on the platform of the rear end of the car, to get off, and actually stopped the car to push him off, when I, from within, with all the emphasis I could throw into my voice, in imitation of my chivalrous friend Marshall of Kentucky, sung out, 'Go on! let the gentleman alone; no one here objects to his riding!' Unhappily the fellow saw where the voice came from, and turned his wrathful attention to me, and said, 'You shall get out also!' I told him I would do no such thing, and if he attempted to remove me by force he would do it at his peril. Whether the young man was afraid to tackle me, or did not wish to disturb the passengers, I do not know. At any rate he did not attempt to execute his threat, and I rode on in peace till I reached Chestnut Street, when I got off and went about my business.

On my way down the Hudson river, from Albany to New York, at one time, on the steamer *Alida*, in company with some English ladies who had seen me in their own country, received and treated me as a gentleman, I ventured, like any other passenger, to go, at the call of the dinner bell, into the cabin and take a seat at the table; but I was forcibly taken from it and compelled to leave the cabin. My friends, who wished to enjoy a day's trip on the beautiful Hudson, left the table with me, and went to New York hungry, and not a little indignant and disgusted at such barbarism. There were influential persons on board the *Alida*, on this occasion, a word from whom might have spared me this indignity; but there was no Edward Marshall among them to defend the weak and rebuke the strong.

When Miss Sarah Jane Clark, one of America's brilliant literary ladies, known to the world under the *nom de plume* of Grace Greenwood, was young, and as brave as she was beautiful, I encountered a similar experience to that on the *Alida* on one of the Ohio river steamers; and that lady, being on board, arose from her seat at the table, expressed her disapprobation, and moved majestically away with her sister to the upper deck. Her conduct seemed to amaze the lookers on, but it filled me with grateful admiration.

When on my way to attend the great Free-Soil Convention at Pittsburg, in 1852, which nominated John P. Hale for President, and George W. Julian for Vice-President, the train stopped for dinner at Alliance, Ohio, and I attempted to enter the hotel with the other delegates, but was rudely repulsed, when many of them, learning of it, rose from the table, and denouncing the outrage, refused to finish their dinners.

In anticipation of our return, at the close of the Convention, Mr Sam Beck, the proprietor of the hotel, prepared dinner for three hundred guests, but when the train arrived, not one of the large company went into his place, and his dinner was left to spoil.

A dozen years ago, or more, on one of the frostiest and coldest nights I ever experienced, I delivered a lecture in the town of Elmwood, Illinois, twenty miles distant from Peoria. It was one of those bleak and flinty nights, when prairie winds pierce like needles, and a step on the snow sounds like a file on the steel teeth of a saw. My next appointment after Elmwood was on Monday night, and in order to reach it in time it was necessary to go to Peoria the night previous, so as to take an early morning train, and I could only accomplish this by leaving Elmwood after my lecture at midnight, for there was no Sunday train. So a little before the hour at which my train was expected at Elmwood, I started for the station with my friend Mr Brown, the gentleman who had kindly entertained me during my stay. On the way I said to him, 'I am going to Peoria with something like a real dread of the place. I expect to be compelled to walk the streets of that city all night to keep from freezing.' I told him 'that the last time I was there I could obtain no shelter at any hotel, and that I feared I should meet a similar exclusion tonight', Mr Brown was visibly affected by the statement, and for some time was silent. At last, as if suddenly discovering a way out of a painful situation, he said, 'I know a man in Peoria, should the hotels be closed against you there, who would gladly open his doors to you – a man who will receive you at any hour of the night, and in any weather, and that man is Robert J. Ingersoll.' 'Why,' said I, 'it would not do to disturb a family at such a time as I shall arrive there, on a night so cold as this.' 'No matter about the hour,' he said; 'neither he nor his family would be happy if they thought you were shelterless on such a night. I know Mr Ingersoll, and that he will be glad to welcome you at midnight or at cock-crow.' I became much interested by this description of Mr Ingersoll. Fortunately I had no occasion for disturbing him or his family. I found quarters at the best hotel in the city for the night. In the morning I resolved to know more of this now famous and noted 'infidel'. I gave him an early call, for I was not so abundant in cash as to refuse hospitality in a strange city when on a mission of 'good will to men'. The experiment worked admirably. Mr Ingersoll was at home, and if I have ever met a man with real living human sunshine in his face, and honest, manly kindness in his voice, I met one who possessed these qualities that morning. I received a welcome from Mr Ingersoll and his family which would have been a cordial to the bruised heart of any proscribed and storm-beaten stranger, and one which I can never forget nor fail to appreciate. Perhaps there were Christian ministers and Christian families in Peoria at that time, by whom I might have been received in the same gracious manner. In charity I am bound to say there probably were such ministers and such families, but I am equally bound to say that in my former visits to that place I had failed to find them. Incidents of this character have greatly tended to liberalise my views as to the value of creeds in estimating the character of men. They have brought me to the conclusion that genuine goodness is the same, whether found inside or outside the church, and that to be an 'infidel' no more proves a man to be selfish, mean, and wicked, than to be evangelical proves him to be honest, just, and humane.

It may possibly be inferred from what I have said of the prevalence of prejudice, and the practice of proscription, that I have had a very miserable sort of life, or that I must be remarkably insensible to public aversion. Neither inference is true. I have neither been miserable because of the ill-feeling of those about me, nor indifferent to popular approval; and I think, upon the whole, I have passed a tolerably cheerful and even joyful life. I have never felt myself isolated since I entered the field to plead the cause of the slave, and demand equal rights for all. In every town and city where it has been my lot to speak, there have been raised up for me friends of both colours to cheer and strengthen me in my work. I have always felt, too, that I had on my side all the invisible forces of the moral government of the universe. Happily for me I have had the wit to distinguish between what is merely artificial and transient and what is fundamental and permanent, and resting on the latter, I could cheerfully encounter the former. 'How do you feel,' said a friend to me, 'when you are hooted and jeered in the street on account of your colour?' 'I feel as if an ass had kicked but had hit nobody,' was my answer.

I have been greatly helped to bear up under unfriendly conditions, too, by a constitutional tendency to see the funny sides of things, which has enabled me to laugh at follies that others would soberly resent. Besides, there were compensations as well as drawbacks in my relations to the white race. A passenger on the deck of a Hudson River steamer, covered with a shawl, well-worn and dingy, I was addressed by a remarkably-religiously-missionary-looking man in black coat and white cravat, who took me for one of the noble red men of the far West, with 'From away back?' I was silent and he added, 'Indian, Indian?' 'No, no,' I said; 'I am a negro.' The dear man seemed to have no missionary work with me, and retreated with evident marks of disgust.

On another occasion, travelling by a night train on the New York Central railroad, when the cars were crowded and seats were scarce, and I was occupying a whole seat, the only luxury my colour afforded me in travelling, I had lain down with my head partly covered, thinking myself secure in my possession, when a well-dressed man approached and wished to share the seat with me. Slightly rising, I said, 'Don't sit down here, my friend, I am a nigger.' 'I don't care who the devil you are,' he said, 'I mean to sit with you.' 'Well, if it must be so,' I said, 'I can stand it if you can,' and we at once fell into a very pleasant conversation, and passed the hours on the road very happily together. These two incidents illustrate my career in respect of popular prejudice. If I have had kicks, I have also had kindness. If cast down, I have been exalted; and the latter experience has, after all, far exceeded the former.

During a quarter of a century I resided in the city of Rochester, N.Y. When I removed from there, my friends caused a marble bust of me to be carved, and since honoured it with a place in Sibley Hall, Rochester University. Less in a spirit of vanity than that of gratitude, I copy here the remarks of the Rochester *Democrat and Chronicle* on the occasion, and on my letter of thanks for the honour done me by my friends and fellow-citizens of that beautiful city:

Rochester, June 28, 1879

FEDERICK DOUGLASS

It will be remembered that a bust of Frederick Douglass was recently placed in Sibley Hall of the University of Rochester. The ceremonies were quite informal, too informal, we think, as commemorating a deserved tribute from the people of Rochester to one who will always rank as among her most distinguished citizens. Mr Douglass himself was not notified officially of the event, and therefore could, in no public manner, take notice of it. He was, however, informed privately of it by the gentleman whose address is given below, and responded to it most happily, as will be seen by the following letter which we are permitted to publish. [Then follows the letter which I omit, and add the further comments of the *Chronicle*.] It were alone worth all the efforts of the gentlemen who united in the fitting recognition of the public services and the private worth of Frederick Douglass, to have inspired a letter thus tender in its sentiment, and so suggestive of the various phases of a career than which the republic has witnessed none more strange or more noble. Frederick Douglass can hardly be said to have risen to greatness on account of the opportunities which the republic offers to self-made men, and concerning which we are apt to talk with an abundance of self-gratulation. It sought to fetter his mind equally with his body. For him it built no schoolhouse, and for him it erected no church. So far as he was concerned freedom was a mockery, and law was the instrument of tyranny. In spite of law and gospel, despite of statutes which thralled him and opportunities which jeered at him, he made himself, by trampling on the law and breaking through the thick darkness that encompassed him. There is no sadder commentary upon American slavery than the life of Frederick Douglass. He put it under his feet and stood erect in the majesty of his intellect; but how many intellects as brilliant and as powerful as his it stamped upon and crushed, no mortal can tell until the secrets of its terrible despotism are fully revealed. Thanks to the conquering might of American freemen, such sad beginnings of such illustrious lives as that of Frederick Douglass are no longer possible; and that they are no longer possible, is largely due to him who, when his lips were unlocked, became a deliverer of his people. Not alone did his voice proclaim emancipation. Eloquent as was that voice, his life in its pathos and in its grandeur, was more eloquent still; and where shall be found, in the annals of humanity, a sweeter rendering of poetic justice than that he, who has passed through such vicissitudes of degradation and exaltation, has been permitted to behold the redemption of his race?

Rochester is proud to remember that Frederick Douglass was, for many years, one of her citizens. He who pointed out the house where Douglass lived, hardly exaggerated when he called it the residence of the greatest of our citizens; for Douglass must rank as among the greatest men, not only of this city, but of the nation as well – great in gifts, greater in utilising them; great in his inspiration, greater in his efforts for humanity; great in the persuasion of his speech, greater in the purpose that informed it.

Rochester could do nothing more graceful than to perpetuate in marble the features of this citizen in her hall of learning; and it is pleasant for her to know that he so well appreciates the esteem in which he is held here. It was a thoughtful thing for Rochester to do, and the response is as heartfelt as the tribute is appropriate.

CHAPTER XVIII

'Honour to Whom Honour'

Grateful recognition – H. Beecher Stowe – Other friends –
Woman suffrage – Failure of male governments

Gratitude to benefactors is a well-recognised virtue, and to express it
in some form or other, however imperfectly, is a duty to ourselves as
well as to those who have helped us. Never reluctant or tardy, I trust,
in the discharge of this duty, I have seldom been satisfied with the
manner of its performance. When I have made my best effort in this
line, my words have done small justice to my feelings. And now, in
mentioning my obligations to my special friends, and acknowledging
the help I received from them in the days of my need, I can hope to do
no better than give a faint hint of my sense of the value of their
friendship and assistance. I have sometimes been credited with having
been the architect of my own fortune, and have pretty generally
received the title of a 'self-made man'; and while I cannot altogether
disclaim this title, when I look back over the facts of my life, and
consider the helpful influences exerted upon me, by friends more
fortunately born and educated than myself, I am compelled to give
them at least an equal measure of credit, with myself, for the success
which has attended my labours in life. The little energy, industry and
perseverance which have been mine, would hardly have availed me, in
the absence of thoughtful friends, and highly favouring circumstances. Without these, the last forty years of my life might have been
spent on the wharves of New Bedford, rolling oil casks, loading ships
for whaling voyages, sawing wood, putting in coal, picking up a job
here and there, wherever I could find one, holding my own with
difficulty against gauntsided poverty, in the race for life and bread. I
never see one of my old companions of the lower strata, begrimed by
toil, hard handed, and dust covered, receiving for wages scarcely
enough to keep the 'wolf' at a respectful distance from his door and
hearthstone, without a fellow feeling and the thought that I have been

separated from him only by circumstances other than those of my own making. Much to be thankful for, but little room for boasting here. It was mine to take the 'tide at its flood'. It was my good fortune to get out of slavery at the right time, and to be speedily brought into contact with that circle of highly cultivated men and women, banded together for the overthrow of slavery, of which Wm Lloyd Garrison was the acknowledged leader. To these friends, earnest, courageous, inflexible, ready to own me as a man and brother, against all the scorn, contempt, and derision of a slavery-polluted atmosphere, I owe my success in life. The story is simple, and the truth plain. They thought that I possessed qualities that might be made useful to my race, and through them I was brought to the notice of the world, and gained a hold upon the attention of the American people, which I hope remains unbroken to this day.

Observing woman's agency, devotion, and efficiency in pleading the cause of the slave, gratitude for this high service early moved me to give favourable attention to the subject of what is called 'Woman's Rights', and caused me to be denominated a woman's-rights man. I am glad to say I have never been ashamed to be thus designated. Recognising not sex, nor physical strength, but moral intelligence and the ability to discern right from wrong, good from evil, and the power to choose between them, as the true basis of Republican Government, to which all are alike subject, and bound alike to obey, I was not long in reaching the conclusion that there was no foundation in reason or justice for woman's exclusion from the right of choice in the selection of the persons who should frame the laws, and thus shape the destiny of all the people, irrespective of sex.

In a conversation with Mrs Elizabeth Cady Stanton, when she was yet a young lady, and an earnest abolitionist, she was at the pains to set before me, in a very strong light, the wrong and injustice of this exclusion. I could not meet her arguments except with the shallow plea of 'custom', 'natural division of duties', 'indelicacy of woman's taking part in politics', the common talk of 'woman's sphere', and the like, all of which that able woman, who was then no less logical than now, brushed away by those arguments which she has so often and effectively used since, and which no man has yet successfully refuted. If intelligence is the only true and rational basis of government, it follows that that is the best government which draws its life and power from the largest sources of wisdom, energy, and goodness at its command. The force of this reasoning would be easily comprehended and readily assented to in any case involving the employment of physical strength. We should all see the folly and madness of attempting to accomplish with a part what could only be done with the united strength of the whole. Though this folly may be less apparent, it is just as real, when one-half of the moral and intellectual power of the world is excluded from any voice or vote in civil government. In this denial of the right to participate in government, not merely the degradation of woman and the perpetuation of a great injustice happens, but the maiming and repudiation of one-half of the moral and intellectual power for the government of the world. Thus far all human governments have been failures, for none have secured, except in a partial degree, the ends for which governments are instituted.

War, slavery, injustice, and oppression, and the idea that might makes right, have been uppermost in all such governments; and the weak, for whose protection governments are ostensibly created, have had practically no rights which the strong have felt bound to respect. The slayers of thousands have been exalted into heroes, and the worship of mere physical force has been considered glorious. Nations have been, and still are, but armed camps, expending their wealth, and strength, and ingenuity, in forging weapons of destruction against each other; and while it may not be contended that the introduction of the feminine element in government would entirely cure this tendency to exalt might over right, many reasons can be given to show that woman's influence would greatly tend to check and modify this barbarous and destructive tendency. At any rate, seeing that the male governments of the world have failed, it can do no harm to try the experiment of a government by man and woman united. But it is not my purpose to argue the question here, but simply to state, in a brief way, the ground of my espousal of the cause of woman's suffrage. I believed that the exclusion of my race from participation in government was not only a wrong, but a great mistake, because it took from that race motives for high thought and endeavour, and degraded them in the eyes of the world around them. Man derives a sense of his consequence in the world not merely subjectively, but objectively. If from the cradle through life the outside world brands a class as unfit for this or that work, the character of that class will come to resemble and conform to the character described. To find valuable qualities in our fellows, such qualities must be presumed and expected. I would give woman a vote, give her a motive to qualify herself to vote, precisely as I insisted upon giving the coloured man the right to vote, in order that he should have the same motives for making himself a useful citizen as those in force in the case of other citizens. In a word, I have never yet been able to find one consideration, one argument, or suggestion in favour of man's right to participate in civil government which did not equally apply to the right of woman.

CHAPTERTER XIX

A Valediction

Interment of the late James A. Garfield – Brief reference to the solemn event – Account of an interview at the Executive Mansion – His recognition of the rights of coloured citizens

On the day of the interment of the late James A. Garfield, at Lake View Cemetery, Cleveland, Ohio, a day of gloom long to be remembered as the closing scene in one of the most tragic and startling dramas ever witnessed in this, or in any other country, the coloured people of the District of Columbia assembled in the Fifteenth Street Presbyterian Church, and expressed by appropriate addresses and resolutions, their respect for the character and memory of the illustrious deceased. On that occasion I was called upon to preside, and by way of introducing the subsequent proceedings – leaving to others the grateful office of delivering eulogies – made the following brief reference to the solemn and touching event –

Friends and fellow citizens – Today our common mother Earth has closed over the mortal remains of James A. Garfield, at Cleveland, Ohio. The light of no day in our national history has brought to the American people a more intense bereavement, a deeper sorrow, or a more profound sense of humiliation. It seems only as yesterday, that in my quality as United States Marshal of the District of Columbia, it was made my duty and privilege to walk at the head of the column in advance of this our President-elect, from the crowded Senate Chamber of the National Capitol, through the long corridors, and the grand rotunda, beneath the majestic dome, to the platform on the portico, where amid a sea of transcendent pomp and glory, he who is now dead, was hailed with tumultuous applause from uncounted thousands of his fellow citizens, and was inaugurated Chief Magistrate of the United States. The scene was one never to be forgotten by those who beheld it. It was a great day for the nation, glad and proud to do honour to their chosen ruler. It was a glad day for James A. Garfield. It was a glad day for me, that I – one of the proscribed race – was permitted to bear so prominent a part in its august ceremonies. Mr Garfield was then in the midst of his years, in the fullness and vigour of his manhood, covered with honours beyond the reach of princes, entering upon a career more abundant in promise than ever invited president or potentate before.

Alas, what a contrast, as he lay in state under the same broad dome, viewed by sorrowful thousands day after day! What is the life of man? What are all his plans, purposes, and hopes? What are the shouts of the multitude, the pride and pomp of this world? How vain and unsubstantial, in the light of this sad and shocking experience, do they all appear! Who can tell what a day or an hour will bring forth? Such reflections inevitably present themselves, as most natural and fitting on an occasion like this.

Fellow citizens, we are here to take suitable notice of the sad and appalling event of the hour. We are here, not merely as American citizens, but as coloured American citizens. Although our hearts have gone along with those of the nation at large, with every expression, with every token and demonstration of honour to the dead, sympathy with the living, and abhorrence for the horrible deed which has at last done its fatal work; though we have watched with beating hearts, the long and heroic struggle for life, and endured all the agony of suspense and fear; we have felt that something more, something more specific and distinctive, was due from us. Our relation to the American people makes us in some sense a peculiar class, and unless we speak separately, our voice is not heard. We therefore propose to put on record tonight our sense of the worth of President Garfield, and of the calamity involved in his death. Called to preside on this occasion, my part in the speaking shall be brief. I cannot claim to have been on intimate terms with the late President. There are other gentlemen here, who are better qualified to speak of his character than myself. I must say, however, that soon after he came to Washington I had a conversation with him of much interest to the coloured people, since it indicated his just and generous intentions towards them, and goes far to present him in the light of a wise and patriotic statesman, and a friend of our race.

I called at the Executive Mansion, and was received very kindly by

Mr Garfield, who, in the course of the conversation said, that he felt the time had come when a step should be taken in advance, in recognition of the claims of coloured citizens, and expressed his intention of sending some coloured representatives abroad to other than coloured nations. He enquired of me how I thought such representations would be received? I assured him that I thought they would be well received; that in my own experience abroad, I had observed that the higher we go in the gradations of human society, the farther we get from prejudice of race or colour. I was greatly pleased with the assurance of his liberal policy towards us. I remarked to him, that no part of the American people would be treated with respect, if systematically ignored by the Government, and denied all participation in its honours and emoluments. To this he assented, and went so far as to propose my going in a representative capacity to an important post abroad – a compliment which I gratefully acknowledged, but respectfully declined. To say the truth, I wished to remain at home, and retain the office of United States Marshal of the District of Columbia.

It is a great thing for the Honourable John Mercer Langston to represent this Republic at Port au Prince, and for Henry Highland Garnet to represent us in Liberia, but it would be indeed a step in advance, to have some coloured men sent to represent us in white nationalities, and we have reason for profound regret that Mr Garfield could not live to carry out his just and wise intentions towards us. I might say more of this conversation, but I will not detain you except to say, that America has had many great men, but no man among them all, has had better things said of him, than he who has been reverently committed to the dust in Cleveland today.

Mr Douglass then called upon Professor Greener, who read a series of resolutions eloquently expressive of their sense of the great loss that had been sustained, and their sympathy with the family of the late President. Professor Greener then spoke briefly and was followed by Professor John M. Langston and Revd W. W. Hicks. All the speakers expressed their confidence in President Arthur and in his ability to give the country a wise and beneficial administration.

CONCLUSION

As far as this volume can reach that point, I have now brought my readers to the end of my story. What may remain of life to me, through what experiences I may pass, what heights I may attain, into what depths I may fall, what good or ill may come to me, or proceed from me in this breathing world, where all is change, uncertainty, and largely at the mercy of powers over which the individual man has no absolute control, if thought worthy and useful, will probably be told by others when I have passed from the busy stage of life. I am not looking for any great changes in my fortunes or achievements in the future. The most of the space of life is behind me, and the sun of my day is nearing the horizon. Notwithstanding all that is contained in this book, my day has been a pleasant one. My joys have far exceeded my sorrows, and my friends have brought me far more than my enemies have taken from me. I have written out my experience here, not to exhibit my wounds and bruises, to awaken and attract sympathy to myself personally, but as a part of the history of a profoundly interesting period in American life and progress. I have meant it to be a small individual contribution to the sum of knowledge of this special period, to be handed down to after-coming generations which may want to know what things were allowed and what prohibited; what moral, social, and political relations subsisted between the different varieties of the American people down to the last quarter of the nineteenth century; and by what means they were modified and changed. The time is at hand when the last American slave, and the last American slave-holder will disappear behind the curtain which separates the living from the dead, and when neither master nor slave will be left to tell the story of their respective relations, and what has happened in those relations to either. My part has been to tell the story of the slave. The story of the master never wanted for narrators. They have had all the talent and genius that wealth and influence could command, to tell their story. They have had their full day in court. Literature, theology, philosophy, law and learning have come willingly to their service, and if condemned they have not been condemned unheard.

It will be seen in these pages that I have lived several lives in one.

First, the life of slavery; secondly, the life of a fugitive from slavery; thirdly, the life of comparative freedom; fourthly, the life of conflict and battle; and fifthly, the life of victory, if not complete, at least assured. To those who have suffered in slavery, I can say, I too have suffered. To those who have taken some risks and encountered hardships in the flight from bondage, I can say, I too have endured and risked. To those who have battled for liberty, brotherhood, and citizenship, I can say, I too have battled; and to those who have lived to enjoy the fruits of victory, I can say, I too live and rejoice. If I have pushed my example too prominently for the good taste of my Caucasian readers, I beg them to remember that I have written in part for the encouragement of a class whose inspirations need the stimulus of success.

I have aimed to assure them that knowledge can be obtained under difficulties; that poverty may give place to competency; that obscurity is not an absolute bar to distinction, and that a way is open to welfare and happiness for all who will resolutely and wisely pursue that way; that neither slavery, stripes, imprisonment, nor proscription, need extinguish self-respect, crush manly ambition, nor paralyse effort; that no power outside of himself can prevent a man from sustaining an honourable character and a useful relation to his day and generation; that neither institutions nor friends can make a race to stand, unless it has strength in its own legs; that there is no power in the world which can be relied upon to help the weak against the strong – the simple against the wise; that races like individuals must stand or fall by their own merits; that all the prayers of Christendom cannot stop the force of a single bullet, divest arsenic of poison, or suspend any law of nature. In my communication with the coloured people I have endeavoured to deliver them from the power of superstition, bigotry, and priest-craft. In theology I have found them strutting about in the old clothes of the masters, just as the masters strut about in the old clothes of the past. The falling power remains among them long after it has ceased to be the religious fashion of our refined and elegant white churches. I have taught that the 'fault is not in our stars but in ourselves that we are underlings', that 'who would be free, themselves must strike the blow'. I have urged upon them self-reliance, self-respect, industry, perseverance, and economy – to make the best of both worlds – but to make the best of this world first, because it comes first, and that he who does not improve himself by the motives and opportunities afforded by this world, gives the best evidence that he would not improve in any other world. Schooled as I have been among the abolitionists of New

England, I recognise that the universe is governed by laws which are unchangeable and eternal, that what men sow they will reap, and that there is no way to dodge or circumvent the consequences of any act or deed. My views at this point receive but limited endorsement among my people. They for the most part think they have means of procuring special favour and help from the Almighty, and as their 'faith is the substance of things hoped for and the evidence of things not seen', they find much in this expression which is true to faith but utterly false to fact. But I meant here only to say a word in conclusion. Forty years of my life have been given to the cause of my people, and if I had forty years more they should all be sacredly given to that great cause. If I have done something for that cause, I am after all more a debtor to it than it is debtor to me.

West India Emancipation

[Extract from a speech delivered by Frederick Douglass in Elmira, N.Y., August 1, 1880, at a great meeting of coloured people, met to celebrate West India emancipation, and where he was received with marked respect and approval by the president of the day and the immense crowd there assembled. It is placed in this book partly as a grateful tribute to the noble transatlantic men and women through whose unwearied exertions the system of negro slavery was finally abolished in all the British Isles.]

Mr President – I thank you very sincerely for this cordial greeting. I hear in your speech something like a welcome home after a long absence. More years of my life and labours have been spent in this than in any other State of the Union. Anywhere within a hundred miles of the goodly city of Rochester, I feel myself at home and among friends. Within that circumference, there resides a people which have no superior in points of enlightenment, liberality, and civilisation. Allow me to thank you also, for your generous words of sympathy and approval. In respect to this important support of a public man, I have been unusually fortunate. My forty years of work in the cause of the oppressed and enslaved, have been well noted, well appreciated, and well rewarded. All classes and colours of men, at home and abroad, have in this way assisted in holding up my hands. Looking back through these long years of toil and conflict, during which I have had blows to take as well as blows to give, and have sometimes received wounds and bruises, both in body and in mind; my only regret is that I have been enabled to do so little to lift up and strengthen our long enslaved and still oppressed people. My apology for these remarks personal to myself, is in the fact that I am now standing mainly in the presence of a new generation. Most of the men with whom I lived and laboured in the early years of the abolition movement, have passed beyond the borders of this life. Scarcely any of the coloured men who advocated our cause, and who started when I did, are now numbered among the living, and I begin to feel somewhat lonely. But while I have the sympathy and approval of men and women like these before me, I shall give with joy my latest breath in support of your claim to justice, liberty, and equality among men. The day we celebrate is pre-eminently the coloured man's day. The great event by which it is distinguished, and by which it will for ever be distinguished from all other days of the year, has justly claimed thoughtful attention among statesmen and social reformers throughout the world. While to them it is a luminous point in human history, and worthy of thought in the coloured man, it addresses not merely the intelligence, but the feeling. The emancipation of our brethren in the West Indies comes home to us, stirs our hearts, and fills our souls with those grateful sentiments which link mankind in a common brotherhood.

In the history of the American conflict with slavery, the day we celebrate has played an important part. Emancipation in the West Indies was the first bright star in a stormy sky; the first smile after a long providential frown; the first ray of hope; the first tangible fact demonstrating the possibility of a peaceful transition from slavery to freedom of the negro race. Whoever else may forget or slight the claims of this day, it can never be other to us than memorable and glorious. The story of it shall be brief and soon told. Six-and-forty years ago, on the day we now celebrate, there went forth over the blue waters of the Caribbean sea a great message from the British throne, hailed with startling shouts of joy, and thrilling songs of praise. That message liberated, set free, and brought within the pale of civilisation eight hundred thousand people, who, till then, had been esteemed as beasts of burden. How vast, sudden, and startling was this transformation! In one moment, a mere tick of a watch, the twinkle of an eye, the glance of the morning sun, saw a bondage which had resisted the humanity of ages, defied earth and heaven, instantly ended; saw the slave-whip burnt to ashes; saw the slave's chains melted; saw his fetters broken, and the irresponsible power of the slave-master over his victim for ever destroyed.

I have been told by eyewitnesses of the scene, that, in the first moment of it, the emancipated hesitated to accept it for what it was. They did not know whether to receive it as a reality, a dream, or a vision of the fancy.

No wonder they were thus amazed, and doubtful, after their terrible years of darkness and sorrow, which seemed to have no end. Like much other good news, it was thought too good to be true. But the silence and hesitation they observed was only momentary. When fully assured the good tidings which had come across the sea to them were not only good, but true; that they were indeed no longer slaves, but free; that the lash of the slave-driver was no longer in the air, but buried in the earth; that their limbs were no longer chained, but subject to their own will, the manifestations of their joy and gratitude knew no bounds, and sought expression in the loudest and wildest possible forms. They ran about, they danced, they sang, they gazed into the blue sky, bounded into the air, kneeled, prayed, shouted, rolled upon the ground, embraced each other. They laughed and wept for joy. Those who witnessed the scene say they never saw anything like it before.

We are sometimes asked why we American citizens annually celebrate West India emancipation when we might celebrate American emancipation. Why go abroad, say they, when we might as well stay at home?

The answer is easily given. Human liberty excludes all idea of home and abroad. It is universal and spurns localisation.

> When the deed is done for freedom,
>   Through the broad earth's aching breast
> Runs a thrill of joy prophetic,
>   Trembling on from East to West.

It is bounded by no geographical lines, and knows no national limitations. Like the glorious sun of the heavens, its light shines for all. But besides this general consideration, this boundless power and glory of liberty, West India Emancipation has claims upon us as an event in this nineteenth century in which we live; for rich as this century is in moral and material achievements, in progress and civilisation, it can claim nothing for itself greater and grander than this act of West India Emancipation.

Whether we consider the matter or the manner of it, the tree or its fruit, it is noteworthy, memorable, and sublime. Especially is the manner of its accomplishment worthy of consideration. Its best lesson to the world, its most encouraging word to all who toil and trust in the cause of justice and liberty, to all who oppose oppression and slavery, is a word of sublime faith and courage – faith in the truth and courage in the expression.

Great and valuable concessions have in different ages been made to the liberties of mankind. They have, however, come not at the command of reason and persuasion, but by the sharp and terrible edge of the sword. To this rule West India Emancipation is a splendid exception. It came not by the sword, but by the word; not by the brute force of numbers, but by the still small voice of truth; not by barricades, bayonets, and bloody revolution, but by peaceful agitation; not by divine interference, but by the exercise of simple human reason and feeling. I repeat that, in this peculiarity, we have what is most valuable to the human race generally.

It is a revelation of a power inherent in human society. It shows what can be done against wrong in the world, without the aid of armies on the earth or of angels in the sky. It shows that men have in their own hands the peaceful means of putting all their moral and political enemies under their feet, and of making this world a healthy and happy dwelling-place, if they will faithfully and courageously use them.

The world needed just such a revelation of the power of conscience and of human brotherhood, one that overleaped the accident of colour and of race, and set at naught the whisperings of prejudice. The friends of freedom in England saw in the negro a man, a moral and responsible being. Having settled this in their own minds, they, in the name of humanity, denounced the crime of his enslavement. It was the faithful, persistent, and enduring enthusiasm of Thomas Clarkson, William Wilberforce, Granville Sharp, William Knibb, Henry Brougham, Thomas Fowell Buxton, Daniel O'Connell, George Thompson and their noble co-workers that finally thawed the British heart into sympathy for the slave, and moved the strong arm of that Government in mercy to put an end to his bondage.

Let no American, especially no coloured American, withhold a generous recognition of this stupendous achievement. What though it was not American, but British; what though it was not Republican, but Monarchical; what though it was not from the American Congress, but from the British Parliament; what though it was not from the chair of a President, but from the throne of a Queen, it was none the less a triumph of right over wrong, of good over evil, and a victory for the whole human race.

Besides, we may properly celebrate this day because of its special relation to our American Emancipation. In doing this we do not sacrifice the general to the special, the universal to the local. The cause of human liberty is one the whole world over. The downfall of slavery under British power meant the downfall of slavery, ultimately, under American power, and the downfall of negro slavery everywhere. But the effect of this great and philanthropic measure, naturally enough, was greater here than elsewhere. Outside the British Empire no other nation was in a position to feel it so much as we. The stimulus it gave to the American anti-slavery movement was immediate, pronounced, and powerful. British example became a tremendous lever in the hands of American abolitionists. It did much to shame and discourage the spirit of caste and the advocacy of slavery in church and state, It could not well have been otherwise. No man liveth unto himself.

What is true in this respect of individual men, is equally true of nations. Both impart good or ill to their age and generation. But putting aside this consideration, so worthy of thought, we have special reasons for claiming the 1st of August as the birthday of negro emancipation, not only in the West Indies, but in the United States. Spite of our national Independence, a common language, a common literature, a common history, a common civilisation makes us and keeps us still a part of the British nation, if not a part of the British Empire. England can take no step forward in the pathway of a higher civilisation without drawing us in the same direction, She is still the mother country, and the mother, too, of our abolition movement. Though her emancipation came in peace, and ours in war; though hers cost treasure, and ours blood; though hers was the result of a sacred preference, and ours resulted in part from necessity, the motive and mainspring of the respective measures were the same in both.

The abolitionists of this country have been charged with bringing on the war between the North and South, and in one sense this is true. Had there been no anti-slavery agitation at the North, there would have been no anti-slavery anywhere to resist the demands of the slave-power at the South, and where there is no resistance there can be no war. Slavery would then have been nationalised, and the whole country would then have been subjected to its power. Resistance to slavery and the extension of slavery invited and provoked secession and war to perpetuate and extend the slave system. Thus, in the same sense, England is responsible for our civil war. The abolition of slavery in the West Indies gave life and vigour to the abolition movement in America. Clarkson of England gave us Garrison of America; Granville Sharpe of England gave us our Wendell Phillips; and Wilberforce of England gave us our peerless Charles Sumner.

These grand men and their brave co-workers here, took up the moral thunderbolts which had struck down slavery in the West Indies, and hurled them with increased zeal and power against the gigantic system of slavery here, till, goaded to madness, the traffickers in the souls and bodies of men flew to arms, rent asunder the Union at the centre, and filled the land with hostile armies and the ten thousand horrors of war. Out of this tempest, out of this whirlwind and earthquake of war, came the abolition of slavery, came the employment of coloured troops, came coloured citizens, came coloured jurymen, came coloured congressmen, came coloured schools in the South, and came the great amendments of our national constitution.

We celebrate this day, too, for the very good reason that we have no other to celebrate. English emancipation has one advantage over American emancipation. Hers has a definite anniversary. Ours has none. Like our slaves, the freedom of the negro has no birthday. No man can tell the day of the month, or the month of the year, upon which slavery was abolished in the United States. We cannot even tell when it began to be abolished. Like the movement of the sea, no man can tell where one wave begins and another ends. The chains of slavery with us were loosened by degrees. First, we had the struggle in Kansas with border ruffians; next, we had John Brown at Harper's Ferry; next, the firing upon Fort Sumter; a little while after, we had Fremont's order, freeing the slaves of the rebels in Missouri. Then we had General Butler declaring and treating the slaves of rebels as contraband of war; next we had the proposition to arm coloured men and make them soldiers for the Union. In 1862 we had the conditional promise of a Proclamation of Emancipation from President Lincoln; and, finally, on the 1st of January 1863, we had the proclamation itself and still the end was not yet. Slavery was bleeding and dying, but it was not dead, and no man can tell just when its foul spirit departed from our land, if indeed it has yet departed, and hence we do not know what day we may properly celebrate as coupled with this great American event.

When England behaved so badly during our late civil war, I, for one, felt like giving up these 1st of August celebrations. But I remembered that during that war, there were two Englands, as there were two Americas, and that one was true to liberty while the other was true to slavery. It was not the England which gave us West India emancipation that took sides with the slave-holders' rebellion. It was not the England of John Bright and William Edward Foster, that permitted Alabamas to escape from British ports, and prey upon our commerce, or that otherwise favoured slave-holding in the South, but it was the England which had done what it could to prevent West India emancipation.

It was the Tory party in England that fought the abolition party at home, and it was the same party that favoured our slave-holding rebellion.

Under a different name, we had the same, or a similar party, here; a party which despised the negro and consigned him to perpetual slavery; a party which was willing to allow the American Union to be shivered into fragments, rather than that one hair of the head of slavery should be injured.

But, fellow citizens, I should but very imperfectly fulfil the duty of this hour if I confined myself to a merely historical or philosophical discussion of West India emancipation. The story of the 1st of August has been told a thousand times over, and may be told a thousand times more. The cause of freedom and humanity has a history and destiny nearer home.

How stands the case with the recently emancipated millions of coloured people in our own country? What is their condition today? What is their relation to the people who formerly held them as slaves? These are important questions, and they are such as trouble the minds of thoughtful men of all colours, at home and abroad. By law, by the constitution of the United States, slavery has no existence in our country. The legal form has been abolished. By the law of the constitution, the negro is a man and a citizen, and has all the rights and liberties guaranteed to any other variety of the human family, residing in the United States.

He has a country, a flag, and a government, and may legally claim full and complete protection under the laws. It was the ruling wish, intention, and purpose of the loyal people, after rebellion was suppressed, to have an end to the entire cause of that calamity by for ever putting away the system of slavery and all its incidents. In pursuance of this idea, the negro was made free, made a citizen, made eligible to hold office, to be a juryman, a legislator, and a magistrate. To this end, several amendments to the constitution were proposed, recommended, and adopted. They are now a part of the supreme law of the land, binding alike upon every State and Territory of the United States, North and South. Briefly, this is our legal and theoretical condition. This is our condition on paper and parchment. If only from the national statute book we were left to learn the true condition of the coloured race, the result would be altogether creditable to the American people. It would give them a clear title to a place among the most enlightened and liberal nations of the world. We could say of our country, as Curran once said of England, 'The spirit of British law makes liberty commensurate with, and inseparable from, the British soil.' Now I say that this eloquent tribute to England, if only we looked into our constitution, might apply to us. In that instrument we have laid down the law, now and for ever, and there shall be no slavery or involuntary servitude in this Republic, except for crime.

We have gone still further. We have laid the heavy hand of the constitution upon the matchless meanness of caste, as well as the hell-black crime of slavery, We have declared before all the world that there shall be no denial of rights on account of race, colour, or previous condition of servitude. The advantage gained in this respect is immense.

It is a great thing to have the supreme law of the land on the side of justice and liberty. It is the line up to which the nation is destined to march – the law to which the nation's life must ultimately conform. It is a great principle, up to which we may educate the people, and to this extent its value exceeds all speech.

But today, in most of the Southern States, the fourteenth and fifteenth amendments are virtually nullified.

The rights which they were intended to guarantee are denied and held in contempt. The citizenship granted in the fourteenth amendment is practically a mockery, and the right to vote, provided for in the fifteenth amendment, is literally stamped out in face of government. The old master class is today triumphant, and the newly-enfranchised class in a condition but little above that in which they were found before the rebellion.

Do you ask me how, after all that has been done, this state of things has been made possible? I will tell you. Our reconstruction measures were radically defective. They left the former slave completely in the power of the old master, the loyal citizen in the hands of the disloyal rebel against the government. Wise, grand, and comprehensive in scope and design, as were the reconstruction measures, high and honourable as were the intentions of the statesmen by whom they were framed and adopted, time and experience, which try all things, have demonstrated that they did not successfully meet the case.

In the hurry and confusion of the hour, and the eager desire to have the Union restored, there was more care for sublime superstructure of the Republic than for the solid foundation upon which it could alone be upheld. They gave freedmen the machinery of liberty, but denied them the steam to put it in motion. They gave them the uniform of soldiers, but no arms; they called them citizens, and left them subjects; they called them free, and almost left them slaves. They did not deprive the old master class of the power of life and death which was the soul of the relation of master and slave. They could not, of course, sell them, but they retained the power to starve them to death, and wherever this power is held, there is the power of slavery. He who can say to his fellow-man, 'You shall serve me or starve', is a master, and his subject is a slave. This was seen and felt by Thaddeus Stevens, Charles Sumner, and leading stalwart Republicans, and had their counsels prevailed the terrible evils from which we now suffer would have been averted. The negro today would not be on his knees, as he is, abjectly supplicating the old master class to give him leave to toil. Nor would he now be leaving the South, as from a doomed city, and seeking a home in the uncongenial North, but tilling his native soil in comparative independence. Though no longer a slave, he is in a thraldom grievous and intolerable, compelled to work for whatever his employer is pleased to pay him, swindled out of his hard earnings by money orders redeemed in stores, compelled to pay the price of an acre of ground for its use during a single year, to pay four times more than a fair price for a pound of bacon, and be kept upon the narrowest margin between life and starvation. Much complaint has been made that the freedmen have shown so little ability to take care of themselves since their emancipation. Men have marvelled that they have made so little progress. I question the justice of this complaint. It is neither reasonable, nor in any sense just. To me, the wonder is, not that the freedmen have made so little progress, but, rather, that they have made so much; not that they have been standing still, but that they have been able to stand at all.

We have only to reflect for a moment upon the situation in which these people found themselves when liberated: consider their ignorance, their poverty, their destitution, and their absolute dependence upon the very class by whom they had been held in bondage for centuries, a class whose every sentiment was averse to their freedom, and we shall be prepared to marvel that they have under the circumstances done so well.

History does not furnish an example of emancipation under conditions less friendly to the emancipated class, than this American example. Liberty came to the freedmen of the United States, not in mercy but in wrath; not by moral choice, but by military necessity; not by the generous action of the people among whom they were to live, and whose good will was essential to the success of the measure, but by strangers, foreigners, invaders, trespassers, aliens, and enemies. The very manner of their emancipation invited to the heads of the freedmen the bitterest hostility of race and class. They were hated because they had been slaves, hated because they were now free, and hated because of those who had freed them. Nothing was to have been expected other than what has happened; and he is a poor student of the human heart who does not see that the old master class would naturally employ every power and means in their reach to make the great measure of emancipation unsuccessful and utterly odious. It was born in the tempest and whirlwind of war, and has lived in a storm of violence and blood. When the Hebrews were emancipated, they were told to take spoil from the Egyptians. When the serfs of Russia were emancipated, they were given three acres of ground upon which they could live and make a living. But not so when our slaves were emancipated. They were sent away empty-handed, without money, without friends, and without a foot of land to stand upon. Old and young, sick and well, were turned loose to the naked sky, naked to their enemies. The old slave quarter that had before sheltered them, and the fields that had yielded them corn, were now denied them. The old master class in its wrath said, 'Clear out! The Yankees have freed you, now let them feed and shelter you!'

Inhuman as was this treatment, it was the natural result of the bitter resentment felt by the old master class, and in view of it the wonder is, not that the coloured people of the South have done so little in the way of acquiring a comfortable living, but that they live at all.

Taking all the circumstances into consideration, the coloured people have no reason to despair. We still live, and while there is life there is hope. The fact that we have endured wrongs and hardships, which would have destroyed any other race, and have increased in numbers and public consideration, ought to strengthen our faith in ourselves and our future. Let us then, wherever we are, whether at the North or at the South, resolutely struggle on, in the belief that there is a better day coming, and that we by patience, industry, uprightness, and economy may hasten that better day. I will not listen, myself, and I would not have you listen, to the nonsense, that no people can succeed in life among a people by whom they have been despised and oppressed.

The statement is erroneous, and contradicted by the whole history of human progress. A few centuries ago, all Europe was cursed with serfdom, or slavery. Traces of this bondage still remain but are not easily discernible.

The Jews, only a century ago, were despised, hated, and oppressed, but they have defied, met, and vanquished the hard conditions imposed upon them, and are now opulent and powerful, and compel respect in all countries.

Take courage from the example of all religious denominations that have sprung up since Martin Luther. Each in its turn has been oppressed and persecuted.

Methodists, Baptists and Quakers have all been compelled to feel the lash and sting of popular disfavour – yet all in turn have conquered the prejudice and hate of their surroundings.

Greatness does not come to any people on flowery beds of ease. We must fight to win the prize. No people to whom liberty is given can hold it as firmly and wear it as grandly as those who wrench their liberty from the iron hand of the tyrant. The hardships and dangers involved in the struggle give strength and toughness to the character, and enable it to stand firm in storm as well as in sunshine.

One thought more before I leave this subject, and it is a thought I wish you all to lay to heart. Practise it yourselves and teach it to your children. It is this, neither we, nor any other people, will ever be respected till we respect ourselves, and we will never respect ourselves till we have the means to live respectfully. An exceptionally poor and dependent people will be despised by the opulent, and despise themselves.

You cannot make an empty sack stand on end. A race which cannot save its earnings, which spends all it makes and goes in debt when it is ill, can never rise in the scale of civilisation, no matter under what laws it may chance to be. Put us in Kansas or in Africa, and until we learn to save more than we spend, we are sure to sink and perish. It is not in the nature of things that we should be equally rich in this world's goods. Some will be more successful than others, and poverty, in many cases, is the result of misfortune rather than of crime; but no race can afford to have all its members the victims of this misfortune, without being considered a worthless race. Pardon me, therefore, for urging upon you, my people, the importance of saving your earnings; of denying yourselves in the present, that you may have something in the future, of consuming less for yourselves that your children may have a start in life when you are gone.

With money and property comes the means of knowledge and power. A poverty-stricken class will be an ignorant and despised class, and no amount of sentiment can make it otherwise. This part of our destiny is in our own hands. Every dollar you lay up, represents one day's independence, one day of rest and security in the future. If the time shall ever come when we shall possess, in the coloured people of the United States, a class of men noted for enterprise, industry, economy, and success, we shall no longer have any trouble in the matter of civil and political rights. The battle against popular prejudice will have been fought and won, and in common with all other races and colours, we shall have an equal chance in the race of life.

Eulogy by George L. Ruffin

Frederick Douglass was born a slave, he won his liberty; he is of negro extraction, and consequently was despised and outraged; he has by his own energy and force of character commanded the respect of the American Nation: he was ignorant, he has, against law and by stealth and entirely unaided, educated himself; he was poor, he has by honest toil and industry become rich and independent, so to speak; he, a chattel slave of a hated and cruelly-wronged race, in the teeth of American prejudice and in face of nearly every kind of hindrance and drawback, has come to be one of the foremost orators of the age, with a reputation established on both sides of the Atlantic; a writer of power and elegance of expression; a thinker whose views are potent in controlling and shaping public opinion; a high officer in the National Government; a cultivated gentleman whose virtues as a husband, father, and citizen are the highest honour a man can have.

Frederick Douglass stands upon a pedestal; he has reached this lofty height through years of toil and strife, but it has been the strife of moral ideas; strife in the battle for human rights. No bitter memories come from this strife; no feelings of remorse can rise to cast their gloomy shadows over his soul and Douglass has now reached and passed the meridian of life, his co-labourers in the strife have now nearly all passed away. Garrison has gone, Gerrit Smith has gone, Giddings and Sumner have gone – nearly all the early abolitionists are gone to their reward. The culmination of his life-work has been reached; the object dear to his heart – the Emancipation of the Slaves – has been accomplished, through the blessings of God; he stands facing the goal, already reached by his co-labourers, with a halo of peace about him, and nothing but serenity and gratitude must fill his breast. To those, who in the past – in *ante-bellum* days – in any degree shared with Douglass his hopes and feelings on the slavery question, this serenity of mind, this gratitude, can be understood and felt. All Americans, no matter what may have been their views on slavery, now that freedom has come and slavery is ended, must have a restful feeling and be glad that the source of bitterness and trouble is removed. The man who is sorry because of the abolition of slavery, has outlived his day and generation; he should have insisted upon being buried with the 'lost cause' at Appomattox.

We rejoice that Douglass has attained unto this exalted position – this pedestal. It has been honourably reached; it is a just recognition of talent and effort; it is another proof that success attends high and noble aim. With this example, the black boy as well as the white boy can take hope and courage in the race of life.

For more than forty years he has been before the world as a writer and speaker.

The first twenty-three years of his life were twenty-three years of slavery, obscurity, and degradation, yet doubtless, in time to come these years will be regarded by the student of history as the most interesting portion of his life; to those who in the future would know the inside history of American slavery, this part of his life will be specially instructive. Plantation life at Tuckahoe as related by him is not fiction, it is fact; it is not the historian's dissertation on slavery, it is slavery itself, the slave's life, acts, and thoughts, and the life, acts, and thoughts of those around him.

Colonel Lloyd's plantation, where Douglass belonged, was very much like other plantations of the South. Here was the great house and the cabins, the old Aunties and patriarchal Uncles, little picanninies and picanninies not so little, of every shade of complexion, from ebony black to whiteness of the master race; mules, overseers, and broken-down fences. Here was the negro doctor learned in the science of roots and herbs; also the black conjurer with his divination. Here was slave-breeding and slave-selling, whipping, torturing and whipping to death. All this came under the observation of Douglass and is a part of the education he received while under the yoke of bondage. He was there in the midst of this confusion, ignorance and brutality. Little did the overseer on this plantation think that he had in his gang a man of superior order and undaunted spirit, whose mind, far above the minds of the grovelling creatures about him, was at that very time plotting schemes for his liberty; nor did the thought ever enter the mind of Colonel Lloyd, the rich slave-holder, that he had upon his estate one who was destined to assail the system of slavery with more power and effect than any other person.

F. Douglass' fame will rest mainly, no doubt, upon his oratory. His powers in this direction are very great, and in some respects unparalleled by our living speakers. His oratory is his own, and apparently formed after the model of no single person. It is not after the Edmund Burke style, which has been so closely followed by Everett, Sumner and others, and which has resulted in giving us splendid and highly embellished essays rather than natural and not over-wrought speeches. If his oratory must be classified, it should be placed somewhere between the Fox and Henry Clay schools. Like Clay, Douglass' greatest effect is upon his immediate hearers, those who see him and feel his presence, and like Clay, a good part of his oratorical fame will be tradition. The most striking feature of Douglass' oratory is his fire, not the quick and flashy kind, but the steady and intense kind. Years ago on the anti-slavery platform, in some sudden and unbidden outburst of passion and indignation, he has been known to awe-inspire his listeners as though Etna was there.

If oratory consists of the power to move men by spoken words, Douglass is a complete orator. He can make men laugh or cry, at his will. He has power of statement, logic, withering denunciation, pathos, humour, and inimitable wit. Daniel Webster with his immense intellectuality had no humour, not a particle. It does not appear that he could even see the point of a joke. Douglass is brim full of humour, at times of the driest kind. It is of a quiet kind. You can see it coming a long way off in a peculiar twitch of his mouth; it increases and broadens gradually until it becomes irresistible and all-pervading with his audience.

F. Douglass' rank as a writer is high, and justly so. His writings, if anything, are more meritorious than the speaking. For many years, he was the editor of newspapers, doing all of the editorial work. He has contributed largely to magazines. He is a forcible and thoughtful writer. His style is pure and graceful, and he has great felicity of expression. His written productions in finish compare favourably with the written productions of our most cultivated writers. His style comes partly, no doubt, from his long and constant practice, but the true source is his clear mind, which is well stored by a close acquaintance with the best authors. His range of reading has been wide and extensive. He has been a hard student. In every sense of the word he is a self-made man. By dint of hard study he has educated himself, and today it may be said he has a well-trained intellect. He has surmounted the disadvantage of not having an university education, by application and well-directed effort. He seems to have realised the fact that to one who is anxious to become educated and is really in earnest, it is not positively necessary to go to college, and that information may be had outside of college walks; books may be obtained and read elsewhere, they are not chained to desks in college libraries as they were in early times at Oxford; Professors' lectures may be bought already printed; learned doctors may be listened to in the Lyceum; and the printing press has made it easy and cheap to get information on every subject and topic that is discussed and taught in the University. Douglass never made the great mistake (a common one) of considering that his education was finished. He has continued to study, he studies now, and is a growing man, and at this present moment he is a stronger man intellectually than ever before.

Soon after Douglass' escape from Maryland to the Northern States he commenced his public career. It was at New Bedford as a local Methodist preacher and by taking part in small public meetings held by coloured people, where anti-slavery and other matters were discussed. There he laid the foundation of the splendid career, which is now about drawing to a close. In these meetings Douglass gave evidence that he possessed uncommon powers, and it was plainly to be seen that he needed only a field and opportunity to display them. That field and opportunity soon came, as it always does to possessors of genius. He became a member and agent of the American Anti-Slavery society. Then commenced his great crusade against slavery in behalf of his oppressed brethren at the South.

He waged violent and unceasing war against slavery. He went through every town and hamlet in the Free States, raising his voice against the iniquitous system,

Just escaped from the prison-house himself, to tear down the walls of the same and to let the oppressed go free, was the mission which engaged the powers of his soul and body. North, East, and West, all through the land went this escaped slave delivering his warning message against the doomed cities of the South. The ocean did not stop nor hinder him. Across the Atlantic he went through England, Ireland, and Scotland. Wherever people could be found to listen to his story, he pleaded the cause of his enslaved and downtrodden brethren with vehemence and great power. From 1840 to 1861, the time of the commencement of the civil war, which extirpated slavery in his country, Douglass was continuously speaking on the platform, writing for his newspaper and for magazines, or working in conventions for the abolition of slavery.

The life and work of Douglass has been a complete vindication of the coloured people in this respect; it has refuted and overthrown the position taken by some writers that coloured people were deficient in mental qualifications, and were incapable of attaining high intellectual position. We may reasonably expect to hear no more of this now, the argument is exploded. Douglass has settled the fact the right way, and it is something to settle a fact.

That Douglass is a brave man there can be little doubt. He has physical as well as moral courage. His encounter with the overseer of the Eastern Shore plantation attests his pluck. There the odds were against him, everything was against him – there the unwritten rule was, that the negro who dared to strike a white man must be killed, but Douglass fought the overseer and whipped him. His plotting with other slaves to escape, writing and giving them passes, and the unequal and desperate fight maintained by him in the Baltimore ship yard, where law and public sentiment were against him, also show that he has courage. But since the day of his slavery, while living here at the North, many instances have happened which show very plainly that he is a man of courage and determination; if he had hot been, he would have long since succumbed to the brutality and violence of the low and mean-spirited people found in the Free States.

Up to a very recent date it has been deemed quite safe even here in the North to insult and impose on inoffensive coloured people, to elbow a coloured man from the sidewalk, to jeer at him and apply vile epithets to him, in some localities this has been the rule and not the exception, and to put him out of public conveyances and public places by force, was of common occurrence. It made little difference that the coloured man was decent, civil, and respectably clad, and had paid his fare, if the proprietor of the place or his patrons took the notion that the presence of the coloured man was an affront to their dignity, or inconsistent with their notions of self-respect, out he must go. Nor must he stand upon the order of his going, but go at once. It was against this feeling that Douglass had to contend. He met it often; he was a prominent coloured man travelling from place to place. A good part of the time he was in strange cities stopping at strange taverns – that is, when he was allowed to stop. Frequently has he been refused accommodation in hotels. And as to riding in public conveyances, mean-spirited conductors at one time made it a rule to put all coloured people, *nolens volens*, in the smoking car. Many times was Douglass subjected to this indignity.

The writer of this remembers well, because he was present and saw the transaction – the John Brown meeting in Tremont Temple in 1860, when a violent mob composed of the rough element from the slums of the city, led and encouraged by bankers' brokers came into the hall to break up the meeting. Douglass was presiding; the mob was armed; the police were powerless; the mayor could not or would not do anything. On came the mob, surging through the aisles, over benches and upon the platform; the women in the audience became alarmed and fled. The hirelings were prepared to do anything, they had the power and could with impunity. Douglass sat upon the platform with a few chosen spirits, cool and undaunted; the mob had got about and around him; he did not heed their howling, nor was he moved by their threats. It was not until their leader, a rich banker, with his followers, had mounted the platform and wrenched the chair from under him that he was dispossessed, by main force and personal violence (Douglass resisting all the time) they removed him from the platform. Free speech was violated; Boston was disgraced; but the Chairman of that meeting was not intimidated.

GEORGE L. RUFFIN
Boston

The Revd David Thomas
on Frederick Douglass and His Work

A book not only reveals but often contains its author. It is a kind of incarnation of himself, a body in which he lives and works, long after the brain that thought it and the pen that wrote it have mouldered into dust. In it may be seen, not merely his passing opinions and floating feelings, but his thinking intellect and throbbing heart. A book may be less but never greater than its author. A small man, however learned, can never produce a great book. A truly great book is the spontaneous outflow of a great soul, it has not the polish of art, but the bloom of nature. A book is not to be judged by the number of its pages, the consecutiveness of its reasoning, or the rhythms of its periods, but by the amount of creative life that impregnates its sentences, and breathes in its pages.

This volume is small in bulk, but overflowing with vitality. The author (with whom I became acquainted soon after my advent to London, and who addressed a crowded audience in the church at Stockwell of which I was minister) gave me an impression which continues fresh to this hour, not only of his unique history, but of his extraordinary ability and genius. In memory I see him now as he appeared on the platform some thirty-six years ago. He was then a runaway slave. In stature tall, and somewhat attenuated, with a head indicative of large brain force, his dark countenance radiating with humour and genius, his large eyes, now flashing with the fire of indignation against tyranny, and now beaming with tender sympathy for his oppressed race.

As an *orator* I have never heard his superior from that day to this. His voice was clear and strong, capable of every modulation, and of conveying all classes of sentiment, from the most terrific to the most gentle. His attitudes were natural, and therefore electrically commanding. He dramatised those awful memories of wrong that were at that time burning in his soul. Ten such men in our House of Commons would make quasi-patriots and hireling statesmen quail, give the genuine lovers of right courage, and effect a moral revolution. Ten such men in our London pulpits would send charlatanic pulpiteers to their 'own place'; all the little *isms* would take their wing at the thunders of their voice, whilst candid enquirers would get firmly rooted in sound ethical convictions.

Having read every line of this book, and being assured that it is re-published in this country with the author's consent, I have heartily acceded to the request of the enterprising publisher to write this brief note. To me, the book itself supplies the interest of *Uncle Tom's Cabin*, and recalls tragic adventures equal to the boldest creations of romance. It will, I trow, run as widely and live as long as *Robinson Crusoe* and kindred works, but exert at the same time a more potent and beneficent influence.

The book is an autobiography, in which a great man tells out the heartrending wrongs which he has endured, and the agonising and tremendous struggles which he put forth for freedom and justice. The author's life was so mixed up with the most tragical period in American history, that this autobiography reveals, in aspects new and grand, the labours of the anti-slavery reformers, such as the illustrious Lloyd Garrison, and his noble colleagues; the characters of Presidents Lincoln and Garfield; and the origin, the progress, and the issues of the great Civil War between the North and the South.

It also reveals the possibilities of a human soul to change external circumstances. Here is a man, born and bred in slavery, subject for twenty-one long years to the most terrible oppression and ruthless cruelty, bleeding under the lash of the slave-holder, incarcerated in dungeons, subject to daily insults even from the conventional sainthood of the churches, as well as from white men everywhere, and what does he do? He breaks through all, like Samson through the 'withs' that bound him, until he becomes one of the first men in the State, an associate of leading Senators, a most distinguished citizen, the 'Marshal of Columbia', wearing the title of *Honourable*. Man need never, ought not ever, to be the creature of circumstances. He degrades his manhood when he yields to externalities. Heaven has endowed him with the power to use the most unpropitious external conditions, as the skilful mariner uses hostile waves and winds, to carry him on to his destination. In truth, to a great soul, as in the case of Frederick Douglass, the most unfavourable circumstances may be turned into triumphant chariots, to bear our manhood on to its ideal power and grandeur.

Mr Lobb, in publishing this volume, does a work of true patriotism and philanthropy. I trust that it will find its way not only to every railway stall and every circulating library, but into every British home. All who, through this work, come in contact with Frederick Douglass, will be impressed with the dignity of human nature, and feel refreshed and encouraged. They will find a *man* here: an existence, alas! somewhat rare.

Amongst millions of bipeds there are not many real men. Jeremiah was commissioned by the Almighty to 'run to and fro through the streets of Jerusalem, and to search the broad places' in order to find a *man*. The city had at that time, not been desolated by war, nor had its inhabitants, so far as is known, been thinned by any catastrophe; its streets resounded with the tread of a crowded population, its broad market-places were thronged with those who bought and sold in 'order to get gain', but amidst this dense concourse of human animals – feeding, thinking, bartering, all acting with more or less energy and some flaunting as local magnates – to find a *man* was a difficult work. A *man* amongst a teeming population of human animals was a rare object. The grand mission of Christianity, as I understand it, is to convert the fleshly into the spiritual, the selfish into the generous, and thus all human animals into men. This book contains a *man* – not a man's portrait, but a man's self – breathing and thinking, weeping and rejoicing, praying and lecturing, hurling fulminations at the wrong, and smiling benedictions on the right. Truly Frederick Douglass is a grand man.

> Nature might stand up
> And say to all the world, this was a man.
>
> *Shakespeare*

DAVID THOMAS
Erewyn, Upper Tulse Hill, Feb. 24th, 1882

Wordsworth American Library

IRVING BACHELLER
Eben Holden

AMBROSE BIERCE
Can Such Things Be?

KATE CHOPIN
The Awakening

JAMES FENIMORE COOPER
The Deerslayer

STEPHEN CRANE
The Red Badge of Courage
Maggie: A Girl of the Streets

RICHARD HENRY DANA JR
Two Years Before the Mast

FREDERICK DOUGLASS
*The Life and Times of
Frederick Douglass*

THEODORE DREISER
Sister Carrie

BENJAMIN FRANKLIN
*Autobiography of
Benjamin Franklin*

ZANE GREY
Riders of the Purple Sage

EDWARD E. HALE
The Man Without a Country

NATHANIEL HAWTHORNE
The House of the Seven Gables
The Scarlet Letter

HENRY JAMES
Washington Square
The Awkward Age

JACK LONDON
The Iron Heel
Call of the Wild/White Fang

HERMAN MELVILLE
Moby Dick

HARRIET BEECHER STOWE
Uncle Tom's Cabin

MARK TWAIN
*The Man That
Corrupted Hadleyburg*
*The Tragedy of Pudd'nhead
Wilson*

HENRY DAVID THOREAU
Walden

EDITH WHARTON
Ethan Frome
The House of Mirth

OWEN WISTER
The Virginian